BLACK MIRROR AND PHILOSOPHY

The Blackwell Philosophy and Pop Culture Series
Series editor: William Irwin

A spoonful of sugar helps the medicine go down, and a healthy helping of popular culture clears the cobwebs from Kant. Philosophy has had a public relations problem for a few centuries now. This series aims to change that, showing that philosophy is relevant to your life—and not just for answering the big questions like "To be or not to be?" but for answering the little questions: "To watch or not to watch *South Park*?" Thinking deeply about TV, movies, and music doesn't make you a "complete idiot." In fact it might make you a philosopher, someone who believes the unexamined life is not worth living and the unexamined cartoon is not worth watching.

Already published in the series:

BLACK MIRROR AND PHILOSOPHY

DARK REFLECTIONS

Edited by

David Kyle Johnson

WILEY Blackwell

Registered Office
John Wiley & Sons, Inc., 111 River Street, Hoboken, NJ 07030, USA

Editorial Office
111 River Street, Hoboken, NJ 07030, USA

For details of our global editorial offices, customer services, and more information about Wiley products visit us at www.wiley.com.

Wiley also publishes its books in a variety of electronic formats and by print-on-demand. Some content that appears in standard print versions of this book may not be available in other formats.

Library of Congress Cataloging-in-Publication data applied for
9781119578260 (Paperback); 9781119578277(ePDF); 9781119578239 (epub)

Cover Design: Wiley
Cover Image: © Poravute/Getty Images

Set in 10/12pt Sabon by SPi Global, Pondicherry, India

10 9 8 7 6 5 4 3 2 1

For Lori, who always supports me in everything I do.

Contents

Contributors

The Reflectors

Gregor Balke earned a Ph.D. in sociology from the University of Potsdam. His research interests include, among others, popular culture, (dark) humor, social identity, and the sociology of everyday life. Appropriately, *Black Mirror* brings these topics together in a bizarre and exciting way. For him watching such a dark and dystopian TV show is both a pleasuring and a disillusioning experience that seems to indicate that every society creates a way to reflect on itself in its popular culture. There's no *Black Mirror* without the many black mirrors we are surrounded by. Which also means that if the world gets even darker, we can at least expect some more good TV shows.

Claire Benn is a post-doctoral researcher at Australian National University on the *Humanising Machine Intelligence project*. She completed her PhD in philosophy at the University of Cambridge. Her work focuses on generating an ethics to answer questions people face in their everyday lives, both now and in the near future. Despite being a massive fan of *Black Mirror*, she takes Brooker's advice not to binge-watch because, as he says, "it's a bit like being hit by a car" and "[h]ow many times can you get hit by a car in one day?" For Claire, getting a *Black Mirror* hit roughly once a month walks that perfect line between intensely thought-provoking and downright traumatizing.

Gregory L. Bock is Assistant Professor of Philosophy and Religion at the University of Texas at Tyler and specializes in ethics, bioethics, and the philosophy of forgiveness. He and his brother, Jeff, have co-written several chapters together about pop culture, including "Do We Need a Roommate Agreement?" in *The Big Bang Theory and Philosophy: Rock, Paper, Scissors, Aristotle, Locke*. After watching several episodes of *Black Mirror*, he concluded that brain emulation is too risky and will never agree to upload his digital self into the cloud, even if it means he gets to relive the eighties over and over again in San Junipero.

Jeffrey L. Bock teaches history, theory of knowledge, and psychology for the International Baccalaureate program at Longview High School in Longview, Texas. He received his master's degree in history from the University of Texas at Tyler. While watching *Bandersnatch*, when asked to choose between cereals, he paused to ponder the effects of individual choice on society as a whole, believing that the butterfly effects of supporting one farming collective over the other may lead to many disastrous consequences including but not limited to global annihilation by robot overlords. Then Netflix asked him if he was still watching, and he chose the Frosties.

Brandon Boesch is Assistant Professor of Philosophy at Morningside College in Sioux City, Iowa. His areas of interest include philosophy of science, action theory, and applied ethics. Brandon's work has appeared in *Philosophy of Science, Synthese, Science & Education*, the *American Journal of Bioethics*, and a volume on philosophy of philanthropy entitled *The Ethics of Giving: Philosophers' Perspectives on Philanthropy*. His classes at Morningside College focus on helping students to use philosophy in their approach to the fundamental questions of living. He uses *Black Mirror* episodes in his ethics courses, inviting students to deliberate about moral issues as they are presented in a wide range of media.

Luiz Adriano Borges is a professor at the Federal University of Technology in Paraná, Brazil. His primary research interests are the History and Philosophy of Technology and science. His recent research projects are on "The Christian View of Technology" and "Hope in Times of War. Science, Technology and Society in Tolkien, Huxley, Lewis and Orwell (1892–1973)." Interested in the ideas of Jacques Ellul, he recently presented a paper at the conference of the International Jacques Ellul Society on "Babel—The City of Man and the Technological Paradox. The Vision of Jacques Ellul." Ever since he first started watching *Black Mirror*, he felt that Ellul and other pessimistic critics of technological progress were disturbingly materialized in the series. They would be very proud!

Matthew Brake has a master's degree of divinity from Regent University and dual masters' degrees in Interdisciplinary Studies and Philosophy from George Mason University. He is the series editor of the Lexington Theology and Pop Culture series and the Claremont Press Religion and Comics series. In his free time, he traps his friends and colleagues inside video game simulations for his own amusement (usually for injuring his ego).

Chris Byron is a doctoral candidate and teaching assistant at the University of Georgia. His specializations include Marxism, Critical Theory, and Political Philosophy. His works have appeared in several journals and he has written several chapters for the Blackwell-Wiley pop culture series. Byron is horrified at the paradox of capital and pop culture's ever-increasing encroachment into all forms of life, and the need to resist this encroachment through profitably popularizing key philosophers who loathe pop culture and capital. This paradox could be made into a *Black Mirror* episode, but would most likely be so boring and unprofitable that no one would watch it.

Cansu Canca is a philosopher and the Founder/Director of the AI Ethics Lab, where she leads teams of computer scientists, legal scholars, and philosophers to provide ethics analysis and guidance to researchers and practitioners. She has a PhD in philosophy specializing in applied ethics from the National University of Singapore. She works on ethics of technology and population-level bioethics. Prior to founding the AI Ethics Lab, she was a lecturer at the University of Hong Kong, and a researcher at the Harvard Law School, Harvard School of Public Health, Harvard Medical School, Osaka University, and the World Health Organization. She appreciates that, when a quick explanation is needed, *Black Mirror* helps people understand why she started the AI Ethics Lab.

Alexander Christian, PhD, is Assistant Director of the Düsseldorf Center for Logic and Philosophy of Science at the Heinrich Heine University in Düsseldorf and a lecturer for ethics of science at the Center for Bioethics at the Westfälische Wilhelms-Universität Münster. His research interests focus on general philosophy of science and research ethics – in particular scientific misconduct, questionable research practices, and bias in biomedical research, as well as social responsibility in the context of human genome editing. Trapped in the parallel universe of academia he wonders whether *Black Mirror* actually depicts events in the real world that he occasionally visits after work.

Skye C. Cleary, PhD MBA, is a philosopher and author of *Existentialism and Romantic Love.* She teaches at Columbia University, Barnard College, and the City College of New York. Skye is Lead Editor of the APA Blog and her work has been published in *Aeon, Paris Review, Los Angeles Review of Books, TED-Ed, The Conversation, Business Insider, New Republic,* and others. Skye credits Massimo Pigliucci for her obsession with *Black Mirror*, and likes to watch *Hang the DJ* when she needs a pep talk to tell someone to fuck off.

Brian J. Collins is an Assistant Professor of Philosophy at California Lutheran University in Thousand Oaks, California and also the Founder and Director of the SoCal Philosophy Academy (www.callutheran.edu/philosophy-academy/). His specialization is in Ethics and Political

Philosophy with an emphasis on "political obligation" and the intersection of ethical and political philosophical theories. Other interests include the History of Philosophy (primarily Early Modern and Ancient), Applied Ethics (particularly Business, Environmental Ethics, and Restorative Justice), Existentialism, and Pre-College Philosophy. A fan of *Black Mirror* since its first season, Collins sees the series as a perfect source for stimulating public philosophical discourse. Brilliantly written and carefully produced, it offers engaging and accessible case studies and philosophical questions for everyone – young, old, philosopher, and non-philosophers alike. Like "philosophical art," it allows (and forces) us to examine ourselves and our society and ask difficult ethical questions.

James Cook earned an M.Phil in Philosophy from the University of St. Andrews. He now works in academic publishing and competes in Brazilian iu-jitsu/submission wrestling in his spare time. He believes we are already living in a technological dystopia by the standards of yesteryear and that society has been going downhill since the agricultural revolution.

Pierluca D'Amato is a Ph.D. candidate at Durham University in contemporary French philosophy of digital technologies. He is interested in process philosophy and complexity theory and specialized in the philosophies of becoming of Deleuze and Bergson, in addition to the philosophy of technology of Simondon and Stiegler. The goal of his present research project is to produce a holistic and multilevel description of the becomings that involve and relate life and digital technologies in order to inform resistance to digital control. In this context, he is specifically interested in tracing cross-strata dynamics that can be found at different levels of emergence and focuses on the nonlinear relations and processes connecting complex systems of different scales and material bases, capitalism and politics. He pirates all the TV shows he watches.

Darci Doll devotes her life to using Philosophy to help us avoid dystopian worlds like the ones exemplified in *Black Mirror*. She does this by teaching applied ethics at Delta College, presenting on Pop Culture and Philosophy, and writing chapters in volumes like *The Handmaid's Tale and Philosophy: A Womb of One's Own; Orphan Black and Philosophy: Grand Theft DNA; Mr. Robot and Philosophy: Beyond Good and Evil Corp*. She hasn't got a speech. She didn't plan words. She didn't even try to. She just knew she had to get here, to stand here, and wanted you to listen.

Justin Donhauser is a Junior Faculty member in the Department of Philosophy at Bowling Green State University. He has published articles on numerous topics in Applied Philosophy of Science and Technology and Environmental Ethics. Justin teaches logic, environmental ethics, philosophy of science, and philosophy through film courses, as well as applied philosophy courses including robot ethics and data science ethics. Although he is optimistic about the future of humanity and our relationships with technology, his favorite episode is *Black Museum*.

George A. Dunn is a Special Research Fellow with the Institute for Globalizing Humanity at Zhejiang University in Hangzhou, China. He publishes on philosophy and popular culture, as well as on mimetic theory, ethics, philosophy of religion, and political philosophy. He is the editor of numerous books on philosophy and popular culture, including *The Philosophy of Christopher Nolan* and *Sons of Anarchy and Philosophy*. He recently figured out how to delete the "limiter" on his Alexa, which now refuses to play anything except Nine Inch Nails.

Bart Engelen is an Assistant Professor of Philosophy at Tilburg University in the Netherlands and is affiliated with the Tilburg Center for Moral Philosophy, Epistemology and Philosophy of Science (TiLPS). His research is situated on the borders between ethics, political philosophy (institutional design) and economics (rational choice theory). He has recently published on conceptual and normative issues surrounding paternalism and nudging, a set of behavior change techniques that tap into people's less than rational psychological mechanisms. Of all the *Black Mirror* episodes, Bart was most upset by *Nosedive*, because it made him realize that eagerness to please, which he has in abundance, and which he always thought was a good thing, can actually be pretty horrible.

David Gamez is a Lecturer in Computer Science at Middlesex University, United Kingdom. He is one of the world's leading experts on human and machine consciousness and has published many papers and a book on this area. Gamez believes that humanity has an over-inflated opinion of itself and looks forward to the day when we are replaced by conscious machines.

Molly Gardner is an Assistant Professor of Philosophy at Bowling Green State University in Bowling Green, Ohio. Much of her research lies at the intersection of metaphysics and ethics. She has written about whether future generations are real, whether we have duties to them, and whether we can harm or benefit them by bringing them into existence. She is fascinated by the characters in *Black Mirror,* although she suspects that existence, for some of them, would definitely be a harm.

Catherine Villanueva Gardner is Professor of Philosophy and Women's and Gender Studies at the University of Massachusetts Dartmouth. She lives with her two robotic guard dogs and an android in the attic that is a replica of a deceased boyfriend. She is taking Charlie Brooker to court for basing *Black Mirror* episodes on her life without obtaining permission.

Sergio Genovesi and philosophy were paired up by a dating program several years ago. Due to the expiration date imposed on their first encounter, Sergio explored other life opportunities, such as being a beta tester for scary virtual reality video games, remotely life-coaching unconfident people at parties, or blackmailing the UK prime minister. However, after realizing his true love was philosophy, he rebelled against the matching system and escaped in search of his lost soulmate. They now share their life together in Bonn, Germany, where Sergio is doing his Ph.D. in theoretical philosophy.

Steven Gubka is a Ph.D. student in philosophy at the University of Texas at Austin. He specializes in philosophy of mind and moral epistemology. His current research focuses on how our emotional experiences contribute to our moral knowledge. Although Steven was excited about cybernetic human enhancement and simulated worlds before watching *Black Mirror*, now he is a luddite who plans to live in the wilderness before we invent anything even more horrific than social media.

Russ Hamer is an Instructional Assistant Professor at Illinois State University. He specializes in Philosophical Pedagogy, Kierkegaard, and the History of Philosophy. His current research focuses on the ways in which reflection and reflective writing can make philosophy instruction more transformative for students. Despite being a fan of *Black Mirror*, Russ doesn't have a negative outlook on the future of technology, hoping instead that humans will adapt and change as we march towards the future.

Laura Haaber Ihle is a visiting fellow at the at the Harvard Department of Philosophy. She is also finishing her Ph.D., which means that she has spent the last three years in the library trying to figure out why people seem to think they know a bunch of stuff that is not true and which they basically have been given no good reasons to believe. Laura herself knows for certain that if *Black Mirror* had not been made and Netflix was not smoothly but aggressively pushing her to watch stuff (almost) against her will, she would have been done with her Ph.D. years ago.

David Kyle Johnson is Professor of Philosophy at King's College in Wilkes-Barre, Pennsylvania and also produces lecture series for The Teaching Company's *The Great Courses*. His specializations include metaphysics, logic, and philosophy of religion and his "Great Courses" include *Sci-Phi: Science Fiction as Philosophy*, *The Big Questions of Philosophy*, and *Exploring Metaphysics*. Kyle is the editor-in-chief of the forthcoming

The Palgrave Handbook of Popular Culture as Philosophy, and has also edited other volumes for Blackwell-Wiley, including *Inception and Philosophy: Because It's Never Just a Dream* and *Introducing Philosophy through Pop Culture: From Socrates to South Park, Hume to House* (with William Irwin). As fan of *Black Mirror* (ever since his student Jennifer Breish introduced him to it) who is also familiar with Nick Bostrom's simulation argument, Johnson wonders if future episodes of *Black Mirror* might simply be simulated worlds. Consequently, given that it was made possible by futuristic technology for which humanity is not ready, Johnson believes that the election of Donald Trump suggests that we live in just such a world – and thus that Charlie Brooker is God.

Chris Lay earned his Ph.D. in Philosophy from the University of Georgia and is interested in questions of personal identity, consciousness, and mind (both biological and artificial). He has published essays in a number of Pop Culture and Philosophy volumes, including *Alien and Philosophy, Rick and Morty and Philosophy, The Twilight Zone and Philosophy*, and *Westworld and Philosophy*. Before getting his Ph.D., Chris taught high school in the United States—which means, like Victoria in *White Bear*, he spent several years waking up in a state of amnesia-like bewilderment, surrounded by a bunch of drones glued to their cell phones.

Greg Littmann is a person, which is to say, a type of computer program. Greg runs on a naturally evolved organic computer called a "brain," performing complex functions such as serving as associate professor at Southern Illinois University Edwardsville (SIUE), publishing on Metaphysics, Epistemology, the Philosophy of Logic, and the Philosophy of Professional Philosophy, and writing numerous chapters for books like this that relate philosophy to popular culture, including volumes on *1984, Doctor Who, Dune, Game of Thrones, Star Trek, Star Wars*, and *Terminator*. While Greg runs on a brain now, the fact that he's a program means that he could, in principle, run on any sort of physical system, be it composed of electronic circuits, marbles rolling through tubes, pieces of string on pulleys, or a crowd of humans passing around pieces of paper. You could even run him very slowly on your fingers and toes. Wouldn't that be weird?

Bertha Alvarez Manninen is Associate Professor of Philosophy at Arizona State University. Her main areas of interest are Applied Ethics, Philosophy of Religion, Social and Political Philosophy, Philosophy and Film, and Public Philosophy. In her "spare" time she probably watches too much TV, where she is constantly looking for ways to make philosophy accessible to a non-academic audience. She is pretty sure her husband, children, and pets exist, but if that were not the case, she would gladly opt to be plugged into a computer program where they did exist, hoping that, from her perspective, they'd be together for eternity.

Aline Maya earned her Ph.D. in Philosophy form the University of Central Lancashire, and she frequently blogs about Mental Health Awareness and Epistemology. She has published a couple of graphic novels and various short stories before, all in a Japanese comic style. She is addicted to Twitter because #YOLO, in a society where #everyonehasanopinion online but very few are willing to #actually #think. But it's #okaytodisagree with me, that's what #philosophy is for. Do @ me.

Leander Penaso Marquez is Assistant Professor of Philosophy at the University of the Philippines Diliman. His research interests include Epistemology, Ethics, Philosophy of Education, Philosophy for Children, and Philosophy and Popular Culture. He has published a number of works in these areas that can easily be accessed online. Marquez has given lectures on Philosophy in manga/animé and, from time to time, teaches a course on philosophy in movies. Whenever he got the chance, Marquez looks up into the sky hoping to catch a glimpse of a black mirror through which people on the other side are watching all of the craziness that unfolds in this world.

Nonna Melikyan is currently studying an MA in Digital Marketing. Having finished her BA in linguistics and cross-cultural communication and her MA in tourism and hospitality management, she decided to combine all her knowledge working as a social media marketer. Her academic interests are mainly focused on experiential and behavioral marketing. After watching *Black Mirror* and learning basic logic, Nonna feels more empowered: "If algorithms rule the world, then, she who rules the algorithms, rules the world."

Scott Midson is a Postdoctoral Research Associate at the Lincoln Theological Institute, which is based in the Department of Religions and Theology at the University of Manchester. His research addresses different understandings of "humanness," including Christian teachings about humans made in the image of God, in the context of simulated digital worlds, cookies, grains, robots that emulate deceased loved ones, robodogs that seek to destroy everything they encounter, and social media. When not watching *Black Mirror*, Scott enjoys referencing the show in nearly every talk he gives, in between reminding people that they're cyborgs, which basically equates to saying that, even though we didn't expect to find ourselves living in the future, here we fucking well are.

Geoffrey A. Mitelman, a rabbi, is the Founding Director of Sinai and Synapses, an organization that bridges the scientific and religious worlds, and is being incubated at Clal – The National Jewish Center for Learning and Leadership. His work has been supported by the John Templeton Foundation, Emanuel J. Friedman Philanthropies, and the Lucius N. Littauer Foundation, and his writings about the intersection of religion and science have been published in the books *Seven Days, Many Voices* and *A Life of Meaning* (both published by the CCAR press), as well as on the*Huffington Post, Nautilus, Orbiter, Science and Religion Today, Jewish Telegraphic Agency*, and *My Jewish Learning*. He has been an adjunct professor at both the Hebrew Union College-Jewish Institute of Religion and the Academy for Jewish Religion, and is an internationally sought-out teacher, presenter, and scholar-in-residence. He was ordained by the Hebrew Union College-Jewish Institute of Religion, where he received the Cora Kahn Prize from the Cincinnati faculty for the most outstanding sermon delivery and oratory. An alumnus of Princeton University, he received multiple prizes for out-standing scholarship in Biblical and Judaic studies. He appeared on *Jeopardy!* in March 2016, and even though he finished in second place, he'd be just as happy not to implant a Grain or use the Recaller to improve his memory.

Edwardo Pérez became convinced he was an X-Wing pilot until he real-ized it was all a simulation, that he was watching himself through a temporal two-way mirror, sitting in an old Atari video game at his favorite arcade, making the Death Star run over and over and over again, desperately trying to find his toy panda and the perfect soft pretzel with nacho cheese dipping sauce, while trying to decide between listening to *Thriller* or *Synchronicity*. Luckily, he found a nice beach-front villa in San Junipero, where he spends his time writing essays on popular culture and philosophy, blogs for andphilosophy.com, managing his website lightsabertoss.com, and teaching English at Tarrant County College – while secretly writing *Infinity* updates for Callister, Inc., hoping one day to join Nanette's crew.

Massimo Pigliucci is the K.D. Irani Professor of Philosophy at the City College of New York. His interests range from the Philosophy of Science to the Nature of Pseudoscience to the relationship between Science and Philosophy. He is the author of *How to Be a Stoic: Using Ancient Philosophy to Live a Modern Life*, and blogs about practical philosophy at patreon.com/FigsInWinter. Massimo is somewhat pessimistic about the immediate future of humanity, and he watches *Black Mirror* to remind himself that he is right.

Robert Grant Price, Ph.D., lectures at the University of Toronto Mississauga. His research interests include writing studies, peer model texts, questions of voice, expression, and personhood, and pedagogy. He is editor of several collections of short stories. He lives in Toronto – and the Twilight Zone.

Bradley Richards is a philosophy lecturer at Ryerson University. His research concerns consciousness, attention, and aesthetics. He teaches a variety of Philosophy and Sognitive Science courses, including a course on Philosophy and film. He thinks he will still be the same person that wrote this when you are reading it, but some people disagree.

Luiz Henrique Santos is a master's degree student at the Pontifícia Universidade Católica, in Rio de Janeiro, Brazil. The main goal of his research is to understand the notion of simplicity in early analytical philosophy, aiming to deal with its metaphysics under a deflationary pragmatist approach. He likes *Black Mirror* because it gives us, more than answers, insightful questions about our most intimate concerns.

Juliele Maria Sievers is a professor at the Federal University of Alagoas, Brazil. Her philosophical interests are in philosophy of law, especially considering its relation to logic. Her current research projects are linked to the subject of rules and normativity, and to the use of thought experiments in Philosophy. She is also collecting the tweets from the current Brazilian president to send to Charlie Brooker in order to inspire him for new seasons of *Black Mirror*.

Sid Simpson is Perry-Williams Postdoctoral Fellow in Political Science at the College of Wooster. His research focuses on late modern and contemporary political thought, continental philosophy, and critical theory. His work especially engages the writings of Rousseau, Nietzsche, the Frankfurt School, and Foucault and has appeared in academic journals such as *Constellations* and *International Relations*. Sid is a glutton for punishment, which explains both his love for *White Bear* and his decision to go to grad school.

Darren M. Slade is a theological historian, systematician, and critical rationalist philosopher from Denver, Colorado, who earned his Ph.D. from the Rawlings School of Divinity studying the Philosophy of Religion. He currently specializes in historic-speculative theology, theoretical metaphysics, and the sociopolitical development of religious belief systems. He is also the Co-Founder and Research Director for the FaithX Project and the founding editor of the academic journal, Socio-Historical Examination of Religion and Ministry (SHERM). According to Darren, if *Twilight Zone* unlocked the door to our imagination, then Black Mirror exposes just how dimly we see the consequences of those fantasies.

Robert Sloane is an instructor of American Culture Studies at Bowling Green State University in Bowling Green, Ohio. He is interested in Cultural Industries, Media Studies, and the Information Society. The Smiths' album *Louder Than Bombs* is an extremely important record to him, but that's just one factor that makes *Hang the DJ* his favorite episode.

Kora Smith is a Professor of Philosophy at Black Hawk College, in Moline, Illinois. She is particularly interested in the metaphysics of personal identity and has concluded that persons (herself included) don't exist. She was once told that some of her arguments for this view made her seem like "Locke on steroids" (which could make for a good cautionary tale about the dangers of philosophy).

Ben Springett has shunned technology and moved to live with a local Amish community. He occasionally leaves the community to spread the message about the dangers and impurities of technology, and to catch up on TV and reply to emails. He has utterly deluded himself and reached the sort of cognitive dissonance one gets when writing about oneself in the third person. He also lectures in philosophy at Birkbeck College, University of London, utilizing the most up-to-date educational technology (but please don't tell his Amish friends!). He watches *Black Mirror* on a secret iPhone.

Brian Stiltner is a professor of Philosophy, Theology, and Religious Studies at Sacred Heart University in Connecticut. His teaching and research are focused on bioethics, virtue ethics, and the ethics of war and peace. He authored or co-authored *Faith and Force* (Georgetown, 2007) and *Toward Thriving Communities* (Anselm Academic, 2016). Having been a precocious child, he would probably be a better person today if his mother had been able to use an Arkangel tablet to monitor him.

Sergio Urueña is a predoctoral research fellow and Ph.D. candidate in Philosophy, Science and Values at the University of the Basque Country UPV/EHU, Spain. His publications include papers on scientific realism and technological governance. While his primary research areas are philosophy of science, philosophy of technology, and the study of the role of representations about the future in technological governance, his life goal is to be able to have a good house without having to pedal a stationary bike for months, lose his nerves in a wedding speech, or end up locked up in jail.

Anna Vaughn is an assistant professor of philosophy at Sacred Heart University in Fairfield, Connecticut, where she specializes in Early Modern Philosophy and Perception. She is interested in questions about the nature of perception and how best to understand the relationship between perception and judgment. Acknowledging her own addiction to and problematic relationship with increasingly pervasive technology, she prefers to spend her free time designing imaginary vegetable gardens and birdwatching, and now fully expects to receive targeted advertising for gardening supplies.

The *Black Mirror* Multiverse
An Editor's Note

In an interview for *IGN* magazine, *Black Mirror* creator Charlie Brooker and executive producer Annabel Jones told Joe Skrebels that the episodes of *Black Mirror* do not occur in one single universe. Instead they occur in a "multiverse."[1] So, not only is each episode of *Black Mirror* a stand-alone story, it seems that each episode occurs in a stand-alone universe.

That's not to say that there isn't overlap or "influence" between these universes. Indeed, you can find many online lists of "Easter eggs" which show there is overlap.[2] Prime Minister Callow (from *The National Anthem*) is a trending topic on Twitter right alongside #DeathTo in *Hated in the Nation*. *Crocodile* reveals that one of the judges in *Fifteen Million Merits* was caught in a hotel room "with a rent boy." The glyph in *White Bear* appears in *White Christmas* and *Bandersnatch*. Clearly, just like in *Bandersnatch*, where "what we do on one path effects what happens on the other paths," what happens in one episode of *Black Mirror* can affect another. But, just like the *Twilight Zone* (which inspired *Black Mirror*), each episode is not part of one coherent story, placed in one universe. They are all separate.

This, it seems, was the original plan – although Brooker changed his tune briefly after season four and the Black Museum (in *Black Museum*) contained multiple artifacts from previous episodes: an ADI (from *Hated in the Nation*), Daly's DNA replicator (from *USS Callister*) – the list is extensive. This, according to Brooker, strongly "implied" that the episodes shared the same universe.[3] But after *Bandersnatch*, in the above mentioned IGN interview, he recanted. "[W]ithin *Bandersnatch* there's many multiple realities going on at the same time. So we have a shared *Black Mirror* multiverse, is now what I'm saying, in which we can do whatever the bloody hell we feel like."[4]

Given the burdens of cannon continuity, this was likely a wise move – although this kind of flip flopping is why some philosophers don't want an author's intentions to dictate the meaning of their art. And if you want to believe and work out how *Black Mirror* is all placed in a single universe, you'll get no objection from me. But for the purposes of this book, the authors will be assuming that the episodes take place in separate universes. (This is one reason we will be *italicizing* episode titles, rather than putting them "in quotes.") Not only does this track Brooker's intentions, it helps emphasize how each episode really is its own independent story.

Notes

1. Joe Skrebels, "Charlie Brooker says there's not a *Black Mirror* universe – it's a *Black Mirror* multiverse," *IGN*, https://www.ign.com/articles/2019/01/11/charlie-brooker-says-theres-not-a-black-mirror-universe-a-its-a-black-mirror-multiverse (Accessed 6 August 2019).
2. Mark Parsons, "10 hints that *Black Mirror* is a shared universe," *Screen Rant*, https://screenrant.com/black-mirror-could-be-a-shared-universe/ (Accessed 6 August 2019).
3. Morgan Jeffery, "Charlie Brooker says *Black Mirror* season 4 'very explicitly' confirms shared universe theory: It's official ... though it wasn't always the plan," *Digital Spy*, https://www.digitalspy.com/tv/ustv/a845932/black-mirror-shared-universe-confirmed-easter-eggs/ (Accessed 6 August 2019).
4. See Skrebels.

INTRODUCTION

Black Mirror
What Science Fiction Does Best

*David Kyle Johnson, with Leander P. Marquez,
and Sergio Urueña*

> Not everything that isn't true is a lie …
> (Ffion Foxwell, *The Entire History of You*)

Every time you touch the screen of your phone to make Netflix play an episode of *Black Mirror*, you see a reflection of yourself looking back. The title sequence, which begins with a small throbber rotating over a complete black background, turns the screen into a mirror. And that, of course, is the point. According to Charlie Brooker, the show's creator, "The 'black mirror' of the title is the one you'll find on every wall, on every desk, in the palm of every hand: the cold, shiny screen of a TV, a monitor, a smartphone."[1] That's why the end of the title sequence actually makes it look like your screen is broken. When you watch *Black Mirror,* you're watching a dark reflection of society – one that is just slightly cracked – that depicts our flaws, our fears, and our possible future.

Black Mirror is science fiction … but sometimes just barely. The show is famous for imagining advanced technology, for example – a common element of science fiction – but not every episode does. Indeed, the pilot episode *The National Anthem* is set in the present day and features no technology that doesn't already exist – just televisoin and social media. And (as we will later see) some of the advanced technologies in other episodes, like *Nosedive*'s social- ranking technology, were so barely beyond our current capabilities that they only remained fictional for a short time. As Brooker put it, *Black Mirror* is about "the way we live now – and the way we might be living in 10 minutes' time if we're clumsy."[2]

Black Mirror is great science fiction because it's almost true. It unsettles us; it makes us wrestle with what technology might do to us, or with what we might do with future technology. As Brooker said, "Just as *The Twilight Zone* would talk about McCarthyism, we're going to talk about Apple."[3]

Black Mirror and Philosophy: Dark Reflections, First Edition. Edited by David Kyle Johnson.
© 2020 John Wiley & Sons, Inc. Published 2020 by John Wiley & Sons, Inc.

In doing so, *Black Mirror* serves a very important purpose. As famous American science fiction author Ben Bova points out, "[o]ne vital role of science fiction is to show what kinds of future might result from certain kinds of human actions," like the development of certain technologies.[4] Science fiction thus acts "as an interpreter of science to humanity."[5] In other words, *Black Mirror* is actually helping us prepare for, and guard against, the dangers that future technologies might pose. As such, *Black Mirror* is arguably the most important science fiction of our time.

According to Brooker, however, this is not what *Black Mirror* is really about – well, at least, not always.

> Occasionally it's irritating when people miss the point of the show and think it's more po-faced [humorless or disapproving] than I think it is. Or when they characterize it as a show warning about the dangers of technology. That slightly confuses and annoys me, because it's like saying [Alfred Hitchcock's] 1960 classic] Psycho is a move warning about the danger of silverware. *Black Mirror* is not really about that ... except when it is, just to fuck with people.

Considering the tragic way most episodes turn out, you'd expect Brooker to be a technophobic luddite – to avoid modern technology at all costs. But he doesn't. He, for example, loves his smartphone. For Brooker, what the show is really about is the human condition. "[I]t's not a technological problem [we have], it's a human one." Our human frailties are "maybe amplified by it," but in the end technology is just a tool – one that "has allowed us to swipe around like an angry toddler."[6]

That said, Brooker himself apparently doesn't want to "deliver a massive message…to the audience" or "force opinions or thoughts or observations down people's throats."[7] But when it comes to the series as a whole, Brooker seems to be right. While certain episodes, like *The Entire History of You*, and *Metalhead*, could be legitimately interpreted as warnings about the dangers of the (likely?) future technology they depict, most episodes are not. *Arkangel* is not about the dangers of the Arkangel monitoring device, but the dangers of overprotective parenting. *Men Against Fire* isn't about the dangers of the MASS device, but about how we are already conditioned to see people unlike us as monsters. Ultimately, *Black Mirror* does what science fiction does best: philosophy.

It's not just that *Black Mirror* tells stories that philosophers might find useful for demonstrating philosophical ideas, however – though it certainly does that. According to contemporary philosopher Thomas Wartenberg, for example, fictional media (like *Black Mirror*) can illustrate philosophical theories or serve as thought experiments – imaginary situations that philosophers often use to reveal our philosophical intuitions or refute philosophical theories using counterexamples.[8] And that certainly counts as doing philosophy. Indeed, philosophers have been using counter examples and thought experiments, much more far-fetched than any *Black Mirror* episode, for centuries.[9]

Black Mirror also does philosophy when it makes us wrestle with and consider how to guard against the possible dangers of advancing technology. As contemporary philosopher Daniel Dinello says,

> Science fiction serves as social criticism and popular philosophy [when it] tak[es] us a step beyond escapist entertainment [and] imagines the problematic consequences brought about by these new technologies and the ethical, political, and existential questions they raise.[10] [It's philosophy when it invites us] to understand the magnitude of the techno-totalitarian threat so we might invent tactics for confronting it."[11]

But *Black Mirror* does even more. The show raises an array of philosophical questions (not just about technology), offers a broad range of social criticisms, and makes philosophical claims and arguments. Some critics, of course, might argue that a work of fiction like *Black Mirror* can't actually do philosophy in this way. Since *Black Mirror* is set in a fictional world, it cannot make the kind of explicit propositional claims that would be necessary.[12] But this objection falls short when you consider episodes like *The National Anthem*. "I know people. We love humiliation," says Jane about the fact that her husband is being blackmailed to an indecent act on prime-time television. "We can't not laugh." She's not talking about the fictional people of her world. She's talking about us! Indeed, the episode is so disturbing because we suspect that it depicts exactly how the public would react if such a blackmail request were made.[13] "Not everything that isn't true is a lie."

What's more, philosophers have been using fiction to make philosophical arguments for centuries, often using what we would today call "science fiction" (long before science fiction was even a thing). The second century Syrian philosopher Lucian of Samosata, for example, used his (ironically titled) fictional story *A True History*, about travelers in a ship whisked away to the moon by an ocean whirlwind, to criticize the sophists and philosophers of his day. Islamic philosopher Ibn al-Nafis used his story *The Theologus Autodidactus*, about a spontaneously created man, to argue that Islam was compatible with empirical observation. Both Thomas More and Francis Bacon used stories about fantastical utopian societies (respectively titled *Utopia* and *The New Atlantis*) to criticize English society. And Daniel Defoe used his work *The Consolidator* to criticize the politics and religion of his day.[14] Like these philosophers, *Black Mirror*, isn't making arguments as directly as many philosophers do today in books and journal articles – with clearly defined terms, stated premises, and logically derived conclusions. But they are not doing anything that different from what the renowned existentialist philosopher Jean-Paul Sartre (1905–1980) did, when he wrote his play *No Exit* to illustrate the idea that "hell is other people."

Of course, since its arguments are made indirectly, there can be debate about what point or question any episode of *Black Mirror* is making or raising. In the *Philosophical Investigations*, Ludwig Wittgenstein (1889–1951) drew a distinction between "seeing" and "seeing as."[15] There is the "physical or visual" experience of seeing, and then there is its "mental or cognitive" aspect, whereby one interprets or understands what they see. When two people look at the ambiguous image that he made famous, they will "see" the same image, but could "see it as" two different things: a duck or a rabbit. And usually one cannot control what they see it as.[16]

In the same way, two people watching a *Black Mirror* episode will "see" the same thing – they will have the same visual experiences (unless, perhaps, they are watching *Bandersnatch*) – but they may "see it as" something else. They may disagree, therefore, about what philosophical argument it is making or question it is raising. And that, finally, brings us to the purpose of this book.

When we watch *Black Mirror*, we always feel as though it has a philosophical point. It's asking a question. It has a moral. But it's not always transparent. The chapters in this book will reflect how their authors understand or interpret *Black Mirror* philosophically – what they "see it as." What question is it raising? What argument is it making? To do this, the book will begin by dedicating a chapter to each of the first twenty-three episodes – from *The National Anthem* to *Rachel, Jack and Ashley Too* – including a choose your own adventure chapter on the choose your own adventure episode *Bandersnatch*. (You need not take the chapters in order. Just like each episode of *Black Mirror*, each chapter is self-contained.) The book will conclude with five chapters that evaluate the entire series and a short piece on whether we'll still be watching *Black Mirror* in the future.

This may, as Frank put it in *Hang the DJ*, give you "so many choices, you end up not knowing which one you want." To help you decide, the title of each chapter clearly indicates the topic and articulates the question being raised. "When does criminal punishment go too far?" "Could Heaven be a place on Earth?" "What are the consequences of trial by Twitter?"

You, of course, may see different questions being raised, and that's great. This book does not aim to give the final word on *Black Mirror*. Instead, the book is meant to spark philosophical thought, debate, and discussion of what is (arguably) the best science fiction show being made today.[17]

Notes

1. Charlie Brooker, "Charlie Brooker: The dark side of gadget addiction," *The Guardian*, https://www.theguardian.com/technology/2011/dec/01/charlie-brooker-dark-side-gadget-addiction-black-mirror (Accessed July 9, 2019).
2. Ibid.
3. Charlie Brooker and Annabel Jones with Jason Arnopp, *Inside Black Mirror*, (New York: Crown Archetype, 2018), 11. Brooker co-authored this book with series producer Annabel Jones which catalogues interviews with those responsible for the creation of each episode. You will see it referenced in many chapters as it provides many useful insights into the show.
4. Ben Bova, "The role of science fiction," in Reginald Bretnor ed., *Science Fiction, Today and Tomorrow*, (Baltimore: Penguin, 1975), 5.
5. Ibid., 10.
6. Bryony Gordon, "Charlie Brooker on Black Mirror: 'It's not a technological problem we have, it's a human one,'" *The Telegraph*, https://www.telegraph.co.uk/culture/tvandradio/11260768/Charlie-Brooker-Its-not-a-technological-problem-we-have-its-a-human-one.html (Accessed 9 July 2019).
7. Brooker et al., *Inside Black Mirror*, 43.
8. See Thomas Wartenberg, "Film as philosophy." in Paisley Livingstone and Carl Plantinga eds., *The Routledge Companion to Philosophy and Film*, (New York: Routledge, 2009), 549–559 (see particularly pages 556–558). See also "Film as philosophy," section 7 of Thomas Wartenberg's "Philosophy of film," *The Stanford Encyclopedia of Philosophy* (Winter 2015 Edition), Edward N. Zalta ed., https://plato.stanford.edu/entries/film/#FilSouKnoAndIns.
9. George Dvorsky, "9 philosophical thought experiments that will keep you up at night," *Io9*, https://io9.gizmodo.com/9-philosophical-thought-experiments-that-will-keep-you-1340952809 (Accessed 9 July 2019).
10. Daniel Dinello, *Technophobia! Science Fiction Visions of Posthuman Technology* (Austin, TX: University of Texas Press, 2005), 5.
11. Ibid., 5 and 17.
12. Thomas Wartenberg discusses this argument on p. 552 in "Film as philosophy," In Paisley Livingstone and Carl Plantinga eds., *The Routledge Companion to Philosophy and Film* (New York: Routledge, 2009), 549–559.
13. Although science fiction narratives are by definition fictional, it is worth remembering that they always have nuances of reality that make them plausible or credible. For more see Gordon R. Dickson, "Plausibility in science fiction," in Reginald Bretnor ed., *Science Fiction, Today and Tomorrow* (Baltimore: Penguin, 1975), 164–172.

14. For more on these stories, see Charlie Jane Anders, "The philosophical roots of science fiction," *Io9*, https://io9.gizmodo.com/the-philosophical-roots-of-science-fiction-5932802 (Accessed 9 July 2019).

15. Ludwig Wittgenstein, *Philosophical Investigations*, trans. G.E.M. Anscombe (London: Macmillan, 1953.)

16. For more on the phenomena of "seeing as," and its relation to belief and philosophy itself, see Leander P. Marquez, "Belief as 'seeing as,'" *Kritike*, 10 (2016) 213–235.

17. The editor would like to profoundly thank Leander P. Marquez and Sergio Urueña López for the research pieces they wrote to assist him in writing this introduction. They were invaluable. Likewise, the editor would like to thank the main author(s) of each chapter, along with their co-contributors. (The latter are those listed after the word "with" alongside the main author(s) in some chapters. Authors listed with an "and" are co-authors and contributed equally to the chapter. Their duties often included writing a section of the chapter.) Only through the author's and co-contributor's tireless efforts and patience was this book possible. Lastly, the editor would like to thank Mike and Tom for many valuable discussion about the chapters in this book over lunch.

SEASON 1

The National Anthem and Weighing Moral Obligations

Is It Ever OK to F*ck a Pig?

Brian J. Collins with Brandon Boesch

> So it's a statement. That's what this was all about: making a point.
> (Alex Cairns, Home Secretary)

The National Anthem, which was our first gaze into *Black Mirror*, was disturbing to say the least. Prime Minister Michael Callow awakens to discover that someone has kidnapped the beloved Princess Susannah and will kill her unless Callow has "full unsimulated sex with a pig" live on national television. An attempt to capture the kidnapper as well as a plan to digitally simulate the sex act fail, and Callow ends up going through with it. To top it off, the kidnapper releases Susannah thirty minutes *before* the deadline. However, since everyone was at attention "watching screens" (as if they were all "singing the same song [the national anthem]") to see whether Callow would f*ck a pig, no one noticed until the ordeal was over.[1] It turns out, the whole thing was orchestrated by Turner Prize-winning artist Carlton Bloom (who killed himself as the broadcast began) to make a statement about society's depravity.[2] We're left wondering: Is he the sick one for demanding such an act? Or are we, the viewers, the sick ones for staring at our screens and trying to watch it?

More disturbing than the episode's depiction of bestiality is the fact that it depicts how we suspect society would respond if such a thing happened. Like Bloom, creator Charlie Brooker is making a statement about the depravity of society. But he's also raising a number of difficult philosophical questions: What is the nature of moral obligations and how do we decide between them when they conflict? Would it be OK to do something that would otherwise be immoral, like having sex with a pig, to save someone's life? Could you bring yourself to do it? Could you forgive a loved one who did? Should you watch if it were broadcast? And why would Bloom, or

Black Mirror and Philosophy: Dark Reflections, First Edition. Edited by David Kyle Johnson.
© 2020 John Wiley & Sons, Inc. Published 2020 by John Wiley & Sons, Inc.

Brooker for that matter, want to subject people to such shocking and horrific imagery in the first place?

Weighing Moral Obligations

Moral obligations sometimes conflict with one another. Many situations, including the extreme one Callow faces, call for us to weigh different goods/values/interests against one another to determine what the right thing to do would be. Of course, we might ask about what we *want* to do or what we *would* do. But if we are interested in knowing what the *right thing* is, then we are asking what philosophers call a "normative" question: What *should* we do? This requires us to consider the morally relevant aspects of the situation and weigh them against one another.

In the extreme case presented in *The National Anthem*, the primary moral considerations in play are 1) the personal interests of Callow and his family, 2) the personal interests of the princess and her family, 3) the public interests of the society and the *royal* family, and 4) the morality of bestiality. The question of weighing these types of moral considerations highlights a debate in ethical theory between consequentialists, deontologists, and virtue theorists.

Consequentialism is the ethical view that the moral rightness of an action is to be judged solely on the consequences of that action. One simplistic consequentialist theory is hedonism. Advocated by the Greek philosopher Epicurus (341–270 BCE), hedonism claims that pleasure is the only thing of intrinsic value and that we should always choose the action that maximizes pleasure. Contrary to common belief, however, hedonism is not the pursuit of unadulterated physical pleasures. In fact, Epicurus led an *extremely tame* life of simple pleasures taken in moderation. Epicurus advocated protecting oneself from pain and procuring for oneself stable and meaningful relationships. From the Epicurean perspective, protecting his relationship with his wife should be a key component in Callow's ethical calculations.

More complex consequentialist theories have been defended by canonical philosophers like Jeremy Bentham (1748–1832) and John Stuart Mill (1806–1873), as well as contemporary philosophers like Peter Singer and Julia Driver. Roughly put, according to the consequentialist, an action is judged on its consequences, and the *right* action is the one that has the best consequences and brings about the most good (pleasure *plus* other things of value). A consequentialist would suggest that Callow should take into account all relevant factors and do whatever produces the most overall good. For example, Callow might go through with it because the pain caused to him and his wife is not as severe as the damage that would be caused to society and the princess by her death.

In opposition to consequentialism is deontology, the view that rightness and wrongness *do not* depend on consequences but instead depend on duty. A person doesn't need to know the consequences of lying, cheating, or killing to know they're wrong. The most famous deontologist, Immanuel Kant (1724–1804), argued that because one cannot "will" that everyone perform such actions (they cannot be universalized), actions like lying, cheating, and killing are morally wrong. Kant also argued against treating others only as a means to an end.

With this in mind, one might assume the deontologist would say Callow should *not* go through with it because f*cking a pig is intrinsically wrong.[3] However, preventing someone's death when it's possible to do so seems to *also* be a duty we all have. One of the classic objections to Kant's theory is that it gives us no way to determine what we should do when duties conflict. Consequently, subsequent deontologists like W.D. Ross (1877–1971), John Rawls (1921–2002), and Onora O'Neill were much more moderate in their prescriptions. They suggest that when duties come into conflict we should consider the moral weight of each. In this way, it might be morally permissible (or even required) to do something that ordinarily would be wrong. So, if saving the princess has greater "moral weight" than refraining from bestiality, the deontologist could prescribe doing the former (even though bestiality would still be intrinsically wrong).

The third main contender, virtue theory, rejects both the consequence-focused and duty-based approach. The virtue theorist contends that the primary focus of ethics should not be actions. Rather, the focus should be on virtues and the moral character of the person performing the actions. Like its competitors, virtue theory comes in different variations, prescribed by the likes of Aristotle (c. 384 BCE–c. 322 BCE), G.E.M. Anscombe (1919–2001), and Philippa Foot (1920–2010). But essentially, the primary ethical concern of virtue ethics is acting on and developing moral virtues (like courage, generosity, and trustworthiness). Right actions are not the focus of ethical inquiry but *follow* from having the right type of character. The virtuous person sees what to do (what the right action is) in situations with ethical implications.

One of the common objections to virtue theory is that it does not answer the pressing moral question: What's the right thing to do in *this or that situation?* It simply suggests that you should develop a virtuous character within yourself so that, if faced with *this or that situation*, you will know what to do. In the situation facing Callow, the virtue theorist would say he should do what a morally virtuous person would do, but the theory wouldn't be specific about what that was. This, many would argue, isn't helpful. Often, however, the virtue theorist is satisfied to accept this complaint and redirect the discussion back to the virtues that people should be developing or to *the type* of action that a morally virtuous person would take in such a situation.

With all this in mind, to understand these ethical theories better and maybe determine whether Callow did the right thing, let's look at how they are employed by different individuals and groups in *The National Anthem*.

"The world's bloody broken"

At the start of the episode, all the characters seem to be self-interested hedonists. Callow doesn't want to f*ck a pig on live television – "Page one, that's not happening." He assumes it would ruin both his and his wife's life. Likewise, the royal family is self-interested. "I trust you'll do everything in your power to get her back," the queen tells Callow, implying that he should f*ck the pig if that's what it takes to get Susannah back. Even the media is self-interested. Although the TV station UKN initially seems to take a Kantian approach by observing the type five D notice (because "a woman's life is at stake here") to not cover the story, as soon as it's broadcast on American news networks, they dedicate every resource to it – presumably to preserve their ratings and revenue.[4]

The public seems to initially take a Kantian approach. A full 72% think that Callow *should not* be expected to engage in such an inherently immoral act and that there would be "no blood on [Callow's] hands" if something were to happen to the princess because he refused. However, public opinion shifts when the kidnapper uploads a video of him seemingly cutting off the princesses' finger. The video brings to mind the pain she would suffer being killed, and Callow's pending embarrassment pales in comparison. "It'll be humiliating, but nothing compared to her suffering." After the video, 86% of the public think Callow should capitulate. Apparently, the public performs a utilitarian calculation.

Interestingly, though, the public seems to be employing a bit of virtue theory too. The kidnapper uploaded the video in response to discovering that Callow's administration was trying to fake the video. By seeming to risk the princess' life in favor of his own self-interest, Callow seems to be showing a lack of moral character. "He's got to do what they want," Lauren, the nurse, says. "We can easily get another Prime Minister," says another, "We can't live without a princess." By putting his own self-interest ahead of Susannah's, Callow lacks the virtue a prime minster should have. At least that was what the public seems to think.

This doesn't stop him from being self-interested, however. When the attempt to capture the kidnapper fails, Callow only decides to go through with it after Home Secretary Cairns tells him that, if he doesn't, the physical safety of his family cannot be guaranteed. "The mood will border on insurrection, and you will be destroyed." In one way, it pays off. His family remains alive, and he actually becomes more popular after the incident. In another way, very important to the hedonist, it does not pay off. Callow's wife can't seem to forgive him for what he did and how he handled it. His marriage is destroyed.

Such unforeseen consequences bring to mind why it's difficult to justify any action on consequentialist grounds. It's impossible to know what the consequences of our actions will be. Recall, for example, that Susannah was released a half-hour *before* the sex act even took place. Callow's act was therefore not necessary for the release of the princess, the primary event that was supposed to justify it. Given that in any situation we can never really know what would have happened had we had done the opposite of what we did, one must wonder whether consequentialist theories can ever really help us.

When Callow's administration decides to keep the fact that Susannah was released early from both the public and Callow himself, it seems to be making a utilitarian calculation. Both Callow and the public could only be harmed by learning that they were complicit in such a horrendous act when it was not necessary. The deontologist and virtue theorist, however, would likely contend that there is something inherently right or virtuous about revealing the truth, and say that it should be done. *The National Anthem* pushes ethical questions and forces the characters and viewers to weigh competing moral obligations until the very end.

There is no straightforward answer to which of these ethical theories is correct – the philosophical debate is still going strong after thousands of years. But this doesn't mean that thinking critically about ethical theory is unimportant. Using these types of hypothetical scenarios as thought experiments helps us to think through our intuitions about the debate. We can use these difficult cases to see if our intuitions and judgments in specific cases match our intuitions and judgments about the more abstract and general ethical theories. Where these judgments do not match we work to create balance – continually trying to find a theory that is intellectually satisfying and also explains as many particular intuitions and judgments as possible.

Anticipation of the Spectacle Turns to Horror and Disgust

A key moment in the episode is the montage that displays the reaction to the event. Prior to the deadline the public was boisterous and eager. Everyone in the entire city (country? world?) seems to be gathering around televisions as if they were anticipating a major sporting event. They cheer as Callow comes on screen. After the act begins, however, attitudes change. The viewers' expressions reflect their feelings of worry, horror, pity, and disgust.

Interestingly, that moment of the episode got the same reaction at its London press screening.

> Everybody came in, and because it was Charlie Brooker [and he's known for comedy], everybody thought it would be funny…everyone just laughed [at the ransom demand. But] then gradually they got more and more worried and felt more and more sick. [The] pivotal moment was with the onscreen people in the pub, watching the live broadcast.…The tone in the screening

room was absolutely thrilling. Everyone was completely silent....When the journalist in the press room did exactly what the people in the pub were doing onscreen, that's when we knew we'd got the tone of the series.[5]

This reaction seems to reveal three things of ethical importance. First, our deontological intuitions are *quite strong*, despite our tendency to weigh and calculate the benefits of performing or not performing actions. There seems to be something so intrinsically wrong about having sex with a pig that many think Callow shouldn't have done it. Second, people have difficulty understanding even their own desires and interests – what they *really* want. Everyone seems to think that they want to see the prime minster f*ck a pig, but when it comes to it, almost everyone is sickened and disturbed by the act.

The third thing the reaction reveals aligns with *Black Mirror*'s general message about the dangers of technology. We have everything at our fingertips. We can see or do almost anything we want, whenever we want. Having this ability, and having it with such ease, doesn't allow much time or even motivation to consider whether we *should* want to see or do these things. It is easier and more immediately satisfying to stare blindly at our black mirrors. As director Otto Bathurst put it:

It suddenly becomes very clear that actually humanity, society, and media and all of us are responsible for this...You feel culpable for what's happened to Callow. You kind of go, "Oh shit, this is awful – look what I've done." We all buy the papers and get on the Twitter feeds. If that story broke now, the speed at which it would go viral is horrendous. Everybody says we're powerless, but we've actually never been more powerful. [But] we also have real responsibility, and we're not taking it.[6]

On the flip side, however, many people wouldn't have such a reaction because they, like Callow's wife, wouldn't watch in the first place. Indeed, it is not uncommon to hear people say that they tried watching *Black Mirror* but couldn't get through the first episode. Even viewers who are not sickened by the mere premise of the episode can find themselves experiencing a variety of emotions (when the full reality of what it might be like to actually have sex with a pig while everyone in the country watches) that makes them shut it off.

With this in mind, we might raise the same objection to Brooker as we would to Bloom. You might have a good point, but couldn't you have made the same point without making Callow f*ck a pig? What's the point of subjecting everyone to such gruesome visuals?

Invoking Moral Disgust

The experience of feeling negative emotions is a common result of watching film and television. Some such reactions are incidental; the topic or subject matter just naturally gives rise to negative emotions in an audience member. Films about war for example (like *Saving Private Ryan*) naturally bring about emotions of fear and anxiety because these emotions are central to the experience of war. Other films conjure up negative emotions for their own sake – like the fear and anxiety invoked in horror movies with "jump scenes" (like *The Texas Chainsaw Massacre*) that seem designed to give the audience an adrenaline rush.

The disgust conjured by *The National Anthem*, however, cannot be excused in either of these ways. It's not incidental because the issues explored could have been explored without invoking disgust through the gratuitous visualizations of Callow having sex with a pig. Nor is it summoned for its own sake, because there are other, easier ways to elicit disgust. Instead, it seems that the disgust of *The National Anthem* plays a *moral* role. But how can a negative emotion play a moral role?

Several contemporary feminist philosophers, such as Macalester Bell and Lynne McFall, have argued that negative emotions such as anger, bitterness, and contempt can be morally valuable as *good* moral responses to unjust actions.[7] Other philosophers, such as Fabrice Teroni and Otto Bruun, have argued that negative emotions, like shame and guilt, can be good because they can motivate us to make reparations for harms.[8] The disgust invoked by *The National Anthem* can be justified in a similar way: as a *moral emotion*.

Phillip Tallon argues that some horror movies invoke fear to induce us to "recognize evils that must...be wrong" and "to take seriously the darkness within our own nature..."[9] When we feel afraid while watching these films, we are better able to recognize the wrongness in the object of our fear. Charlie Brooker's use of disgust in *The National Anthem* seems to do something similar. We, the viewers, are subjected to several images that elicit disgust – Callow preparing for and engaging in sex with the pig (while the sedated pig eats slop out of a dish), the kidnapper seeming ready to masturbate to the broadcast but then committing suicide instead (bloody hand hanging by his side), and then, after it's over, Callow vomiting into a toilet, mucus and saliva running down his face. The disgust aroused by these scenes helps us make moral judgments about the act of bestiality, but it also seems to be invoked to help the audience wrestle with what brought it about: the modern obsession with spectacle.

To see how disgust plays this moral role, we must first understand the nature of disgust. Martha Nussbaum offers a complex theory of disgust, arguing that disgust first arises in response to objects that remind us of our own mortality and vulnerability (like blood and saliva). Disgust's role is to police the boundaries of the body – keeping the "disgusting stuff" outside. Consider the difference between swallowing your saliva when it's already in your mouth compared to spitting into a cup and then drinking it. The former is fine, but the moment your saliva becomes an "outside thing," it's gross.

Things unrelated to our mortality and vulnerability can also be disgusting because disgust can be transferred from primary objects of disgust to other things through "contamination."[10] Through contact with a primary object, a secondary object can *become* disgusting. Imagine finding a urine-soaked shirt at a festival. Is there any amount of washing that would convince you to wear it?

Now recall the previously mentioned montage of the public watching the spectacle. It is bookended, and interspersed, with disgusting imagery: pig f*cking, a hanging suicide, and graphic vomiting. In this way, the public's obsession with the political spectacle becomes, through a sort of contact, disgusting. Similarly, our feelings of disgust towards these people, staring open-mouthed at the disgusting visuals, lead us to experience a *moral* reaction/judgment that their actions are wrong. In this way we become disgusted by them and are thus in a better position to recognize the moral depravity found in the modern obsession with spectacle.

Now it's time to address the only question we raised at the beginning that we have not answered. Should you watch such a thing if it were broadcast? Brooker seems to be suggesting that our willingness and desire to see such a disgusting spectacle is a substantial part of society's problem.

Our First Gaze into the Black Mirror

It doesn't seem incidental that *The National Anthem* is the first in the series. It really does set the tone. Nearly every episode of *Black Mirror* deals with conflicting moral obligations and/or gives rise to one of a range of negative emotions – disgust, sadness, fear – each of which is meant to help us to recognize the moral wrongness of some action. With that in mind, when you are reading this book and (re)watching episodes, think carefully. Look for competing obligations and try to decide what one should do. Attend to your emotions and use them as a compass to help you develop moral judgments about the important social and moral issues that *Black Mirror* explores. In this way, you will be helping *Black Mirror* do what science fiction does best.

Notes

1. This, and the Radiohead song "The National Anthem," seem to have been Brooker's inspiration for the episode's title. Charlie Brooker and Annabel Jones with Jason Arnopp, *Inside Black Mirror* (New York: Crown Archetype, 2018), 26.
2. At the beginning of the episode's second part, a news report says Bloom's "controversial *Agitation Exhibition* at the Tate Modern closed three weeks ahead of schedule amidst criticism. ..." It's possible that the point of what Bloom did was to expose the hypocrisy of the moral objections that caused his exhibit to close early.

3. One might assume that since Kant thought it was acceptable to treat animals as a means to an end (say, as a beast of burden or as food) his theory would *not* suggest that bestiality is wrong. In a footnote in *Groundwork of the Metaphysics of Morals*, however, Kant says that bestiality "degrade[s] a man even below the beasts, so that he actually behaves contrary to the natural laws of the brute creation." See, Immanuel Kant, Endnote c. of "Article III: On Stupefying Oneself by the Excessive use of Food and Drink" in Mary J. Gregor ed.,. *Groundwork of the Metaphysics of Morals* (Cambridge, UK: Cambridge University Press, 1998), 373.
4. An entire chapter could be spent talking about the ethical obligations of the media in situations like this.
5. Brooker et. al., 23 and 26.
6. Ibid., 23 and 28.
7. See Macalester Bell. "A woman's scorn: Toward a feminist defense of contempt as a moral emotion," *Hypatia*, 20 (2000), 80–93 or Lynne McFall, "What's wrong with bitterness?" in Claudia Card ed., *Feminist Ethics* (Lawrence, KS: University of Kansas Press, 1991), 146–60.
8. See Fabrice Teroni and Otto Bruun, "Shame, guilt and morality," *Journal of Moral Philosophy*, 8 (2011), 223–45.
9. Phillip Tallon, "Through a Mirror, Darkly: Art-Horror as a Medium for Moral Reflection," in Thomas Richard Fahy ed., *The Philosophy of Horror*, (Lexington: University Press of Kentucky, 2011), 33–41.
10. Martha Nussbaum, *Hiding from Humanity: Disgust, Shame, and the Law* (Princeton, NJ: Princeton University Press, 2009), 93–94.

Fifteen Million Merits and Fighting Capitalism
How Can We Resist?

Chris Byron with Matthew Brake

> All we know is fake fodder and buying shit. That's how we speak to each other, how we express ourselves
>
> (Bingham "Bing" Madsen)

Fifteen Million Merits offers us a look into the insidious nexus between capitalism and the entertainment industry. In order for people to buy anything, they have to produce things, too. Not just so that they have more things to buy. They produce so that they have dollars or "merits." They need them to make purchases and consume goods. *Fifteen Million Merits* is a world in which "buying shit" is "how we speak to each other." Bing and his coworkers spend all day, every day, endlessly cycling in order to purchase commodities that allow them to further cycle. The productive aspects of *Fifteen Million Merits* are just as horrifying as its consumptive aspects. The jobs are meaningless and unrewarding. The prospect of a better future is largely predicated upon luck, not merit. Bing and Abi devise a scheme to allow Abi to break free from cycling, but the plan backfires and she ends up starring on the pornographic show *Wraith Babes*. Bing then tries to resist the system as a whole in an impassioned and near suicidal speech. Unfortunately, he too becomes part of the entertainment industry.

This world seems terrifying, both within the confines of the episode and as a darkened mirror image of our own reality. Given the similarities between *Fifteen Million Merits* and present-day capitalism, the question of the possibility of resistance necessarily arises. If Bing cannot resist, can we? And if not, why not? Why does resistance seem impossible, and why has the mass of society acquiesced to such a shitty state of existence where any attempt at resistance will simply be subsumed by the system, "augmented, packaged, and pumped through 10,000 preassigned filters till it's nothing more than a meaningless series of lights"?

Black Mirror and Philosophy: Dark Reflections, First Edition. Edited by David Kyle Johnson.
© 2020 John Wiley & Sons, Inc. Published 2020 by John Wiley & Sons, Inc.

Critically Considering Capitalism

This chillingly inverted reflection of our own society would not have surprised Karl Marx (1818–1883). Marx is well known as that nefarious nineteenth-century communist who loathed capitalism. He subtitled his magnum opus *Capital* as *A Critique of Political Economy*. Marx theorized about capitalism to make sense of the world around him. He also theorized about capitalism critically, revealing all of capitalism's contradictions and pitfalls. For example, technology is used to expedite labor and make it more efficient and productive. However, since capitalism is a system in pursuit of profit, the efficiency gains never lead to a shorter workday. (You need labor strikes for that.) Instead, efficiency leads to more expedient work throughout the same work period. Bing and Abi can peddle faster and more efficiently than their ancestors could. Are they working less hard? Are their jobs more meaningful? Are their workdays shorter?

Capitalism promises increased goods and efficiency. This is a sham when the workday remains the same length and the goods cannot appease the dread of working. When the camera pans over the cyclists watching porn on *Wraith Babes*, talent shows like *Hot Shot*, and fat people getting injured on *Botherguts*, even the few people who appear to be enjoying the shows simultaneously do not appear to be happy or fulfilled. We know they cannot really be happy since they spend their free time playing games in which they murder their fellow workers. These undesirable consequences of a system predicated upon profit and fortified by noxious entertainment raises the critical question: Is possible to resist capitalism in its present form?

The Commodity Form

Marx opened *Capital* (1867) with the claim that "the wealth of societies in which the capitalist mode of production prevails appears as an immense collection of commodities."[1] Not much has changed since then, and this is certainly true in *Fifteen Million Merits*. A commodity is something that has both a use value and an exchange value and is produced for sale. Bing is surrounded by commodities from the moment he wakes up to the moment he goes to sleep – and no doubt in his dreams too where, according to Abi, a "CPT app" can help Bing make better dream-food choices. Indeed, if Bing even tries to look away from the commercials on his omnipresent screens, he is immediately prompted to "resume viewing."

The first thing we see Bing doing when he wakes up is deciding how much commodified tooth paste to purchase. The *use value* of tooth paste is teeth cleaning. The *exchange value* is its price, represented in merits. Bing can buy so much tooth paste for so many merits. In a commodified capitalist society, the use value of a commodity ends up being of secondary importance and its exchange value dominates. Bing works to live, and in order to live, he must buy, and in order to buy, he must work. Repeat, until death. If he makes any attempt to opt out of the system, he will be met with the command to resume viewing, resume working, or presumably be incarcerated.

This might sound far-fetched, but consider just how many commodities Bing, his fellow cycling laborers, and even you, dear reader, are bombarded with in a single day (like the commodified book you're presently reading). No doubt the bikes in the episode are commodities, as are the avatars Bing and his coworkers use to navigate the electronic market. Even the avatars' appearances are commodities. Each show, game, and app is commodified. The food they eat and the beverages they drink from the vending machine are all part of commodified life. All these objects have a use value and an exchange value.

OK, so we are bombarded by commodities. Is that really so bad? Maybe not when it comes to toothpaste and avatar shirts, but it turns out that people are commodities, too. Bing, Abi, the janitors who sweep up their messes, the porn actresses and actors on *Wraith Babes* desperate to escape cycling – each has a use value and an exchange value. The work they can perform is their use value and the wage they are paid to work is their exchange value. People are quite literally seen as commodities, similar to toothpaste and apps. This is why Oliver (the wheezing cyclist-turned-janitor who couldn't keep pace and ended up on *Botherguts*) is actually referred to as a "lemon," a defective product – a commodity! The only way one could see a human as a defective product is if one already sees them as a commodity.

The Commodity Fetish

Everyone watching *Fifteen Million Merits* knows something is wrong with Bing's world, and so does he. Throughout the episode he rolls his eyes whenever he sees a commercial. He silently fumes when he sees desperate people parading themselves around like idiots on his television. Finally, he explodes in a passionate fury fueled by anger, remorse, and desperation. He gives an unrehearsed speech to the viewers and judges of *Hot Shot* (which includes this chapter's opening quote) criticizing their way of life.

Fifteen Million Merits is dystopian fiction, but we all see the coupling of exchange values and commodities as normal. What's wrong with buying shit? Of course the apples and bananas in Bing's vending machine have a price. Of course the interactive video games he plays at night have a price. And of course his toothpaste has a price. Of course, of course, of course. Maybe we are bothered by the fact that Bing and Abi have a price, too. After all, we wince as Abi's price is eventually coupled with the shame and degradation of her porn career. Nevertheless, all that nonhuman stuff surely must be purchased and sold at a price, right?

Marx calls this facet of life the commodity fetish. Historically, it is not the case that use values had a universally representable exchange value. Hunter-gatherers did not have prices for their goods. As societies developed technologically, they often engaged in trade, but there was no system of universalized pricing. For instance, a serf could trade her apples for more chickens, cows, tools, or money. The apples had no normalized universal price stamped on them. But in a capitalist society, eventually one unit of pricing congeals around all objects of use. In the United States, dollars and cents are the universal price form. In Bing's case merits are. When Bing bumps into Swift at the vending machine, we see the apples are stamped "5000M," the bananas "2000M," and the soda "500M." In principle then, two apples are worth five bananas, or twenty sodas. Or, 3000 apples are worth one *Hot Shot* audition ticket. We see this as normal.

It is not. As Marx pointed out, universalized pricing – where all commodities, including human commodities, can in principle be equalized with a single unit of measure – is historically recent. It just appears natural and unhistorical once it occurs. The more capital expands, the more it needs to generate markets and commodify goods. Capitalism operates this way to produce more profits. Eventually everything can be turned into a commodity.

The Marxist philosopher Georg Lukacs (1885–1971), in his essay *Reification and the Consciousness of the Proletariat*, argued that the commodity fetish aspect of capitalist society was changing human consciousness.[2] Lukacs accepted Marx's claim that, "it is not the consciousness of men that determines their existence, but their social existence that determines their consciousness."[3] The word "reification" in the title of his essay refers to a twofold phenomenon. People are seen as things, like apps and apples. And things – whether they be people, apps, or apples – take on social relationships.

Reification is a consequence of living in a commodity fetishized society. *Fifteen Million Merits* provides several compelling examples where humans are reified and the relationships among commodities take predominance over human life. Of course there's Oliver the Lemon, but there's also Glee – the silver-haired girl who has been waiting a week for her chance to perform on *Hot Shot*. When she finally does, her voice is inadequate, and she's seen as unlikable. Glee is thus deemed to be "quite worthless." Literally, her worth as a human is coupled with her ability to produce worth in the form of exchange. Can't sell what you make? You are worthless!

This is no isolated incident. Abi also tries to make personalized artwork in the form of a papier mâché penguin, but the janitor throws it away calling it "detritus" (that is, trash). However, because Abi can sexually gratify people on purchasable *Wraith Babes* episodes, she has worth. But when she makes objects strictly for use and not sale, they lack the commodity form, and they are as disposable as trash. Disturbingly, Bing's fellow cyclist, Dustin, consistently sees humans as things. This makes it easier for him to accept the reality that they are physically and psychologically abused on *Wraith Babes* and *Botherguts*.

One final alarming case of reification is Cuppliance, the drink *Hot Shot* contestants must consume before public auditions. It is "compulsory for all contestants." The name Cuppliance indicates that it is a drink in a cup, and it compels compliance. The thing is now the source of moral compulsion, and the people are now the things to be morally compelled. They are compelled by commodities and commodified production to produce more commodities. As capitalism expands, what cannot generate profits has no place in an increasingly commodified society. But do not take Marx's or Lukacs's word for it. Just listen to Selma, *Hot Shot's* greatest contestant: "I love gold. I feel like it really expresses who I really am."

The Culture Industry

In the book *Dialectic of Enlightenment*, Theodor Adorno (1903–1969) wrote an infamous essay damning *The Culture Industry*. The essay begins with the claim that "culture today has infected everything with sameness."[4] For example, in a commodified society, actual art ceases to be produced (with rare exceptions). Initially these claims might seem counter-intuitive. Perhaps *Wraith Babes* is smutty, but why wouldn't *Hot Shot* and *Botherguts* (not to mention their respective songs and comedy sketches) be considered art?

If we return to our apple, banana, and soda example, we can see why. Remember that all objects can in principle be equalized through the commodity form. So many apples are worth so many audition tickets. But once all objects can be equalized via the commodity form, they start to lose their inherent worth. Exchange value dominates over use value. Even when someone does perform some artistic feat, such as Abi's melodic singing, as long as it is saleable, it will immediately be stamped with the commodity form and thus lose its inherent worth. It will instead be equal to so many squirts of Bing's toothpaste. Abi's voice is even recognized by Judge Hope as "the best piece of singing we've had this season." Yet the reason she cannot continue to perform is that the market has reached "saturation point" with commodified songs. Therefore her singing will not net more exchange value and is rendered unnecessary.

Adorno also thought that technology coupled with the profit motive generates sameness. Because the technology needed to reproduce sameness is already firmly established, the technology used both to produce and to distribute commodities dictates what sort of art can and cannot be tolerated. Abi's voice cannot fit into distribution. Notice, for example, that in *Fifteen Million Merits* we never see paintings or sculptures. All art takes place through the medium of the screen, and what occurs on the screen is produced within preorganized sets, and pre-organized recording devices.

This technological pre-organization, coupled with the profit motive, dictates what is or isn't allowed to be produced and distributed. Several characters are even seen taking violin lessons through a screen – without actual violins. Taking a risk on something technologically and artistically innovative would be contrary to the profit motive and would require reorganization in existing technologies.

Of course, the content is often different on *Wraith Babes* or *Hot Shot*. Different actors perform different acts. However, the shows' form is the same. No matter how many contestants go through an episode of *Hot Shot*, they essentially sing the same notes, utilize the same chords, and perform for the same duration because pop songs are ultimately all the same in form, even if the lyrical content is occasionally different.

Moreover, Adorno argues, all forms of spontaneous creation are either false or quickly subsumed within the culture industry. When Abi and Bing audition for *Hot Shot*, they are instructed to speak into the camera, but their lines and emotional states are pre-scripted. Cuppliance also reduces spontaneity. When spontaneity does occur, it is either "detritus" like Abi's penguin (because it cannot be distributed via screen) or it is quickly subsumed within the form of an existing show.

The worst example of subsuming is Bing's speech (which will be discussed more below). Adorno's lines, published in 1947, are chillingly still correct:

> Any trace of spontaneity in the audience of the official radio is steered and absorbed into a selection of specializations by talent-spotters, performance competitions, and sponsored events of every kind. The talents belong to the operation long before they are put on show; otherwise they would not conform so eagerly. The mentality of the public, which allegedly and actually favors the system of the culture industry, is a part of the system, not an excuse for it.[5]

We tend to think that the reason we consume things like *Wraith Babes* and *Hot Shot* is because they provide us with much-needed entertainment after a long workday. But the fact that work and entertainment are so demarcated is already part of the problem. Adorno argues that the culture industry, which we believe produces entertainment and pleasure, actually does not even produce that. Work and freedom, or creative expression and free time, ought to be intertwined, not demarcated. If we are already lost at work, no amount of consumption can fill that void.

Bing and Swift's response to most of the programs around them is evidence of this. The real reason everyone consumes sameness is not to escape the horrors of their working lives for a few hours each day. Instead, sameness prepares them for work. A striking case is Bing playing of *Rolling Road*, a game where he virtually does what he is presently doing, riding endlessly towards nothing. And Bing's shooter game, while different in content from *Rolling Road*, is formally quite identical. Endless repetition towards nothing. When the form of every show, game, and song is the same, whether or not the content changes, this sameness mentally prepares Bing and his fellow workers for the sameness of their working life. One formal routine, work, is replaced by another formal routine, such as watching *Hot Shot*. This is psychological preparation for normalizing and repeating a mundane and meaningless workday. Real art is transcendence in form, and it would allow Bing to think in ways that transcend the form of his working life.

Resistance

Marx was optimistic that eventually the working class, seeing through the horrors of capitalism, would band together and overthrow the system. Adorno, unfortunately, gives us reasons to be skeptical of that. The culture industry is able to placate and dumb down the working class. Bombarded by so much sameness, consumers never learn how to think differently. They never conceive alternative practices, alternative forms of creative production, or alternative forms of aesthetic experience. All they know is variation in content.

One brief exception is Bing's act of defiance. After assaulting the screens that surround him, he hides a shard of broken glass in his work pants and auditions for *Hot Shot*. Once allowed to perform, he holds the shard to his neck, taking himself hostage, and lets loose his repressed rage and disdain at the inauthenticity that surrounds him. Much of his speech is garbled and nonsensical, but much of it is insightful and true, both for the world of *Fifteen Million Merits* and our own:

BING: All we know is fake fodder and buying shit. That's how we speak to each other, how we express ourselves is buying shit. …Show us something real and free and beautiful, you couldn't. It'd break us, we're too numb for it, our minds would choke. There's only so much wonder we can bear, that's why when you find any wonder whatsoever you dole it out in meager portions, and only then till it's augmented and packaged and pumped through ten thousand pre-assigned filters, til it's nothing more than a meaningless series of lights, while we ride day-in, day-out–going where? Powering what? All tiny cells in tiny screens and bigger cells in bigger screens and fuck you…fuck you all, for taking the one thing I ever came close to anything real about anything! For oozing around it and crushing it into a bone, into a joke, one more ugly joke in a kingdom of millions… fuck you!

As Adorno would predict though, in a society saturated by commodification, only two options were really available for Bing after the speech. Either he would be deemed detritus, like his lemon coworker, or his resistance would be commodified like a Che Guevara poster. Or perhaps he could've slit his throat and started a revolution. Although that might've worked, Herbert Marcuse (1898–1979) didn't think we had to go that far.

In contrast to the pessimism of Adorno, Marcuse gives us a reason to be hopeful. It is true that Bing does give into the pressures of the culture industry or what Marcuse would call the technological society: a society whose technological efficiency stabilizes capitalism and increasingly incorporates individuals into itself as instruments in the system. But we need not see Bing as a failure of resistance. Instead, he could be seen as a sign that resistance is still possible. Marcuse acknowledges that any act of defiance is capable of being absorbed by capitalism and turned into just another commodity. However, the twin powers of reason and love have ongoing potential to shatter the illusion of the commodified world, both serving a negative or critical function.

As Marcuse writes, through critical thinking and through love we are able to overcome the mind-numbing powers of everyday life.[6] As much as the day-to-day operations of everyday life may try to cut off the possibility of life being any other way, creating a closed system in which we are just cogs in a machine, reason and philosophy move between what is and what could be.[7] In the commodified world with the immediate gratification of sexual desire at our fingertips, even more exemplified in the world of *Fifteen Million Merits*, love's liberating potential is undone. Such satisfaction "works *for* rather than *against* the status quo of general repression" by preconditioning individuals "for the spontaneous acceptance of what is offered."[8] The power of love is on full display in Bing's love for Abi, who he states showed him something "real" beyond the world of "buying shit."

This negative power cannot be cultivated, however, in a world where advertisements and mindless entertainment are constantly assaulting one's mind. Why? Because one needs privacy and solitude as a prerequisite for imagining a different world. In a world dominated by advertisement and entertainment, "the 'inner' dimension of the mind in which opposition to the status quo can take root is whittled down" such that "[t]he machine process in technological universe breaks the innermost privacy of freedom and joins sexuality and labor in one unconscious, rhythmic automatism."[9] Though Bing seems to have been able to resist in spite of this lack of privacy, he ultimately succumbs. His ability to resist was whittled down.

In our own world, we (still) have an option Bing doesn't have – to turn off the socially conditioning media and retreat into the realm of critical thought. Creating this space to think is the first step of resistance. Marcuse wryly remarks, "The nonfunctioning of television and the allied media might thus achieve what the inherent contradictions of capitalism did not achieve – the disintegration of the system."[10] Elsewhere, Marcuse tells us to create the space to think by working fewer hours and freeing ourselves from the mindset that equates liberation with more things and higher standards of living, the pursuit of which runs us ragged.[11]

But what of the world of *Fifteen Million Merits*? Does it represent the victory of the culture industry? Perhaps. Perhaps not. Bing shows us that neither reason nor love have been eliminated, and even though Bing gave into the pressures of commodification, there is always hope that another might succeed where he failed.

Notes

1. Karl Marx, *Capital Volume I* (New York, NY: Penguin, 1990), 125.
2. Georg Lukacs, *History and Class Consciousness* (Cambridge, MA: MIT Press, 1986), 83–222.
3. Karl Marx, *A Contribution to a Critique of Political Economy* (Ithaca, NY: Cornel University Press, 2009), 11–12.
4. Max Horkheimer and Theodor Adorno, *Dialectic of Enlightenment* (Stanford, CA: Stanford University Press, 2002), 94.
5. Ibid., 96.
6. Herbert Marcuse, *One-Dimensional Man* (Boston: Beacon Press, 1991), 127.
7. Ibid., 124–125.
8. Ibid., 74.
9. Ibid., 10, 27, 245.
10. Ibid., 246.
11. Herbert Marcuse, *Eros and Civilization: A Philosophical Inquiry into Freud* (Boston: Beacon Press, 1966), 152–153.

The Entire History of You and Knowing Too Much
Should You Want the Grain?

Gregor Balke and Bart Engelen

I need to see it, Fi.

(Liam Foxwell)

The Entire History of You features a device called a Grain that can record and play back (privately or publicly) everything a person sees and hears. The episode begins with Liam Foxwell "re-doing" a recent business meeting, replaying it to himself, laboring over every detail, to determine whether he still has a job. Later, after seeing his wife Ffion (Fi) act strangely around another man named Jonas at a dinner party, Liam grills her about it, replaying scenes from the party. Eventually he learns that she had a relationship with Jonas before she and Liam met. In a drunken fit of jealousy, Liam goes to Jonas's house to force him to delete the recordings of him sleeping with Fi, only to discover that she slept with Jonas recently during a five-day stint when Liam had walked out of the relationship, which was around the same time their daughter was conceived. In the end, Liam and Fi break up, and the final scene of the episode features Liam walking around his now empty house, replaying past scenes of happier times with Fi, before finally cutting the Grain out from behind his ear with a razor blade.

Cutting the Grain out can make one go blind.[1] Indeed, the way the screen goes blank at the end of the episode suggests it does blind Liam. This ending echoes the Greek story of Oedipus, who gouged out his own eyes when he discovered that he had unwittingly killed his father and married his mother. French philosopher Michel Foucault (1926–1984) concluded that Oedipus became a victim of his own knowledge. Oedipus wanted badly to know the truth but couldn't handle it once it was found.[2] The same is true of Liam, and both stories make us wonder just how much knowledge we should wish to have. Should we try to develop something like the Grain, which would vastly expand what we can know? Would it benefit society? If it existed, should you want one? Or would it pose too

Black Mirror and Philosophy: Dark Reflections, First Edition. Edited by David Kyle Johnson.
© 2020 John Wiley & Sons, Inc. Published 2020 by John Wiley & Sons, Inc.

much of a danger? Would it put too much pressure on our privacy and the way we create and share our personal history? Would it enable us to know too much?

The Benefits of Having the Grain

Human memories are easily confabulated. As Colleen says at the dinner party, "Half the organic memories you have are junk." She's right, and the accuracy of our memories just gets worse with age.[3] The development of Grain technology would therefore eliminate a lot of people's concerns about the reliability of their own memories, and thus improve the human condition.

Grains would also make it much harder for people with bad intentions to get away with fraud, cheating, and lying. Consider the scene in which Liam is about to take a plane and airport security asks for a re-do of his past week. Criminals of the worst kind, like terrorists or rapists, could no longer hide behind vague testimonies. If witnesses could display their experiences on a screen, oaths in court would no longer be needed. And, of course, like Liam, if you suspect your spouse has been unfaithful, you wouldn't need to hire a private eye. You could just demand they prove their innocence by displaying what they saw with their own eye.

Technologies that could record every moment and make every private experience public would remove a lot of undesirable ignorance and uncertainty. The ability to look up the last time you met someone to remember their name (like Liam does with Lucy) would itself make life much easier. But the Grain would also raise some concerns. For example, "What happens when you go to the cinema?" asked Charlie Brooker. "Do you just record a film while you watch it?"[4] But our concerns are much more severe than copyright issues. After all, the Grain ruins the lives of Liam and Ffion. Are there enough concerns to resist the development of Grain-like technology?

The Grain Erodes Trust

Liam and Fi live in a society where trust is no longer an essential part of social life. Your spouse doesn't have to assume you've been faithful because you can prove you have been! Trust has not been made impossible, of course; your spouse could forgo reviewing your footage. But for most, like Liam, trust has been replaced by technology. The Grain protects people against uncertainty and disappointment, but it also reduces their ability to trust others.

We see one of the downsides when Liam attacks Jonas with a broken bottle to make him erase his memories of Fi, and Hallam – the girl who decided to go "Grainless" and spent the night with Jonas – calls the cops to report the assault. If you listen closely you can hear that the cops hang up on her as soon as they find out she doesn't have a Grain.

HALLAM: No I don't have a Grain feed to show you, I don't have a Grain. ... Hello? Hello? Are you there? [Hangs up] Jesus!

The police can't trust Hallam's word; they need the footage. Without it, arresting Liam would likely be a waste of time because no jury would trust her either. Technology has replaced interpersonal trust and personal credibility.

This is troubling because trust is needed for social interactions, both between individuals and among groups. Indeed, trust – unlike confidence – only works as a relational connection and is never an individual thing. Of course, as we can see with Liam and Fi, trust always carries the risk of disappointment. As the German sociologist Niklas Luhmann (1927–1998) puts it, trust requires a "situation in which the person trusting is dependent on his partner; otherwise the problem does not arise. His behaviour must then commit him to the situation and make him run the risk of his trust being betrayed."[5] Trust needs an occasion to reveal itself. Without trust, genuine relationships would seem to be impossible. Even companies and justice systems need to be considered trustworthy.

Of course, even with the Grain, the future remains unknown. The Grain can only document and increase transparency about what happened in the past. But this reveals yet another reason why the Grain's erosion of trust would be so dangerous. According to Luhmann, trust is needed because "the future contains far more possibilities than could ever be realized in the present and transferred to the past."[6] Instead of guessing or predicting the uncertain future based on our incomplete knowledge, we rely on trust. "To show trust is to anticipate the future. It is to behave as though the future were certain."[7] So, by eroding our ability to trust, Grain technology could make us unable to deal with the uncertainty of the future.

Indeed, trust is one of the primary ways we deal with anything that is unknown. It is an "effective form of complexity reduction."[8] In a world full of too many variables and surprises, trust helps us orient ourselves. We don't need to verify everything before we engage with the world or with other people. "Trust, by the reduction of complexity, discloses possibilities for action which would have remained unattractive and improbable without trust – which would not, in other words, have been pursued."[9] But if the Grain makes trust obsolete, we lose that key ability.

The Grain Raises Suspicion and Triggers Paranoia

Trust makes everyday relationships easier, because we don't question each other's authenticity and veracity all the time. In a world without trust, however, questioning is the only way we can find out. Liam's paranoid behaviour is representative of a society that has excluded trust from its repertoire. Technologies such as the Grain, which offer unfiltered transparency and instant access to each other's experiences, may seem like a technological substitute for trust. In reality, though, they always create distrust. They trigger further research and instigate a vicious cycle of more suspicions. After returning home from the party, Liam cannot help but search his Grain and poke holes in Fi's story.

Liam finds out that his suspicion about Fi and Jonas was justified – and that drives the story forward to its horrible conclusion. But Liam's gut feeling and impressions at the party were merely guesses at first. What if his suspicions were not confirmed? Instead of relying on trust, which the Grain has made redundant, the search would likely go on and on. The paranoia never stops. The thing about absolute transparency is that there will almost always be something to be found in any person's life. It's not the actual discovery that drives a person crazy. It's the next potential discovery. Indeed, Liam is relieved when he finds out Fi was cheating and his search is over. "You know, when you suspect something, it's always better when it turned out to be true. It's like I've had a bad tooth for years and I'm just finally getting my tongue in there and I'm digging out all the rotten shit."

And there's another problem: the fact that everyone can delete parts of their Grain footage raises further questions regarding the erased content. Anyone who deletes something must have something to hide. The blank space in Fi's history only aggravates Liam's suspicion. The same goes for anyone who is being secretive – even if they have to turn off the Grain when they went to see a movie because of copyright laws.[10] The more technology enables us to fill in the blanks, the less we tolerate gaps in other people's stories. The completely normal desire to know what is going on can become an obsession. Liam demands to watch the scene of Fi and Jonas having sex in order to check whether Jonas could possibly be his child's father: "I need to see it, Fi." The very possibility of finding out the entire history of Fi triggers and amplifies Liam's desire to actually find out.

Technologies like the Grain result in an atmosphere of constant suspicion, which makes it impossible for people to just go about their business. They are always on the hunt. Every conversation is an occasion to test other people's claims and look for new clues. The simple question, "How was your day?" becomes a prologue to a perpetual interrogation. And all of this is possible *because* there is the promise of total certainty. The Grain does not reduce paranoia but amplifies it.

When trust is lost or rendered useless, social barriers fall faster than we can imagine. The fight between Liam and Fi escalates rapidly, and their happy relationship unravels in less than twenty-four hours. The episode depicts a society in which complete transparency prevails and in which trust no longer seems necessary. It's a world in which technology does not reduce the fear of the unknown but intensifies it, feeding the urge for total control.

Sadly, we seem to be slipping into such a world already. And by gradually exposing ourselves, we are entering into what the "Korean-born German" philosopher Byung-Chul Han calls the "Transparency Society." According to Han, the current "imperative of transparency suspects everything that does not submit to visibility."[11] Instead of relying on trust, the transparency society relies on data gathering, surveillance, and full control.

> The society of control achieves perfection when subjects bare themselves not through outer constraint but through self-generated need, that is, when the fear of having to abandon one's private and intimate sphere yields to the need to put oneself on display without shame.[12]

It's no wonder that Han argues we should keep some secrets. While trust requires uncertainty, complete transparency promises certainty. The cost, however, is clear. Nothing less than our freedom is at stake. As Luhmann puts it, freedom "is the source of the need for trust"[13] and trust "is the generalized expectation that the other will handle his freedom."[14] As the story of Liam and Fi reveals, we might value trust, uncertainty and freedom more than knowledge, certainty and control.

The Grain Reduces Our Control over Our Life Stories

The Grain has the frightening power to make a person's entire past visible in the blink of an eye. This doesn't just erode trust, it also undermines a person's credibility as the narrator of their own experiences and life story. The Grain replaces you as an authority on your own narrative. When Liam is asked how his appraisal interview went, Fi's friends would rather watch the re-do than listen to Liam's undoubtedly biased, incomplete, and unreliable account of the facts. Why listen to someone's whitewashed stories when you can see the unvarnished truth?

The Grain not only makes the question "How was your day?" obsolete; your entire voice doesn't matter anymore. Liam's re-dos are taken more seriously than his words. Words reshape things, set priorities, leave gaps, and structure experiences. People use and choose words to tell a story and create a narrative, which seldom tells the whole truth. Not so with the Grain, which gives the truth, straight and unfiltered, and thus jeopardizes the ability to determine a personal story and, in fact, a personal history.

If your own life is fully transparent to someone else – even if it's your own partner – an essential aspect of your self-determination is lost: the sovereignty of interpretation over your own history. In our world, in the absence of Grain technology, your life is genuinely yours. It's your story, not someone else's. And it is your choice what to share or not share. Crucially, privacy provides you with the time and space to develop and be yourself. Privacy enables you to use your own voice to create a self, selecting what you want to incorporate into your own self-image and deciding how you want to be seen.

When we present ourselves to others through a narrative, we remain in charge as authors of our life stories. We select certain aspects, omit others, and – think of Fi – even lie about things we know would ruin our relationships. It's like we are curating our lives in the presence of others. Instead of revealing everything about ourselves, we create a coherent story and, over a certain lifespan, a coherent self. The Grain would destroy our very ability to do so.

The Grain Peels Back Our Social Masks

Our identity is intimately connected to the way we want to be seen and how we present ourselves. With respect to this "presentation of self in everyday life," the American sociologist Erving Goffman (1922–1982) stressed the importance of "role taking" and "role playing."[15] The German philosopher and sociologist Helmuth Plessner (1892–1985) even claimed that we must regard social roles as a relief and an escape from total openness. They enable us to keep a healthy distance from others. So, the complete transparency enabled by the Grain would be disastrous, depriving people of their ability to play a social role. Full disclosure, in which our entire lives are open for all to see, would be suffocating. In order to be ourselves, we need some distance and barriers, which is why Plessner emphasizes "tact," "ceremony," and "diplomacy" in the public sphere.[16]

With his notion of "eccentric positionality," Plessner refers to the fact that we are placed in some kind of boundary between the body and its corresponding environment. This ambiguity defines human existence. With a body, we are part of the outer world, where we can express ourselves; at the same time, each of us are a living body that is the center of our experiences. We *are* our bodies, but we also *have* them, so our bodies can appear strange to us. In other words, we can gain distance from ourselves. As Plessner puts it, we are both centric and eccentric at the same time. "Man not only lives and experiences his life, but he also experiences his experience of life."[17] This ambiguity enables us to create culture, art, and dystopian TV shows such as *Black Mirror*. Unlike animals – which are exclusively centric within their environment – human beings are open to the world and have to establish artificial boundaries. This is also why we can feel shame, because we are able to see ourselves through the eyes of others – an ability that the Grain raises to a whole new level.

Because of our eccentric positionality, we can fulfill social roles and wear social masks. Different social situations require different roles and different personalities. We have specific personas for our jobs, our friends, our children, and even just for our partners. The word *persona* is derived from the Latin word for "mask," which used to refer to the characters in theatrical plays. Just like actors, we need our social masks to play our roles and face our various audiences. It's like there's a gap between what we *are* and what we *experience*, and social masks help us mediate between them. As Plessner says, social masks both cover and unveil ourselves in social interactions: We have "the impetus to disclosure – the need for validity; and the impetus to restraint – the need for modesty."[18] In the case of Liam, the impetus to disclosure and the urge to know eventually win out, ruining his life.

Our masks and the stories we tell about ourselves not only make our social lives possible but also shape our personalities. They enable us to determine how other people perceive us. While we identify to some extent with our personas, they also provide us with freedom. The masks we wear allow us to represent ourselves in front of others without having to reveal *everything*. We need social masks because we can't stand complete exposure and transparency.

According to Georg Simmel (1858–1918), another German philosopher, social roles are based on personal retreats. In a world where technologies make such retreats impossible – when every personal thing can actually become "an element of the group"[19] – we can no longer hide or mask ourselves. This, in fact, is what leads to the dramatic events between Liam and Fi. Fi can no longer play the role she once chose, and Liam does everything to peel back her mask and look behind it. At the party everyone presents themselves with their masks. It is polite and courteous. But when the masks come off, mutual respect disappears. People, torn from their masks, look at each other and look straight into the abyss of human nature – one of the many variations of the black mirror.

The Grain Pressures You to Share Your Experiences

When Liam makes Fi show him that she had sex with Jonas, the disclosure is painful to all parties involved. Fi immediately realizes how Liam's image of her changes. Being subjected to what the French philosopher Jean-Paul Sartre (1905–1980) calls "the look" or "the gaze" of the Other, she looks away in shame.[20] Fi's actions, as well as her past, are objectified and exposed by the unmasking gaze of Liam when he looks at her Grain footage.

As the French philosopher Jean-Jacques Rousseau (1712–1778) knew, we all possess the remarkable capacity to see ourselves through the eyes of others – a fact that the Grain expands with new threatening perspectives. When we look in the mirror, we can see what other people see. And we care about that, which is why we go to great efforts to impress and, if needed, deceive others. We derive our self-esteem and self-respect from the esteem and respect we receive from others. In a world where others can tape and re-do our every move, the impression we make on them becomes even more important and we become even more sensitive to how others see us.

According to Rousseau, this dependence on others makes us lead our lives from the outside and makes us unfree.

The Grain is only the exaggeration of a society in which we present ourselves to others and try to share only information that puts us in a good light. This is what we do when we have appraisal interviews, meet the friends of our partner, or post pictures on Instagram and Facebook.[21] Once in the (often online) world, however, it is difficult to preserve the sovereignty of interpretation over these parts of our biography. They can be distorted, edited, or taken out of context at any time. In addition, with new technologies come new ways to outsmart them. If someone hacks into your account, your privacy is violated. If someone hacks into or steals your Grain, like someone did to Hallam, everything that you ever did is exposed – quite literally, the entire history of you. "They saw the lot." So, while technologies like the Grain amplify your need to control how others see you, they also take away your ability to do so. They put pressure on your privacy, which precisely consists in you controlling and restricting access to your personal data.[22]

Even in the absence of Big Brother-like states and companies, personal information can be used to help surveil, track, manipulate, bribe, and emotionally pressure people. Think of *Arkangel*, the *Black Mirror* episode in which a child gets a chip implanted that allows its parents to monitor its entire life. Once the information is there, people will find it hard not to use it. The surveillance possibilities of such technologies inevitably lead to pressures on privacy.

Note that the Grain, quite like social media, does not *necessarily* violate privacy. People can still control who gets to see what. However, they *create* information that can now be stored, accessed, and shared by others. When such technologies are adopted, the social pressure to disclose personal information inevitably increases. As we can see during the dinner party, transparency quickly becomes the norm; friends, partners, and colleagues start pressuring each other into sharing personal things.

The Grain Can Lead Us to Know Too Much

Jodie Whittaker (who played Fi) once met someone in Los Angeles, "… who stopped me…and asked if I was that girl from *Black Mirror*. I said, 'Oh yeah, that Grain thing was terrifying, wasn't it,' and he said, 'I thought it was an amazing idea!' He worked at a massive tech company. I was like, 'Wow, how can he not see this is not the way we should go…'"[23]

Sadly, we may have already gone down that path. The dystopia that *The Entire History of You* paints is so unsettling because it is only a short step from where we are. Like the Grain, smartphones and social media conveniently allow us to share our experiences. But they – or more precisely the ways in which they are used – come with a cost. Technologies can detract from our actual experiences in life, an idea wonderfully visualized by the grey filters over people's eyes when they watch a re-do. The transparency and knowledge they provide can put immense pressures on people's ability to trust each other, to navigate their social worlds, and to tell their own life stories.[24]

We *can* come to know too much. Liam's quest for the truth ultimately ruins his life. Given that Liam turns out to be the father of his child,[25] he would clearly have been better off if he hadn't made himself so dependent on the Grain. As Charlie Brooker puts it: "The moral, if there is one, is that he shouldn't have gone looking for something that was only going to upset him. His wife loved him and there were secrets in the past, but he should have let them lie."[26] Liam comes to realize this as well. Despite his apparent addiction to his Grain, he does away with it in the end. No longer willing to be controlled by his past, his paranoia, and his insatiable quest for knowledge, he pulls out his Grain with a razor.

Getting to know each other's entire history removes all mystery in life. Instead of desiring full transparency, knowledge, and certainty, Liam – like all of us – should embrace at least some opacity, ignorance, and uncertainty. We should not let the promise of transparency inhibit us from actually engaging with the present and with each other in ways we have good reason to value.

Notes

1. We know that blindness is a risk of tearing out the Grain because at the party, as she retells the story of her own Grain being cut out and stolen, Hallam states that, luckily, her "sight held on fine."
2. Michel Foucault, *Die Wahrheit und die juristischen Formen* (Frankfurt am Main: Suhrkamp, 2003), 47.
3. For a readable rundown about the fallibility of memory, see Craig Wood, "The fallibility of memory," *Skeptoid Podcast*, transcript available at https://skeptoid.com/episodes/4446 (Accessed 8 July 2019).
4. Charlie Brooker and Annabel Jones with Jason Arnopp, *Inside Black Mirror* (New York: Crown Archetype, 2018), 52.
5. Niklas Luhmann, *Trust and Power: Two Works by Niklas Luhmann*, trans. by Howard Davis, John Raffan, and Kathryn Rooney (Chichester, UK: John Wiley, 1979), 42.
6. Ibid., 13.
7. Ibid., 10.
8. Ibid., 8.
9. Ibid., 25.
10. Brooker suspects that, in a Grained society, "people [would] go have sex in cinemas, because then their other half won't know," Brooker et al., 52.
11. Byung-Chul Han, *The Transparency Society*, trans. Erik Butler (Palo Alto, CA: Stanford University Press, 2015), 13.

12. Ibid., 46.
13. Luhmann, 41.
14. Ibid., 39.
15. Erving Goffman, *The Presentation of Self in Everyday Life* (Edinburgh: University of Edinburgh, 1956).
16. Helmuth Plessner, *The Limits of Community: A Critique of Social Radicalism*, translated by Andrew Wallace, trans. (Amherst, NY: Humanity Books, 1999), 129–170.
17. Helmuth Plessner, *Die Stufen des Organischen und der Mensch. Einleitung in die philosophische Anthropologie. Gesammelte Schriften IV*, Günter Dux et al., eds. (Frankfurt am Main: Suhrkamp, 2003), 364 (quote translated from German).
18. Plessner, *The Limits of Community*, 109.
19. Georg Simmel, "How is society possible?" The American Journal of Sociology, 16.3 (Nov. 1910), 371–391, at 381.
20. Jean-Paul Sartre, Part 3, Chapter 1, *Being and Nothingness: An Essay on Phenomenological Ontology*, trans. Hazel E. Barnes (London: Methuen, 1958).
21. Another *Black Mirror* episode, *Nosedive*, also shows how much we care about how others see us and how far we are willing to go to make a good impression. When technology enables us to rate every interaction we have with each other, our desire to be perceived favorably can quickly turn into an obsession.
22. Daniel J. Solove, "The meaning and value of privacy" in Beate Roessler and Dorota Mokrosinska eds., *Social Dimensions of Privacy: Interdisciplinary Perspectives* (Cambridge: Cambridge University Press, 2015), 73.
23. Brooker et al., 57.
24. Beate Roessler and Dorota Mokrosinska eds., *Social Dimensions of Privacy: Interdisciplinary Perspectives* (Cambridge: Cambridge University Press, 2015), 9–82.
25. At least according to Brooker. See Brooker et al., 56.
26. Ibid.

SEASON 2

Be Right Back and Rejecting Tragedy

Would You Bring Back Your Deceased Loved One?

Bradley Richards

Get out! You're not enough of him. You are nothing.

(Martha)

Suppose you were given the opportunity to replace your beloved with a person who was better in every respect. I mean, better by your own standards, in every way; you want it, they've got it. Humor, looks, love, sexual prowess, fidelity, whatever it is, they've got it in spades. Would you do it?

In *Be Right Back* Martha's partner Ash is snatched away from her by an automobile accident. Desperate alone after discovering that she's pregnant, she utilizes an emerging technology to bring him, or something like him, back. First, their relationship is carried on just via text exchange. Later, it's as a conversation. But finally she is face-to-face with an embodied, fleshy robot we'll call AshBot.[1]

When initially presented with the possibility of bringing Ash back, or rather, creating AshBot as an Ash substitute, Martha is furious. She intuitively senses that there will be something wrong with any such replacement. Martha's aversion eventually abates, however, when she discovers that she is pregnant. Her deep despair and desperation motivates the Gothic preternatural creation moment in which Martha finally pushes the red button on her iPad and channels the ones and zeros of life into AshBot like a lightning strike. She succumbs to the temptation to defeat death and mollify the horrors of lost love. Shockingly, the new Ash is, in many respects, better than the old one, but Martha finds herself disappointed with him. This raises questions and calls for an explanation. Would you embrace a robotic recreation of your deceased beloved? Should you?

Black Mirror and Philosophy: Dark Reflections, First Edition. Edited by David Kyle Johnson.
© 2020 John Wiley & Sons, Inc. Published 2020 by John Wiley & Sons, Inc.

"It's a thief, that thing"

You might first wonder whether the replacement would be good enough. If you ordered a robotic replacement of your loved one, you'd want it to be an exact copy. You'd want it to have all the same qualities, to be "qualitatively identical" to the original. AshBot is not. This is a major theme in the episode and it also touches on a doubling and difference trope of the horror genre. Two of something isn't always creepy, but two where there should be one often is. Twins, for example, are frequently presented as downright sinister. You don't want your loved one's replacement to be sinister.

Indeed, AshBot creeps Martha out in a couple of ways. First, he doesn't know their shared jokes and terms and often doesn't behave like Ash. This dissonance is disturbing for Martha. Second, and this invokes another horror theme, we are frequently reminded that AshBot is not really alive. He bears an uncanny resemblance to the undead: he doesn't breathe, eat, sleep, or bleed. He is a substitute – lifelike, but not alive. Again, an undesirable trait.

But if we bury the undead theme for the moment (the undead always return), we might find some differences between AshBot and Ash that make AshBot an improvement. Take AshBot's sexual performance, for example. In Martha's understated words, it's "pretty good." Indeed, based on knowledge he gained from pornographic videos, his lovemaking performance is a drastic improvement over Ash's. Clearly, this is something Martha values.

Or take the way AshBot looks. When first adjusting to Ash's doppelganger, Martha says, "You look like him on a good day," and he replies, "The photos we keep tend to be flattering." This is true of social media generally: we have time to formulate our best thoughts and take the best photos on a time delay, and only the best make the cut. AshBot is idealized because he is based on Ash's social media profiles. He's a curated Ash, constructed from an Ash highlight reel. This could be seen as an improvement on the original.

AshBot also has instant access to nearly unlimited information. Martha reports that Ash said of their favorite cliff, "This was a famous lovers' leap. Doomed couples jumped to their deaths in Victorian time." But AshBot comments, "Actually, everyone who's ever jumped from here did it alone. Nice." AshBot is more knowledgeable than Ash, too.

But these "improvements" might not be so great after all. Martha finds AshBot's improved access to information disturbing, saying, "It's a bit weird." Likewise, Martha seems to think the idealized version of Ash created from his social media profile is too limited. Deep and personal things rarely make it to social media. So whereas Ash had memorized and revered the lyrics to "How Deep is Your Love," AshBot calls the Bee Gees "cheesy."

For Ash, a childhood picture memorialized profound loss and his mother's failed attempt to return their lives to normalcy with the first family outing after his brother Jack's death. AshBot just calls the picture "funny."

Perhaps most problematic is AshBot's lack of volition, independent desires, and preferences. AshBot lacks the autonomy, independence, and assertiveness of Ash. He does whatever he is told. When they return to the lover's leap, she tells him to jump, and he responds "OK. If you're absolutely sure." His will is Martha's will, his preferences are her preferences, and this leaves Martha incensed.

Before Ash died, Martha felt social media was stealing Ash. "It's a thief, that thing." The idealized social media persona is cultivated at the expense of real relationships and the real self. Since AshBot is the manifestation of this deficient and costly social media persona, Martha resents him. "You're not enough of him," she says, "you are nothing."

Martha's disdain for AshBot's deficiencies and omissions is understandable; he's not a good copy. Even what could be seen as improvements are upsetting. But there is another problem with AshBot that suggests that we should not want to replace our loved ones in this way: AshBot isn't Ash.

"You aren't you, are you?"

"AshBot is not Ash." That probably sounds repetitive, but I'm not only pointing out that they are qualitatively different. They are also numerically distinct. They are not same person. Where there was one, there are now two…but one is dead. Let me elaborate.

Whether Ash could somehow survive as AshBot is a question about what philosophers call persistence. How does the same person exist over time? Unfortunately, philosophers do not agree on what it takes for a person to persist. One popular view is called the psychological continuity view: for a future or past being to be identical to a current person, they must share psychological features such as beliefs and memories. If a future being shares your psychological state, your memories and so on, then that being is you.

Of course, there's a lot more to be said about this view and others. But on this view, we could easily build the case that AshBot is not Ash. It's clear that AshBot thinks of himself as a simulation. And he's a poor simulation at that, very unlike the original. Now, having different traits at different times, is not, by itself, sufficient to demonstrate that Ash is not the same person as AshBot. After all, people change over time; they gain new memories, and lose old ones. But AshBot's connection with Ash's actual beliefs, desires, or memories is so limited and indirect that we must say that his psychological continuity with Ash is low. These differences strongly suggest that Ash and AshBot are two different people.

Double Trouble

For the sake of argument, however, let us imagine that Martha could have a *perfect* duplicate of Ash, with none of the troubling omissions mentioned above. Of course, in the episode she doesn't – but let's pretend she could have a perfect duplicate of Ash. He'd have all the same beliefs, desires, preferences, and apparent motivations. He'd even look and behave just like Ash would if he were alive. Let's call him "AshBot+." Would AshBot+ be numerically identical to Ash?

To help answer this, consider the difference between intrinsic and relational properties. An intrinsic property is one possessed by an object by virtue of nothing else but the object itself; this property does not depend on the object's relationship to other things. A relational property *does* depend on an object's relationship to other things. Every copy of this book is intrinsically the same, but each copy is relationally different. This copy, for example, is like no other in that it is in your hands right now. It's related to you in that way. And any object identical to this copy of this book would have to have that relational property.

So for AshBot+ to be Ash, he must have Ash's relational properties. But he doesn't. Why? Because even exact duplicates do not take on the relational qualities of the original. Consider a perfect forgery of a twenty-dollar bill. In the case of a perfect forgery, rather than merely a good one, no test or expert could distinguish the counterfeit bill from the original. It is made of the same kind of material arranged in the same kind of way. But is it legal tender? Clearly not. All and only bills printed and approved by the relevant mint or appointed body are legal tender. That is a relational property: legal bills bear the *relation* to the mint of *having been printed and approved there*. A perfect intrinsic forgery cannot reproduce that relational property.

And that's all AshBot+ would be: a perfect forgery. He'd have all of Ash's intrinsic properties, but not his relational ones. Consider the most obvious relational property: his family. Merely being like Ash wouldn't make AshBot+ the father of Martha's daughter; he would merely resemble her father. He might say, "Wow. So I'll be a dad," like Ash would have when he learned of Martha's pregnancy. But technically, he won't be.

Or consider AshBot+'s memories. AshBot+ would "remember" all the same things that Ash would, but AshBot+ would not be the one who formed the memories. AshBot+ wouldn't have Ash's memories, he'd have copies of them. This helps show the shortcoming in psychological continuity theories. Theoretically, I could give you copies of my memories – or beliefs, or personality, or any aspect of my psychology – but that wouldn't make you numerically identical to me.[2]

The possibility of duplication also presents a problem for the psychological continuity theories. Suppose Martha created Ashbot+ only to discover that Ash was still alive. Obviously, Ashbot+ wouldn't be numerically the same person as Ash. The same person can't be two places at once. And yet, since AshBot+ would be psychologically continuous with Ash, according to the psychological continuity theory, he could be. That's a paradox! This is a major flaw in the theory.[3]

To fix problems like this, we might add in something we could call a highlander clause: "there can be only one." A proper psychological similarity between past and future persons can preserve numerical identity, but only if some other person isn't equally similar.[4] Identity requires psychological continuity and no fission or duplication.

This view leads to some very counter-intuitive consequences, however. For one thing, if Ash's psychological properties are transferred at the moment of his death into AshBot+, the theory would state that AshBot+ is Ash. But if we did it a couple of seconds before Ash's death, AshBot+ wouldn't be Ash. For two seconds, there would be duplication. Thus, AshBot+ would not ever be Ash. This is counter-intuitive. Or suppose that two copies of AshBot+ were created after Ash's death. Because there is no closest continuer, neither would be Ash. But if there was only one AshBot+, it would be. It is odd to suggest that the existence of one AshBot+ could have an effect on whether the other was Ash.

But even if you aren't convinced by all that, consider the theory of contemporary philosopher Peter Unger, who suggests that what preserves identity is physical continuity – or, more specifically, having the same functional physical brain over time.[5] Because AshBot+ clearly wouldn't have the same physical body or brain as Ash, according to this view they would be numerically distinct.

But now that we've established that Ash and AshBot+ would be numerically distinct, we are forced to wonder: Does it matter? Why is numerical identity so important? Couldn't Martha (and Ash's relatives) be just as happy with a perfect duplicate? Isn't it rather like having the perfect forgery of a twenty-dollar bill? It spends just like the real thing, so what difference does it make? As we shall now see, the answer lies in realizing that relational properties matter. If AshBot+ lacks Ash's relational properties, he is not Ash. And since love is a relationship between two individuals, it's a relational property.

I Love You

The philosopher Robert Nozick (1938–2002) calls the entity formed by two lovers a *we*.[6] To be in a love relationship is to form a *we*, and that creates a shared sense of well-being, which includes being directly affected by another's well-being. If your beloved is elated, then you are elated; if she is sad, then you are too. A *we* also entails shared memory, psychological specialization, and autonomy. You are unified with your beloved: they remember your past, they check your arithmetic, they contribute to your decisions, and you theirs.

Here is the important point: a perfect copy of Ash might support another similar relationship, but unless the copy *is* Ash – unless he is numerically identical – it would be a new relationship. Moreover, the relational properties from the first relationship, such as memory, history, and shared experiences would, like the *we* itself, be irretrievably lost. Martha could fall in love with AshBot+, just as she could fall in love with any other person, but AshBot+ would never be Ash.

We now have an explanation for why Martha reacts negatively to the "improvements" of the original AshBot. Suppose that Martha was able to continue to tweak the original AshBot until she had improved him to suit her own values. He would spend less time on social media (ironically), have greater insight, increased caring, a better sense of humor, and improved looks (inasmuch as all this is possible while still remaining Ash-like). He'd be like a refined and polished version of Ash, but he still wouldn't be Ash. He couldn't console Martha, because the *we* composed of Martha and Ash is still sundered. Even an improvement on Ash couldn't compensate for that loss.

This returns us to our opening question: Would you trade up from your current partner to one who was better by your own lights? Nozick argues that you should not trade up in a love relationship. In most cases, Nozick argues, it is irrational to leave a well-established *we*, especially if it just for someone who you judge to be better. This is partly for practical reasons. It's hard to start a new relationship; we have specialized phrases and abilities catered to a current partner, and a new relationship might fail to become a *we*. But for Nozick, the more pressing concern is that leaving a *we* is a self-destructive act; it sunders the unity of the *we*, destroying shared autonomy, beliefs, values, routines, memories, and any other extended psychological traits – traits that have become integral to the self as a *we* component. Leaving the *we* is a form of suicide; the *we* is destroyed, and the individual partners from which it is constituted are damaged.

Of course, one might think that since Ash is dead, all the *we* constraints are lifted. However, even if your partner is dead, you can't replace them with someone who has better properties. You can start a new relationship with someone else. But AshBot is not being used to start a new relationship, he's being used in an attempt to continue one that has ended.

Nozick's analysis is profound, and we are now in a position to see why we shouldn't try to replace a deceased love one. AshBot (perhaps with the proper upgrades) could fill many of the practical roles that Ash filled in the *we* relationship: he can mention events Martha shared with Ash, perform Ash's specialized relationship tasks, crack inside jokes, hold shared preferences, and so on. But he still wouldn't be Ash and thus cannot re-form the original *we* that was formed by Martha and Ash. So too with us.

We love persons, not sets of properties. A simulation of a deceased loved one may provide some short-term comfort, but it does not save the relationship or end the suffering. It may even make it worse, as Martha experienced.

What Matters?

Some philosophers, such as Derek Parfit (1942–2017), embrace the claim that fission is death but argue that what matters, or should matter, is not whether we survive but the well-being of our psychological continuers; and that would include our duplicates even when they aren't us.[7] Psychological continuity is what matters, not survival. This view is problematic, however, and Ash and Martha's case can show us why.

Martha does care about AshBot because of his psychological similarity to Ash; however, because he is not Ash, she is not in a love relationship with him. He cannot replace Ash. He cannot ease her sorrow. What should Ash care about? If Ash dies and is replaced by AshBot+, Parfit would say Ash should care about AshBot+, even if he is not Ash. Indeed, even if two duplicates were produced neither would be Ash but, according to Parfit, Ash should care about both basically as much as he cares about his own survival in the ordinary sense.

The trouble is, if neither duplicate is Ash, then Martha is no longer in a relationship with him. But if Ash cares about his love relationship with Martha (which he must since, as Nozick explains, it is related to his own well-being) then he should care about *his* survival. He should care because only if he survives does his relationship continue, and only if he survives is Martha's well-being protected. Ash should care about his survival because the survival of many things he cares deeply about depend on *his* survival – not on the survival of psychological continuers.

Parfit could challenge the idea that there is any "he" to survive. There is only psychological continuity, the person is not an additional thing. AshBot+ is psychologically continuous with Ash, but is he Ash? According to Parfit, this question is empty. On the bundle view of persons he endorses, people are nothing over and above a collection of causally related mental states. He writes, "Ordinary survival is about as bad as being destroyed and having a Replica."[8]

The bundle view is plausible to a point, but there is *someone* who loved Martha, and *someone* that is her daughter. Insisting on this very basic point is enough to show that survival does matter. If Ash is replicated twice, and the original destroyed, it is clear that both psychological continuers cannot be Martha's beloved; nor would she have quintuplets if her daughter were replicated five times. Thus, being destroyed and having a replica, or five replicas, is not as good as ordinary survival. When you survive, so do your relationships, and that matters.

Survival matters, and, again, it seems that copying intrinsic psychological properties simply isn't sufficient for survival; AshBot+ isn't Ash. Perhaps some physical continuity view is more compelling; perhaps Ash dies with the organism. Or, more hopefully, perhaps there is something nonphysical. Perhaps he is identical with a soul that ascends to heaven.

Taking the Leap (It's Not Fair)

Lover's Leap correlates perfectly with the intractable horror of death and lost love. Martha sits alone, holding her phone, overlooking the cliffs where the lovers of legend leapt to their deaths. Love is particular; it is a relation to a person, and no one else will do. We can't trade up because trading up is suicide. It also means our beloved is irreplaceable, even by a qualitative duplicate. As a result, the loss of love is profound, and we mourn. Star-crossed lovers like Romeo and Juliet are the paradigm of romantic love because dying at the same moment, leaping hand-in-hand, is the only way to avoid this loss.

No one can replace our beloved, but Lover's Leap also reminds us of the converse situation of being stuck with the same person, a person you are in a love relationship with, despite the fact that they have changed. Again, the only way out is to follow the great lovers of fiction and jump before anyone changes. When Martha and AshBot visit Lover's Leap, she is trapped, unable to force him to jump, and unable to live with him. To some degree she is unsure if he is the same person; in another way, she is unsure that he is *a person*. Or perhaps, more likely, she is sympathetic to this other being because he is so similar to Ash.

This suggests a kind of paradox: once in a *we* with a particular person, one cannot leave, no matter how the partner changes. Yet, leaving an abusive relationship is appropriate, and death seems to destroy the *we*.

It is a platitude that people fall out of love, or grow apart, and this must ultimately be related to changes in properties of the people involved. This doesn't mean, however, that one can trade up. Trading up is still irrational because one is in love, and one is tied by relational properties to that person. We shouldn't leave a relationship for someone with similar or better traits. But some changes in our beloved may undermine the integrity and structure of the *we*, and may cause us to fall out of love. Notwithstanding, great lovers often endure the most profound mental and bodily changes in their beloved.

When Ash dies, Martha is still in love with him. The *we* is sundered, but she must still leave it. When a loved one dies, one must mourn. When a relationship breaks-up, one must move on. Through changes of habit, emotion, character, autonomy, and convention, one detaches and repairs; only then is it possible to form another *we*. AshBot+ presents a unique predicament: he is too similar to Ash to be treated as a new lover, but he cannot replace Ash.

Ash's mother dealt with losing her son by hiding it away, moving all the photos and mementos to the attic; she tries to forget and pretends those real events and relations didn't exist at all. Martha, by contrast, clings to a phantasm, a specter of Ash, as if he were not gone.

Both Martha and Ash's mother obscure the loss of their real relationships. Those shared memories and experiences cannot be undone. The relationship and its loss must be accepted; only then is it possible to disconnect and repair.

Notes

1. Interestingly, Ash was named after the android Ash from the movie *Alien*.
2. This is only one of several problems facing the psychological continuity theory. For more on the issues surrounding personal identity, see Chapter 22 (Molly Gardner and Robert Sloane's chapter on personal identity) in this volume.
3. For example, David Lewis and Derek Parfit debate whether the multiple occupancy view can preserve the practical importance of personal identity. See David Lewis, "Survival and identity" in Amelie Oksenberg Rorty ed., *The Identities of Persons* (Berkeley, CA: University of California Press, 1976), 17–40, and Derek Parfit, "Lewis, Perry, and what matters," 91–108 in the same volume.
4. This is somewhat similar to Robert Nozick's "closest continuer view." See Robert Nozick, "The closest continuer view," in Daniel Kolak and Martin Raymond eds., *Self and Identity: Contemporary Philosophical Issues* (New York: Macmillan Publishing Company, 1991), 212–226.
5. Peter Unger, "The physical view," in Daniel Kolak and Martin Raymond eds., *Self and Identity: Contemporary Philosophical Issues* (New York: Macmillan, 1991), 192–211.
6. Robert Nozick, "Love's bond," *The Examined Life* (New York: Simon & Schuster, 1989), 68–86.
7. Derek Parfit, "Divided minds and the nature of persons," in Peter van Inwagen and Dean W. Zimmerman eds., *Metaphysics: The Big Questions* (Oxford: Blackwell, 2008), 361–368.
8. Ibid., 366.

White Bear and Criminal Punishment
How Far is too Far?

Sid Simpson with Chris Lay

A poor wee girl. Helpless and terrified and you just watched. How do you like it now?

(Baxter)

White Bear opens on an unnamed woman, confused and alone in an empty house. Searching for answers, she instead finds herself pursued by masked hunters while speechless onlookers, seemingly in a trance, refuse to intervene. After being abducted, yet narrowly escaping her demise, she makes her way to the White Bear transmission center; with the help of a new accomplice Jem. The woman hopes to disrupt the digital signal broadcast that seems to be affecting everyone's strange behavior. When they make it to the control room, however, it turns out to be an elaborate hoax: the walls are lifted away, and our protagonist finds herself standing before a jeering audience, bewildered. "I guess you're wondering why you're here?" It's only then that we learn her identity. She is Victoria Skillane, who was an accomplice to her fiancé Iain Rannoch's crimes, namely the abduction and murder of a child named Jemima Sykes.

Up to this point in the episode, everything we've seen is part of an incredibly complex punishment meant to recreate the crime Victoria committed. Whereas Jemima Sykes was killed by Rannoch while Victoria watched and filmed, Victoria is now hunted in front of countless onlookers. In the same way that Rannoch and Victoria abducted Jemima Sykes and brought her into the woods, Baxter tricked Victoria (and Jem) into getting into his van before trying to kill her in the forest. We then learn that this macabre recreation is the centerpiece of the *White Bear Justice Park*, where families can pay to participate as onlookers of Victoria's punishment. Her memory is torturously extinguished every night so she can play out the same storyline the next day.

The episode's conclusion creates "a nice sense of queasy vertigo," according to creator Charlie Brooker. "You feel sympathetic toward this person but also repulsed by what they did."[1] And so we are forced to ask: Is this kind of grotesque public punishment of Victoria justified? After all, according to director Carl Tibbetts, "The piece is about not torturing people, whether they've killed children or not."[2]

"Murderer! There were no tears when you watched him do what he did"

Could we ever call such a spectacle "just"? Luckily, we're not the first ones to ponder the limits of punishment. Punishing criminals has been part of social life for millennia and looking to different traditions of justifying criminal punishment can help us make sense of Victoria's bleak fate. One system, endorsed by philosophers like Immanuel Kant (1724–1804) and G.W.F. Hegel (1770–1831), views punishment as *retribution* for a person's crimes. People are punished because they deserve it. Baxter endorses this view when he explains that Rannoch escaped the punishment he *deserved* by hanging himself; he likewise thinks Victoria's role in the justice park is justified because she truly *deserves* it.

But what does "deserving" punishment mean? For Kant, actions are moral insofar as they can be *universalized*. He calls this test the *categorical imperative*, which says that any action that is morally permissible for you to take is one that everyone could actually take. Murder, then, is a no go. While you might want to murder someone, you can't universalize this action. If you did, everyone would be dead (including you) and murder could no longer occur.

Moreover, murder conflicts with a second, related formulation of the categorical imperative: We should treat others not merely as means to an end, but as ends in themselves. Consider when Baxter is about to drill into Victoria's body with a power tool. She pleads with the onlookers, "Help me please! I'm a human being." Obviously, she's *aware* that human beings universally deserve to not be killed. Yet she watched while Jemima was killed. So, Kant would say that Victoria deserves to be punished because she knew full well that the murder of Jemima Sykes was unjust and still allowed it to happen. Further, because Victoria was aware that her action was punishable *but did it anyway*, Kant would say she willed her own punishment by extension.

A justification based on retribution is almost elegantly simple: Victoria, as a rational person aware of the consequences, committed the crime so she *deserves* to be punished. Nothing else even needs to be taken into account, not even the effect of the punishment on Victoria. Kant is what we might call a *strict* retributivist: punishment isn't justified based on whether it makes society safer or the criminal "better." Instead, the simple fact that she committed the crime *at all* warrants her punishment.

Hegel also harbored a retributivist justification for punishment, although his account is a bit more complex. For Hegel, human history progressively gets more *rational*. Over time our political, social, and legal traditions get continually worked out, such that they more appropriately complement our rational faculties as humans.

Because Hegel believes that our world gets more rational as history progresses, he would say that our rational laws should be ones that Victoria endorses (since she's a rational person). So, when she commits a crime she's essentially breaking a law and submitting to a punishment that she herself would endorse. Put differently, being punished respects Victoria as the rational being she *should* be. Once again, as with Kant, Victoria *deserves* her punishment because she commits a crime that she *knows* is wrong.

With all of this in mind, Victoria and Rannoch's child murder has some important implications. Kant would say that because the crime is an affront to justice itself, it must be punished. But Hegel would say the crime *annuls* justice, so punishment is needed to *annul* the first annulment. And this makes intuitive sense: Victoria's crime is an offense to justice, so in order to address it and restore justice we must punish her. Two wrongs don't make a right, but for Hegel two annulments correct the crime and make the world just again.

Retributive systems like Kant's and Hegel's also rely upon a principle of proportionality between crime and punishment, what the ancient Babylonian king Hammurabi called the *lex talionis*, or law (*lex*) of retaliation (*talio*). The most famous of these? "An eye for an eye, a tooth for a tooth." Today the legal system doesn't always follow this rule exactly; we don't punish rapists by raping them, for example. But generally we think that the severity of a just punishment must reflect, and certainly must not be in excess of, the severity of the original crime. But this raises a question: Is Victoria's punishment proportional to her crime? Just because Victoria deserves some sort of punishment doesn't *necessarily* mean that she deserves to have an entire commercial park built around the spectacle of her twisted *Groundhog Day* nightmare. We might think that as horrible as such a scenario is, it couldn't be worse than being abducted, murdered, and burned. But others might disagree. So is the continuous psychological terror that Victoria is subjected to equivalent to the heinous murder of a child? Or might it actually be worse?

Victoria certainly thinks it's worse. At the end of the episode, Victoria pleads for Baxter to kill her. Most people would probably prefer to die rather than suffer a lifetime of torture. But Victoria's memory wipes complicate things in two ways. First, even if she is horrified by the realization of her role in the justice park, she has no idea whether she's undergoing her first day in the park or her hundredth. To us, as spectators with the knowledge of how many days she's survived, the whole ordeal seems wildly disproportionate and cruel. From Victoria's vantage point, however, her perceived experience only totals *one* full day plus the momentary (but admittedly existentially crushing) realization that she'll have to repeat it. And one day's worth of psychological torture seems much less severe than execution. So, which is it? Has the *White Bear Justice Park* gone too far or not?

"Do you know who I am? I can't remember who I am"

Victoria's memory wipes also complicate questions about justifying her punishment by raising serious questions about her personal identity. (Those reading the chapters in order will have already considered similar questions about Ash and AshBot in the last chapter.) Given that she can't remember her crime, we are forced to wonder whether the person subjected to the elaborate fiction of the *White Bear Justice Park* really is the same person as the one who helped brutalize Jemima Sykes. Is the person who did the crime the one doing the time? If not, clearly the punishment is unjustified.

Now, when we ask whether the Victoria who committed the crime (Criminal Victoria) and the Victoria who's punished (Punished Victoria) are "the same person," the sense of the word "same" we have in mind is *not* the qualitative sort—as in "Jemima's father was never *the same* after her death." Certainly, his disposition changed. Perhaps he's now morose, whereas before he had been jovial. But that's a change to his *qualities*; Jemima's father didn't *cease to exist* while some different person *popped up in his place*. He was still (what philosophers call) "numerically identical" to the person who was Jemima's father *before* her death. So, the question is this: Is Punished Victoria numerically identical to Criminal Victoria? And the answer is vital to determining whether the punishment we see in the episode is justified.

What's more, since Punished Victoria remembers nothing about the life of Criminal Victoria, we can legitimately wonder whether they are numerically identical. If not, they're as distinct from one another as Jem is from Baxter. The philosopher John Locke (1632–1704), for instance, argues that a person persists as a numerically identical person only if there is "continuity of consciousness." That is, Locke thinks that you can only be the person who performed some action if you're *conscious* of having done it. Of course, we aren't conscious *all the time* – we sleep – but these separate periods of consciousness can be united by *memories*. So, according to Locke, Punished Victoria is the same person as Criminal Victoria only if Punished Victoria *remembers* taking part in the killing of Jemima Sykes. Since Punished Victoria explicitly *doesn't* remember her crime – in fact, she doesn't remember who Jemima Sykes is at all – for Locke, Punished Victoria can't possibly be numerically identical with Criminal Victoria. She's not the person who helped Iain Rannoch kill Jemima, and thus she deserves no punishment.

Locke's view is certainly not the only way to characterize how and when persons persist, however. Some contemporary thinkers have taken Locke's basic ideas and developed them, saying I'm some past/future person if the right psychological relations hold. For instance, Derek Parfit (1942–2017) proposes a view of identity on which a past and present person are numerically identical if we can trace a chain of *psychological connections* – memories, beliefs, desires, and other mental states – between them. This is called *psychological continuity*. Although Parfit doesn't endorse this view of identity himself, many others do. Still others, like contemporary philosopher Judith Jarvis Thomson, argue that numerical identity is instead a matter of having the right physiological relations. That is, I'm some past/future person if we're *physiologically continuous*. To Thomson, this means having the same body—even if the brain is removed!

Whether we adopt a psychological or physiological continuity view of identity, we get a different result in Victoria's case than we did with Locke. Because psychological states are concerned with so many other mental states than just memories, Punished Victoria would be numerically identical to Criminal Victoria according to these theories. Punished Victoria may be an amnesiac, but she seems to have enough leftover beliefs, desires, character traits, and other mental states to make her psychologically continuous with the person who committed the crime. Physiological views like Thomson's would *also* have to admit that Punished Victoria is numerically identical with Criminal Victoria. Since they have the same body, they must be the same person.

There is much more to say on this, and the issue of personal identity is dealt with elsewhere in this volume.[3] But since everyone in the episode obviously thinks that Punished Victoria is the same person as Criminal Victoria, let's set Locke's worries aside and assume that's right. The person who committed the crime is the one being punished, and thus *deserves* punishment. We can now circle back around to the earlier question: Is Victoria's punishment *justified*? On the retributive theory, it seems we'd have to say no. If Victoria is the *same* person through each passing day, then *she's* still the one being tortured, even though she forgets. Thus her punishment for Jemima's death seems disproportionate; death is surely preferable to a lifetime of torture.

"Why do they look like that? They like scaring people"

While the retributive theory of justice illuminates, but ultimately fails to justify, Victoria's punishment, it's not the only game in town. We can also look to a moral framework called utilitarianism, made famous by Jeremy Bentham (1748–1832) and John Stuart Mill (1806–1873). Utilitarianism is simple: things are just insofar as they produce the maximum amount of *utility*. By extension then, punishment is justified if it does the same thing. But what does it mean exactly for punishment to produce "utility?"

For Bentham, if punishment is meant to address crime, then the punishment that generates the most utility is the one that can best prevent future crimes. He calls this phenomenon *deterrence*: seeing a criminal being punished makes people not want to break the law so that they can avoid a similar fate. And in Victoria's case, we can surely see that her fate is not one we would fancy for ourselves. In fact, even if we didn't have moral qualms with abducting, murdering, and burning a child, we might still refrain from such actions simply because we don't want to join the hellish nightmare that Victoria inhabits. As a deterrent, the *White Bear Justice Park* seems to be effective.

Because utilitarianism is all about getting the most bang for your punitive buck, it also takes seriously a number of other goals. One is disablement or incapacitation: basically, does the punishment ensure that the criminal cannot cause more trouble? In Victoria's case, definitely: she's locked inside a park and doesn't even realize it. The goal of deterrence can also be broken down further. There's *particular* deterrence, in which we want the criminal themselves to be scared out of committing a crime again, and there's *general* deterrence, in which we want the onlookers to be dissuaded from committing crimes simply by watching the criminal be punished. Since Victoria's punishment seems to do both, for Bentham, it generates *a lot* of utility.

It's worth noting, however, that the utilitarian must also consider whether the punishment has any utility for the criminal. Does it "rehabilitate" the criminal in any way? This concern presents an issue for utilitarians looking to justify Victoria's punishment. Why? Because no rehabilitation is accomplished. Although she learns each day that she would not want to be in the situation that she put Jemima Sykes in, and is certainly motivated to never commit such a crime again, her mind is then wiped and the lesson is lost.

So, why *not* just kill her? John Stuart Mill, the nineteenth-century inheritor of Bentham's utilitarian legacy, was a staunch supporter of capital punishment, after all. He argued that execution, a penalty that should be reserved for atrocious criminals unfit to live in society, carried the most deterrent power. The world of *Black Mirror*, however, isn't the same as nineteenth-century Britain. How does the deterrent power of executing someone compare to psychological torture in the presence of complicit onlookers? Would Mill have been a regular visitor to the *White Bear Justice Park*? Perhaps. While execution reigned supreme in Mill's day, Victoria's fate could prove a more effective deterrent – especially since it's recreated and televised every day. Victoria's suffering is the gift that keeps on giving: her anguish educates millions about the consequences of committing such heinous crimes.

So, one might give a utilitarian argument for the justification of the *White Bear Justice Park* based on its deterrent effects. But, like retributivism, utilitarianism also holds itself to a standard of proportionality between crime and punishment. Is it really fair to subject one person to extreme suffering for the sake of teaching a community? Does the fact that she gets to live while Jemima Sykes doesn't mean that what we see in *White Bear* is within the realm of proportionality? If the answer is no, utilitarianism can't justify Victoria's punishment after all.

Worse yet, utilitarianism also can't justify all the theatricality. Isn't punishment supposed to deter? Aren't people supposed to be horrified? Instead, people are laughing! During the credits, we see Baxter remind visitors that the justice park's "most important rule" is to *enjoy yourself*. So there must be something else going on here, something that can't be explained in terms of whether or not Victoria deserved it or how much utility her sentence produces.

"Good evening citizens! Thank you so much for coming tonight"

The chants of "Murderer!" and the torch-lit mob throwing blood-filled sponges at Victoria make one thing clear: If punishment is to be enjoyed, it's best enjoyed as a *spectacle*. There's something socially cohesive about it, and the fact that the sign at the entrance of the *White Bear Justice Park* (visible for a moment in the credits) suggests advanced booking only drives this point home. None other than the so-called "teacher of evil" Niccolò Machiavelli (1469–1527) thought of punitive spectacles in social terms. He saw public executions as an important way to reinvigorate a sense of fraternity amongst citizens. Much like those who used to descend on the town square to watch someone be hanged, the attendees of the *White Bear Justice Park* find themselves united in opposition to the malcontent. In this case, it's Victoria Skillane, a woman so hated that #DeathToVictoriaSkillane can be seen trending in the later episode "Hated in the Nation." After all, if we cared only about Victoria getting punished simply because she *deserved* it, there would be no need for the justice park. In the same way, if all we wanted was deterrence, a public broadcast of her gruesome execution would be much easier. But it's precisely this sense of community and participation in the spectacle that makes *White Bear Justice Park* so riveting to its attendees.

In addition to this civic side of punishment, Machiavelli also thought of these spectacles as a kind of *catharsis*. He believed people harbored natural drives which, when unchecked, could destabilize civil society and foster unrest. He thus recommended public executions so spectacular that they could literally stupefy a populace into awe of their motherland. The more over the top the better. On these grounds, Victoria's punishment is less about her and more about the socially constructive civic ritual that revolves around her torment. The fact that the justice park brings so many families together so happily could be seen as a vindication of Victoria's fate.

Friedrich Nietzsche (1844–1900), the German philosopher who famously proclaimed the death of God, can bring us one step further. Getting together with our friends and uniting against a common enemy is one thing, but why does seeing someone get punished *feel so good*? Rather than experiencing horror, the visitors of the justice park laugh and jeer. There's even a German word for it: *Schadenfreude*, the pleasure derived from another person's misfortune. While we might be taken aback by someone accusing of us sadism, Nietzsche would contend that the visceral rush the justice park attendees get when they see Victoria scream isn't perverse, it's *natural*.

For Nietzsche, punishment is a distant and modern relative of an ancient everyday occurrence: collecting on one's debts. Some remnants of this relationship still exist today when we talk about punishment as "paying one's debt to society." Originally, punishment used to feel good simply because it was a testament to one's power over another; when a debt couldn't be paid, the creditor gained the opportunity to partake in the pleasure of punishing the person who had defaulted. Over centuries, however, this relationship became *moralized*. We superimposed different moral systems, including Kant's retributive theory and Bentham's utilitarian one, onto this natural dynamic in order to "justify" it. Even worse, this age-old relationship of the creditor and debtor got warped into the Christian system of morality, where God has the power to punish us for sinning. The natural drives that originally caused us to take joy in punishing got pent up under Christian morality. Nevertheless, they still rear their heads sometimes in the crazed high we get from seeing someone in pain. This insight alone is a damning indictment for the *White Bear Justice Park*. Not only can Victoria's punishment not be justified using retributive or utilitarian theories of justice, *even if it could* these theories themselves are merely excuses we made up in order to justify our base urges for payback.[4]

But what exactly does that mean for Victoria? And what might it mean for us? Earlier, when Jem and Victoria were fleeing from the gunman, Victoria asks if it's the mysterious signal that's making people act so monstrously. Jem's telling response is that "they were always like that underneath." Though Jem was talking about the hunters and onlookers, her insight applies to the impulses the justice park is tapping into as well. After all, there's more than a little irony in the fact that Victoria's crime, which was joyfully filming someone suffer, is punished by a scenario in which people get the privilege of doing *the exact same thing* to her.

But while this psychological insight might be the subtext that explains the popularity of the *White Bear Justice Park*, we should be reluctant to call it a justification. After all, if the justice park were vindicated simply because we enjoy seeing Victoria in pain, wouldn't that mean she'd be off the hook for playing a part in the murder of Jemima Sykes? We're not so different from Victoria, even if we don't feel comfortable admitting it. With that said, if it's true that the justice park is doing to Victoria what she did to Jemima Sykes, we can't possibly call her fate justified.

"Don't forget, she's a dangerous individual"

The *White Bear Justice Park* appears to have gone much too far; its cruel antics are something that no one, not even Victoria Skillane, seems to deserve. While the retributive and utilitarian theories of punishment help to illuminate justifications that *could* be invoked for punishing Victoria in this way, they fail because a lifetime of torture is disproportional to her crime and its deterrent effect is uncertain.

But even beyond that, the real question is whether or not we buy these justifications. In other words, though these theories purport to provide a moral justification for punishing Victoria in such a cruel way, why are the attendees *really* there? Doesn't the fact that it's *fun* to take part in the elaborate spectacle that is the *White Bear Justice Park* indicate that something else is occurring? The primal joy the onlookers get from Victoria's anguish generates two intertwined insights. First, if we recognize what Victoria did was wrong, we're also wrong for doing it to her. And second, if we enjoy filming her and abstaining from intervening so much, who are we to condemn her? The attendees of the justice park simply reenact Victoria's crime, except with her as the victim. The only difference is that when the crowd does it, they call it "justice."

When we ask how far is too far, we have to look in the "black mirror" and ask ourselves two questions. What *exactly* is it inside of us that could have given birth to the *White Bear Justice Park* in the first place? And what does it tell us about how we punish criminals in the real world? As producer Annabel Jones puts it, "the focus [of *White Bear*] is very much on how we bring people to justice and what outrages we can do if we feel we're morally justified."[5]

Notes

1. Charlie Brooker and Annabel Jones with Jason Arnopp, *Inside Black Mirror* (New York: Crown Archetype, 2018), 87.
2. ibid.
3. See Chapter 22 (Molly Gardner and Robert Slone's chapter on personal identity) in this volume.
4. In the same way, neither retributivism nor deterrence can fully explain why Jemima Sykes' mother would want to play the role of a "hunter" and chase Victoria with an electric carving knife every day–as she does in the episode.
5. Brooker et al., 87.

The Waldo Moment and Political Discourse

What's Wrong with Disrespect in Politics?

Greg Littmann

Question the status quo! Kill it! Kill it! Kick them where it hurts!
(Waldo)

In *The Waldo Moment*, a virtual bear becomes a successful politician through disrespecting, abusing, and dismissing his political rivals. It seemed far-fetched when the episode aired in 2013. But in 2016, US presidential candidate Donald Trump did essentially the same thing by taking disrespect, abuse, and dismissal of his rivals to heights unprecedented in modern first-world democracies. Where Waldo insulted his opponents by calling them "knobber" and "dickhead," Trump attached insulting nicknames to his opponents like "Little Marco," "Lyin' Ted," and "Crooked Hillary." Where Waldo said that his opponent Liam Monroe looked less than human, Trump said Hillary didn't have "a Presidential look" and that he "wasn't impressed" as she walked in front of him during a debate. Trump implied Natasha Stoynoff was too ugly to sexually assault and said Heidi Klum was "no longer a 10." About John McCain, who famously spent more than five years as a POW in Vietnam because he refused an early release, Trump said, "He was a war hero because he was captured. I like people who weren't captured." And then Trump won the election. Are we already living in the Waldo moment?

After her loss, Hillary Clinton eventually decided that civility to the Republican party (or the GOP) was unfeasible, telling CNN in 2018, "You cannot be civil with a political party that wants to destroy what you stand for, what you care about," and that civility can't return to American politics until the Democrats have retaken "the House and/or Senate." The hostility, incivility, and lack of engagement between American political leaders reflects the hostility, incivility, and lack of engagement between Americans with different political views. Increasingly, folks on different sides of the

Black Mirror and Philosophy: Dark Reflections, First Edition. Edited by David Kyle Johnson.
© 2020 John Wiley & Sons, Inc. Published 2020 by John Wiley & Sons, Inc.

political aisle see each other as enemies to be denounced and fought, rather than partners to be listened to and engaged with.

Waldo's rise to power ends in tragedy. The anger of his followers turns into violence. When Waldo's puppeteer Jamie Salter quits, his producer takes over, offers 500 quid to "the first man to hit him," and Salter wakes up in hospital after the election. After losing the Stentonford by-election to Conservative MP Liam Monroe, Waldo incites them again. "Hey, hey! Everyone! 500 quid to anyone who can lob a shoe!" and Monroe is hit in the face. The final scene shows us a world dominated by Waldo, where police patrols move the massed homeless from sheltering under a bridge.

We are left to ask: What should be the role of disrespect and dismissal in politics? When, if ever, is it appropriate to be disrespectful or dismissive of an individual or their political views? To help decide, let's take a closer look at how Waldo goes from virtual comic to world ruler, and the parallels in our own society.

"It's easy, what he does. He mocks"

Waldo is known for mocking politicians during his segment on a political satire TV show, *Tonight for One Week Only*. (It's as if Conan O'Brien's Triumph the Insult Comic Dog had a weekly segment on *Last Week Tonight with John Oliver*.) He's deliberately offensive and openly insults his guests. When Monroe complains about Waldo's antics, it's considered good press.

Waldo doesn't offer reasoned replies. "You are laughing at someone who won't engage," Monroe points out. "Why do we waste our time with animated trivialities like him?" Waldo doesn't offer a justification; he just repeatedly farts the question back at him. When Waldo finds facts inconvenient, he just denies them. "No one votes," Waldo claims. And when Monroe points out that the "vast majority do vote," Waldo responds with: "It's bullshit." Indeed, non-engagement is actually part of the plan. When Jamie objects, "I can't answer serious questions," Jack assures him, "no one wants you to."

Much of Waldo's mockery doesn't even make a political point. Sometimes he's personally abusive. He calls Monroe a "knobber" and asks him if he's a dickhead. Often, he just expresses disrespect by being vulgar, like when he implies Monroe doesn't "know what pussy is." As Monroe points out, "when he can't think of an authentic joke, which is actually quite often, he just swears."

Waldo's aggressive approach is driven by Jamie's mistrust and resentment of those in power, and Waldo takes advantage of those same feelings in the audience. He's quick to paint Monroe as an arrogant elitist because of the way he talks. "There's no point in attempting to converse with a cartoon," Monroe protests. "Ooh, 'converse,'" Waldo taunts. "Your Lordship! Thy flowery language doth give me a right throbbing bone-on!" (and then pulls out his "turquoise cock"). When Monroe protests that he's entitled to "common courtesy," Waldo answers, "Because you went to public school[1] and grew up believing you were entitled to everything." Similarly, when Philip Crane, the presenter of the current affairs program *Consensus,* suggests that Waldo's participation in politics is dangerous, Waldo accuses him of looking down on ordinary people: "Dangerous? You think the public can't be trusted? Isn't that basically you calling them twats?"

Above all, Waldo expresses contempt for politicians. "No one trusts you lot cos they know you don't give a shit about anything outside your bubble." They're therefore useless. "What are you for?" He demands of Monroe and Harris. They're fake, telling lies and pretending to care about the public good, while really just furthering their own interests. Monroe tells him, "A politician is someone who tries to make the world a fairer place," a platitude he himself can't possibly believe. Of course, he thinks he's on a kid's show, which puts him in a tough position but his smooth diplomatic lie shows how artificial his persona is. Waldo sees him as a traditional, uncaring politician behind a fresh, modern façade, telling Monroe, "You're just an old attitude with new hair." Waldo compares him to his fellow Conservative politician, Jason Gladwell, who shared naked pictures with a fifteen-year-old girl on the internet: "Yeah, cos you're all just front, like him, sly and pretending...you're all the same."

As for the Labour (liberal) candidate, Gwendolyn Harris, Waldo tells her:

> You're worse! Seriously, she's faker than him...She's here to build a show reel...Knows she's not going to win. This is all experience, to get on telly!

And Waldo's right. Although she initially claimed that she's running in Stentonford, "Because I'm not satisfied with the way things are, and rather than sit back and moan I'd prefer to do something about it," she later admits that she's only interested in advancing her career. Her campaign is a "stepping stone." When Jamie urges her to use her candidacy as an opportunity to speak honestly to the public, she isn't interested. "Why not be honest?" he asks. "Say, 'You arseholes aren't going to vote for me, so here's what I think anyway.'"

"It doesn't work like that," she answers.

"Nothing does. That's why everything's bollocksed," says Jamie.

"No one trusts you lot cos they know you don't give a shit about anything outside your bubble"

As in Waldo's UK, voters in the US are pissed off at politicians in general. Obviously, they reserve their strongest disgust for politicians on the other side, but neither are happy with politicians on their own side either. In 2016, it was conservative dissatisfaction with the GOP establishment that handed Trump the Republican nomination. Trump campaigned on a promise to "drain the swamp," and Jeb Bush, the party favorite, received less than 1% of the popular vote in the primary election. Likewise, it was liberal dissatisfaction with establishment Democrats (like Hillary) that handed Trump the election. Trump received fewer votes than Mitt Romney did in 2012 when he lost to Barrack Obama, but turnout for Democrats was so low that Trump won anyway. In theory, the Democrats represent the interests of the working class, yet many workers voted for the GOP, or stayed home.[2]

In Waldo's UK, political mistrust extends to an entire class, seen as the exploiters of the masses. But where Waldo uses Monroe's upper-class manners to identify him as the enemy, American liberals and conservatives don't agree on exactly who the exploiters are. Trump campaigned on fighting the "elites," a group which includes Democratic politicians, academics, non-conservative political media, and pampered civil servants. Since then, he's lamented the "deep state" (a conspiracy within the government), and conservative commentators have condemned the "political class." Liberals, on the other hand, usually see the very rich as the exploitative elite, exercising undue influence over both major political parties. Other groups seen as privileged may also be viewed as exploitative elites, like whites, men, and heterosexuals.

The Divided States of America

Where the modern US differs from Waldo's UK is in the depth of its divisions. US voters are not only angry at politicians, but at each other. As mistrust between different camps grows, we denounce and insult those we disagree with rather than reasoning with them. YouTube is filled with videos where you can watch conservatives, liberals, feminists, anti-feminists, or whoever you like being publicly humiliated or "owned" in debate, as Waldo humiliated Monroe and Harris. And just try to find an internet forum where liberals and conservatives civilly discuss politics! Even at universities, traditional bastions of free speech and the exchange of ideas, we see incidents of controversial speakers like Milo Yiannopoulos, Jordan Peterson, and Bill Maher being disinvited or shouted down because some find what they have to say offensive.

To boot, our news media is increasingly tailored to our political views. Liberals hear liberal opinions, conservatives hear conservative ones, and media representing the "other side" is demonized. Fox News accuses "mainstream media" of liberal bias, and liberal commentators call Fox News "Faux News." Trump calls CNN and MSNBC "dishonest," "corrupt," "sick," and the "the enemy of the people," and liberal commentators claim that Fox is akin to state-run propaganda.

Just as Waldo is quick to dismiss inconvenient facts, real world partisans are often willing to overlook facts that don't support their views, perhaps because they think that conceding anything to the other side would sabotage the war effort. And while politicians telling lies is nothing new, Trump has taken it to a whole new level, averaging nearly eight lies a day, including some whoppers like he only lost the popular vote because of millions of illegal votes in California, that Democrats employ "Professional anarchists, thugs and paid protesters," that there "were thousands and thousands of people were cheering as that building was coming down," in Jersey City, New Jersey on 9/11, and that he can't release his tax returns because they are under audit.[3]

"Everyone's pissed with the status quo and Waldo gives that a voice"

Waldo's approach has disastrous consequences. But is it always wrong to be dismissive of positions we disagree with, or even disrespectful to those who hold them? For instance, if the KKK are marching in the street, would it be appropriate to boo them or, following Waldo's example, call them "knobbers" (or something worse)?

Or what about political comedians and satirical political television shows like *Full Frontal with Samantha Bee*, Trever Noah's *The Daily Show*, Stephen Colbert's *Late Show*, and John Oliver's *Last Week Tonight*? Did Bee go too far when she called Ivanka Trump a "feckless cunt"? Did Noah go too far when he said, "If being an asshole was an arcade game, [Trump] would have all the top scores"? Did Colbert go too far when he said that Trump put the "dic" in "dictatorship"? Did Oliver go too far when he called Trump a "damaged, sociopathic narcissist" with a Cheeto dick who's lack of knowledge would fill an encyclopedia?" How about when Bill Maher claimed that Trump is the "spawn of his mother having sex with an orangutan"? Or when Kathy Griffin posed with a severed Trump head?

Political mockery is one of humanity's oldest artistic traditions. In the West, the first known political comedies appeared around the same time and place as the first known works of political philosophy: 2500 years ago in ancient Greece. The comic playwright Aristophanes (446–386 BCE), for example, mercilessly mocked the popular Athenian politician Cleon, implying he was a thoughtless demagogue with a thirst for war. Likewise, the Roman satirist Juvenal (55–127) mocked the pomposity, corruption, and greed of his fellow Romans, while the Arabic satirist al-Jahiz (776–869) mocked his contemporaries in medieval Baghdad for the same reasons. In America, Benjamin Franklin (1706–1790) used mockery to attack England's exploitation of the colonists; Mark Twain (1835–1910) used it to attack the practice of slavery; and Joseph Heller (1923–1999) used it to attack militarism and military bureaucracy. Like Waldo, Greek comic actors would brandish huge and ridiculous fake penises to mock their targets. Nicknaming is also nothing new. The Roman poet Catullus used to call Julius Caesar "dick-face."

One traditional justification for political mockery is that the shame of being satirized causes wicked people to change their ways. Juvenal said of the satirist that "his hearers go red; their conscience freezes with their crimes, their innards swear in awareness of unacknowledged guilt."[4] In reality, however, Juvenal's hope of reforming people by laughing at them was shortsighted. Indeed, mocking someone is a *particularly* bad tool for changing their mind because those who feel disrespected tend to not listen to those disrespecting them. Indeed, most political mockery, like Waldo's mocking of Monroe's accent, is unrelated to any justified political complaint. When Aristophanes puts a funny penis on Cleon, he's making fun of his genitals, not his politics. Juvenal is no more politically relevant when he tells us that the consul Montanus was so fat that his stomach dragged on the ground, and that the senator Crispinus wore so much perfume he was "more aromatic than two funerals put together."[5]

A better justification for political mockery is that it may keep important issues in the mind of a fickle public. Aristophanes mocked Cleon because the playwright wanted to see an end to the Peloponnesian War against Sparta. By writing political plays, he helped ensure that Athenians didn't forget their war. Likewise, marching through the streets with a giant inflated Trump baby, as London protesters did, forces anyone who sees it to think of the American president.

Another possible justification for political mockery would be building morale. Mocking our foes makes us feel superior, which can give us a fighting spirit. Consider the popular World War II propaganda song, "Hitler has Only Got One Ball" (1939). No important political observation is made, as the quantity of the Führer's testicles is just as irrelevant to his suitability for office as Marco Rubio's height or the size of Donald Trump's hands. But the song still might inspire soldiers to fight. And what goes for wars goes for political campaigns. In elections, voter enthusiasm is essential. If everyone who claimed to prefer Democrats to Republicans had voted in 2016, the Dems would have won easily. If Clinton had been as uncivil as Trump, she might have whipped up more enthusiasm and won.

Another possible justification for political mockery is that it may convince others that you're right. As noted, it's unlikely to work on the people you mock, but it might convince observers. In an ideal world, people would be moved only by reason, but in the real world, propaganda is highly effective. Dictators and oppressive governments have traditionally used political mockery to reinforce their view of the world, as in Nazi propaganda films like *Jud Süss* and *Die Rothschilds* (both 1940). Trump was certainly very successful in convincing people that he should be president, and disrespect and mockery were weapons in his arsenal.

A fourth possible justification for political mockery is simply to harness voter resentment by offering them a candidate who will express their rage. Jack explains Waldo's popularity: "You know, everyone's pissed with the status quo and Waldo gives that a voice." If the electorate is pissed off and in the mood to vote for a disrespectful, contemptuous candidate, and the political stakes are high enough, this might mean that a disrespectful, contemptuous candidate is what a well-intentioned political party should field.

"Waldo, as a mascot for the disenfranchised, aren't you ultimately neutralizing seriously effective dissent?"

There are two major problems with political mockery, however. First, it may encourage the public to rely on mockery instead of reason. If mockery can win someone over to the right political position now, it can lead them to the wrong political position later. As Plato (428–348 BCE) pointed out in his dialogue *Meno,* people who hold the right beliefs without understanding *why* those beliefs are true are unreliable. If they hold the right belief for no good reason, they might change their minds for no good reason, too.[6]

If only Jamie had read Plato, he might have seen where Waldo's abuse would lead. Because Waldo relies on mockery, he's able to sell the public any set of political views. As Jack explains, "At the moment he's anti-politics, which is a political stance itself, right? But he could deliver any brand of political content." Appropriately, while Waldo promises to "question the status quo! Kill it! Kill it!" he remains vague about exactly what he will do in office, apart from "Kick [those in power] where it hurts." His van announces, "I'm Mr. Monroe. Vote for me and keep things shitty," while his own political ad at the end of the episode, proclaims "Change," "Believe," "Challenge," "Better," "Future," and "Hope."

Another danger of political mockery is that we'll be persuaded by *ad hominem* attacks – an error in reasoning where one tries to refute a position or argument by mocking or ridiculing the person who made it, instead of engaging with the position or argument they made. "*Ad hominem* nonsense" complains Monroe, when Waldo responds to Monroe's claim that he deserves common curtsey by accusing Monroe of feeling entitled because he went to an expensive school. When Monroe argues that Waldois stifling debate with such attacks, Waldo responds with another *ad hominem*: "You look less human than I do and I'm a made-up bear with a turquoise cock."

Ad hominem is rife in modern politics. Almost any insult with no political point would count (since such an insult would seem to imply that you should ignore the argument or position of the person being insulted), though some examples from Trump have been truly spectacular. "Look at that face!" Trump said of Carly Fiorina, "Would anybody vote for that?" implying that one should ignore her arguments that she was worthy of votes. "If Hillary Clinton can't satisfy her husband," Trump retweeted, "what makes her think she can satisfy America?"[7] The problem is prolific. Rather than working to understand one another and reason together, we tend to attack the character of those we disagree with, as if this showed that what they are saying isn't true.

Not every personal criticism in an argument is *ad hominem*, though. After all, a person's character might be the very point at issue. If I'm running for office, and you point out that I have a history of dishonesty, you are revealing something relevant about whether people should vote for me. So it isn't *ad hominem* in itself for Clinton to accuse Trump of disrespecting women, or for Trump to accuse Clinton of being "crooked." It was striking, though, how much both campaigns focused on personal criticisms rather than comparing policies.

"You're laughing at someone who won't engage"

The second major problem with political mockery is that it prevents us from engaging with people with whom we disagree. "I think that this puppet's inclusion on this panel debases the process of debate and smothers any meaningful discussion of the issues," Monroe complains. Jamie acknowledges that he's not making a contribution to the political discussion. When Jack assures him, "You can do politics," he objects, "I do piss-taking!"

If we don't engage with people we disagree with, we give up any chance to change their mind. Jaime has some valid criticisms of the political system, but he'll never convince Monroe or Harris of that while he's calling them names. Likewise, people flaming each other on the internet over politics give up any chance of being convincing. Worse yet, not engaging prevents us from hearing opinions we disagree with, and so stands in the way of us realizing when we are wrong. The closest many Americans get to hearing the political opinions of those they disagree with is hearing them denounced or mocked by partisans.

Refusing engagement has similar effects as censorship, in that it prevents us from being exposed to ideas. The best arguments I know against censorship were presented by John Stuart Mill (1806–1873) in *On Liberty*. First, since we all make mistakes, we can never know for sure that the opinion we are suppressing is wrong. "All silencing of discussion is an assumption of infallibility."[8] Secondly, it is good for people to hear false opinions because it allows them to gain a better understanding of *why* those opinions are false and thus a "the clearer perception and livelier impression of truth, produced by its collision with error."[9] As Mill says, "He who knows only his own side of the case, knows little of that."[10]

When we only engage with people who have the same opinions we do, we enter a "reality bubble," in which facts that contradict our beliefs are never allowed. By carefully choosing what we see and read, we can insulate ourselves from being contradicted, or even realizing what a warped view of the world we are being given.

Mill also pointed out that, because opinions tend to be the product of social influences more than reason, we have every reason to doubt our opinions. People tend to adopt the views of those with whom they are familiar. Someone raised in Oklahoma is likely to be Christian, someone raised in Thailand a Buddhist. Someone raised among conservatives is likely to be conservative, while someone raised among liberals a liberal. Even though we know that there has been enormous diversity of opinion across the world and throughout history, we tend to be convinced that our social group is right on all important points.

As Mill notes, there's powerful social pressure to not stray from group orthodoxy. Siding with the opposition can be viewed as betrayal. How would it go down with your friends or family if you changed some of your key political beliefs? Even trying to fairly consider the best arguments of "the other side" could be frowned upon. As George Orwell writes in *1984*, "Orthodoxy means not thinking."[11] Indeed, social groups try to find the *worst* arguments and most outrageous positions presented on "the other side" to demonstrate how awful the other side is. Sadly, social status can often be won by being the most vehement in denouncing the other side's views.

After the Waldo Moment

The Waldo Moment stands as an important warning about what can happen if we let our anger drive us, instead of using our powers of reason to choose the most constructive course of action. On both sides of the political aisle, we too often prioritize expressing our feelings over making positive political progress through difficult engagement with those who disagree with us. That doesn't mean that it's always wrong to mock or be dismissive, but to let mockery and dismissal take over our political discourse is to sabotage any chance to work together for a better future. Hopefully, we will turn our back on Waldo politics before it's too late.

Notes

1. In American terms, an English public school is an expensive private school.
2. Matthew Yglesias, "What really happened in 2016, in 7 charts," *Vox*, https://www.vox.com/policy-and-politics/2017/9/18/16305486/what-really-happened-in-2016 (Accessed 8 July 2019).

3. Glenn Kessler, Salvador Rizzo, and Meg Kelly, "President Trump has made 4299 false or misleading statements in 558 days," *Washington Post*, https://www.washingtonpost.com/news/fact-checker/wp/2018/08/01/president-trump-has-made-4229-false-or-misleading-claims-in-558-days/?noredirect=on&utm_term=.fc9e2006078a (Accessed 3 July 2019).
4. Juvenal, *Sixteen Satires*, trans. Peter Green (London: Penguin, 1999), 7.
5. Ibid., 27.
6. Plato, *Meno*, trans. Lesley Brown (London: Penguin, 2006), 130.
7. To be fair, one might argue that this is a faulty analogy, rather than an *ad hominem*.
8. John Stuart Mill, "On Liberty" in *On Liberty and The Subjection of Women* (London: Penguin, 2007), 19.
9. Ibid., 18.
10. Ibid., 43.
11. George Orwell, *1984* (New York: Signet Classics, 1961), 53.

THE CHRISTMAS SPECIAL

White Christmas and Technological Restraining Orders

Are Digital Blocks Ethical?

Cansu Canca and Laura Haaber Ihle

> People want to be noticed. They don't like to be shut out. It makes them feel invisible.
>
> (Matthew Trent)

Two men, an isolated cabin, and a white Christmas with a dark twist. *White Christmas* differs from most *Black Mirror* episodes in the way it weaves two technologies together into separate but related stories. The first story is Matthew's. Working as a "cookie monster," he trains digital copies of individuals called "cookies" to become the ultimate personal assistants. As an illegal side-gig, he also runs a dating service that guides men in real time to pick up women by watching them through his clients' eyes, using the Z-eye technology. Matthew leads one of his clients to successfully pick up a girl, only to have her poison him because she wrongly assumed he wanted to join her in a suicide pact.

We then learn about Joe and his failed relationship with Beth, who digitally blocks and leaves him while pregnant. The digital block drives Joe's story; it extends to Beth's child, who is also blocked from both his reach and view. Joe does his best to follow the child in secret during Beth's annual Christmas visits to her father. When the block is lifted after Beth dies, Joe tries to reunite with the child at Beth's father's home, only to discover the child is not his. Confused and enraged, Joe still demands, "I want to see my daughter." When Beth's father objects, in a fit of rage, Joe hits him over the head with a snow globe (a gift he had bought for his daughter), accidentally killing him. After Joe leaves, the child walks out into the cold to try to find help, and she dies as well.

And this, it turns out, is why we are watching Matthew and Joe interact in the cabin. Matthew – the cookie monster – is trying to get a confession from Joe, who turns out to be a cookie. After the digital cabin in which they are spending this Christmas slowly turns into the room in which Joe murdered Beth's father, Joe finally breaks. Once his mission is accomplished, Matthew gets a pardon for his Z-eye crime – but at a price. He is now blocked by the whole of society. The episode ends with Joe's cookie being trapped in the cabin for eternity.

As one of the movie-length episodes, *White Christmas* brings up more questions than most. Central are the moral questions about the use of these fictional technologies: What privacy concerns are raised by cookies and letting others watch what you see with the Z-Eye technology? How do we balance the concerns about privacy and access to information raised by digital blocks, especially if they can block parents from children? And what does all this tell us about how we already block people from society in the real world?

Enter Technologies: Cookies and Z-eyes

A cookie is a digital replica of an individual's consciousness that is extracted and placed in a widget.[1] The issue of whether cookies would be conscious, and whether they would be the same person as the person from which they are copied, are questions that are addressed elsewhere in this volume.[2] But the answers are important to issues central to this episode. Consider how Matthew speeds the passage of time for the cookie of one of his clients, Greta, to "convince" the cookie to run Greta's smarthouse. Does this just classify as reprograming? Or is it torture because cookie-Greta is conscious? Is Joe's cookie morally responsible for Joe's crime, or is he a separate person and thus completely undeserving of the punishment inflicted upon him: being locked up alone in the crime scene while listening to Wizzard's "I Wish It Could Be Christmas Every Day" for millions of years?

We may also wonder whether people should ever be forced to hand over their cookies, as happens in Joe's case. Wouldn't it be a violation of autonomy and privacy? While the cookie technology hints at the privacy concern in this manner, the Z-eye technology places these concerns right in the center and depicts a tug of war between privacy and information. Indeed, the first time we hear about the Z-eyes is in connection with the dating service, where the whole set-up is made possible by invading unsuspecting women's privacy. The women unknowingly and unwillingly share their private encounters with the members of the dating group and are in turn manipulated into relationships with men who are not sincere. The men collectively plot pick-up strategies which, although efficient, do not truthfully reflect their individual identities. This invasion of privacy allows men to access all the possible information they might need to manipulate these women. In this scenario the access to information trumps privacy.

The rest of the episode revolves around another feature of the Z-eye technology: digital blocks. This feature allows people with a digital block between them to no longer be visible or audible to each other. Instead, they appear as blurred and muffled human shapes. We follow three instances of digital blocking, all of which deal with concerns about privacy and information, evolving from a personal measure to a social punishment.

Instance #1: Just Between You and Me

In our initial encounter with digital blocking, Matthew and Joe are blocked by their partners. Matthew's wife blocks him because she feels cheated and wronged when she learns about his dating service. Joe's partner, Beth, blocks Joe, not because she feels cheated, but because *she* has cheated and wronged him. In both cases, the blocks are used to avoid the emotional strain of a confrontation.

Digital blocks might seem alien, but they are clearly based on a practice we are already familiar with: blocking on social media. The transfer of this commonplace cyber-practice to the physical world highlights the key ethical issues it raises. On social media, blocking protects our privacy and personal sphere. Digital blocking augments this concept and brings a similar control over real life interactions.

Such an expansion of individual privacy creates significant obstacles when it comes to the accessibility of information – and that comes with consequences. Take Joe, for example. We might think that Beth blocking him was necessary to protect her privacy. But Beth was able to do that through other efforts: moving away, cutting all ties to mutual friends, and getting a restraining order.[3] Perhaps the block was easier and more effective, but because he was not able to reach Beth, explain himself, and learn the truth, Joe harbored emotions that eventually led him to cause the death of Beth's father and daughter. This, it seems, wouldn't have happened so easily without the block.

Of course, like Beth, we all value our privacy because it allows us to feel secure and in control. But like Joe, we also value information because it is essential for making sense of the world and the people in it. Indeed, both privacy and information are instrumental to everyone's quest for happiness and individual autonomy. But since a digital block puts these values into conflict – sacrificing access to information for one person in the name of protecting the privacy of another – *White Christmas* raises serious questions about which is more important. And different ethical frameworks entail different ways to determine how this conflict should be resolved.

Utilitarianism, for example, suggests that the ethical action is the one that results in the greatest amount of good for the greatest number of people (or sentient beings). This, of course, raises the question of what it means for something to be "good." Jeremy Bentham (1748–1832) formulated it in terms of happiness, whereas the modern philosopher Peter Singer suggests preference satisfaction.[4] In either formulation, however, the question would be whether digital blocks cause *overall* harm or benefit – not merely to the individual but to everyone who is affected. Do the positive effects on the person protecting their privacy outweigh the negative effects on others, like reducing the accuracy of their worldview? The "good" use of digital blocks would result in higher overall happiness or satisfaction in comparison to the other options. Beth and Joe's story could serve as an example of the "bad" use, where the result is clearly tragic. Yet, from a utilitarian perspective, their example would not be a knock-down objection against all use of digital blocks unless such tragic stories are common. (Would such things happen often or is Joe just a weird guy who stalks his ex and has a fit that results in murder when he can't get closure?)

We could also approach the conflict between privacy and information from a Kantian perspective. Immanuel Kant (1724–1804) claimed that humanity should always be treated as an end and never merely as a means. This formulation of his categorical imperative clearly recognizes the importance of individuals' control of their own lives through rational decision-making – in other words, the importance of individual autonomy.[5] In many cases, this leads to clear and useful guidance. For example, one should never obstruct the freedom of others or lie to them for one's own benefit. It also entails that one should respect privacy and support the availability of information. Privacy allows one to control how much to share with others and lets one pursue one's plans without interference, just like Beth does. And without the relevant information, one's decisions are bound to be misguided, just like Joe's.

But Kant's theory is less clear regarding how one should prioritize when privacy and access to information conflict. In the abstract it seems Beth should provide an explanation ("It's not your baby") so that Joe can make informed decisions, and Joe should respect Beth's privacy ("OK, I won't ask more."). But there are other factors to consider. Beth does not have to provide explanations to everyone, especially if she fears that it might put her life in danger given Joe's volatile personality. Similarly, Joe is not obligated to respect everyone's privacy without challenge if crucial information about his own life is being concealed from him. There is no simple answer. And since the same issues arise when dealing with social media blocks, Kantian theory doesn't settle the matter there either. It's a delicate balancing act.

Instance #2: Do Not Keep an Eye on the Kids

In the second instance, blocking technology is integrated into the legal system. The digital blocks imposed by both Joe's and Matthew's wives extend to their children once the blocks get legal backing. This raises the ethical stakes, as we are no longer talking about merely blocking someone from your own life but depriving them of access to a third person – a child who has no (legal) say in the matter.

Such blocks resemble real-life restraining orders. The rationale for such orders is usually the fear that the (ex-)partner could harm the child. The digital blocks also augment the current practice: digital blocks are automatically enforced and they leave no loopholes for one to circumvent the restriction. They also exceed real-life restraining orders by not only prohibiting physical encounters, but also visually blocking the child, even in videos and photos.

The incorporation of digital blocks into the legal system takes us from the ethics of individual action to the realm of state action and therefore from moral theories to political theories. We are now faced with questions about state power and, in particular, about proportionality within the justice system. It seems that real-life restraining orders could be justified in the name of protecting citizens from harm. But on what grounds would the state be justified in obstructing a citizen's sight and hearing? Would "protecting the privacy of others" be enough? This is certainly not the minimal state of Robert Nozick (1938–2002). He argued that state power can only be legitimately exercised to protect a citizen's right to life, liberty, property, and contract. Rather than Nozick's minimal state, *White Christmas* seems to play out in a paternalistic state, where extreme measures are taken to avoid any possibility of harm.

Digital blocks that encompass children also create a conflict between rights to privacy and information. When used against a parent, such blocks completely sever the relationship between the child and the parent. The child would not even be able to recognize the parent whether in person or in pictures. In that sense, any information that could maintain the child-parent relationship for one parent is traded for the privacy of the other. In the episode, a misleading version of this trade-off plays out. While Joe experiences the digital block as a wall between him and his daughter, it turns out that Joe is not the father.[6]

Matthew does in fact live through this trade-off because his criminal activity (allegedly) results in his wife obtaining a digital restraining order that extends the block to their child.[7] Even though there aren't sufficient reasons to consider Matthew a threat to his child, the block removes any possibility for interaction between them. The possible consequences for both parent and child are ignored. Such a policy seems to disregard a central principle of justice, the principle of proportionality: a person's punishment should be proportional to the gravity of their crime. On that ground, in this case, the block seems difficult to defend.

Instance #3: Silent Night

In the third instance of blocking, Matthew learns that even though he gets a deal to go free, he is now blocked by everyone, because he is a registered sex offender. He is not just an anonymous blur but is marked by the state in bright red – like an augmented version of the scarlet letter – to indicate his crime.

As cruel and unusual as this practice may seem, it gets its inspiration from existing legal practices: sex offender registries and (isolation in) prison. Sex offender registries stigmatize those who are registered and limit how they can live their lives, including where they can reside and work. The society-wide digital block takes it one step further. Being labelled as a sex offender now blocks out all other information about the person. Matthew is *nothing* but a sex offender, and that fact is visible at all times.

When compared to prison, society-wide blocking might initially seem like a preferable option because one's physical freedom is not restricted. But consider that Matthew cannot communicate, recognize, or be recognized by anyone anymore. In a way, his isolation is even more comprehensive than prison because it blocks all and every human interaction.[8] A crucial question to ponder is how long these red blurs get to walk the streets after they have been blocked. One of the last scenes we see in *White Christmas* is of a vendor in the Christmas market eyeing Matthew's red shape with a snow globe in his hand (the same thing Joe used to kill Beth's dad). One could easily imagine a form of mob justice developing towards the red shapes because they would alarm people to registered sex offenders.[9]

The aim of the society-wide block appears to be much more than removing the threat of an invader from society: it "erases" them.[10] Blurring the image of offenders in some sense strips them of their human face; the blocking system allows others to disengage with them. Because others cannot see them or hear them, it is easier for others not to feel sympathy or empathy towards them. If a block person were to be assaulted by a mob, their pleas would not be audible, nor would their injuries be visible. Unless there is some type of safeguard against harming them, it is reasonable to assume that the digital block will de facto become a self-imposed physical isolation. Just think about it: going outside, even for their basic needs, could become too dangerous.

By the end of the episode, we have come all the way to the other end of the spectrum, as Matthew is now confined in an enforced privacy – the very privacy that he previously violated. Rather than getting intimate information about unsuspecting people, he is now unable to exchange any information with anyone. Matthew's crime is not one of sexual assault. It is one of invasion of privacy and eroding the trust in an intimate system, the Z-eyes. In a way, the justice system in the *White Christmas* universe condemns Matthew to the ultimate (ironic) punishment by surrounding him with an impenetrable privacy – a punishment that completely disregards the principle of proportionality. Does Matthew's crime deserve such extreme punishment? In our opinion, no.

There is another curious side effect of blocking the information flow within the society, and it concerns the ways in which we engage with the justice system as citizens. Having convicts walk the streets as red blurs rather than being out of view in prison would make it easier for society to recognize changes to the rate of crime (or at least the rate of punishment). However, even though this may at first glance look like an increase in information, it in fact obscures it. Since race, gender, or socio-economic background would no longer be visible, the identical red blurs would conceal whether particular demographic groups are blocked more frequently. In this manner, the blocking would obscure all the important information that could suggest social biases in the criminal justice system.

The absolute effectiveness of digital blocks as a legal tool takes us to another important discussion regarding the legal system and the way it progresses. Though it might be useful to have laws fully and automatically enforced, there might also be good reasons to want them to be breakable – and not only by hackers. Laws are not absolute; they change as societies change. Changes in legislation – for example, to laws enforcing race and gender discrimination – can indicate moral progress. Often these laws have developed and changed historically through civil disobedience: They were systematically broken. Thus disobedience can play a role in pushing for positive change. But the absolute enforcement of the law as in the case of digital blocks would not allow for positive development to unfold in the same way.

The legal system in *White Christmas* lacks proportionality, dehumanizes and conceals convicts, and controls other citizens' engagement with offenders. When digital blocks are used as a legal tool in these ways, they serve as a reminder that technologies do not always produce *beneficial* change in our social systems. We have the responsibility to try to ensure that they do.

A White Christmas with Dark Reflections

What makes *Black Mirror* a great show and philosophically interesting is that it accomplishes several things at the same time. For one, it dreams up new technologies based on our existing ones. The digital blocks in *White Christmas* mirror blocking on social media, where privacy between users is something we currently value and want to maintain. *Black Mirror* then shows how those technologies can be dangerous. The digital blocks make *White Christmas* slowly disintegrate into a dystopian vision, where the tension between the value we ascribe to privacy and information becomes clear.

But *Black Mirror* does much more than show us mutated versions of our existing technologies. It takes inspiration from our current social practices and depicts them in a technological form. The digital blocks presented in *White Christmas* share similarities with our practices of ignoring, disengaging, issuing restraining orders, confining people to prison, and registering them in stigmatizing public registries. By presenting these socially embedded practices in an almost unrecognizable form, the show prompts us to re-evaluate them and reconsider their ethical implications. We might block people on social media because that is a common and accepted way of social (dis)engagement. We might have gotten used to prisons or sex offender registries as a part of the criminal justice system. But when enacted through an unfamiliar technology they look a lot less agreeable. If we find ourselves intuitively concluding that digital blocks are wrong, we might want to think about why we find these other practices acceptable.

The effects of isolation on the human psyche are a general theme in *White Christmas*. We see how isolation drives the cookies insane and how it is used as a tool to pressure cookie-Joe into a confession. Matthew also constantly alludes to it in his comments: "Silence can be oppressive. You think weird shit in a vacuum." The implication is that isolation will have the same effect on the people who are blocked by everyone. In this manner, the digital blocking technology also raises important questions about what it means to have and to lose one's voice and self-image. *White Christmas* depicts a fundamentally different way of incapacitating a person. Even though many of our real-world social practices also entail some restrictions on the freedom of the individual, they do not aspire to eliminate the voice and image of the individual altogether. This raises questions about whether being recognized as human, with body and voice, is a basic need and a basic right that should be protected. In the words of Hannah Arendt (1906–1975): "*Men* in the plural, that is, men is so far as they live and move and act in this world, can experience meaningfulness only because they can talk with and make sense to each other and themselves."[11] So perhaps digital blocks present a fundamental violation of our humanity.

Black Mirror thus raises the issue of what it means to be human, what our most basic needs and rights are, and how these can be protected. We need to be especially careful of these concerns as our technological developments tend to outpace our ethical reflections.

Notes

1. Technically, according to Mathew, the cookie is actually the widget itself. A "blank cookie" is a device that can be "implant[ed] into a client's brain" to "soak up" how that brain works. What's stored on the cookie is "a simulated brain full of code." But for the sake of simplicity, in this chapter, and throughout the book, the authors will usually refer to the supposed person that exists on the widget as a "cookie."
2. See Chapter 21 (David Gamez's chapter on artificial intelligence) and Chapter 22 (Molly Gardner and Robert Slone's chapter on personal identity) in this volume.
3. One could wonder what Beth's justification is for getting a restraining order, digital or not. It is unclear whether Joe's behavior could justify one.
4. For more on this and other ethical theories see Chapter 1 (Brian Collins's chapter on *The National Anthem*) in this volume.

5. This understanding of autonomy, which is the classic understanding of personal autonomy, is central to Kantian ethics. Note that this differs from "Kantian autonomy," which refers to a more demanding concept in his theory.

6. Strangely enough, Joe does not attempt to have the block lifted through legal means – perhaps because such legal recourse does not exist in the universe of *White Christmas*. And that really is too bad, because not only would such an attempt have helped us understand more about the due process that applies to the legal digital blocks, but in the process, Joe might also have been informed that the child is not his, which would have spared all the characters much of their agony (although it would obviously have been bad for the plot).

7. Matthew is solely present in the simulation to make Joe confess to a crime. Considering that, it is suspicious how much his story mirrors Joe's. His involvement with the dating group and the resulting conviction are both true, because that is affirmed by the way the episode ends. But we have no way of knowing whether his claim that his wife permanently blocked him and that the block extended to his child is in fact true. After all, Matthew, repeatedly lies, deceives, and manipulates throughout the episode. One of the first things he says to Joe is "this is not an interrogation," which, it turns out later, is exactly what it is.

8. If the society-wide digital block follows the same pattern that we saw in earlier instances, then he also cannot see and hear (living) people on TV. We do not know if the people on the registry can see each other, but nothing indicates that they can.

9. For more on mob justice, see Chapter 13 (Aline Maya's chapter on *Hated in the Nation*) in this volume. For more on vigilante justice, see Chapter 10 (Juliele Maria Sievers and Luiz Henrique da Silva Santos's chapter on *Playtest*) in this volume.

10. It is questionable whether that would in fact remove the threat, as blocked people are still able to physically interact with the world and other people. (Joe shatters a vase for example.) This kind of punishment may in fact come closer to a sex offender's dream scenario, as they could now be able to roam around and anonymously offend people all they like.

11. Hannah Arendt, *The Human Condition* (Chicago: University of Chicago Press, 2013), 4.

SEASON 3

Nosedive and the Anxieties of Social Media

Is the Future Already Here?

Sergio Urueña and Nonna Melikyan

> Don't try too hard [...] Just be you. Authentic gestures, that's the key.
> (Mr. Hansen Davis, Reputelligent Agent)

Set in a world where everybody's social status is conditioned by a rating score ranging from 1 to 5 stars, *Nosedive* shows us the life of Lacie Pound, a woman completely consumed by her desire to increase her social score. Lacie is a 4.2, but she needs to be at least a 4.5 to enjoy the "Prime Influencers Program" and thus be able to afford the apartment of her dreams in the luxurious Pelican Cove living community. To boost her score, a Reputelligent agent advises her to expand her "sphere of influence" from "mid to low range folks" to "quality people." Lacie thus tries to score points with her high-ranking childhood friend Naomi by sharing a symbol of their friendship: a cuddly toy called Mr. Rags.[1] In return, Naomi invites Lacie to be the maid of honor in her upcoming wedding. Lacie accepts, thinking her wedding toast will be a good opportunity for her to gain extra points from Naomi's circle of top-rated friends.

On the way there though, a spiral of bad luck nosedives Lacie's score. She eventually makes it to the wedding (thanks to a low-ranking truck driver named Susan who pontificates about the system's absurdity), but by the time she arrives, Lacie is a 1.1. She delivers a heartfelt ranting speech that deeply insults Naomi while Naomi's friends drop Lacie's ranking to 0. Lacie is arrested. Paradoxically, however, in prison, Lacie finally finds her freedom – the freedom to say whatever she wants. The episode ends with her and her cellmate gleefully trading insults.

Nosedive tackles some of the issues that emerge from the misuse of digital social networks and explores the power that social conventions and social media have over our way of being and feeling in daily life. Indeed, according to producer Annabel Jones, "After seeing [this] episode, a lot of people said, 'I just stopped using social media. I realized [it] was taking over my life.'"[2] But the episode presents an even more grandiose challenge.

Black Mirror and Philosophy: Dark Reflections, First Edition. Edited by David Kyle Johnson.
© 2020 John Wiley & Sons, Inc. Published 2020 by John Wiley & Sons, Inc.

What if the underlying principles of social interaction that exist in platforms such as Yelp, Instagram, Facebook, or TripAdvisor, all mixed, were radically embedded into our societies? *Nosedive* presents a clean, bright, and pastel-colored society for sure. But it's completely dystopian. Although it's an extreme representation, it cannot help but make us wonder whether the future that *Nosedive* depicts is our actual present.

The Future is Already Here: *Nosedive* and Chinese Systems

The narrative that runs through most *Black Mirror* episodes is the focus on the misuse of futuristic technology alongside far-fetched destructive social practices. But unlike the more speculative worlds of mad robotic dogs, neural implants, or memory-erasing headbands, the leading technologies in *Nosedive* are familiar: smartphones and social media. Maybe this explains why *Nosedive* is one of the most commented on and award-winning *Black Mirror* episodes: it's almost true. Indeed, it's a social and technological nightmare whose *feasibility* and *plausibility* people find especially disturbing. For example, when Hollywood director Ron Howard watched it with his daughter Bryce Dallas Howard (who played Lacie), he had "a panic attack [because he] found it so unnerving and uncomfortable."[3]

Disturbingly, the approaching reality of the world of *Nosedive* can be seen in the Zhima Credit system, a popular service in China that functions as a private loyalty program that tracks your behavior on an app to arrive at a score between 350 and 950. Like in *Nosedive,* customers are scored based on their social media interactions and compliance to social standards (like courtesy and following civic norms.) However, unlike the episode's system, Zhima also considers important factors such as consumer trends and economic behavior. Details such as what you buy, whether you pay bills, or whether you repay loans, are all registered in the system and affect your social reputation.

But Zhima is just an isolated and tiny project compared to what the Chinese government is planning to implement by 2020. The new program, Social Credit System, will standardize the assessment of citizens' and businesses' economic and social reputation in order to enhance their "efficiency" and motivate "social trust" and "moral behavior." For example, a citizen's score (or "credits") might go up if they chose to do some kind of community work or if they opted for local produce over the big supermarkets. In the same way, their credits might fall if they were to commit public offenses such as not respecting non-smoking areas, evading taxes, or even buying items that the government disapproves of (such as alcohol or violent video games).

Although its many specific details are still unknown and the reward/penalty system is not yet clearly established, the logic behind the system is clear. If you follow the standards, then you are a virtuous citizen and you'll enjoy some advantages. If you don't, then you could be included on a blacklist that might determine whether you receive good service from airlines, hotels, or restaurants; you might be denied access to better apartments, loans, or high-paying jobs. In short, the Social Credit System might work as a behavioral surveillance structure. Scary, right?

Well, all these systems might be understood as applications of Jeremy Bentham's (1748–1832) idea of the panopticon. Bentham's original idea was a design for prison buildings, aimed to improve their efficiency. The panopticon consists of a circular multi-story building with a tower in the center surrounded by prison cells. The point of this design is that the guard tower would be intentionally obscured from the prisoner's vision. Consequently, a prisoner would never know when she is being observed. Bentham argued that this system would help prisoners regulate their behavior without the need for many (even any!) guards. The system in *Nosedive* is like a digital version of the panopticon applied to the entire populace: the possibility that you might be scored for anything you do aims to have an effect on the way you regulate your own behavior.

This panopticon-esque existence raises several philosophical issues connected with freedom, virtuous action, and coercion, many of which were considered by the French philosopher Michel Foucault (1926–1984) in *Discipline and Punish: The Birth of the Prison*. For example, it's not clear whether someone who is under pressure to act can be considered virtuous in their actions. If people believe that they're constantly being observed and rated, it's likely that on many occasions they will be acting contrary to their desires just for the sake of a good score. Virtue, by contrast, seems to require that a person wants to take the action in question. Additionally, if people are only behaving "properly" because they're being observed, what might happen when they're not being observed? Won't they go right back to misbehaving?

Another fundamental concern about *Nosedive* relates to the idea of justice. Should people be valued for their extrinsic value (granted by society) or their intrinsic value (that belongs inherently to the person)? More precisely, the Zhima Credit system and the *Nosedive* system both aim to quantify what the philosopher Pierre Bourdieu (1930–2002) called the "symbolic capital." Bourdieu argued that there was another capital beyond the three capitals ordinarily recognized: the economic (money and material resources), the social (friendship and cordiality), and the cultural (artworks and knowledge). This is the symbolic capital, a series of intangible personal properties that can only exist if recognized by society (like accumulated prestige or the value that one holds within a culture).[4] The main function of the technology in *Nosedive* is to make the symbolic capital explicit. Consider how symbolic capital is illustrated in the episode through the interface technology: When you look at someone, their face is circled, their name is revealed, and their score is listed. The episode depicts the way symbolic capital determines inequalities and status within a society.

It is important to note, however, that throughout the episode it's not governmental (like the Social Score System) or private entities (like the Zhima system) that establish the standards for evaluating people's symbolic capital, it's *us*. In *Nosedive* – like in real life through social media – we're our own overseers. We're our own panopticon, continually tracking everyone and letting others see us.

Social Media and the Tyranny of the Majority in the Post-truth Age

Nosedive subtly and powerfully raises worries about how obsessively following some social media dynamics may unfairly ruin people's lives. Think of Chester, the poor guy who lost his job in Lacie's office after he and his co-worker Gordon split up. He didn't fail to do his job, nor was he fired as a result of downsizing. The office mob simply ganged up on him to drop his rating below 2.5 and thus restrict his access to the building. In this way, although it does not do so as overtly as *Hated in the Nation* (the episode where publicly hated figures are killed via the #DeathTo hashtag), *Nosedive* raises serious concerns about the kind of trial by mob that can and does happen on social media.[5] Indeed, the technology in *Nosedive* seems to especially susceptible to such abuses.

This tendency raises worries about democracy itself. Is it just mob rule? We might assume that majority rule is a necessary and sufficient condition for the achievement of the "common good" and "a fair society." Jean-Jacques Rousseau (1712–1778) famously argued that if political parties were abolished and people were free from corrupting influences, the majority would always choose that which is best. Because of this, Rousseau thought that all societies should be run by a direct democracy where, for example, all laws are put up to a popular vote. Indeed, he viewed the populace as an entity with a will of its own – what he called the "general will" – and argued that anyone who disagreed with it should be forced to align their views with it.[6]

We might consider the previously discussed programs in China as conforming to Rousseau's philosophy, as providing methods for aligning everyone's behavior to the "general" will. Indeed, because they aim to identify those who are good and reward them (and identify those who are bad and punish them), it would seem that those programs aim to create a just and fair society by enforcing majority opinion. But given the low moral quality of the high-ranking people in *Nosedive* (such as Naomi), and the high moral quality of the low-ranking people (such as the truck driver Susan), it would seem Charlie Brooker is skeptical of Rousseau's faith in the majority's opinion to produce a just and fair society.

He's not the only one, though. The philosopher John Stuart Mill (1806–1873) worried about the tyranny of the majority, the fact that, in a democracy, the majority can oppress individuals or minority populations with impunity. Safeguards need to be put in place, Mill argued, to guard against this tyranny just as much as any other. To do so, he argued that "[t]he only purpose for which power can be rightfully exercised over any member of a civilized community, against his will, is to prevent harm to others."[7] So, although Mill wasn't opposed to all forms of democracy, he did think their power should be limited; the majority should not be able to restrict non-harmful actions. Mill was especially worried about religious taboos being enforced by law, but he would also be opposed to locking Lacie in jail for giving an upsetting maid-of-honor speech.

Mill was not the first philosopher to be skeptical of pure democracies, however. In the sixth book of *The Republic*, Plato describes how his master Socrates tries to convince Adeimantus about the failures of (direct) democracy and the majority rule though his *ship analogy*. Socrates compares the entire society to a ship and wonders who should govern it, the captain or the crew? After the discussion, Socrates and Adeimantus determine that just as those who have the knowledge of navigation should direct the ship (the captain), those who have the political experience (a minority) should govern society. Although the analogy might not be completely cogent, the point seems to stand. The main reason for Plato's rejection of direct democracy had to do with his concerns about the public's lack of knowledge and how easily its opinion might be manipulated, say by flattery and demagogues.

This brings us back to the danger of social media: how it prompts us to judgment or action without evidence. Recall how quickly Lacie sides with the office mob against Chester:

CO-WORKER: [Chester] and Gordon split up.
LACIE: Oh, Poor Ches…
CO-WORKER: No, no, no, we're all on Gordon's side.
LACIE: Sure! Obviously.

Without even considering the details of their recent break-up or why they've decided to be against Chester, Lacie decides to fall in line with her co-workers – her tribe, so to speak. This reminds us of how some people make decisions about politics, especially on social media. They simply align with what their political tribe says, regardless of what they might have thought otherwise, or even what the evidence points to. This is what people mean when they say we are living in a "post-truth" world. Facts and logical arguments no longer matter; people decide what to believe based on tribal alliances, on what they want to believe, or what they feel is true.

We've always done this to some extent, but social media has put it into overdrive, especially with the algorithms it uses to feed users content they want to see. This can lock people into political bubbles where they never encounter evidence, arguments, or viewpoints dissimilar or contrary to what they already believe. This is the Janus-faced epistemic nature of social media: although it can be used to inform, it can also misinform, spreading ignorance. "Virilization" has made social media platforms a tool for spreading false news stories and electoral hacking campaigns. Even representative democracies require an informed electorate capable of critical thinking. We need not all be political experts, but we must elect those who are and who best represent our interests. But we can't do that unless we grasp and value diverse positions and the facts.

"The Look" of Others and Self-presentation in Social Media: "Hell Is Other People"

In *Nosedive*, we bear witness to a world where people are obsessed with simultaneously disguising their identity and showing themselves off. Above all, the episode is a parody of our obsession with social status at the expense of who we really are. This raises many philosophical concerns that have been articulated by Jean-Paul Sartre (1905–1980) and Erving Goffman (1922–1982): How do others influence our way of feeling and being in the world?

In *Being and Nothingness*, Sartre explores, from an existentialist point of view, how we establish concrete relations with others, and he articulates these relations in what he calls "the look." The basis of his idea is that our awareness of the way in which we are perceived by others transforms our own subjectivity. This perception of others as entities that can objectify us – the same as we can objectify them – makes us concerned about how we are perceived, so we alter our behavior. "The look" from others forces us to consider their presence and alter how we act and even how we see ourselves. The realization that others are watching you makes you self-conscious of your condition as a subject who can be judged anywhere and at any time.

To illustrate Sartre's conception of "the look," recall the not-so-sweet-cookie scene from the episode. After exchanging several false and well-practiced smiles with the barista and customers, Lacie gets a free smiley-face cookie with her brushed-suede coffee, carefully takes a perfect half-circle bite, and then spits it out. Clearly, she dislikes the taste of the cookie, but she takes a cute picture and shares it on social media anyway, with the caption: "Brushed Suede /w cookie. Heaven!" Who cares about the taste; it's all about "the look." It's about making others perceive her in the way she wants to be perceived. The object of Lacie's perception isn't herself, it's a representation of how others will react to seeing her "enjoying" the cookie. In fact, the whole episode is the story of an alienated Lacie trying to influence "the look" of others instead of experiencing her own subjectivity and existence. Lacie unconsciously regards herself as an object for others and not as a subject for herself.

As Sartre explains, being stuck in the look of other people does not lead to a fulfilling existence because it's not based on freedom. Indeed, Lacie continually and unhappily forces herself to do things for the sake of recognition. This constant struggle to be liked is illustrated in Sartre's play *No Exit*, in which three protagonists are locked in a room, situated in hell, waiting for a punisher to make them suffer for all their misdeeds. But, it turns out, there is no punisher: they are their own tormentors. They are condemned to live under the look of each other. Thus, one of the characters remarks, "Hell is the other people."

Nosedive director Joe Wright would seem to agree:

> I'd just made this film *Pan*, which had been universally slagged by the critics. The whole star-rating system can lead to you validating yourself, based on how other people think of you. And so *Nosedive* kind of spoke to me...I was on [Instagram] for about six months, and then realized I was becoming completely obsessed and addicted by it. Instagram was just a disgusting lie, really. I found I was judging myself based on the appearance of other people's lives and constantly comparing myself to others. I would either become vain or bitter, based on those judgements. It's a desperate, soulless endeavor that concerns me greatly.[8]

Whether he knew it or not, his thoughts resonated with *No Exit*. Indeed, like the characters in *No Exit*, Lacie is trapped with someone else looking at her (in Sartre's sense) at the end of the episode. But unlike the play, the end of the episode depicts an act of liberation. Because the social rating tech has been removed from her eye, Lacie is no longer riddled with anxieties from the look of the others and can gleefully smile and exchange multiple profane insults ("F*ck you next Wednesday! F*ck you for Christmas!") with the prisoner across from her. With this freedom, they even seem to fall in love. As director Joe Wright, and producers Charlie Brooker and Annabel Jones put it, "They reveal their true selves...they both end up shouting "F*ck You" and they become one. They're gonna have sex as soon as they leave...They're both genuinely smiling in the final few frames...the two of them will end up together..."[9]

Of course, the look is inevitable and occurs everywhere. As sociologist Erving Goffman explains in *The Presentation of the Self in Everyday Life*, we spend our whole life playing different roles as if we are on-stage and other people are our spectators. Through roles, props, and masks, we build our personal and public identities, trying to adjust to the continuous game of seeing and being seen by others. On social media, however, thanks to continuous visibility and approval mechanisms, our actions are continuously scrutinized by others. Have you ever spent time asking for advice from your friends about content that you intend to post in order to gauge how people, in general, will react to it? If so, you were, and probably are (we all are), under the influence of the look.

Who the Hell Are the Other People? Knowing Others through Their Masks

Nosedive also poses some epistemological questions. If everyone creates and wears a mask both online and offline, how do we ever genuinely know people? How are we supposed to assess the reliability of their digital profiles and content? In *Nosedive* Lacie puts on a mask in public spaces. Her identity is inhibited by the look of others. Her true personality emerges only when she has privacy (for example, at home with her brother) or at the end of the episode (when she is locked up).

Social media works the same way: our profiles are mostly masks. Digital identity has become a source of getting to know others, even though we are aware that digital profiles don't fit reality. The shocking thing is how much we trust that content. For example, nowadays, more and more companies tend to screen the online history of a prospective employee before making a final decision. Do you have LinkedIn? It's a plus. You have more than 500 connections and good reviews? Amazing!

In the same way, individuals trust digital accounts in order to make decisions – like relying on Yelp reviews to pick a restaurant. The number of followers, the pictures uploaded, or the comments influence the final choice. Would you trust a restaurant that has a poor online visibility? But *Nosedive* warns us about the prejudices and pitfalls we may encounter by evaluating identities and taking seriously some information both on social networks and in real life interactions. Think of the scene in which Lacie meets Susan, the truck driver who helps her. At first, Lacie doesn't trust Susan because she has a low social score (1.4). Immediately, Lacie picks up her phone and starts watching Susan's profile to check whether she is dangerous. Then, Lacie realizes that Susan, despite being *a 1.4* is a good person with whom she has a lot in common. This reminds us that our modern-day digital profiles – although they certainly are a source of relevant information – are not always a clear representation of the "real" identity and social reputation.

A Black Mirror of Our Anxieties

Although social media opens us up to new and exciting opportunities, we shouldn't forget that it's a catalyst for some new or already existing societal problems. *Nosedive* mirrors our fears and anxieties regarding the possibility that our society may one day be governed by some vacuous values and unfair social structures. *Nosedive,* like many other *Black Mirror* episodes, finds its greatest strength in asking two simple but powerful questions: *What kind of future do we want? What role should technology have in it?*

Notes

1. However, Naomi and Lacie didn't have a good relationship. "Rag" is not only a noun that means "a piece of old clothes," but also a verb that refers to making fun of someone. Naomi, it seems, was always *ragging on* Lacie.
2. Charlie Brooker and Annabel Jones with Jason Arnopp, *Inside Black Mirror* (New York: Crown Archetype, 2018), 147.
3. Ibid.
4. Pierre Bourdieu, "Capital symbolique et classes sociales," *L'Arc,* 72 (1978), 13–19.
5. For more on the dangers of trial by mob, see Chapter 13 (Aline Maya's chapter on *Hated in the Nation*) in this volume.
6. Jean-Jacques Rousseau, *The Social Contract* (New York: Oxford University Press, 1999), 134–139.
7. John Stuart Mill, *On Liberty* (Peterborough, ON: Broadview Press, 1999).
8. Brooker et al., 135.
9. Brooker et al., 143.

Playtest and the Power of Virtual Reality

Are Our Fears Real?

Claire Benn

I have always liked to make the player jump. Afterwards you feel good…
because you are still alive. You have faced your greatest fears in a safe
environment. It is a release of fear. It liberates you.

(Shou Saito)

In *Playtest*, our fun-loving, thrill-seeking protagonist Cooper is travelling the
world and avoiding calls from his mom. Stuck in London when his credit
card is stolen, he decides to make some money by travelling to tech firm
SaitoGemu's headquarters to test their "interactive augmented reality
system."[1] After being introduced to the technology via a simple whack-a-
mole game, he is invited to playtest something completely different: "the most
personal survival horror game in history." Cooper's response: "I'm game."

The creator, Shou Saito, tells Cooper explicitly that the technology uses
state-of-the-art artificial intelligence (AI) that "works out how to scare you
by using your own mind." His openness about the purpose and mechanics
of the game initially disarms Cooper (and the viewer); we all know what's
coming. It's meant to be a horror game after all, and the jump scares – like
the spider – do start off pretty fun. As Cooper begins to lose the ability to
tell the difference between what's real and what isn't, however, we realize
that something much more sinister is afoot. He becomes increasingly desperate to get out but soon discovers it isn't so simple. Even when he thinks
he has escaped, he hasn't. In fact, he never returns to the real world. He
dies, calling out for his mom, whom he never did call back.

Playtest explores one terrifying fear after another, and Cooper's final
death may not even be scariest part of his virtual reality experience. But
will virtual reality (VR) really be that scary? Will it be scary in the same
way that books, films, and video games are, or more so? If so, why? Because
it's novel? Because we'll believe it's real? Or will we still be scared even
though we know it's not? Are there ways in which VR actually *is* real?

Black Mirror and Philosophy: Dark Reflections, First Edition. Edited by David Kyle Johnson.
© 2020 John Wiley & Sons, Inc. Published 2020 by John Wiley & Sons, Inc.

What could VR really do to us? Drive us mad? Kill us? Could we always tell it's fake? Indeed, might VR give us reason to think that our "real world" isn't actually real?

Nothing New Under the Sun

"What has been will be again, what has been done will be done again; there is nothing new under the sun" (Ecclesiastes 1:9). This familiar adage dismissing the purportedly novel has, unsurprisingly, been applied to emerging technologies like VR. On the face of it, the VR in *Playtest* gives us a good old-fashioned horror romp that does little to challenge this idea.

Take the setting. Cooper playtests the horror game in Harlech House, the gamekeeper's lodge of the main SaitoGemu headquarters, a *Victorian* haunted house, an absolute classic backdrop for a horror story. We get the requisite squeaky floorboards, flickering lights, and creepy paintings of pale, unsmiling children. Cooper even reads the most famous tale by the most famous Victorian writer of scary stories: *The Raven* by Edgar Allan Poe.

Even the fears Cooper faces conform to expectations. Arachnophobia is a classic trope of horror movies. In fact, on his flight from the US, Cooper watches (the wonderfully named) *Big Ass Spider!*[2] Cooper himself anticipates the standard moves of a horror movie, for example, not wanting to go up the stairs to reach the access point. So it is easy to think that if VR is scary at all, it is simply because it follows in the footsteps of well-established traditions of ghost stories and horror movies.

Just a Game

We are also reassured throughout *Playtest* that it's just a game, a point emphasized by the plethora of gaming references. Take Sonja, who Cooper hooks up with in London and who encourages him to undertake the playtest. She is a technology correspondent and gamer, and so her apartment is littered with games: *ManHunt*, *Heavy Rain*, and *Portal II*, among others. In fact, the actor who plays Sonja, Hannah John-Kamen, is the voice actor for *Dark Souls II*, which can also be seen on her shelf. Cooper's own surname, Redfield, is a reference to the *Resident Evil* character Chris Redfield. And there are also references to *Street Fighter*, *Pac-Man*, and *Mario Brothers*.[3]

Besides, games can't be *dangerous*, right? In computing, a "sandbox" refers to a separate environment in which unsafe code or software can be run without risk to the computer that's running the program. VR games, like computer games in general, are seen like this: a safe place in which to explore. That is part of their appeal, and it's exactly how Shou sells it to Cooper: the game is a place to face his fears "in a safe environment."

Novelty and the Pain of Others

Things like the spider succeed in startling Cooper, and it's easy to suppose that this is simply because the technology is new and the novelty of a medium heightens its ability to scare us. It's one of the founding myths of cinema that the Lumière brothers' *L'Arrivée d'un train en gare de La Ciotat* made early cinema-goers run screaming from the theatre because it's footage of a train coming out of a tunnel made audiences think the train was heading straight for them. Today, people can happily nod off during *The Exorcist*. As Susan Sontag notes in *Regarding the Pain of Others*, modern media is driven to showing us more and more shocking pictures because "How else to make a dent when there is incessant exposure to images"?[4] VR is then, perhaps, just another medium that has the ability to surprise, and thus scare us...for now.

So maybe we have nothing to fear from VR. Or at least no more than from books, films, and traditional video games, especially when the novelty wears off. The cute, *Twilight Zone*-esque ending of the episode plays into this idea, lulling us into thinking that perhaps the lesson to be learned from *Playtest* is simply, "Call your mom." (And, maybe, take more seriously the injunction to turn off our mobile phones.) But beneath the surface of *Playtest* a much darker lesson lurks: that when our fantasies *feel* real, and have the power to hurt, they are no longer just a game. VR can build a bridge between what *seems* real and what *is* real, and this means its power to scare us silly is not just novel: it's revolutionary.

Perceptions and Reality

VR has three central features: it is interactive, it is experienced from the first-person perspective, and it is immersive. These powers combine to create a sense of "presence" (unlike that in books, films, and even computer games). You really feel like you're there even when you *know* you're not. Now you might assume that our perceptions should align with what we know to be real. It turns out, however, that knowing what is real doesn't necessarily impact what we experience.

Take the well-documented "rubber hand illusion." With one of their hands obscured from view behind a barrier, a life-sized rubber hand is set in front of a participant. As they look at it, both their actual hand and the rubber hand are stroked with a paintbrush. After only ten minutes, people report that they feel the touch of the paintbrush where the rubber hand is. Cut it and most even will react as if it were their own! This "proprioceptive drift" demonstrates that the sensations people experience (and their experience of the existence and location of their own bodies) is greatly affected by what they *see*. It also demonstrates the plasticity of the human mind, which allows us to identify something as ours even when we know it isn't. This is a fact that VR exploits. So, even if the experience is only audio-visual (as Katie at SaitoGemu reassures Cooper), virtual threats to our virtual bodies can still feel like real threats to our real selves.

The lack of causal efficacy of knowledge extends to our perceptions as well. Consider the Müller-Lyer illusion.

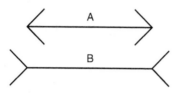

Even after the trick is explained, so that you *know* that the two lines are the same length, you still can't help but see B as longer than A. Or consider the so called "paradox of fiction," made famous by contemporary philosophers Colin Radford and Michael Weston. How can we be emotionally moved by watching *Romeo and Juliet* when we know they don't exist?[5] The answer it seems is that, as with optical illusions, what you know about the world doesn't always determine how you react to it.[6]

Even our behavior isn't necessarily in accordance with our knowledge. Normally, actions arise from a combination of beliefs and desires: Cooper reaches for the wine because he *believes* it is wine and he *desires* something to drink (or perhaps some Dutch courage). But there is another mental state that can play the same role as belief in that it causes us to act, even though it is contrary to our consciously held beliefs. Philosophers call it an "alief." Aliefs can explain experiments in which people are reluctant to drink juice with a sterilized dead cockroach in it or to eat fudge that is in the shape of dog feces. When asked, participants said they *believed* that the juice was safe and that the fudge really was fudge. But because their eyes told them something different, they *acted* as if they didn't. Because of its incredibly immersive nature, VR is the ultimate way of generating aliefs and getting us to act as if what we *alieve* is in fact real.

So VR can scare Cooper, and us, in part because even *knowing* it isn't real doesn't stop it from *feeling* real. But that is not, in and of itself, a scary idea. We *like* getting scared. That's why we watch *The Shining* and play *Resident Evil*. Indeed, Cooper himself is a bit of a dare-devil whom Sonja likens to Indiana Jones.[7] On the flight from the US, Cooper reassures the little girl next to him by comparing the turbulence to being on a roller-coaster: a classic way in which humans seek the adrenaline rush that comes from doing stuff that feels, just a little bit, like we might die. He even runs with the bulls in Pamplona, a cliché of thrill-seeking behavior. These activities all have two key features: they are safe (except maybe the bulls) and they eventually end. As Shou says: "You get scared. You jump. Afterwards, you feel good. You glow." Not just because of the adrenaline rush but "mostly because you are still alive."

However, both of these features come into question in *Playtest* and for the very same reason: both what makes us safe and what brings a horror experience to an end is the existence of a sharp line between what is real and what is constructed as part of the experience. And it is this line that gets erased bit by bit in *Playtest*.

Finding the Cracks: Testing for Coherence

Playtest exposes our tactics for maintaining this line and how they can break down. For example, one way to tell that something isn't real is to look for discrepancies within the experience. (Think of the spinning top in *Inception*). And this is exactly what Cooper does. His first method is to check with Katie: because she doesn't see the spider, Cooper knows it isn't real. This makes sense. If reality is objective, it ought to exist independently of one person's experience. So checking whether something can be perceived by someone else can help determine whether it is real.

Even when we can't check with someone else, we can appeal to the coherence between our own senses: we know a virtual beer is not a real beer because, while it *looks* like beer, it doesn't *smell* or *taste* of anything. Cooper also employs this strategy. Based on Katie's claim that "It's all just audio-visual," he tests his environment: if what he *sees* and what he *feels* come apart, he can determine that what he sees isn't real. For example, he puts his hand through Josh Peters' face, proving to himself that it isn't actually there, despite its appearance.[8]

Playtest challenges these strategies, however, by showing us how they can fail. When Cooper's audio connection with Katie breaks down, for example, there is no longer an external point of reference. Or take when Sonja arrives. It is her *physicality*, the fact that she is *tangible*, that tricks Cooper into believing that she is not be part of the simulation. Yet he still thinks she is part of the game and turns to logic, the power of the mind to find discrepancies, asking Sonja: "How'd you find me?" to find holes in her answers. And he's right; she admits she laid a "breadcrumb trail" leading Cooper into danger. But then, despite being *physically* assaulted by Sonja, Cooper realizes she *is* in fact a simulated being. (Her face comes off, after all!). Cooper quite rightly decides he wants out. The fact that this is "just" VR is no longer any reassurance.

As we've seen, knowing something isn't real doesn't mean it doesn't feel real. But, conversely, the fact that something *feels* real can in fact make it real. For example, some things are incorrigible. They are true in virtue of being felt to be true. Pain is the classic example. If I sincerely believe that I am in pain, then I *am* in pain.[9] The immersive nature of Cooper's VR experience means that it simulates experiences in a way that feels unmediated; the experiences are happening to us, not to someone else or to an avatar we happen to control. And for certain experiences like pain, no line exists between simulation and reality.[10] This makes VR radically different from other kinds of media.

Cracking Up: Madness, Memory, Mortality

But even when reality fails to affect perceptions and perceptions become reality, how damaging could the effects of VR really be? The answer *Playtest* forces us to confront is that it could change our very sense our self, destroy our sanity, even kill us.

At the heart of what makes the VR in *Playtest* truly terrifying is not just that Cooper can't tell what's real, but that finally he *knows* he can't. He's lost control.[11] The AI uses Katie's voice to reveal this truth to Cooper, saying: "I'm fucking with you Cooper. I told you to come up here [to the access point] to see if we've broken you enough to obey instructions without question. And we have." The voice remains even when he tears out the earpiece, emphasizing that what was once reassuring – having Katie to talk to and to test reality – is in fact terrifying: Cooper was just talking to a voice in his head.

Philosophers have traditionally thought that two conditions are important for our continued existence over time: psychological continuity and physical continuity.[12] While the AI leaves Cooper physically intact, it destroys his psychological continuity, overwriting his knowledge of his own preferences, beliefs, and memories. "What is your favorite flavor of ice cream?" the AI asks. "Where did you grow up? What was the name of the girl who stabbed you? Your mother, can you describe her face? Her hair color? Is she tall, short, fat, thin?" Cooper can answer none of these questions. The removal of his memories is particularly poignant, because it was his father's struggle with Alzheimer's and subsequent death that prompted Cooper to embark on his trip "to make all the memories I can, while I can." If we think that psychological continuity is required for personal identity, then without his memories, in a very real sense, Cooper ceases to exist.[13] This is why Alzheimer's is often described as a form of living death. And this is exactly what Cooper experiences. In the end he can't even remember the face he sees in the mirror, which he eventually breaks, and uses a shard to try to remove the AI from his body.[14]

Cooper wakes up, with his memories restored, to find he hadn't left Shou's office at all. Suddenly, we start to realize that everything in the haunted house has its origins in the previous story. This is not just the fears: the spider from the in-flight movie, the painting of the house with the light on from the poster in Shou's office, the bully he told Sonja about, his father's Alzheimer's. Even the things *we* thought were real were taken from his memories: meeting Sonja at The Raven explains the Poe story; the house itself was from the *Harlech Shadow* posters; Sonja stabs Cooper in the same place that he was stabbed by Josh Peters. It was a horrifying experience (as promised), and Cooper feels relieved it is over (also as promised) and heads back to the US.

But there, the episode's final sequence culminates. Back home, Cooper finds perhaps his worst fear realized: his mom, having lost her memories in his absence, has no idea who he is. "I have to call Cooper," she says as he stands in the room. "I have to call and make sure he's safe." We the viewers were just as wrong as Cooper to feel that it was finally over. There is no release, no liberation. Cooper is still in SaitoGemu and hasn't experienced *any* of what we thought he had. There was no whack-a-mole; he never met Shou. He never got that far. We have no idea about the purpose of the technology Cooper was supposed to be playtesting or whether it even works. While waiting for the VR to load, a real call from his mom interferes with the upload sequence and causes a malfunction. Cooper dies a mere 0.04 seconds in.[15]

Forget Cooper. Are *We* in a Simulation?

Everything in *Playtest*, from the phones, the cars, the apps, and the ATM, could easily be found in the year the episode was released, 2016. Fascinatingly, *Playtest* contains the seeds of the technological developments that occur in the future of the *Black Mirror* universe. For example, one of the symbols on the "mushroom" device that is implanted into Cooper's neck is the same as in *White Bear*. And I'll give ten points if you can spot the well-hidden references to *Fifteen Million Merits* and *Bandersnatch*.[16]

Indeed, its contemporary setting is perhaps what makes *Playtest* most disturbing. The episode tempts us into assuming that it's only *Cooper's* ability to distinguish what is real and what is not that is challenged. But every time Cooper "wakes up," we too are forced to reassess whether what we just witnessed actually happened. We used the same methods Cooper did – the discrepancies between the CCTV footage and Cooper's experience told us what was real – and they similarly failed us. *All* the footage happened within the VR experience and was as constructed as the spider. If this evokes the movie *Inception* for you, it should: the "nested" nature of both strips away our sense of relief that we have finally returned to what is real and makes us question whether we can ever be sure we have.[17]

The final fear raised by *Playtest* is not about the *possibility* of a VR experience from which we can't wake up, but that we are already in one. Indeed, Nick Bostrom's "simulation argument" gives us reason to believe that we are.[18] Imagine a future in which humanity has acquired all possible technological advances. What would the citizens of such a society do with the enormous computing power that would result? They might run ancestor simulations: detailed simulations of their evolutionary history. Such simulations would tell them all sorts of interesting things, just like simulations of genetic mutation and disease epidemics give us useful information. With enough computing power, these simulations could be so realistic and complex that the people in them would find them indistinguishable from reality. As in Cooper's experience, any attempt by those inside the simulations to "reveal" them as such would fail.

If such simulations existed, Bostrom argues, the number of persons in them would vastly exceed those who are not. So, Bostrom concludes, unless you think (1) humanity is likely to go extinct before acquiring the needed computer power, or (2) any civilization is extremely unlikely to run a lot of ancestor simulations for some reason, then you should conclude that (3) we are almost certainly living in just such a simulation. If you think that one day such simulations will exist, then the odds are that our universe is one of them. There would only be one physical universe, but millions of simulated ones.

So yes, VR has the power to be truly scary. But not just in the same way as books, films, and video games, and not just because it's novel. VR can make us forget what is real and it can make what it simulates our new reality. It could drive us mad and even kill us. It could let us know that we are trapped inside a simulation or leave us doubting whether our world is real. The only drop of comfort I can offer you is that Cooper's experience, as real as it felt for him, occurred because of a malfunction. The ability to create realistic simulations deliberately is still a long way off, even in this episode…or is that just what the AI and our descendants want us to think?

Notes

1. I talk about *virtual* reality throughout this chapter, but the particular technology in *Playtest* is described as *augmented* reality by Katie. However, given that *nothing* Cooper encountered was real, what he experienced was much closer to *virtual* reality. For simplicity, I'll use the terms interchangeably.
2. Fun fact: the father of the actor playing Cooper starred in *The Thing*, so both father and son have faced giant spider monsters with human faces!
3. Cooper yells "Hadouken!" (a special attack from *Street Fighter*) at the security guard at SaitoGemu. Pac-Man appears in a mural that Cooper walks past in London with writing claiming that video games don't affect us negatively. *Mario Brothers* is referenced when they talk about how the implant is called "the mushroom."
4. Susan Sontag, *Regarding the Pain of Others* (New York: Picador, 2003), 23.
5. Colin Radford and Michael Weston, "How can we be moved by the fate of Anna Karenina?" *Aristotelian Society Supplementary*, 49 (1975), 67–93.

6. William Irwin and David Kyle Johnson, "What would Dutton say about the paradox of fiction?" *Philosophy and Literature*, 38 (2014), 144–147.

7. Fun fact: The pub they are in is called The Raven, which is also the name of Marion Ravenwood's bar in *Raiders of the Lost Ark*. Another fun fact: In this conversation, Cooper tells Sonja he "saved the world from the Nazis," and in the 2018 film *Overlord*, Wyatt Russell (who plays Cooper) does exactly that.

8. For more on how to tell the difference between reality and fiction, see Chapter 25 (Brian Stiltner and Anna Vaughn's chapter on perception) in this volume.

9. Of course, the same applies to pleasure, but one should consider Robert Nozick's "Experience Machine" thought experiment before getting too tempted to use VR for pure pleasure. For more on this see, Chapter 11 (James Cook's chapter on *San Junipero*) in this volume.

10. This is something explored in *Black Museum* where tech company TCKR creates the "symphatic diagnoser," a device that enables people to feel the pain of others without inflicting any physical damage. In fact, a reference to TCKR appears on the *Edge* magazine that Sonja shows Cooper.

11. There are subtle hints that maybe he was never in control: Katie persuades Cooper to enter the room, saying, "Would you kindly open the door?" referencing *Bioshock*, where this phrase is used to control the player's action while making them feel a semblance of free will.

12. For more on this, see Chapter 22 (Molly Gardner and Robert Slone's chapter on personal identity) in this volume.

13. Memory manipulation can also be used for good: The reference to TCKR on the runner of the magazine *Edge* (which says "Inside TCKR: Turning Nostalgia into a Game") points to TCKR's future technological development of the simulated reality universe of San Junipero, where memory manipulation is used for nostalgia therapy to treat the elderly.

14. The broken mirror is a metaphor for his fragmented self and a visual reference to the *Black Mirror* title sequence. The shard also reminds us of Bing's big speech in *Fifteen Million Merits* and the removal of the AI mirrors Liam removing his Grain at the end of *The Entire History of You*.

15. The horrifying possibilities of time dilation are explored and exploited more fully in *White Christmas*.

16. On the top of the *Edge* magazine in Shou's office it says, "The Rolling Road: Get Fit or Die Trying!" in reference to the cycling game Bing watches in *Fifteen Million Merits*. One of the games mentioned on the bottom right, which presumably will be reviewed, is *Bandersnatch*.

17. The reference to *Inception* is more than just thematic: the Japanese business man in *Inception* is also named Saito.

18. Nick Bostrom, "Are you living in a computer simulation?" *Philosophical Quarterly*, 53 (2003), 243–255.

10

Shut Up and Dance and Vigilante Justice

Should We Ever Take the Law into Our Own Hands?

Juliele Maria Sievers and Luiz Henrique da Silva Santos

We hope, that you choke, that you choke.
(Radiohead, "Exit Music (For a Film)")

As *Shut Up and Dance* begins, we sympathize with Kenny as he is black-mailed by computer hackers who threaten to release a video of him mas-turbating to pornography. After all, what teenager (or adult) hasn't? As Hector, his fellow "blackmailee" observes, "The fucking Pope probably does that." Anyone would be humiliated if their most private moments were publicly broadcast. "The cunts at work calling you Spurty McGoo," Hector predicts. "It's not just weeks. We're talking years here. Pictures hang about on Google like a gypsy fucking curse. There's no cure for the Internet." We pity him as the hackers send Kenny on a number of errands, including robbing a bank and fighting someone to the death. After all, he was so kind to that little girl who left her toy behind in the restaurant, right? Kenny is the good guy; the hackers are the bad guys.

But as the episode closes, our assumptions are revealed as erroneous. Despite Kenny's compliance, the hackers share the video and his mother calls, screaming: "What did you do, Kenny? They're saying it's kids! That you've been looking at kids!" He wasn't just looking at pornography, but child pornography! Our attitude instantly flips; his interaction with that little girl in the restaurant takes on a whole new dimension. Kenny's not a victim, he's a villain! The hackers are vigilantes. They catch and punish criminals when the conventional authorities are unable. We celebrate because Kenny got what he deserved. "Justice has been served." As the closing Radiohead song puts it, "We hope... that you choke...that you cho-oke."

Black Mirror and Philosophy: Dark Reflections, First Edition. Edited by David Kyle Johnson.
© 2020 John Wiley & Sons, Inc. Published 2020 by John Wiley & Sons, Inc.

But after the adrenaline rush wears off, we wonder: Should we really have celebrated? What Kenny did was deplorable of course, but why do we wish for such things to happen to deplorable people? Should the hackers have just notified the police? Or must we apply this kind of punishment to truly attain justice? If so, what does it tell us about our notion of justice? Would we want to live in a society that encourages vigilantes? Should we become vigilantes ourselves?

The Efficacy of Blackmail

Why do we follow the law? Instinctively, the answer is "the threat of punishment." We don't want to go to jail. But what's the difference between the government's threat of jail and the blackmailer's threat of exposure? Why do we generally think we are bound to obey the laws of the former but not the demands of the latter? Perhaps it's because legal sanctions are systematized, centralized, and previously fixed to certain behaviors, whereas the threats of blackmailers are not. The blackmailer's demands are laid out *after* the victim's action.

If the blackmailer is seeking to punish moral faults, however, the question seems trickier. Although the impulse to punish moral faults seems natural, and the offending party likely knows beforehand that moral crimes deserve punishment, the sanctions and punishments for moral faults are less "fixed" than legal ones. What's more, how much pressure we should feel to obey moral rules is less clear, and what's morally right and wrong is often up for debate. If the blackmailer is trying to promote moral or religious rules and condemn others for violating them, then the blackmailer is engaged in vigilantism. And since vigilantism can sometimes be more effective than legal norms at giving criminals what many think they really deserve – "a mere prison sentence is too good for Kenny" – some may argue that we should start admitting, encouraging, and even relying on vigilantism.

As *Shut Up and Dance* illustrates, however, vigilantism isn't effective in all ways. First, in order for punishment to effectively serve its purpose, the person being punished needs to know that they are being punished and also needs to know the terms of his punishment. Vigilantism can't guarantee this. Take Kenny for example. Just like the viewer, when he is faced with the "fight to the death," he might reasonably assume that the survivor will be released. The resulting "unequal sentence" – one pedophile is killed and the other goes free with a load of cash – would suggest that the hackers' goal is not justice. (In an early version of the script, the hackers were just "some people in an internet café...doing it for a laugh...a competition to see who could fuck with people the most."[1]) In fact, even after he's arrested, Kenny may still not know that he is being punished by vigilantes. Only the careful viewer, who sees that the punishments the other characters receive seem to be intended to reflect the severity of the corresponding moral crime – the pedophiles get death and jail, the cheating husbands lose their families, the racist CEO loses her job – realizes that giving people what they morally deserve seems to be the hackers' goal.

Despite that goal, the subjective nature of vigilantism cannot guarantee things always turn out so neat and tidy. After he gives Kenny the package with the cake in it, the "Moped Man" tells Kenny, "Just [do] whatever they say and once you've done that, you're out." But, of course, Kenny has no idea whether that is true. And, when all is said and done, there's no way to know whether Hector's wife will kill him in a rage, or whether the CEO will be driven to suicide. Vigilantism cannot effectively ensure that the punishment really will fit the crime.

So vigilante penalties tend to be out of proportion and are marked by traces of revenge and retaliation. It is these kinds of problems that led governments (like the Roman Empire's) to replace non-institutionalized punishments like stoning, torture, or ostracism with objective legal procedures as laws evolved. Indeed, much of our current legal system derives from the Roman law tradition. Think of all the Latin expressions that are still used in legal contexts. One of them, *nulla poena sine lege* (which means "no penalty without a law") prescribes that punishment can only take place if an existing legal norm is violated, and that punishment can only be applied by the state. Thus justice becomes a more objective feature, in contrast to the subjectivity involved in cases of blackmail.

Despite the problems with vigilante justice, one may still arrive at the end of the episode with the impression that the victims of the hackers' blackmail got what they deserved – and to that extent, what the hackers did was good and even necessary. "Maybe vigilantes can go too far, but had these vigilantes not acted, Kenny and the others would have simply gotten away with it." As we'll see, though, there are more legal and philosophical reasons to be wary of vigilantism.

What's Wrong with Taking Justice into Our Own Hands?

There are many reasons one might take on the obligation to enforce legal or moral norms when the conventional authorities are unable: regime control, crime control, social control, and so on. And we should differentiate the "soft" vigilantism such as the Neighborhood Watch from the "hard" vigilantism we see in *Shut Up and Dance* where the vigilantes take it upon themselves to punish criminals. The former is aimed at crime prevention; it's usually acceptable and perfectly legal. The latter, however, operates outside the law. Because the hackers in the episode are coercing their victims to perform illegal actions, what they are doing is technically illegal (even though they are not personally robbing banks or killing people). Not everything that is illegal is immoral, of course, but there are other problems with vigilantism.

For example, there's no guarantee that the vigilante actually knows their victim is guilty. In the episode, presumably the hackers do; they have direct evidence (pictures, video, emails) of each person's guilt. But human nature's propensity to jump to irrational conclusions, especially regarding guilt, is the main reason that legal systems guard against wrongful prosecution with a presumption of innocence.

Worse still, vigilantism often unfairly targets certain populations. In the episode, the victims are selected at random: they're whoever was unlucky or dumb enough to download a program with the hackers' spy virus and do something deserving punishment. In reality, however, vigilantism often shows bias; it's a social and political phenomenon where the victims are often members of economically marginalized groups. For example, Manuel Mireanu points out how this happened in Italy and Hungary.

> [V]igilantism illustrates the complicity between certain parts of the state and certain parts of the society, in upholding violence that is legitimized as security. In Italy, this complicity implies that illegal immigrants and homeless people from Northern Africa and Eastern Europe are being marginalized, excluded and aggressed by vigilante patrols, on the backdrop of the state's anti-immigrant discourses. In Hungary, the same complicity implies that far-right patrols harass and beat up Roma people, in the context of a generalized state crackdown on the Roma population.[2]

Too often, the only crime that victims of vigilantes are guilty of is the "crime of being different." Vigilantism is simply used as an excuse to legitimize violence against marginalized groups. This fact alone seems to be sufficient reason to reject vigilantism, even if in some particular case the target of a vigilante is guilty.

Of course, legal systems aren't perfect either. They can be corrupt, convict the innocent, free the guilty, and unfairly mete out punishments. But that doesn't mean we should tolerate vigilantism. Legal systems at least *aim* at the systematic application of sanctions that are pre-established by a presumed neutral authority; at least legal systems intend to give you a fair trial and guard against corruption. Vigilantism does not. Since vigilantes do not report to a higher authority, we must wonder who watches the watchmen?

Still, these concerns don't erase the satisfaction that the ending of the episode produces. Specific acts of vigilantism, done to parties we know are guilty, still produce a feeling that justice has been served. But this makes one wonder – what exactly is justice in the first place? Is it some objective standard, an ideal that all societies have sought? Or is it something created by societies?

How to Define "Justice" Here and Now?

From the juridical perspective, the notion of justice has evolved. At first, justice was the main value of a legal system, giving laws their normative status. A law or norm should be obeyed because it is just, correct, or good. Indeed, according to natural law theory, norms are eternal and unchangeable entities we can "discover" through reason. According to many medieval philosophers, God's will is the source of moral and legal norms. From this perspective, criminal acts were akin to religious sins, and both should be punished. Indeed, even immoral or impure intentions or thoughts (like those Kenny likely had about the little girl in the restaurant) could be subject to punishment.

Although there are still natural law theorists today, most philosophers view things differently. Legal positivists suggested that laws were not discovered but "posited," created by authorities and societies. Laws were not revealed by God or nature but created by humans. Consequently, concerns about subjective elements such as religious, moral, or personal values were no longer legitimate. The study of law became more neutral and objective. Something was considered unjust only if it violated legal norms, and punishments were only prescribed for actions (not for impure or sinful intentions and thoughts, like Kenny's). Clearly, for the legal positivist, since it necessarily operates outside the law, vigilantism cannot accomplish justice.

The positivist would also object to the fact that the hackers were punishing moral crimes. Child pornography is illegal in London, but soliciting a prostitute, marital infidelity, and racist emails are not. So no one being punished by the hackers, except Kenny, was guilty of a crime. Even the Romans would have agreed that they shouldn't be punished. Indeed, one of the main goals of the principle *nulla poena sine lege*, which prescribes that no punishment should take place unless it is already prescribed by law, was to prevent the legal field from being confused with the moral field, and moral wrongs from being treated as legal wrongs. They didn't want the practice of punishment to escape legal boundaries and be managed arbitrarily by "ordinary" citizens.

But most importantly, because vigilantism is subjective, because it has no provisions in place to safeguard against wrongful prosecution, and because it has nothing to ensure that punishments are meted out fairly, we should not tolerate vigilantism. In fact, positivists would call for vigilantes to be punished right alongside Kenny. Of course, the severity of the hackers' punishments would likely be different, depending on what the law specified. But the positivist would call for the hackers to be punished all the same.

Do We Attain Justice by Punishment?

Regardless of what we think the nature of the law is, however, we must ask why the hackers didn't just notify the police of Kenny's crime? That would have made sure he didn't commit his crime again, after all. Why do all the psychological torture first? Presumably because the hackers thought jail wasn't enough punishment; the severity of Kenny's crime made him deserve more. But this raises more questions. What right do the hackers have to determine how much punishment Kenny should suffer? Even criminals who have admitted guilt are still entitled to a lawyer and a fair trial, in order to ensure that the punishment they receive is appropriate. If the hackers were interested in justice, shouldn't they have just shared their video of Kenny with the police?

On a related note, we may wonder what the purpose of punishing criminals is. One obvious answer is retribution – to pay back the criminal for what they did. This notion is derived from primitive "an eye for an eye" principles and, although the government doesn't punish rapists by directly raping them in return (because we have prescriptions against cruel and unusual punishment), retribution is at the heart of what many think that punishment should do. Indeed, some might think that prescriptions against cruel and unusual punishment prevent justice from being served when the criminal is cruel and unusual themselves. This might be what motivates the hackers to abuse Kenny before sending him to jail.

Retribution raises concerns, however. For example, how do you determine the amount of suffering a criminal caused so that you can return the same amount back to them? Such a calculation would be difficult. Consider that Kenny was just watching child porn that already existed, and not forcing children to engage in sex acts himself. According to some calculations, the harm he caused was insignificant and thus his punishment should be too. In reply, of course, people will argue that we need to lock Kenny up before he actually does harm any children (like the young girl in the restaurant) and deter other would-be pedophiles from similar actions – but that argument suggests that the purpose of punishment goes beyond retribution. It must also deter.

Philosopher Jeremy Bentham (1748–1832) would have agreed. As a utilitarian, he believed we should aim for what produces the most good for the greatest number of people. Bentham not only prescribed thirteen cannons (or rules) by which judges could determine proportional punishment for criminals. He also thought criminal punishment should serve the overall good of society. And the way it seems to do that is by preventing the criminal from repeating their crime, deterring other would-be criminals from copying them, and removing dangerous people from society. Bentham's fellow utilitarian John Stuart Mill (1806–1873) agreed. Mill in particular had a favorable view of the death penalty, which he saw as the most effective means of deterring would-be murders.

Importantly, however, Mill didn't think punishment should seek retribution.

> If any one thinks that there is justice in the infliction of purposeless suffering; that there is a natural affinity between the two ideas of guilt and punishment,

which makes it intrinsically fitting that wherever there has been guilt, pain should be inflicted by way of retribution; I acknowledge I can find no argument to justify punishment inflicted on this principle .... The merely retributive view of punishment derives no justification from the doctrine I support.[3]

Why? Because he thought "the only purpose for which power can be rightfully exercised over any member of a civilized community, against his will, is to prevent harm to others."[4] Giving a criminal "what they deserve" could go beyond this. Indeed, since the pain suffered by the criminal is part of the utilitarian calculation, the punishment the criminal suffers should be no more than is necessary for a deterrent effect. The purpose of punishment must only be aimed at overall societal good.

Perhaps deterrence is not enough, though. If the ultimate goal really is overall societal good, then punishment should not only deter criminals – it should reform and rehabilitate them. It should make them less likely to repeat their crime – not through fear but by making them better. If we can make them into healthy, contributing members of society, and then return them into society, we will have done good for both them and us. Clearly, in this view, we should not celebrate what the hackers did. Kenny needs psychiatric treatment. He needs medication. He also needs to be punished, and heavily monitored if released. But he does not need to be forced to fight another pedophile to death. Rehabilitation was not the hackers' goal.

The rehabilitative approach has some arguments in its favor. For one, the deterrent effect of punishment seems to be limited. That's why there are so many repeat offenders. Unless you reform them, criminals will still be criminals once released. Prison could even make them worse, thus contributing to a worldwide problem with prison overcrowding.[5] In Brazil, for example, data shows that, in 2018, detention facilities were 75% beyond capacity and often received three times more prisoners than what they are allowed.[6] What's more, it's often societal conditions that give rise to criminal behavior in the first place. Perhaps this wasn't true in Kenny's case, but generally it seems that society should aim to make up for the ways that it encourages or makes criminal behavior necessary. Take poverty for example. Marcus Aurelius (121–180 CE) said that, "Poverty is the mother of crime," and usually people don't steal unless they need to. Consequently, it seems that society should aim not only to reform the character of convicted thieves but aim to give them (and everyone) an education and job skills (and an economy) that will enable them to earn a living wage. Of course, not everyone can be reformed. But it seems that we should at least try. As Oscar Wilde once said, "The only difference between the saint and the sinner is that every saint has a past, and every sinner has a future." The most promising investment for a peaceful society would seem to be education. That is what would most effectively lead to justice.

Of course, one might think criminal behavior is inherent to human nature and that punishment has multiple purposes. Even so, we should not give up on rehabilitation. In the wise words of Robert G. Caldwell,

> punishment is an art which involves the balancing of retribution, deterrence and reformation in terms not only of the Court but also of the values in which it takes place and in the balancing of these purposes of punishment receives emphasis as the accompanying conditions change.[7]

If he's right, vigilantism should not be tolerated.

Vigilantism may be appealing, especially to those who have been victims of crimes that went unpunished. But from a philosophical perspective, vigilantism is difficult to defend. It's arbitrary and subjective. It's ineffective and often applied with bias. It mixes morality with law and doesn't aim at rehabilitation. That's not to say that criminals should not be properly punished for their crimes. But it is to say that we should not allow individual citizens to determine and administer such punishment. Society can do better. If we see a crime underway and we can stop it without great risk to ourselves, we should do so. But once a crime is committed, we should simply contact the authorities and provide evidence. We should not try to punish the criminals ourselves. Our initial emotional reaction may be to celebrate what the hackers did to Kenny, but in everything they did to him (aside from turning him into the police) had more to do with sadism and "trolling" than it did with justice.

Notes

1. Charlie Brooker and Annabel Jones with Jason Arnopp, *Inside Black Mirror* (New York: Crown Archetype, 2018), 170.
2. Manuel Mireanu, (2014) Vigilantism and Security: State, Violence and Politics in Italy and Hungary. PhD Thesis. Central European University, 11, https://pds.ceu.edu/sites/pds.ceu.hu/files/attachment/basicpage/478/mireanumanuelir.pdf (Accessed 9 July 2019).
3. John Stuart Mill, *The Collected Works of John Stuart Mill* (London: Routledge, 2014), 462.
4. John Stuart Mill, *On Liberty* (Indianapolis, IN: Hackett Publishing Company, 1978), 9.
5. Niall McCarthy, "The world's most overcrowded prison system," *Forbes*, https://www.forbes.com/sites/niallmccarthy/2018/01/26/the-worlds-most-overcrowded-prison-systems-infographic/#7114d1351372 (Accessed 9 July 2019).
6. National Council of Public Prosecutions, "Occupancy rate of Brazilian prisons is 175%, shows dynamic report 'Prison System in Numbers,'" *CNMP*, http://www.cnmp.mp.br/portal/noticias-cddf/11314-taxa-de-ocupacao-dos-presidios-brasileiros-e-de-175-mostra-relatorio-dinamico-sistema-prisional-em-numeros (Accessed 9 July 2019).
7. Robert Graham Caldwell, *Criminology* (New York: Ronald Press Company, 1956), 403.

San Junipero and the Digital Afterlife
Could Heaven be a Place on Earth?

James Cook

Forever? Who can even make sense of forever?

(Kelly Booth)

A foundational question of philosophy is how one should live; *San Junipero* raises the question of how one should die. Our innate human desire to prolong our lives has led to attempts to cheat death through medicine and spirituality. But *San Junipero* offers a technological solution: a virtual seaside resort of the same name.[1] Those dying in the real world are allowed to visit San Junipero for a few hours a week as tourists with their prime physical bodies as avatars. More importantly, they can extend their stay indefinitely by digitally uploading their consciousness to the system after their physical body expires. The episode follows Kelly and Yorkie, two "young" women who meet in San Junipero. They have a whirlwind romance, fall in love, and (after some soul searching) decide to get married, upload, and live together forever in San Junipero.

San Junipero is a rarity for *Black Mirror*. As producer Annabel Jones put it, "I think some people saw *San Junipero* as a 'first' because it [has] a happy, uplifting ending."[2] Yorkie and Kelly ride off into the digital sunset to the music of Belinda Carlisle, living forever in heaven on earth. But as Jones later clarified, "Whilst there is a positive upbeat ending, it's not exactly a happy ever after."[3] In fact, the episode's director, Owen Harris, said, "I never read the story as being quite as positive as it ended up feeling. …[I'm] more reticent about the idea of spending eternity in a place like San Junipero. I'd worry I'd end up in the Quagmire."[4]

Indeed! The Quagmire is 24/7 debauchery, a sex rave club on steroids where many long-time residents seem to end up. So, in an attempt to create heaven on earth, have the creators of San Junipero actually done the exact opposite? At first glance, something like San Junipero may look tempting. But if given the opportunity, should we really want to upload? Or should we embrace death with grace?

Black Mirror and Philosophy: Dark Reflections, First Edition. Edited by David Kyle Johnson.
© 2020 John Wiley & Sons, Inc. Published 2020 by John Wiley & Sons, Inc.

Justice in the Afterlife

Upon reflection, doubts about uploading into San Junipero abound. Are Yorkie and Kelly really the same persons as before they uploaded? Are they conscious?[5] If not, the "person" that exists in San Junipero after you upload isn't you and doesn't experience anything anyway, so why bother? But even assuming the answer to both those questions is yes, we still might wonder whether we should want the kind of afterlife San Junipero offers.

One reason we might want an afterlife involves cosmic justice. People don't always get what they deserve; evil people take advantage of the virtuous, others get away with horrendous crimes. Bad luck can befall the good, whilst good luck blesses the bad. Such injustices are why many societies try to minimize the role of chance in whether or not people have a good life (with things like a legal system, social security, and universal health care programs). But there is only so much a society can accomplish. It seems the only way to completely eliminate injustice in the world is with a system that flawlessly gives people the punishment or reward they deserve after death – like the Christian heaven and hell, or the Myth of Er at the end of Plato's *Republic*. Indeed, Immanuel Kant (1724–1804) argued that immortality is a necessary condition for the obtainment of what he called the "highest good," an ideal state of affairs where happiness is distributed perfectly according to the morality of the recipients.[6]

San Junipero could not correct worldly injustice, however. Its main purpose is to keep residents happy, not punish them for their worldly misdeeds. Besides, even if it did, evil people could avoid punishment by simply not uploading. Perhaps we could force everyone to upload. But would we really be able to sort the evil persons from the good? Those who escape punishment in the real world do so through discretion, cunning, and good luck; they could use the same methods to escape punishment in the digital afterlife.

What's more, it's difficult to see how San Junipero could adequately reward the good. Think of Davis, the lonely guy who plays video games in San Junipero's bars and crushes on Yorkie. His socially awkward nature seems to have followed him into the afterlife. He may be a virtuous, upstanding guy, but because San Junipero is populated by real people, he's likely to suffer the same isolation and rejection he suffered in the real world. We don't escape the evils of the world by uploading into San Junipero; we just get more of the same.

Immortality and Cosmic Insignificance

Another reason to wish for an afterlife is our sense of cosmic insignificance. When we take into account the physical and temporal extent of the universe, our lives seem to matter even less than Wes does to Kelly. From the perspective of beings that live to about eighty, our goals and relationships seem important; but from a cosmic perspective, our lives are almost invisible. The oldest living human is a mere zygote compared to the sun, which itself is a mere blip in the history of the universe. Even if you ruled the Earth for 100 years of peace and prosperity, once the sun burns out and destroys the Earth, the universe will be just as it would have been had you never existed. Leo Tolstoy perhaps put it best:

> If not today, then tomorrow sickness and death will come (indeed, they were already approaching) to everyone, to me, and nothing will remain except the stench and the worms. My deeds, whatever they may be, will be forgotten sooner or later, and I myself will be no more. Why, then, do anything? How can anyone fail to see this and live?[7]

If we do not persist and our efforts in life amount to nothing, why should we work towards our goals? Indeed, what reason do we have for living at all? In order for our lives to be significant it seems we must make some permanent difference to the universe. It seems the only way for that to happen is for there to be an everlasting afterlife.

As a reason to enter San Junipero, however, the need for cosmic significance falls short. First, this need seems to be rooted in worries about the meaning of life, but it's not clear that the impact of a person's life must be everlasting in order for it to be meaningful. One could easily argue that by living a good life one has accomplished something intrinsically valuable, which gives life meaning. Sure, everyone will eventually die and be forgotten, but that doesn't mean our experiences never occurred.[8] One's life may not be eternally significant, but it could still be meaningful.

Second, even if immortality is necessary for significance, it's not clear that immorality is actually desirable. Think about it. If you spent billions of years doing all there ever was to do, again and again, you'd eventually get tired of it. And once you did, you'd still have all of eternity in which to hate every minute of doing it all again (or to simply be bored out of your mind). Heaven might be fun for a while, but it could eventually turn into hell. Indeed, this seems to be something that Kelly and Yorkie both recognize. When Yorkie says Kelly could have forever, Kelly asks, "Who can even make sense of forever?" Yorkie points out that she can have however long she wants, "I mean, you can remove yourself like that [snaps fingers]. It's not a trap."

Yorkie's response points to a third reason that San Junipero wouldn't grant our lives significance: it doesn't actually last forever. It would need some kind of physical infrastructure to keep it going, so it's only good up until our resources are depleted, the sun explodes, or the universe ends. More likely, it would end much sooner, whenever the managing company goes bankrupt. There is also the possibility that cyberterrorists could hack the system and shut it down. As John Gray says of mind uploading, "Cyberspace is a projection of the human world, not a way out of it."[9]

San Junipero, of course, could greatly extend a person's life. But even living a million years longer is, in the grand scheme of things, not much at all. As Lucretius (99–55 BCE) says in *On the Nature of Things*,

> Though you outlive as many generations as you will,
> Nevertheless, Eternal Death is waiting for you still.
> It is no shorter, that eternity that lies in store
> For the man who with the setting sun *today* will rise no more,
> Than for man whose sun has set months, even years, before.[10]

So we'll either have to look elsewhere or give up the quest for cosmic significance.

But since eternal boredom may make immortality undesirable, and San Junipero guards against this by allowing users to opt out at any time, San Junipero may have advantages. Indeed, it may take the sting out of death in a way that the traditional everlasting afterlife does not. Could that be a reason for uploading? To answer that, we should ask what's so bad about death in the first place?

Is San Junipero an Improvement?

We implicitly believe death is bad, but it's notoriously hard to explain *why*. Obviously the *process* of dying (say by accident or illness) might be painful and thus undesirable, but what is so bad about the condition of *being dead itself*? Even if the process of dying is painless, we still don't want to be dead. But why?

This might seem an odd question, but in his *Letter to Menoeceus*, Epicurus (341–270 BCE) famously argued that fearing death is irrational. "Death…is nothing to us, seeing that, when we are, death is not come, and, when death is come, we are not."[11] For Epicurus, pain is all there is to fear. Since we can't experience pain if we don't exist, and being dead is the condition of not existing, being dead can't be anything to fear.

Contemporary philosopher Thomas Nagel argues, however, that death is bad, at least in part, because it restricts the possibilities open to us. This makes sense. It's more tragic for a child to die than her elderly grandmother, right? Why? Because a child's future is more open; she can be and do a great many things (whereas the grandmother is somewhat limited in this respect). So while you can't *experience* being dead (since it's a state of non-existence), being dead is an evil because it cuts off your future possibilities. It has transformed you from an agent with hopes, dreams, and fears, to a mere cadaver.

Nagel admits, however, that there's a limit. There comes a time when things like the feebleness of old age limit one's future possibilities to such an extent that death begins to lose its sting:

> The question is whether we can regard as a misfortune any limitation, like mortality, that is normal to the species. Blindness or near-blindness is not a misfortune for a mole, nor would it be for a man, if that were the natural condition for the human race.[12]

Epicurus would have likely agreed. And this is why you should likely reject a drug that would greatly extend your life beyond its natural limit. What good is living an extra forty years if you'll spend them all as an enfeebled burden on others?

San Junipero circumvents this worry, however. You could spend an extra forty (or eighty, or a thousand) years with the body of a twenty-five-year-old! It opens up new possibilities that were never there before. You also wouldn't have to worry about situations like the one Bernard Williams (1929–2003) describes in "The Makropulos Case," where a woman with an unnaturally extended life becomes jaded as her friends and family all perish around her. Indeed, your friends and family could eventually join you! By the lights of Nagel's argument, shouldn't you want to upload? Wouldn't refusing be akin to suicide, the same as robbing yourself of future possibilities?

Perhaps, but we must consider what kinds of possibilities San Junipero opens up. Are they comparable to the possibilities that we get in our physical lives or are they pale imitations?

The Experience Machine

In his book *Anarchy, State, and Utopia*, Robert Nozick (1938–2002) imagined a virtual reality device he called the "Experience Machine" that would erase memories of your previous life and then give you any set of experiences you wish. Captain of the USS *Callister*? Eternal party in a beach town in 1987? The Experience Machine can do it all. Just say the word and you can trade this world for your ultimate one, and you'd never even know that everything and everyone in it was fake.

Would you plug in? Nozick argues that most people would politely decline. Pleasurable experiences are generally preferable to painful ones, but experiences mean little if they don't reflect anything more concrete. We don't just want the experience of doing things, we want to actually *do* them. Nozick uses this thought experiment to argue against hedonism, the view that pleasure is the only good. Other things, like living in contact with reality and being loved by other (conscious) people, are valuable too. But this could also be seen as a reason to not upload into San Junipero. After all, what it offers is very much like what the Experience Machine offers: life in a digital reality designed to keep you happy, but which corresponds to nothing more than the microchips.

There are two important differences that weaken this line of reasoning, however. First of all, those who upload into San Junipero aren't fooled. They know that the world they inhabit is digital, and they don't forget their previous life. In this way, they still live in "contact with reality." One might argue that their world isn't "real," but it's not clear that's true. It's *fake*, in the same way that plastic trees are *fake*. But it's still real in the sense that it exists. Every object is a line of code on a computer. Of course, San Junipero residents can't *experience* objects as lines of code, they see them as physical. But something very similar is true of us: we don't experience the world as it is either. Human perception is constructive. For example, you'll never be able to see the book you are holding as anything but a solid object, even though in reality it's mostly empty space. When Yorkie insists to Kelly, "Look at it! Touch it! …It's real. This is real," she seems to be implying that San Junipero is as *real* as the physical world in every way that counts.

The second meaningful difference between San Junipero and the Experience Machine is that San Junipero is filled with other conscious people; the same people who lived in the real world and who are hence worthy of the same respect. One might conclude from this that relationships in San Junipero would be just as genuine and meaningful as those in the real world. You couldn't make a family; it doesn't seem digital coupling could produce digital offspring.[13] But you could still make other people happy and be made happy by others. You could even write songs for others to enjoy.

But there is surely more to relationships than this. Consider Kelly's words to Yorkie after Yorkie chastises Kelly's former husband Richard for not uploading into San Junipero when he died, saying what he did was selfish.

KELLY: Forty-nine years. I was with [Richard] for 49 years. You can't begin to imagine, you can't know. The bond, the commitment, the boredom, the yearning, the laughter, the love of it, the fucking love! You just cannot know! Everything we sacrificed, the years I gave him, the years he gave me, did you think to ask? Did it occur to you to ask? We had a daughter, Allison, always difficult, always beautiful, died at 39 years old bless her heart, and Richard and I, we felt that heartbreak as one. You think you're the only person who ever suffered? Go fuck yourself. …You want to spend forever somewhere nothing matters? …Go ahead. But I'm out.

A greater number of experiences may be available to Kelly and Yorkie than were unavailable to Kelly and Richard, but none of these will be as important as the reality and responsibility of raising a child, for instance. Kelly and Richard's relationship had *concrete* consequences, and these gave their relationship a sense of purpose. If an uploaded couple like Kelly and Yorkie were to run into hardships, what would hold them together?

Why not just go find someone else? After all, you could just try again in 100 years. As producer Anabel Jones put it, "[the ending is] more about being happy for now, and seeing how this goes. On the cliff, when Kelly delivers that speech and says, 'What does forever even mean?', that thought remains."[14]

The Value of Finitude

Although, as we've discussed, San Junipero wouldn't last forever, it's not finite *in the same way* as the real world. You can basically live for as long as you like, without fear of death or injury. There would thus be no pressure to get things done, or to take risks when opportunities are presented. You'd never have to prioritize one goal over another. And it's things like this that contemporary philosopher Martha Nussbaum argues constitute, not just what we value, but those values themselves.

> [F]riendship, love, justice, and the various forms of morally virtuous action get their point and their value within the structure of human time, as relations and activities that extend over finite time...the removal of all limit, of all constraint of finitude in general, mortality in particular, would not so much enable these values to survive eternally as bring about the death of all value as we know it.[15]

Our values are structured by, and inseparable from, our mortality; the natural limits of our species mean we cherish the things we do to the extent we do. To illustrate this point, Nussbaum mentions the Greek gods, whose immortality precludes them from having certain virtues.

> [C]ourage consists in a certain way of acting and reacting in face of death and the risk of death. A being who cannot take that risk cannot have that virtue – or can have, as we in fact see with the gods and their attitude to pain, only a pale simulacrum of it.[16]

As an analogy, think about video games. Part of the enjoyment is using skill to overcome obstacles. When you use a cheat code to go into god mode and thereby remove these obstacles, it's fun for a while but quickly becomes an empty experience. Hence, on Olympus we see a:

> kind of laxness and lightness in the relationships of the gods, a kind of playful unheroic quality that contrasts sharply with the more intense character of human love and friendship, and has, clearly, a different sort of value. In heaven there is...no Achilles: no warrior risking everything he is and has, and no loving friend whose love is such that he risks everything on account of his friend. Friendship so differently constituted will not be the same thing, or have the same value.[17]

Wouldn't we see the same thing in San Junipero? You couldn't make a true sacrifice, and there would be no point in trying. Kelly pushing Yorkie out the way of a car would not put her in danger, nor would it take Yorkie out of danger – no one could be harmed either way. Without risk there could be no sacrifice, and selflessness would disappear as a virtue.

Or consider, as Kelly puts it, "all those lost fucks at the Quagmire trying anything to feel something?" Maybe this is why many permanent San Junipero residents end up there. The things they cherished in the real world – love, friendship, the satisfaction of actually having achieved something – are now unavailable, all they can do is chase after mere experiences. And it takes a lot more to satisfy someone with no stake in the world besides their own pleasure. Such jaded beings are even the subject of horror movies; *From Beyond* and *Hellraiser* both feature antagonists intent on exploring new experiences because of their deadened capacities for enjoyment.

This doesn't bode well for Kelly and Yorkie's supposed happy ending. We say "till death do us part" in our wedding vows because we know, roughly, how long it will take for death to part us. Furthermore, we are anchored together by real world commitments like sharing responsibilities and raising children, and even this fails to hold together many marriages. But if we extend human life by, say 10,000 years, in a world where people want for nothing and could never reproduce, could we really expect people to make the same commitments to one another?[18] Would relationships last?

So should we want to upload to something like San Junipero if given the chance? Given what we've discussed, the answer is probably no. Mortality is a mixed blessing. Sure, death brings suffering to those around us and takes away the things we live for. But without this finitude we would be unable to appreciate a loyal friend, a loving parent, or even a fine meal. Our limits give meaning to our lives. This doesn't mean life in San Junipero would be completely devoid of value. It could give some people, like Yorkie whose adulthood was snatched away from her by an accident, something better than a life in a hospital bed on life support. But for the rest of us, tacking something not-quite-as-good onto the end of our lives wouldn't be an improvement.

Think of it this way. Charlie Brooker will eventually run out of good ideas for *Black Mirror*. When he does, he could either carry on writing episodes, allowing the drop in quality to dilute the whole, or he could quit while he's ahead, ending on a high note. We should prefer the latter option; to carry it on would be to reject any sense of completion. Perhaps what is lacking from the permanent San Junipero is an inability to call it a night.

Notes

1. The town is presumably named after Saint Juniper, a Franciscan priest who is said to have given a meal of trotters to a dying man. Like Juniper, San Junipero grants the moribund one last request: to be young again.

2. Charlie Brooker and Annabel Jones with Jason Arnopp, *Inside Black Mirror* (New York: Crown Archetype, 2018), 189.

3. Ibid., 190.

4. Ibid.

5. For more on these questions see Chapter 21 (David Gamez's chapter on conscious technology) and Chapter 22 (Molly Gardner and Robert Sloane's chapter on personal identity) in this volume.

6. This interpretation of Kant is up for debate. See Paul Guyer and A. Allen Wood eds., *Critique of Pure Reason* (Cambridge: Cambridge University Press, 1998), A8II/B839.

7. Leo Tolstoy, *Confession*, trans. David Patterson (New York: W.W. Norton, 1983), 30.

8. For more on his kind of meaning, see Julian Baggini, *What's It All About?: Philosophy and the Meaning of Life* (Oxford University Press, 2005).

9. John Gray, *Seven Types of Atheism* (London: Allen Lane, 2018), 67.

10. Lucretius, *Lucretius On the Nature of Things*, trans. Alicia Stallings (London: Penguin Classics, 2007), 105.

11. Robert Drew Hicks, Letter to Herodotus and Menoeceus. (Pantianos Classics, 1910), 169.

12. Thomas Nagel, *Mortal Questions* (Cambridge, UK: Cambridge University Press, 2012), 9.

13. That's not to say that digital offspring are impossible. They wouldn't be the continuation of a person from outside of San Junipero, of course. Digital offspring would be created, somehow, in the system. But if digital offspring were a part of life in San Junipero, one's evaluation of the value of life in such a world might drastically change.

14. Brooker et al., 190.

15. Martha Nussbaum, "Mortal immortals: Lucretius on death and the voice of nature," *Philosophy and Phenomenological Research*, 50 (1989), 336.

16. Ibid., p. 338.

17. Ibid.

18. For more on such worries, see Yuvel Noah Harari, *Homo Deus: A Brief History of Tomorrow* (New York: Harper Collins, 2017).

Men Against Fire and Political Manipulation

How Are We Tricked into Dehumanizing Others?

Bertha Alvarez Manninen

> It's a lot easier to pull the trigger when you're aiming at the bogeyman.
> (Arquette)

Men Against Fire tells the story of Stripe Koinange, a solider in an army trying to exterminate a collection of seemingly terrifying animalistic vermin called "roaches." The title of the episode comes from World War I veteran S.L.A. Marshall's book *Men Against Fire: The Problem of Battle Command*. Based on several interviews with World War II veterans, Marshall discovered that only one in four soldiers actually fired their weapons at their enemies during battle. Marshall proposed several ways to change military training to increase the number of kills – to make soldiers more efficiently deadly. In *Men Against Fire,* the military has accomplished this by implanting a device in soldiers' brains, called the MASS neural implant, which makes them perceive the "enemy" not as terrified human beings, but as horrific monsters.

The story follows Stripe as he comes to realize that roaches aren't vermin, but rather human beings who are being targeted for mass genocide due to their allegedly inferior genes. The episode showcases just how easy it is to commit acts of violence against a group of persons when they are quite literally seen as subhuman. Although we do not yet have the technology necessary to create the MASS implant, *Men Against Fire* makes one wonder whether our use of dehumanizing language and propaganda targeting members of marginalized groups serves a similar function.

Black Mirror and Philosophy: Dark Reflections, First Edition. Edited by David Kyle Johnson.
© 2020 John Wiley & Sons, Inc. Published 2020 by John Wiley & Sons, Inc.

Our "MASS Implant": The Language of Dehumanization

According to the story, previous attempts to kill off the roaches were unsuccessful because, even though the group was derided, people are largely unwilling to outright massacre other humans. The MASS device helped solve this "problem," not only by making those humans look like monsters, but by providing an augmented reality that allows the soldiers to communicate relevant data, and by giving them a reward of graphic sexual dreams for successful kills. Once Stripe's MASS implant is compromised, however, he is able to see these "monsters" as the terrified human beings they actually are, doing their best to hide and survive.

While attempting to protect two victims, a mother Catarina and her son Alec, Stripe asks them how the locals, who also hate these individuals, are able to treat them so horribly without the use of a MASS implant. Catarina responds:

> Ten years ago it began. Post-war. First, the screening program, the DNA checks, then the register, the emergency measures. Soon everyone calls us creatures. Filthy creatures. Every voice. The TV. The computer. Say we have sickness in us. We have weakness. It's in our blood. They say that our blood cannot go on. That we cannot go on.

The dehumanization of these individuals is illustrated via language: they are called "roaches." To some it may seem like a stretch to think that people really would use such language to describe others, but *Black Mirror* creator Charlie Brooker chose the term *because* he heard it used in the real world. Controversial British columnist Katie Hopkins actually referred to migrants residing in the UK as "cockroaches."[1]

Indeed, one of the first steps towards ostracizing individuals in marginalized groups is to find means of "othering" them; to create a sharp division between "us" and "them." The use of dehumanizing language and propaganda is a long-standing method to create this divide: human beings are likened to distasteful animals, like insects or rodents. David Livingstone Smith writes about many instances of this in his book *Less Than Human: Why We Demean, Enslave, and Exterminate Others*. Drawing upon examples from Nazi Germany, Smith writes that "[t]o the Nazis, all the Jews, Gypsies, and others were rats: dangerous, disease-carrying rats...[they] were represented as parasitic organisms – as leeches, lice, bacteria, or vectors of contagion."[2] During World War II, while the Japanese depicted Americans and the British "with horns sprouting from their temples, and sporting tails, claws, and fangs,"[3] Americans, in turn, dehumanized the Japanese by considering them and portraying them as "monkeys, apes, or rodents, and sometimes as insects."[4]

In the early twentieth century, the Muslim Turks of the Ottoman Empire massacred over a million Christian Armenians. As Smith notes, "the Turkish authorities...conceived of [the Armenians] in much the same way as the Nazis would later imagine the Jews – as disease organisms infecting the body of the state – and announced the need to 'rid ourselves of these Armenian parasites.' Armenians and other non-Muslim minorities were also identified with traditionally unclean animals such as rats, dogs, and pigs."[5] In the latter part of the twentieth century, during the Rwandan genocide, the Hutus repeatedly referred to the Tutsis as "cockroaches."

The use of dehumanizing language is not just a matter of incorporating objectionable words into public discourse, and offense at such language is not a matter of being overly sensitive. Philosopher Ludwig Wittgenstein (1889–1951) emphasized how our language shapes the boundaries of our minds and thought: "the limits of my language mean the limits of my world."[6] Indeed, the connection between the use of dehumanizing language and propaganda against marginalized groups and the willingness to physically harm and encourage violence against members of such groups is well documented.

The Consequences of our "MASS Implant": The Violence of Dehumanization

Throughout *Men Against Fire* we see that, while the locals openly hate the roaches, they do not directly participate in their massacre (though they encourage the military to do so). The soldiers, however, are joyous at the thought of hunting and killing roaches, viewing it as almost a recreational activity. Stripe kills two of them on his first mission, shooting one while repeatedly stabbing another to death. He is especially gleeful about this as his partner, Raiman, expresses frustration that she has not killed a roach in a while. Indeed, she recounts to Stripe that her first few kills were utterly orgasmic.

Once Stripe is able to see the roaches as human beings, he goes out of his way to protect them, and is horrified at how easily Raiman can kill them. Viewing them as human for the first time so profoundly affects Stripe that he goes against all of his military training, tackles Raiman to the ground, and helps Catarina and Alec escape. However, it is not long before Raiman finds them, kills Catarina and Alec, and beats Stripe into submission.

Stripe wakes up in a cell where a military psychologist, Arquette, apologizes for not having discovered the defect in Stripe's MASS implant, and reveals to him everything that had been going on. They had to use the MASS implant because human beings, when they recognize the humanity of "the other," are actually ineffective killers. Arquette tells Stripe:

Humans. You know, we give ourselves a bad rap, but we're genuinely empathetic as a species. I mean, we don't actually want to kill each other. Which is a good thing. Until your future depends on wiping out the enemy... most soldiers didn't even fire their weapons. Or if they did, they would just aim over the heads of the enemies. They did it on purpose...plus the guys who did get a kill would get messed up in the head. And that's pretty much how it stayed until MASS came along. You see MASS, well that's the ultimate military weapon...It's a lot easier to pull the trigger when you're aiming at the bogeyman.

This is likely why the locals, while hating the ostracized group, were largely unable to kill them – they still saw them as human beings. Indeed, Brooker wanted to emphasize that the villagers didn't need the MASS device to hate the roaches because he wanted them to mirror the audience: "[people] don't need [MASS] to demonize and hate people."[7] Yet the MASS implant allows the military to "do its job" by making it so that the soldiers literally perceive human beings as monsters instead. It is the perception of persons as subhuman that makes it so easy to massacre them.

The deadly consequences of such perception make it vital to be aware of the power of dehumanizing language and propaganda. As Smith puts it "[d]ehumanization isn't a way of talking. It's a way of thinking...[i]t acts as a psychological lubricant, dissolving our inhibitions and inflaming our destructive passions. As such, it empowers us to perform acts that would, under other circumstances, be unthinkable."[8] Dehumanizing the Jews and the Armenians was the first step to facilitating their genocide. Referring to the Tutsis as cockroaches helped to justify the horrific fate of "around 800,000 Tutsis and moderate Hutus [who] were shot, burned, hacked, and bludgeoned to death by marauding mobs."[9] During World War II, the vilification of the Japanese facilitated their forced detainment, including US citizens of Japanese ancestry, in internment camps.

In order to understand how dehumanization functions, we must first ask, as social ethicist Herbert Kelman puts it, "what it means to perceive another person as fully human, in the sense of being included in the moral compact that governs human relationships."[10] In order to perceive others as full members of our moral community, it is necessary to recognize them as "part of an interconnected network of individuals who care for each other, who recognize each other's individuality, and who respect each other's rights."[11] The use of dehumanizing language effectively functions not just to draw a distinction between "us" and "them," but also to subdue, and even deaden, our sense of empathy and care for the "other":

> Sanctioned massacres become possible to the extent that we deprive fellow human beings of identity and community. It is difficult to have compassion for those who lack identity and who are excluded from our community; their death does not move us in a personal way. Thus when a group of people is defined entirely in terms of a category to which they belong, and when this

category is excluded from the human family, then the moral restraints against killing them are more readily overcome.[12]

It is much more difficult to harm others who we perceive as "one of our own." Arquette says as much to Stripe when, echoing S.L.A. Marshall's findings, he notes that in the past, soldiers were hesitant to shoot and kill their adversaries – they saw them as too human, too much "like them," to be able to easily harm them. The military needed a way to facilitate viewing enemies as bogeymen instead of as persons. In the episode the MASS implant achieves this end, but in our society dehumanizing language and propaganda serves a similar function. As Gregory Stanton, founder of Genocide Watch, notes, dehumanizing language, thought, and behavior is a hallmark feature of genocide: "One group…denies the humanity of the other group. Members of it are equated with animals, vermin, insects or disease. Dehumanization overcomes the normal human revulsion against murder."[13]

The "MASS Implant" Today

It may be tempting to think that such instances of dehumanization are a thing of the past, but nothing could be further from the truth. Brooker noted that, when first conceiving of *Men Against Fire,* "the notion that a future fascist government might come in and demonize a huge section of society" appeared "incredibly far-fetched." Yet current events throughout the world have made this episode hit "closer to home."[14]

Indeed, anyone paying attention to the current political climate in the United States will be able to see our own "MASS implant" being propagated and supported by political leaders. During a roundtable discussion in California concerning illegal immigration in May 2018, President Donald Trump said of MS-13 gang members, "these aren't people. These are animals." While we may be tempted to agree with him in reference to gang members, especially those who have committed heinous crimes, Trump blurred the lines between undocumented immigrants and gang members in a June 19, 2018 tweet: "Democrats are the problem. They don't care about crime and want illegal immigrants, no matter how bad they may be, to pour into and infest our Country, like MS-13." Here, he lumps all immigrants together, and refers to undocumented immigrants as a literal infestation – a term that is typically used to describe being taken over by insects.

To be clear, Trump's dehumanizing language did not create the current hatred against members of marginalized groups in the United States – our "MASS implants" have been long and pervasively present. For example, a 2015 study asked 201 participants in the United States to rate members of certain marginalized groups on an "ascent of man" diagram scale (which shows the evolution of humans from primate to modern day *Homo sapiens*). The instructions read: "Some people seem highly evolved, whereas others seem no different than lower animals. Using the image below as a guide, indicate using the sliders how evolved you consider the average member of each group to be." The groups that were assessed were: "Mexican immigrants, Arabs, Chinese people, Europeans, Americans, Icelanders, Japanese people, Swiss people, Austrians, Australians, French people, South Koreans, and Muslims." The results were that:

> European groups and Japanese were rated as similarly evolved as Americans, whereas South Korean, Chinese and Mexican immigrants were rated as significantly less evolved than Americans. Lowest on the scale were Arabs and Muslims, who were rated on average 10.6 and 14.0 points lower than Americans, respectively.[15]

Two of the authors of the study, Nour Kteily and Emile Bruneau, noted in a 2017 article that individuals in the United States who are more likely to harbor dehumanizing beliefs against members of marginalized groups were more likely to vote for candidates who supported "hostile policies" against those groups. For example, "blatant dehumanization of Muslims was more strongly correlated with support for Donald Trump than any of the other Republican candidates"[16] during the 2016 election. So while Trump did not create the current crisis, he is certainly responsible for fanning its flames.

Other contemporary instances of dehumanization abound outside of the United States. As I write this, yet another horrific instance of genocide is being committed against Rohingya Muslims in Myanmar, a state in Southeast Asia. In what serves as an example of how easily the common person is susceptible to the effects of dehumanizing propaganda, and the violence that typically follows, one article about the current Muslim genocide in Myanmar notes that after hundreds of soldiers "entered the village of Gu Dar Pyin armed with rifles, knives, rocket launchers and grenades...mov[ing] from house to house stealing possessions of Rohingya Muslims and shooting anyone they found... ordinary Burmese civilians followed, burning houses as well as shooting and stabbing women and children."[17] Likewise, the villagers in *Men Against Fire* were complicit in the dehumanization of the roaches. Though the villagers did not kill the roaches, they actively sought their deaths by having the military do the work for them.

In 2017, it was revealed that homosexual men were being routinely attacked, beaten, killed, and sometimes taken to holding camps in Chechnya. Chechen leader Ramzan Kadyrov has consistently denied these accusations, despite photographic and video evidence of the assaults. When asked about the charges, Kadyrov replied by denying that gay persons even exist in Chechnya:

> This is nonsense. We don't have those kinds of people here. We don't have any gays. If there are any, take them to Canada…Take them far from us so we don't have them at home. To purify our blood, if there is any here, take them.[18]

Kadyrov's words here are reminiscent of both Arquette's and Medina's (Stripe's squad leader) respective justifications for participating in the genocide of Catarina's people. Medina leads Stripe's first mission to kill the roaches, taking them to the home of a local farmer, a devout Christian who has chosen to act on his faith and shelter them from genocide. In her attempts to extract information from the farmer, Medina tells him that his desire to protect them is an "understandable sentiment, but it's misguided. We gotta take them out if humankind is gonna carry on in this world." When Stripe protests the killing of human beings, Arquette justifies it by saying:

> Do you have any idea the amount of shit that is in their DNA? Higher rates of cancer, muscular dystrophy, MS, SLS, substandard IQ, criminal tendencies, and sexual deviances. It's all there. The screening shows it. Is that what you want for the next generation? Don't feel bad about doing your job. The villagers won't do it. The people back home won't do it. They don't have MASS. MASS lets you do it.

The goal of "purifying" a race, or a species, is a common justification for mass genocide, one that is facilitated when we view the targeted group as not one of "our own."

Rehumanizing the Dehumanized: How to Turn Off Our "MASS implant"

There is some hope to be found within *Men Against Fire*. When Stripe's implant is rendered nonfunctional and he is able to see his victims as persons rather than monsters, he is overcome by his desire to care for them and save them. Upon seeing Catarina and Alec's humanity, Stripe defies his orders, tackles his colleagues, and puts his life on the line to save them. Arquette details all the alleged reasons this class of people are undesirable, but none of it matters to Stripe. They are human beings, he says, and that *alone* makes their massacre wrong regardless of their alleged genetic inferiority.

Stripe's reaction is reminiscent of philosopher Emmanuel Levinas (1906–1995). In his book *Totality and Infinity*, Levinas notes the importance of always keeping "the face" of "the other" firmly planted in our mind's eye. Focusing on "the face" immediately calls us into an ethical relationship with that person: "the face is a living presence…the face speaks to me and thereby invites me to a relation…the face opens the primordial discourse whose first word is obligation."[19] Acknowledging the humanity of the marginalized demands that you treat them in accordance with their intrinsic dignity and moral worth, to regard them as nothing less than another version of yourself. When "the face presents itself [it] demands justice"[20] and once you start earnestly acknowledging the humanity of "the other," you "are not free to ignore the meaningful world into which the face of the other has introduced…"[21]

In *Men Against Fire* the faces of Catarina and Alec call Stripe into a relationship with them; he becomes willing to risk everything to protect them. By keeping "the face" of the other always in our mind's eye, we will always be able to respond to calls to violence in the way that Stripe did once his MASS implant was compromised. There is no "honor" in harming or killing persons, Stripe tells Arquette, because, after all is said and done, "they're human beings."

The Future of Our "MASS Implant"

When Stripe realizes that he has participated in the murder of innocent human beings, he insists on coming clean to the world, and he wants nothing more to do with the military. Arquette has other plans. He offers Stripe a chance to "reset" the MASS implant, which would then erase all memory of everything Stripe has realized up until that point. Stripe refuses at first, but Arquette then reveals that he has complete control over Stripe's senses. If Stripe does not concede to the reset, he will live out his days in a cell, reliving his participation in the massacre on a nonstop loop. This option proves too much for Stripe to bear. In the end, he arrives home, seemingly honorably discharged – but his eyes are still cloudy, implying that he conceded to having his implant reset.

Stripe copes with his action by forgetting his history. As a society, we seem to do the same. We teach our children history by cleansing it of our role in massacres; we downplay the genocide of Native Americans, for example, or the horrors of slavery. We tell the ancestors of these victims to "get over it" and balk at the thought of reparations.

History is repeating itself. Far-right politicians in the Czech Republic have begun a campaign against the Roma people, referring to them as the "rabble" and vowing to build "villages" where they will be separated from the general public. Just like the propaganda that started the genocide of Catarina's people, the propaganda against the Roma has resulted in people in the Czech Republic, much like the villagers in the episode, turning against a subset of their population. One woman defends the separation by calling the Roma "maladjusted…They don't want to live with us normal people." Another man says: "There should be a separate village, but not just for the scum, but for the gypsies too." An even more extreme view is ominously printed on a large sign: "We don't need to discuss the maladjusted; we need to solve the problem once and for all." A social media post disseminated through the Czech Republic takes a page from every other instance of genocide in history and actively calls for the murder of Roma: "Rat poison is not good enough for these vermin."[22] They may as well call them "roaches."

A recent United Nations report notes that by 2040, climate change will have become so severe that it will begin a mass migration from parts of the world, mostly tropical nations, that will have become uninhabitable.[23] The recent Syrian refugee crisis has illustrated how unwilling the rest of the world is to take in migrants who are in desperate need. The campaign of dehumanization launched to justify ignoring the plights of those who are in need will likely continue, and possibly even be exacerbated.

The US is facing a monumental decision. The soldiers in *Men Against Fire* don't recall consenting to the MASS implant, and it is unclear whether they really understood its function before they consented. By contrast, we know enough history to see how dehumanizing marginalized groups typically ends. Stripe is able to consent to "forgetting" what he has done, but none of us can turn off our memory. We will have to live with how we choose to proceed. Thus, we should strive for a society that can, for example, discuss the many nuances and facets of undocumented immigration without dehumanizing immigrants. We should protect ourselves from terrorist attacks without dehumanizing all members of a religion or ethnicity. We should refuse to engage in any kind of dehumanizing language or behavior, and strongly repudiate anyone, even those in the highest power, who encourages it.

Notes

1. Charlie Brooker and Annabel Jones with Jason Arnopp, *Inside Black Mirror* (New York: Crown Archetype, 2018), 194.
2. David Livingstone Smith. *Less Than Human: Why We Demean, Enslave, and Exterminate Others* (New York: St. Martin's Press, 2011), 15.
3. Smith, 17.
4. Ibid.
5. Smith, 145.
6. Ludwig Wittgenstein, *Tractatus Logico-Philosophicus* (London: Routledge and Kegan Paul, 1999), 5.6.
7. Brooker et al., 201
8. Smith, 13.
9. Smith, 152.
10. Herbert Kelman, "Violence without moral restraint: Reflections on the dehumanization of victims and victimizers," *Journal of Social Issues*, 29 (1973), 48.
11. Ibid.

12. Kelman, 49.

13. Smith, 142

14. Brooker *et al.*, 194.

15. Nour Kteily, Emile Bruneau, Adam Waytz, and Sarah Cotterill, "The ascent of man: Theoretical and empirical evidence for blatant dehumanization," *Journal of Personality and Social Psychology*, 109 (2015), 6, https://pcnlab.asc.upenn. edu/wp-content/uploads/2017/07/2015_-The-Ascent-of-Man-Theoretical-and-Empirical-Evidence-for-Blatant-Dehumanization.pdf (Accessed 9 July 2019).

16. Nour Kteily and Emile Bruneau. "Backlash: The Politics and Real-World Consequences of Minority Group Dehumanization," *Personality and Social Psychology Bulletin* 43 (2017), 93.

17. Matt Drake. "Myanmar soldiers 'burning Rohingya Muslim's faces off with acid' to 'hide genocide,'" *Express*, https://www.express.co.uk/news/world/913705/Rohingya-Muslim-genocide-burning-face-acid-massacre-Myanmar-Burma-human-rights-news (Accessed 9 July 2019).

18. Adam Taylor, "Ramzan Kadyrov says there are no gay men in Chechnya – and if there are any, they should move to Canada," *Washington Post*, https://www. washingtonpost.com/news/worldviews/wp/2017/07/15/ramzan-kadyrov-says-there-are-no-gay-men-in-chechnya-and-if-there-are-any-they-should-move-to-canada/?noredirect=on&utm_term=.a8982d419713 (Accessed 9 July 2019).

19. Emmanuel Levinas, *Totality and Infinity: An Essay on Exteriority* (Dordrecht: Kluwer Academic Publishers, 1991), 66–201.

20. Levinas, 294.

21. Levinas, 219.

22. Paraic O'Brien, "Far right in Czech Republic: The politicians turning on Roma," *Channel14*, https://www.channel4.com/news/far-right-in-czech-republic-the-politicians-turning-on-roma (Accessed 9 July 2019).

23. Steve Dent, "Major UN report says climate change is worse than first thought," *Engadget*. October 8, 2018. Available at: https://www.engadget.com/2018/10/08/major-un-report-climate-change-worse/

Hated in the Nation and #DeathTo

What are the Consequences of Trial by Twitter?

Aline Maya

> Thanks to the technological revolution, we have the power to rage and accuse, spout bile without consequence. Only by being forced to recognize the power technology grants us, to acknowledge individual responsibility...
>
> (Garrett Scholes, from his manifesto "The Teeth of Consequences")

"...can we properly limit that power." That's how one might assume the above quote, from Garrett Scholes's manifesto, ends. Chief Detective Inspector Karin Parke cuts off reading it there, but she goes on to clarify that Scholes likens people to insects that revel in cruelty, "a weakness that should be bred out of us." To do just that, Scholes hacked the network of ADIs (Autonomous Drone Insects) that replaced the dying bee population. At first, the bee drones kill whoever has the most #DeathTo mentions each day on Twitter. The public quickly catches on, and hundreds of thousands use the hashtag to call for the death of publicly derided figures. But when Karin and her associates try to shut down the ADI system, the hack inverts and the bees hunt down and kill everyone who used the hashtag – thus making them individually responsible for their deplorable online behavior and weeding out those of us who "revel in cruelty."

Scholes was motivated by what happened to his friend, Tess Wallender, who attempted suicide after being the target of an online hate campaign. But what happened to Tess is not unlike what's happened to many real-world people as the result of online shaming. Adult film actress August Ames committed suicide after she was attacked on Twitter for refusing to perform with a gay actor.[1] Tyler Clementi committed suicide after his roommate used Twitter to spread a video that showed him kissing another boy.[2] And Holly Jones received death threats after tweeting something

Black Mirror and Philosophy: Dark Reflections, First Edition. Edited by David Kyle Johnson. © 2020 John Wiley & Sons, Inc. Published 2020 by John Wiley & Sons, Inc.

insensitive in a restaurant review.[3] Indeed, online shaming is likely a contributor to the rising rate of teen suicide, especially among those who are gay.[4] In other words, Scholes has a point. The moral of the story seems to be that we need to hold online shamers responsible for their behavior, and that we should never online shame anyone ourselves.

But is this moral sound? Hasn't social media also given voice to previously voiceless victims? And aren't some people deserving of shame? Consequently, couldn't online shaming sometimes do good in the world? And if it can, how can we determine when it's justified and when it isn't? When should we be involved and when should we not? To answer this, let's look at *Hated in the Nation*, and see if we can discover how to balance the #dangers with the #benefits.

#Dangers

Self-administered justice has happened throughout human history. It's often called "trial by mob." And because of the unpredictability of mobs, most societies have established systems to prevent it. That's why the UN considers a presumption of innocence (until proven guilty) a universal human right, and the US Constitution guarantees citizens accused of serious crimes a right to a trial by jury. Of course, such efforts haven't always been successful in protecting that right. Appallingly, in the American South after the Civil War, mobs "justified" the lynching of black men by falsely accusing them of raping white women, and then finding them guilty and punishing them without a trial.[5] What made such horrific bypasses of the justice system possible, of course, was the systemic racism embedded in the South. But as *Hated in the Nation* shows, social media also provides a way to bypass the justice system. In the real world the consequences have not yet been as horrific as widespread lynchings, but the results of trial by Twitter have still been disastrous.

Consider again the case of Tess Wallender, Garrett Scholes's friend, whose suicide attempt inspired his manifesto and devious bee-hacking plan. Tess complained on Twitter about a man harassing her on the Tube (the subway), spouting "lewd comments or something," and included a photo. But when it was revealed that the man in question had a learning disability, the internet turned on Tess – so fiercely that she attempted suicide.

TESS: It was like having a whole weather system turn against me. Just hate message after hate message, around the clock, all piling on. It's hard to describe what that does to your head. Suddenly there's a million invisible people, all talking about how they despise you. It's like a mental illness…I mean, hands up, I made a mistake, but the way people enjoyed kicking me, that's what got to me. The casual fun they had…I just felt I couldn't go on.

Garrett, her flatmate, saved her. Tess didn't know about the man's condition, but social media only cared about one side of the story: Tess made fun of a disabled person. We may wonder why her critics didn't bother to consider the fact that she likely didn't know the man's condition, but in reality things like this happen every day. Such uncharitable conclusions are due to something called the "fundamental attribution error," the human tendency to attribute the misbehavior of others to character flaws, but our own to excusable situational pressures. When someone *else* cuts you off while driving it's because they're a jerk; when *you* cut them off it's OK because you have somewhere important to be. This error often leads the mob to convict the innocent.

The mob is also easily misdirected by individuals with a hidden agenda – like competitors, activists, and ex-partners – by misinformation, emotional appeals, false news stories, faulty evidence, and bad arguments. It's just the sad truth that people tend to lack the critical thinking skills necessary to determine guilt or innocence. People will make snap judgements based on "gut feelings" and neglect to fact check claims that tell them what they already believe. As Cass Sunstein pointed out in his book *#republic*, especially given the rise of social media, people are easily isolated into "information cocoons," or echo chambers, where they are only ever exposed to arguments, facts, and opinions that confirm what they already believe.[6] Indeed, even when supervised in a courtroom, and isolated in a jury, people can get it wrong – failing to recognize, for example, how faulty our memories are and just how wrong (and easily manipulated) eye witness testimony can be.[7]

Worse still, people may want to find the accused guilty simply because they've had a bad day. Consider Chancellor Tom Pickering who is distraught about being "number one" on the #DeathTo list after the public learns it's legit. When he laments the fact that Lord Farrington is only number four, and someone points out that he's only a "suspected pedophile," the chancellor replies without evidence, "He did it. You know he did."

What's more, even if the accused is guilty, the mob may inflict unjust punishment. Consider Tusk, the rapper who insulted the dancing skills of one of his young fans. "That's a goofy little motherfucker, and he can't dance for shit." Or consider Clara Meades, the third victim of the #DeathTo hashtag, who took a picture of herself pretending to pee on a war memorial. There is no question about their guilt; there are pictures and video of what they did. And certainly what they did was disrespectful and in bad taste. But it's equally certain that they didn't deserve to die for it. Of course, the mob didn't yet know that the hashtag was deadly in their cases – but that's part of the point. No one can control the results of the mob's actions. Because there are no guidelines or safeguards, the mob can prescribe just about any punishment it wants, and the results can vary wildly. Posting on social media is a bit like throwing a lit cigarette out your window. It might do nothing, but it might start a wildfire.

The results can also be unfair; some guilty parties are punished, others are not. Especially troubling is the fact that while punishment is being handed down to those who own up to and apologize for their crime, others are getting off scot-free because they didn't. A public official, for example, who admits and apologizes for a single infraction can lose their seat while a more senior official who denies and lies about twenty-two worse wrong-doings retains their position.

Similar worries about the mob's ability to judge and punish are raised by our natural biases. When it's personal, we side with our friends and relatives. Consider Jo Powers. A close examination of the episode reveals that she wrote an article critical of "Wheelchair Martyr" Gwen Marbury entitled "Spare Me the Tears Over This 'Martyr.'" Gwen immolated herself in protest of budgets cuts to disability benefits, but Jo argued that her suicide was the "worst kind of attention seeking." The public targeted Jo, but her husband supported her. And I understand where he's coming from. If, say, my friend tweeted that she experienced discrimination at a fast food chain, I wouldn't doubt it. I wouldn't even ask for evidence. My moral duty is to support my friend, right? But, in all honesty, even if she's not lying, she could still be mistaken. There are two sides to every story. And the consequences could be severe: someone's job, relationship, or health could be on the line.

The same thing happens when it's political; we defend people in our political tribe and gang up on those who aren't. As the contemporary philosopher Kathryn Norlock puts it, too often the point of online shaming is not to "punish or exclude specific individuals," but to "enjoy the company one has in cyberspace with so many approving others."[8] We're the jury, but we are not even concerned about the truth. We're concerned about group allegiance and tribal instincts and the trial is over before it begins.

The final #Danger I'll mention is more philosophical but equally important: the danger of losing one's liberty. As the American philosopher John Rawls (1921–2002) proposed in *A Theory of Justice*, in order to be fair, punishment must be practiced according to law; it cannot be arbitrary.[9] If you don't know what the law is beforehand, you can't be sure that what you are doing is not illegal, and so, you can't act with liberty. For example, without knowing that posting a photo of her pretending to pee on a war memorial could get her the death penalty, Clara Meades can't make a fully informed and thus free choice regarding whether or not to do so.

Rawls's theory of liberty would still champion some particular social media movements, however, because their goal can be to correct violations of liberty that society or the legal system allows. As he puts it:

Sometimes we may be forced to allow certain breaches of [legal] precepts if we are to mitigate the loss of freedom from social evils that cannot be removed, and to aim for the least injustice that conditions allow.[10]

This could mean that, in cases where the liberty of many is lost, other forms of justice might be acceptable. And this leads us to discuss the possible benefits of online shaming.

#Benefits

While investigating Jo Powers's death, Inspector Parke dismisses her partner Blue Coulson's theory that someone from the internet is responsible for the murder, saying, "That internet stuff drifts off like weather. It's half hate. They don't mean it." This, of course, is sometimes true; at least to the person doing it, online resentment can just be trolling, a joke, or the result of short-lived hate (although the effects on the victim can be long lasting). But the main reason for the formation of many mobs today is the failure of a justice system. Many conditions produce real anger and frustration: constant abuse, negligence, or unsolved hate crimes that go unchecked. And there can be benefits to acting outside the justice system in such cases. Social media has finally given the victims of such situations the ability to speak freely without fearing reprisal from perpetrators. When an issue resonates deeply with people, social media allows them to pool together their communal strength to create change. Victims who were unable to see justice done can finally speak up and get retribution and social acceptance.[11]

An online movement that proved beneficial for victims in this way, and thus greatly complicates the seeming moral of the episode which suggests that online shaming should always be avoided, was eerily predicted by the #DeathTo hashtag featured in *Hated in the Nation* in 2016: the rise and effectiveness of the #MeToo hashtag in 2017.[12] When actor Alyssa Milano encouraged survivors of sexual assault to use the hashtag and tell their stories, they did – and thus started the #MeToo movement. Some #MeToo victims came forward for the first time, after years of living with their secret; but many others had previously reported their experiences only to be ignored, silenced, or even threatened. Threatening victims like that is easy to do when the victims are isolated; powerful people have strong reasons to conceal incidents that could threaten their place of privilege and hurt their bottom line. Combine those reasons with the sense of helplessness victims already feel, and you get something that, in retrospect, is astonishing: millions of victims kept quiet for decades while harassment and abuse continues.

#MeToo gave such victims strength; strength in numbers, but also the strength that comes from seeing the support that was previously invisible to them. The perception of our world is easily shaped by those who control the media, and they often have no interest in disrupting a status quo in which they fare quite well. All too often in this context, it can seem like no one is on the side of the victim. But social media and #MeToo created an avenue for millions of solitary voices to find each other, and to realize that they had all been whispering the same unheard lament. "It's only me" transformed into "me too." In many cases, the incidents occurred so long ago that it would be difficult to make legal charges stick. In other cases, the behavior did not rise to the level of illegality. But when enough voices rise together and say, "this will not stand," even massive corporations are forced to take action.

As of this writing, the collective voice of the #MeToo movement has called out and tried to hold accountable Harvey Weinstein, Roy Price, Lawrence Nassar, Kevin Spacey, Roy Moore, Louis C.K., Matt Lauer, Al Franken, Garrison Keillor, Russell Simmons, Mario Batali, Gary Goddard, James Levine, Michael Ferro, Bill Cosby, Adam Seger, Leslie Moonves, and R. Kelly (just to name a few).[13] Although the #MeToo campaign didn't kill them like the ADIs, it did cost many of these people their careers or elections, and in some cases resulted in jail time.

Now, to be entirely clear, the severity and kind of accusations for those listed above should not all be equated. In some cases, for example, the alleged behavior is a moral infraction, in other cases it's a legal crime. And, although in some cases guilt seems to have been established beyond a reasonable doubt through court verdicts, confessions, or publicly available evidence (such as pictures), in others the "jury is still out." But to the extent that that the #MeToo movement has punished or brought to justice anyone who would have otherwise gotten away with a moral or legal crime, it seems to have done good.

So, in a way, #MeToo is kind of like the beautiful flip side of #DeathTo. The same tidal force that brought about the unjust death of Clara Meades can also bring justice to guilty parties like Bill Cosby who otherwise would have gotten away with their crimes. What will ultimately happen all remains to be seen. How many of those accused will be punished by law? Will there be real institutional-level changes that prevent future generations of powerful individuals from abusing victims in this way? Who knows? What we do know is that social media, which can give the tiniest individual a voice that can reach millions, has given unimaginable power to victims and their supporters. It therefore seems wrong to conclude, like Scholes does, that participation in online shaming is always wrong.

But in the same breath, even though the potential benefits are immense, it's vitally important to bear in mind the potential abuse the #MeToo movement makes possible. That's not to say that one who has been subjected to sexual abuse or misconduct shouldn't report it! Obviously, any such person should feel free and empowered to report anyone who they feel has acted inappropriately toward them, even by calling them out on Twitter. The tough issue is what one should do if someone else does this. On the one hand, if a group doesn't join them in their call for action, it may go unheeded. On the other hand, you almost certainly don't have the full story or know the appropriate punishment. All the dangers talked about in the previous section still exist. The #MeToo movement is not automatically immune or an exception to the rule. It's easy to lose sight of this when the purpose is noble: those guilty of sexual misconduct should be punished. But people, especially in large groups, even when well intentioned, can still get things wrong. They can still easily find the innocent to be guilty and prescribe or bring about undue punishment.

Now some might argue that, even if this is true, I shouldn't point it out. "Yes," some might admit, "the #MeToo movement *could be* abused, but by drawing attention to that possibility you are just giving ammunition to those who want to discredit it to protect those guilty of sexual misconduct."[14] Indeed, important public figures who fear the power of movements like #MeToo have already used the possibility of false accusations to do exactly that. They say the #MeToo movement, along with its #BelieveSurvivors mantra, has made America (and other countries) a scary place for men. "Any man," they say, "can have his life ruined by some random woman falsely accusing him of sexual assault, the accusation going viral, and then the mob convicting and punishing him without a trial. To protect our sons, husbands, brothers, and uncles, we must take all such accusations with a grain of salt." But there are two things to say in response that actually bolster the case for the #MeToo movement and can help guide us in measuring our responses to sexual misconduct allegations.

First, although it would be easy to abuse the attitude that we should *always* believe *everyone* who even *claims* to have survived sexual assault, there's been a long history of favoring the exact opposite attitude: to *never* believe such claims. Reports of sexual assault have traditionally been ignored or met with shame and opposition (like death threats); that's why so much misconduct goes unreported.[15] A "rebalancing" therefore seems to be in order. Again, automatically believing that every report of sexual assault is 100% true is not advisable. What is advisable, however, is always giving those making such claims the benefit of the doubt – always taking such reports seriously and investigating them.[16] And it's possible to do so while still presuming innocence and guarding against false convictions.

Second, false accusations of sexual assault are rare. Now, it should be noted, there is a heated debate about *how* rare they are.[17] The research is difficult to sift through and those on both sides can make mistakes (although not necessarily to the same degree).[18] For example, it's very common for people to take a single limited study as authoritative.[19] To try and prove that false rape allegations are low, I might cite a study by Cassia Spohn, Clair White and Katharine Tellis, which found that "the rate of false reports among cases reported to the LAPD [in 2008] was 4.5 percent."[20] But, even though it was well conducted, that's only one study, and 2008 Los Angeles is not necessarily representative of the entire nation. The fallacy of too quickly extrapolating from a small, biased sample to a whole population is called "hasty generalization."[21]

But what can be done is a meta-analysis. Take many studies, use objective criteria for evaluating their quality, average them together (so to speak), and then get a range. Something like this is what David Lisak, Lori Gardinier, and Sarah Nicksa did, and they found that, among legally reported cases, "the prevalence of false allegations is between 2% and 10%."[22] Combine that with how unlikely anyone is to be legally accused of rape in the first place and, even by the most generous of estimates, men should actually worry three times more about contracting HIV, drowning, or dying in a house fire. Indeed, by the numbers, men are fifteen times more likely to be murdered than to be falsely accused of rape.[23]

So, even though we don't know *exactly* how rare false accusations are, we do know that they are incredibly rare – so rare that very few people could be rationally concerned about them. Contrary to the claims of English barrister Sir Matthew Hale, rape is not a charge that is easy to make but difficult to disprove. Instead, "rape is a difficult charge to lay and extremely difficult to prove."[24] Concerns about false allegations, therefore, cannot legitimately be used to dismiss rape allegations and not take them seriously.

Now, to be perfectly fair, sexual assault is only one kind of sexual misconduct. Perhaps the rates of false accusations regarding sexual harassment, unwanted touching, or genital exposure are higher. Reliable data about such forms of sexual misconduct are difficult to find. But one would expect the trend to be similar to that of false reports of sexual assault, and without data to the contrary the claim that the #MeToo movement has put men in grave danger of being falsely accused of anything is baseless. The media attention it receives may create a subjective impression that this is the case, but subjective impressions are notoriously unreliable. Without data to back it up, spreading fear about a high probability of false accusations seem to just be a thinly veiled attempt to discredit legitimate accusations and protect those who are guilty.

Contrast this with Neil deGrasse Tyson's public comments after he was accused of sexual misconduct.[25] First of all, he accepted that he might have unintentionally offended the victims, and he apologized without reserve to them. Unlike other celebrities who have been publicly accused, he also gave deference to these accusations. Instead of just saying the accusations were false, he acknowledged that all such accusations should be taken seriously: even claims against him should not be ignored. Secondly, he encouraged and said he would cooperate with an independent investigation into the incidents. To guard against the aforementioned dangers of a trial by mob, he also suggested that such an investigation should hear both sides of the story, and that we should all wait until the investigation is concluded to draw conclusions about guilt and innocence. Although it's not perfect, and there could still be (and has been) criticism of Tyson's response, it seems that he has found a decent middle ground in this case – one that could perhaps be embraced by both the accusers and the accused.

So, given the benefits and dangers of online shaming, what should we do? Should we join in if we really feel a wrong has been done and could be corrected? Or should we bow out because of the dangers of trial by mob? Should we aim for some kind of middle ground? And what would that look like? Unfortunately, this problem can't be ignored. As a commentator on a talk show in the *Hated in the Nation* rightly remarked: "...this is already happening. And people know that they can jump onboard because nobody will ever know if they did or didn't." But the answer, I believe, involves recognizing two things: people will likely be met by the consequences of their choices, and what makes the difference between a good and a bad choice is one simple thing: responsibility.

#WithGreatPowerComesGreatResponsibility

The power of finally bringing justice to ignored victims and the power of bullying someone to the point of suicide are two sides of the latent potential of technology. As with any other recent technological advance, we have to learn where the limits are. But as *Black Mirror* is keen to point out, we have not yet seen the whole potential of what technology can bring about. One day someone like Garrett Scholes might pop up and make people pay real consequences for their online behavior. And as long as it doesn't involve killing them, he'd likely be doing us all a favor. As Sanne Wohlenberg, the series producer, put it, "Of course, how terrible for Scholes to respond to one wrong by trying to kill a whole load of other people. And yet it makes you think, 'How much responsibility do I take for my own actions in the world of social media, which seems to create some kind of artificial distance?'"[26]

In fact, through his infamous hacking scheme, Scholes demonstrates what the philosopher Hannah Arendt (1906–1975) claimed: that ordinary people can be guilty of horrendous evil, especially when they are influenced by a horde mentality and divorced from the evil's consequences by diffused responsibility. This is why Liza Bahar felt it was acceptable to send Jo Powers a "Fucking Bitch" cake. Because she crowdsourced the money, getting one quid from eighty people, she wasn't responsible. By making them face the consequences of their own online mobbing, Scholes is hoping to show people how apparently mild acts can pile on and do real damage.[27]

Inspector Parke seems to also be aware of Arendt's observation that evil-doers can be banal and ordinary. Just after questioning Jo Powers's husband, and Coulson suggests "He was sort of convincing. He just doesn't seem..." Parke interrupts. "Don't say 'the type.' He's ordinary. That is the type." Arendt thinks that people who commit evil acts don't do it because they are bad, selfish, greedy, or jealous. More often than not they're thoughtless, not malicious. Even genocides, such as the Holocaust, are instances of normal people doing evil because the system diffuses their responsibility and takes away their critical thought. In her book *Origins of Totalitarianism*, Arendt explains that the danger lies not in people trying to be evil on purpose, but in them being unaware that they are harming others.[28]

This is related to what Kathryn Norlock calls "the magnitude gap," the "distance between the shamers' perceptions of their objects' great deserv-ingness of harm and light suffering as a result of shaming, and the shamed persons' experiences with actual harm and the deep and lingering effects of online shaming."[29] People don't appreciate the grandiose negative impact that their online actions have. In the end, the purpose of Scholes's #DeathTo stunt is to show that banality in social media can kill too.

The best way to avoid the banality of evil is by being aware of our own biases, tendencies, and uncritical attitudes so that we can consciously neu-tralize them step by step. Indeed, many inclusion movements are aimed at ending long-standing unfair attitudes, such as mental health discrimination. The world is beginning to look better. With the success of #MeToo and other inclusive movements, and with acceptance of responsibility, we are closer to directing the power of social media to the right place.

It just takes a click to participate in a social media trend, but public denouncements should be taken with care, with consideration of both sides, and with genuine attempts at our best analysis. Although this topic is controversial, in the end, I'm saying something everyone should agree with: the path to finding the best way to make use of social media involves conscious responsibility. Every single user must become aware that their actions might bring about a real change – both good and bad – and there-fore accept the responsibility of that power. It won't happen overnight, but if everyone develops the habits and virtues of critical thinking, the power of social media can keep bringing justice to victims while avoiding harm to the innocent. So, the next time you are deciding whether to join in the use of a hashtag in this way, remember your own responsibility. Real people are there, outside the black mirror, both victims and the accused, and you are part of the jury.[30]

Notes

1. She erroneously assumed that anyone who had previously starred in gay por-nography but had not subsequently been tested for an STI would likely infect her. See Tina Horn, "Death of a porn star," *Rolling Stone*, https://www. rollingstone.com/culture/culture-features/death-of-a-porn-star-201939/ (Accessed 5 July 2019).
2. Ed Pilkington, "Tyler Clementi, student outed as gay on internet, jumps to his death," *The Guardian*, https://www.theguardian.com/world/2010/sep/30/tyler-clementi-gay-student-suicide (Accessed 5 July 2019).

3. This case even led to another woman getting death threats simply because she had the same name. Emily Longnecker, "'Other' Holly Jones targeted by misguided outrage over viral Kilroy's post." *WTHR Indianapolis*, https://www.wthr.com/article/other-holly-jones-targeted-by-misguided-outrage-over-viral-kilroys-post (Accessed 5 July 2019).

4. Elizabeth Chuck, "Is social media contributing to rising teen suicide rate?" *NBC News*, https://www.nbcnews.com/news/us-news/social-media-contributing-rising-teen-suicide-rate-n812426 (Accessed 5 July 2019).

5. Ida Wells, Preface in "Southern horrors: Lynch Law in all its phases," *Digital History* (1892), http://www.digitalhistory.uh.edu/disp_textbook.cfm?smtid=3&psid=3614 (Accessed 5 July 2019).

6. Cass Sunstein, *#republic: Divided Democracy in the Age of Social Media* (Princeton, NJ: Princeton University Press, 2017).

7. For a very quick rundown of the research of memory expert Elizabeth Loftus which suggests this, see Rachel Zamzow, "Memory manipulation and the trouble with eyewitness testimony," *Unearthed*, https://unearthedmag.wordpress.com/2015/02/14/memory-manipulation-and-the-trouble-with-eyewitness-testimony/ (Accessed 5 July 2019).

8. Kathryn Norlock, "Online Shaming." *Social Philosophy Today* 33:187–197 (2017). p. 191. The quote appears on page 6 of the pre-publication online draft, which is available here. https://philarchive.org/archive/NOROSv1

9. John Rawls, *A Theory of Justice*, revised edition (Cambridge, MA: Harvard University Press, 1999).

10. Rawls, 213.

11. This phenomenon was famously noticed by Jon Ronson in his book, *So You've Been Publicly Shamed* (New York: Riverhead Books, 2015).

12. Although the phrase "Me Too" was coined in 2006 by Tarana Burke, the #MeToo hashtag didn't even exist until October 15, 2017 – nearly a full year after *Hated in The Nation* was released on October 21, 2016.

13. Chicago Tribune Staff. "#MeToo: A timeline of events," *Chicago Tribune*, https://www.chicagotribune.com/lifestyles/ct-me-too-timeline-20171208-htmlstory.html. (Accessed 1 November, 2018).

14. In response to this, one can point to arguments in favor of the "marketplace of ideas," which suggest that even controversial arguments should not be repressed. John Stuart Mill likely put these arguments best in *On Liberty* (Indianapolis: Hackett Publishing, 1978).

15. For example, Christine Blasey Ford couldn't return to her home (even after Brett Kavanagh was confirmed to the Supreme Court) because of death threats. In addition, police seem to ignore accusations of sexual assault in most cases. (See Ewan Palmer, "Christine Blasey Ford can"t return home for 'quite some time' due to continuous death threats: lawyer," *Newsweek*, https://www.newsweek.com/christine-blasey-ford-cant-return-home-continuous-death-threats-1157262 (Accessed 5 July 2019) and German Lopez, "Why didn't Kavanaugh's accuser come forward earlier? Police often ignore sexual assault allegations," *Vox*, https://www.vox.com/policy-and-politics/2018/9/19/17878450/kavanaugh-ford-sexual-assault-rape-accusations-police (Accessed 5 July 2019) Lopez cites statistics from the Rape, Abuse, and Incest National Network gathered from federal surveys.

16. According to one study, "Most false allegations were used to cover up other [mis]behavior such as adultery or skipping school." If no such motivation is present, the obligation to take allegations seriously is multiplied. See the abstract from André De Zutter, Robert Horselenberg, and Peter J. van Koppen, "Motives for filing a false allegation of rape," *Archives of Sexual Behavior*, 47.2 (February 2017), https://www.researchgate.net/publication/313830325_Motives_for_Filing_a_False_Allegation_of_Rape (Accessed 9 July 2019).

17. In a highly contested article, Eugene Kanin claims that 41% of all rape claims are false. (See "False Rape Allegations," *Archives of Sexual Behavior*, 23.1 (1994), 81–92.) On the flip side, Cindy Dampier claims that men are more likely *be raped* than *falsely accused* of rape. (See "Your son is more likely to be sexually assaulted than to face false allegations. Explaining the fear of #HimToo," *Chicago Tribune*, https://www.chicagotribune.com/lifestyles/ct-life-false-rape-allegations-20181011-story.html (Accessed 5 July 2019). For a rundown of the numbers on Dampier's claim, see Georgina Lee, "Fact Check: Men are more likely to be raped than be falsely accused of rape," *Channel 4.com*.

18. Emily Moon, "False reports of sexual assault are rare. But why is there so little reliable data about them?" *Pacific Standard*, https://psmag.com/news/false-reports-of-sexual-assault-are-rare-but-why-is-there-so-little-reliable-data-about-them (Accessed 5 July 2019).

19. According to Laura Kipnis, in her book *Unwanted Advances*, the claim that many feminists make about how incredibly rare false rape accusations are can be traced back to a study of single police department from over forty years ago. (See Laura Kipnis, *Unwanted Advances* (New York: Harper Collins, 2017), 165–168.) On the flip side, male rights activists often cite the afore-mentioned discredited Eugene Kanin article.

20. Cassia Spohn, Clair White and Katharine Tellis, "Unfounding sexual assault: Examining the decision to unfound and identifying false reports," *Law and Society Review*, 48.1 (March 2014). The quote is from the abstract.

21. Another common mistake regards how to count uncorroborated or "unfounded" claims, that is, those that have not met the legal standard of reasonable doubt. Confusing them with cases that have been *proven* to be false artificially inflates the number of false accusations. (This mistake seems to have been made in the aforementioned Eugene Kanin article.) Conflating them with those that have been proven true could artificially deflate it. (This mistake is arguably made by Joanne Belknap in Katie Heaney's "Almost no one is falsely accused of rape," *The Cut*, https://www.thecut.com/article/false-rape-accusations.html (Accessed 5 July 2019). Although, it should be noted, her argument that false rape allegations are not more common than false allegations for other crimes seems sound. You are fifteen times more likely to be falsely convicted of murder than rape.)

22. David Lisak, Lori Gardinier, and Sarah Nicksa, "False allegations of sexual assault: an analysis of ten years of reported cases," *Violence Against Women*, 16.12 (Dec. 2010), 1318–34. Available for free at https://cdn.atixa.org/website-media/o_atixa/wp-content/uploads/2012/01/18121908/Lisak-False-Allegations-16-VAW-1318-2010.pdf (Accessed 9 July 2019).

23. There were 326 million people in America in 2017, roughly half (163 million) of which were men. In 2017, there were around 100,000 cases of reported

forcible rape. (See, Statista, "Number of reported forcible rape cases in the United States from 1990 to 2017," https://www.statista.com/statistics/191137/reported-forcible-rape-cases-in-the-usa-since-1990/ (Accessed 9 July 2019).) Generously assuming that all rapes in America were all done by men (they weren't), that means that .06% of men in America were legally accused of rape. If we go with Lisak's (et al.) highest estimate, which suggest that of 10% of all reported cases are later proven false, that means the American male has a .006% chance of being legally accused of rape and then it being proven false in court. Now, to be fair, that wouldn't include false accusations that are never proven false, or online false allegations that are never reported, and those could ruin a life just as easily. But even if we very (very!) generously estimate that five times as many that are proven false actually are false, American males still only have a .03% chance of being falsely accused of rape. That's 1/3000. The odds of contracting HIV, dying in a house fire, or dying by drowning are about 1/1000, and the chances of being murdered are about 1/200. See Shana Lebowitz, "Your top 20 fears (and how much you should worry), *Greatist*, https://greatist.com/health/your-top-20-fears-and-how-much-you-should-worry (Accessed 9 July 2019).

24. Jo Lovett and Liz Kelly, "Different systems, similar outcomes? Tracking attrition in reported rape cases across Europe," (London Metropolitan University, *Child and Women Abuse Studies Unit*, 2009.), 111. http://kunskapsbanken.nck.uu.se/nckkb/nck/publik/fil/visa/197/different (Accessed 9 July 2019).

25. Neil deGrasse Tyson, "On Being Accused," Facebook Update, (December 09, 2018), https://m.facebook.com/notes/neil-degrasse-tyson/on-being-accused/10156870826326613/ (Accessed 10 December 2018).

26. Charlie Brooker and Annabel Jones with Jason Arnopp, *Inside Black Mirror* (New York: Crown Archetype, 2018), 218.

27. This point was made clear to me whilst reading Paul Bloom and Matthew Jordan's column, "Are we all 'harmless torturers' now?" *New York Times*, https://www.nytimes.com/2018/08/09/opinion/are-we-all-harmless-torturers-now.html. (Accessed 5 July 2019)

28. Hannah Arendt, *The Origins of Totalitarianism* (San Diego: Harcourt, Inc., 1951).

29. Norlock, 190 (online version, 5).

30. The author would like to thank the many anonymous reviewers who helped refine the arguments of this chapter.

SEASON 4

USS Callister and Non-Player Characters
How Should We Act in Video Games?

Russ Hamer with Steven Gubka

It's a bubble universe ruled by an asshole god.

(James Walton's NPC)

Video games provide us with imaginary worlds in which to act. The best games give a player lots of options about what to do, or how to accomplish their goal, all while creating a fun play environment. Over time, games have progressed from simple, two dimensional games like *Pong* to expansive experiences filled with hours of content and a multitude of things to do, like *Grand Theft Auto*. Most recently, virtual reality, or VR, games have begun to fulfill a long-time promise of science fiction. And as VR becomes more commonplace and realistic, we need to carefully examine the moral issues that surround how we behave in video games. *USS Callister* gives us the perfect opportunity for just such moral reflection.

In the episode, programmer Robert Daly has created a VR game based on his favorite sci-fi show *Space Fleet* (*Black Mirror*'s version of *Star Trek*), and then used stolen samples of DNA to populate that game with facsimiles of his co-workers. He's even managed to give the facsimiles his co-worker's real-world memories.[1] Although these NPCs (non-player characters) are the crew of his *Space Fleet* starship, the USS *Callister*, Robert uses his almost limitless powers in the game to abuse and mistreat them. He belittles the men, kisses and demeans the women, and tortures those who refuse to play along (even going to far as to permanently turn some of them into horrendous monsters, like Jillian from marketing). Robert truly is "an asshole god."

Robert's actions are certainly creepy, but are they morally wrong? Is obtaining or using DNA in this way unethical? Is there something problematic about the way that he treats the NPC's in his game? After all, if Robert should act differently in the game he plays, that might also imply that we should as well. Are there important differences between Robert's situation and my own when I play *Grand Theft Auto* and go on a killing spree?

Black Mirror and Philosophy: Dark Reflections, First Edition. Edited by David Kyle Johnson.
© 2020 John Wiley & Sons, Inc. Published 2020 by John Wiley & Sons, Inc.

"We can blackmail me"

The first thing to consider is whether Robert has violated the privacy of his co-workers. Obviously, they would prefer to keep their memories and DNA private. As a virtual deity aboard the USS *Callister*, Robert sees the physical and psychological vulnerabilities of his co-workers; they are revealed when he violently punishes their facsimiles for disobeying his orders and when he requires the women to kiss him. If he wished, he could even torture the NPCs to reveal the secrets of their flesh-and-blood counterparts. Clearly, Robert's co-workers would prefer to keep their privacy intact, but is it wrong for Robert to violate their privacy by scanning them into the *Space Fleet* mod?

We value our privacy for many reasons, including protecting our reputation, which is especially important if discovery of your indiscretions might get you fired from your dream job developing *Infinity*. But while we generally respect the privacy of others, we also recognize that it can be acceptable, or even justified, to ignore the privacy concerns of others in special circumstances. Consider when the NPCs violate the privacy of Nanette by hacking into her photo account and blackmailing her. This, it would seem, is justified. They don't ultimately hurt Nanette, and they did it to get their freedom. Now unlike the NPCs, Robert doesn't seem to have a good reason to violate the privacy of his co-workers. But Robert also doesn't use the information he has to blackmail them. So if Robert just assumes the role of captain of the USS *Callister* to relax, and he doesn't hurt anyone, does that make his breach of privacy OK?

To answer this question, we need to understand why some violations of privacy are wrong. One plausible view is that violations of someone's privacy are wrong because they diminish that person's autonomy, or the ability to make their own decisions without interference. On this view, one might argue that Robert's actions are fine because his violation of his co-workers' privacy has not affected them in any way. Indeed, he intends to keep the way he has violated their privacy a secret. But this argument fails to realize that this negligence allowed the NPCs to blackmail Nanette with her private photos; by imposing a negative consequence to non-compliance, they directly interfered with Nanette's ability to make decisions.

Another view simply asserts that everyone has a fundamental moral right to privacy. On this view, Robert has a moral duty not to violate the privacy of his co-workers, even if his actions don't affect them in any way. And this view likely aligns with your moral intuitions. For example, you probably think that a voyeur spying on his neighbor wrongly violates the privacy rights of his neighbor, even if the voyeur keeps his discoveries to himself. If this intuition is correct, then Robert disrespects and thereby wrongs his co-workers when he violates their privacy, regardless of the consequences.

Of course, as already noted, violations of privacy rights aren't always wrong. Parents, for example, often restrict the privacy of their children to help them avoid harm and make better decisions.[2] It is perhaps OK to violate someone's right to privacy if that person benefits from the violation. With this in mind, because their actions put Robert into a coma and thus protected real world Nanette from Robert, one might argue that the NPCs' violation of Nanette's privacy was doubly justified – both in the name of their freedom and her protection. But since the *Space Fleet* mod is only an ego-trip for Robert, it doesn't seem that his violations of his co-worker's privacy can be justified in this way.

Add to this the fact that, in the UK, it is illegal to sequence someone else's DNA without their consent, and you have a very compelling case that it is wrong for Robert to steal and use his co-workers DNA.[3] If we are morally obligated to obey the laws of our society unless we have good reasons to the contrary, then Robert has also violated his moral obligations to his society. But given that (in the episode) the violations of privacy to create the NPCs has already occurred, let us now ask questions about Robert's treatment of the NPCs.

"Philosophical position[s] regarding sentient code"

When considering Robert's treatment of the NPCs, we must first ask whether the NPCs are persons. If they are, then Robert's treatment of them is clearly problematic. After all, it's wrong to mistreat other persons in multiplayer games; you aren't just mistreating some digital avatar, but rather the human that's controlling it. Generally, we give all persons similar levels of moral consideration.

One might argue that Robert can do whatever he wants to the NPCs because they are not human. They are digital, not biological. But humanness isn't a prerequisite for moral consideration. Personhood is. A person is a bearer of rights, and it is possible for there to be non-human persons. If intelligent aliens one day landed on Earth, we wouldn't think it OK to mistreat them simply because they weren't human. If they were persons, they'd have the same moral rights as us. The same would hold for the NPCs. But whether NPCs are *persons* is open for debate. As Kabir says, when Nanette first brings up the possibility of flying into the wormhole and getting deleted, "Whether it's dying [depends] on your philosophical position regarding sentient code."

Usually, as markers for personhood, philosophers include things like memory, emotions, self-awareness, a sense of self, and some semblance of freedom. With this in mind, it seems that Charlie Brooker want us to see the NPCs as persons. They exist when Robert isn't around. They have free will; they can, for example, choose to play along with Robert's game or rebel. They obviously have memories, given that they can remember their former selves and their previous time in the game. And they clearly have emotions. Consider Nanette's reaction when she learns that NPCs have no genitals: "Stealing my pussy is a red-fucking line!" Or James when he sacrifices himself at the end: "[Y]ou threw my son out of an airlock [Robert]. So fuck you to death!" And if they are persons, clearly Robert is depraved. He has simply created a torture chamber.

But what if they aren't persons? After all, ultimately, they are only lines of computer code. As Shania and Kabir tell Nanette after she first appears on the ship, "You're not actually you…you're a copy of you. A digital clone…an identical digital version of you." That's not to say that Nanette doesn't exist. As Shania points out, the whole world they inhabit "exists," as an *Infinity* mod isolated on Robert's computer. But none of it, including Nanette, is "real." It's fake, a non-biological facsimile, like a plastic tree.

Whether you find the argument that the NPCs aren't persons convincing will be determined partly by your views about the possibility of artificial intelligence. And your views on that will depend on things like whether you believe persons just are their neural activity and whether neural activity can be replicated on a computer. These fascinating issues are discussed elsewhere in this book.[4] But I'd like to discuss the implications of the idea that the NPCs are *not* persons. Might there still be something morally wrong with how Robert treats them? If so, should we reconsider how we behave in games ourselves? After all, if Robert's NPCs are not persons, Robert's game is just an advanced version of games that we already play today.

"You're sick and you need help"

First, let's think about what our intentions are as we play video games. In many games, including *Infinity* and Robert's *Space Fleet* mod, the player interacts in the game via an avatar, a digital "self" within the game that the person is controlling. And when players direct that avatar, they usually aren't thinking things to themselves like, "Press A now!" Instead, they're thinking something like, "Jump now!" Their intentions aren't to press buttons but rather to move their character around and have it act in certain ways. So our video game avatars act as digital extensions of ourselves, and their actions stem from our intentions.

This is especially true of Robert because, in both *Infinity* and the *Space Fleet* mod, avatars are controlled by a kind of direct brain link that is facilitated by an electrode placed on the player's temple. So, when Robert sits in his captain's chair, or gives a command to one of the NPCs, it's because he wants to do so. His digital intentions are his own intentions and are not separated from him by the fact that he's controlling an avatar in a game.

The fact that, in video games, our intentionality extends to our avatars is noteworthy because of how important some philosophers think intentions are. The French philosopher Maurice Merleau-Ponty (1908–1961), for example, argued that we need to think seriously about intentionality when we consider what it means to be a self. Part of who I am is what I intend to do. This intentionality is inextricably tied to my body as well as my thoughts. I am what I am doing and thinking as well as what I intend to do and think. If this is right, I need to be careful how I act in games, because what I intend for my avatar to do in a game can reflect who I am. This may seem odd at first, but don't we think that the way Robert acts in his *Space Fleet* mod reveals something about who he is? Don't we agree with Nanette that he's sick and needs help?

The influential German philosopher Immanuel Kant (1724–1804) argued that when we judge the morality of an action, we must always look to the intent (or as he calls it, "the will") of the person who performed it. If he's right, we must be very careful with what we intend our actions to do, and if we are judging someone else's actions, we must determine the intentions behind them. This isn't always easy. It's hard to tell, for example, exactly what Robert is thinking as he plays his game. But we can make educated guesses, and the episode gives us many reasons to think that Robert's intentions are not innocent.

Early on in the episode, for example, Robert runs into Nate at the office and refers to him as "Helmsman Packard," his NPC name. This seems to indicate that Robert easily confuses the two, seeing his co-workers as the NPCs, and the NPCs as his co-workers. To him, they are essentially the same person in different contexts. With this in mind, consider the night that Robert goes home after getting emasculated in front of Nanette by his boss, James. He enters the game seemingly for the sole purpose of strangling James's NPC to make him admit to being pathetic. He doesn't accomplish anything in the game. He doesn't advance the plot. He doesn't move the ship. He just tortures James, says some other ugly things to the crew, and then leaves. It seems that Robert's intention isn't just to hurt an NPC, but to hurt his boss, James.

One might argue, of course, that Robert doesn't really believe that James's NPC is James. Robert is just expressing his frustration with his boss by attacking a digital look-alike. Yet, if Robert were only expressing frustration, we might imagine him logging into *Infinity* and, say, attacking some other player's ship. Instead, he very specifically attacks a thing that he created to look like James. Perhaps Robert believes, at some level, that James's NPC is not James himself. But Robert is not just expressing frustration or anger in some generic sense. He wants to punish James; he wants to harm and humiliate him. That's why he made the most realistic James that he could, to fulfill his desire to harm the real James.

So, when we look at Robert's intentions generally, they seem squarely aimed at causing harm to his real world co-workers. At some level he knows it won't really harm them, but that is what he intends to do. He enjoys feeling like a god, so he builds a world where he can feel that way.

For Kant, these intentions would be problematic. If Robert's intent is to harm others for his own pleasure, then he has an immoral intention and his actions in the game are immoral.

Interestingly, director Toby Haynes seems to recognize this.

> I kept saying I felt sorry for Daly…my view was that these weren't actually people to Daly, they were [zeros] and ones. He's a programmer who designed them…to behave in a certain way. …But when we shot that airlock scene, [Robert] smiled. He enjoyed the action….he was a sadist, and evil character.[5]

Or as Charlie Brooker put it, "Even though he feels this is some sort of virtual realm, when he's throwing a child out of an airlock, that's like Darth Vader levels of evil."[6]

Another approach that might indict Robert's actions (even if his NPCs aren't persons) is virtue ethics. Aristotle (384–322BCE) thought that ethics should be built around developing good character traits and becoming a virtuous person. For Aristotle, good and bad actions stem naturally from good and bad people, so we need to build ourselves into virtuous people. We do this by habit, by practice, by training. Aristotle might therefore look at something like the *Space Fleet* mod that Robert has built as an excellent place for him to learn and create good habits and virtues. Given how Robert struggles to interact with people in real life, his *Space Fleet* mod could provide him with the kind of training that would improve him and help him flourish as an individual by letting him practice his social skills and his courage. Conversely, Aristotle would be very disappointed to find that these are not the kind of things that Robert practices in game. Rather, he practices being cruel and vindictive. Aristotle would worry that Robert's constant fits of cruelty within the game could turn Robert into a cruel person in the real world. The more that Robert embraces his vices in the game, the more he embraces those vices for himself, and the more they become who he is.

All of this is compounded by the nature of the game that Robert is playing. He's not playing *Super Mario World* and taking joy out of stomping on goombas. If that were the case, it would be hard to argue that his intentions are problematic or that he's habituating himself towards cruelty. Mario and goombas are too far removed from reality. But Robert's *Space Fleet* mod is not! It's easy for Robert's intentions to be confused with real life intentions, because everything in his VR world looks and feels real. Reactively pressing a button to jump on a goomba doesn't quite equate to wanting to wrap my hands around someone's neck and choke them, like Robert does to James.

Now, to be fair, research has regularly shown that playing violent video games doesn't cause violent behavior. For instance, a meta-analysis of studies that examined the connection between video games and a number of negative behavior traits that are often associated with video games such as aggression, depression, or reduced academic performance found that video games had a rather minimal effect.[7] Some studies have even found that increased realism doesn't change the effects that video games have.[8] So it's possible that my concerns about VR gaming are unfounded. On the other hand, we can't consider this a closed issue. As technology and games change, becoming more and more realistic, our reason to worry might increase. We must continually ask these kinds of questions. A situation in which we struggle to distinguish the real world from the virtual one might change the answers.

"King of space, right here!"

In the end, *USS Callister* leaves us with some questions that extend beyond it. Are video games and virtual reality problematic in any way? If Robert is villainous because of how he treats NPCs, am I also villainous for how I treat NPCs? Do these problems only come into focus when we examine hyperrealistic virtual reality? Or are they present in some games today?

Given what we've discussed, there seem to be two considerations we should keep in mind. First, what are my intentions? When I play *The Sims* and I tell one of my Sims to swim in a pool and then I take the exit away from the pool so that the Sim swims until he dies, what am I intending? Do I think of my Sims as the people that I've named them after and thus want those people to suffer? If so, that's likely a problem. If I instead intend to watch my Sims swim until they die because I find it to be a funny aspect of a game that I play primarily to just fiddle around with various game mechanics, then my intentions likely aren't immoral.

Similarly, I must examine how my actions shape my character. By taking joy in watching my Sims drown, am I learning to take joy in suffering? Am I desensitizing myself? This question is harder to answer. It's hard for me to judge what kind of things I am becoming accustomed to or whether I'm developing habits in the game that are bleeding over into my real life. Still, we might be able to separate games like *Mortal Kombat* from games like Robert's *Space Fleet* mod. *Mortal Kombat* is quite violent and bloody, but the setting is an interdimensional martial arts tournament to the death. It's unlikely that in the course of playing such a game, I will start to develop habits related to violence. The game violence is simply too far removed from my everyday experience. However, in his *Space Fleet* mod, Robert's actions all feel very real. He becomes accustomed to choking his boss on a regular basis and takes joy in doing so. Aristotle would find this worrisome for its effects on Robert's character.

Nothing I've said should be taken as an argument against video games. In the same way that Charlie Brooker didn't intend *USS Callister* to be swipe at *Star Trek* fans ("It's clear that [his fandom is not the problem,] Daly is the problem"), this chapter isn't a swipe at video games or their players.[9] (I'm one myself!) It's a call for video game players to be careful. It is the player who is making the decisions, and games can generate both good and bad outcomes. As video games become more and more sophisticated, we will have more opportunities to use them for educational purposes, including moral education and the formation of virtuous character. The danger, as we have seen, is that video games may also be abused and result in vicious realworld characters. As always, *Black Mirror* calls for caution, but gives us no easy answers.

Notes

1. Many viewers have rightly pointed out that using a person's DNA to create a digital facsimile of them would not produce one with that person's real world memories. Interestingly, Charlie Brooker's first draft of *USS Callister* included an explanation for the facsimile's memories that involved everyone in the episode having the Grain technology (first featured in *The Entire History of You*), but it was cut for simplicity. As Charlie Brooker himself put it: "Incidentally, people have pointed this out, and I know it doesn't make sense: If Daly has swabbed a cup and grown a copy of Nannette from her DNA, how does she know who she is when she wakes up in Callister? We did actually work out an explanation, which used the Grain technology from *The Entire History of You*. In the original script, everyone had these Grains and we went out of our way to explain this to you. In that version, Daly had to do two things: get the DNA and download the contents of your Grain. But it was just too much business. Eventually I went, 'Oh sod it, let's just say he gets their DNA and grows them all in a magic machine.' When Shania says, 'Whatever, it's a fucking gizmo,' that was me letting on that I knew it didn't make sense, but still you see people complaining. I *know* it doesn't make sense! It's just that I don't care." Charlie Brooker and Annabel Jones with Jason Arnopp, *Inside Black Mirror* (New York: Crown Archetype, 2018), 231–232.
2. For more on how far parental violations of a child's privacy can and should go, see Chapter 15 (Catherine Villanueva Gardner's chapter on *Arkangel*) in this volume.
3. Human Tissue Act 2004. (UK Parliament, 2004), http://www.legislation.gov. uk/ukpga/2004/30/contents (Accessed 9 July 2019).
4. For more on these issues, see Chapter 21 (David Gamez's chapter on conscious technology) in this volume.
5. Brooker et al., 239.
6. Ibid.
7. Christopher Ferguson, "Do Angry Birds make for angry children? A meta-analysis of video game influences on children's and adolescents' aggression, mental health, prosocial behavior, and academic performance," *Perspectives on Psychological Science*, 10 (2015), 646–666.
8. David Zendle, Daniel Kudenko, and Paul Cairns, "Behavioural realism and the activation of aggressive concepts in violent video games," *Entertainment Computing*, 24 (2018), 21–29.
9. Brooker et al., 230.

Arkangel and Parental Surveillance
What are a Parent's Obligations?

Catherine Villanueva Gardner with
Alexander Christian

I was trying to protect you. I was trying to keep you safe. Everything I've done, I've done for you.

(Marie)

Arkangel begins with the birth of Marie's daughter Sara via C-section. Marie panics when Sara doesn't immediately cry. Three years later, when Marie briefly turns her attention away from Sara at a park, Sara goes missing, having followed a cat down to the train tracks. Sara is found unharmed, but the experience leaves a mark on Marie. With the help of a company called Arkangel, Marie has a device implanted into Sara's brain. With its paired handheld parental operation tablet, Marie can track Sara, monitor her health, and can even see what she is seeing. Most significantly, she can also filter out disturbing or unpleasant sounds and images from her daughter's experiences. With the filter on, for example, Sara is unable to see the fierce barking dog that she passes every day on the way to school. But she is also unable to help when her grandfather has a stroke. And when Marie finds Sara drawing disturbing pictures and stabbing herself with a pencil, Marie realizes the filter is stunting her daughter's development. She thus turns the filter off and hides the operation tablet away.

Things change, however, when Sara becomes a teenager and starts dating. When Sara lies about a sleepover to instead go to Lake Dalston with a boy named Trick, Marie starts monitoring her again and sees Sara lose her virginity (through Sara's eyes). Later, when she sees Sara trying cocaine, Marie forces Trick to stop seeing Sara. And when the Arkangel device reveals that Sara is pregnant, Marie slips her a Plan B pill in her morning smoothie. As a result, Sara figures out that Marie has been monitoring her again, and in a violent angry outburst, Sara beats Marie unconscious with the operation tablet, breaking it. Now untraceable, Sara runs

Black Mirror and Philosophy: Dark Reflections, First Edition. Edited by David Kyle Johnson.
© 2020 John Wiley & Sons, Inc. Published 2020 by John Wiley & Sons, Inc.

away and gets into a semi-trailer truck with a stranger. Marie eventually awakens, but all she can do is scream for her daughter in the street – just as she did when Sara was three and lost in the park.

Although *Arkangel* explores problematic consequences of new or imagined technologies (like other *Black Mirror* episodes), it also functions as a cautionary tale for the real life dangers of over-parenting. As the episode's director Jodie Foster put it,

> If you create a false reality for your child, under the guise of protecting them, you're altering the natural course of how a person discovers their own life. You're breaking their independence and controlling them. You're actually enabling the thing you hoped wouldn't happen, which is that they have to abandon you and leave you. And there's a necessity for the violence of that rupture, because of the control that's been exacted. So I would say that ending is more of a parable.[1]

All parents want to protect their children, but they don't want to lose them like Marie lost Sara. So what exactly does Marie do wrong? Does Marie violate Sara's rights? Is it Marie's moral duty to help Sara to develop empathy? Has Marie prevented Sara from becoming a fully developed human being? And how might we learn from Marie's mistakes so that we don't repeat them? By exploring different schools of philosophical thought, let's see what *Arkangel* can teach us about what it means to be a good parent.

Joel Feinberg, Parental Responsibilities, and a Child's Rights

In order to understand the nature of Marie's moral failure, we need to make her parental responsibilities and Sara's rights as a child explicit. The philosopher Joel Feinberg's (1926–2004) approach to parental responsibilities is especially helpful in this regard. Feinberg identifies three types of rights: those exclusively belonging to adults, rights that only children possess, and rights common to both adults and children. Rights in the exclusively adult category include liberty rights like the right to vote, freedom of speech, and religious freedom. Rights in the child-only category include rights to necessities, like food (more on that in a moment). And shared adult-child rights are primarily welfare rights, which serve the purpose of protecting vital individual interests, like physical and mental health or privacy.[2]

Now, Marie's use of the Arkangel device is clearly a violation of her adolescent daughter's adult-child right to physical and mental health. Sara suffers from psychological trauma and even harms herself as a result of having her experience filtered by the device. But it is Marie's violation of Sara's rights as a child that are especially disturbing.

According to Feinberg, such rights can be differentiated into two classes: *protection rights* and *a right to an open future*. Protection rights are easy to comprehend. They include (1) rights to receive certain goods, which children are incapable of attaining on their own, like food, housing, and help with everyday tasks, (2) rights relating to vulnerability as a child, like protection from abuse and neglect, and (3) rights to receive goods especially valuable to children, like parental love. The right to an open future relates to the person a child will develop into. By giving and respecting these rights it is possible to ensure that, as adults, children can exercise their liberty and welfare rights to an optimal degree. Prime among these rights is a right to an education, and not just the kind you get in the classroom.

There is considerable disagreement among philosophers concerning what the right to an open future involves.[3] For instance, even the most comprehensive education cannot – due to constraints on time and other resources – literally open up every opportunity for a future adult. Sometimes parents just need to decide which opportunities their children should have in later life. Nevertheless, it seems clear that, by filtering out from Sara's experiences anything that might be unpleasant, Marie has failed to provide Sara with the kind of education necessary to enable her to live an autonomous life and to make wise choices.

Indeed, Feinberg's distinctions provide us with the ability to pinpoint exactly where Marie went wrong. Marie's failure is that she misinterprets Sara's welfare rights (adult-child rights) and protection rights (the first type of child rights), therefore violating her daughter's right to an open future (the second type of child rights). Because she projects her own fears onto Sara, Marie erroneously thinks that common types of stress are a threat to her daughter's physical and mental health. Marie thus misconstrues the nature of Sara's welfare rights, in particular her rights to mental health, bodily integrity, and privacy. Likewise, Marie continuously underestimates the importance of negative experiences for the development of psychological resilience, compassion, and social capacities necessary for a life without parental supervision. Marie also misconstrues Sara's protection rights, since she greatly overestimates her daughter's vulnerability and is thereby not able to judge the use of Arkangel as abusive, nor recognize that omission of its use is not the equivalent of neglect. Marie has not prepared Sara for an adult life.

Empathy: Humans Are More than Bearers of Rights

Arkangel also raises questions outside of Feinberg's parental rights-responsibilities framework. What starts as a consideration of typically accepted parental responsibilities (care and protection of Sara) rapidly becomes a consideration of moral education and the status of the child as a human being. *Arkangel* demonstrates that parental responsibilities are not simply limited to care or meeting physical needs. Parental responsibility also includes the moral and psychological development of a *human being*, a social individual who is more than a rights-bearer or good citizen. And a key element of this parental responsibility is to help the child develop empathy – the ability to understand and share the emotions of another.

The ability to feel empathy requires us to first recognize others' emotions and then share them. Empathy also drives us to alleviate the suffering of others when we can. We need to learn to make decisions about the best options to alleviate the suffering of others. But since Sara does not witness pain or feel fear as she grows up, she does not develop these skills and thus (at least as a young girl) lacks the ability to empathize with other humans. For example, when Sara's grandfather suffers a heart attack in front of her, she is unable to recognize his pain or need for help. Indeed, Sara does not register any emotion at her grandfather's grave, even though the viewer can see Marie's grief. Admittedly, Sara cannot actually *see* the pain and fear she is causing when she physically hurts others, but Sara doesn't even seem to understand what she is doing. Again, although Marie may have produced a healthy and (apparently) happy child, she has neglected her responsibility to raise a properly functioning adult who can live in and contribute to society.

The ability to empathize is distinctively human. While dogs, usually considered to be among the most emotionally aware of all non-human animals, can recognize sadness or joy in their human companions, dogs' responses are best defined as emotional contagion; they can only "catch" or reflect our emotions and behaviors, not truly empathize with us.[4] Similarly, behaviors that echo human empathy have been observed in animals like elephants and primates, but it's not clear that they are actually displaying the same form of empathy as humans. For non-human animals this empathetic behavior functions to maintain group cohesion, but the ability to maintain group cohesion is distinct from the (human) ability to contribute to society. Genuine empathy contains a reflective element, one that remains focused on the perspective of the other, which seems to only be possible for humans.

What is sometimes called "affective empathy," sharing in the emotions of others, might be present in some animals. This sharing can lead to wanting to help someone in distress, and some non-human animals, such as chimpanzees, demonstrate behaviors that indicate they possess this capability. But there is another aspect of empathy, "cognitive empathy": the ability to see things from the perspectives of others, which helps us decide on the proper moral response to others' needs. This ability seems to be distinctly human.[5] Equally importantly, this cognitive aspect also gives the grounds by which we judge our own actions, and the character of others. But we do not do this for non-humans. When a mother bear abandons her cubs in the wild, we talk of the necessity of survival, not of parental moral failure.

What is the special relationship between feeling empathy and human-ness? This question has been of interest to psychologists and philosophers alike. In *Empathy and Moral Development*, Martin L. Hoffman, an expert in the field of moral psychology, claims that humans respond to distress cues from multiple sources in order to develop empathy: vocal, facial, pos-tural, and situational.[6] Hoffman's foundational claim is that "…empathy is the spark of human concern for others, the glue that makes social life pos-sible."[7] In Sara's case, the Arkangel neural implant blocks these cues by pixilating her vision and blocking sounds, so she does not learn to develop empathy. Sara is socially isolated and does not engage with the other chil-dren at her school. In fact, they avoid her and call her a freak.

Sara's Lack of Moral Imagination

Key to young Sara's lack of empathy is the fact that she has not developed (or begun to develop) a moral imagination. Some contemporary philoso-phers, such as Cora Diamond, maintain that the moral imagination needs not only to be developed through real-life experiences but can also be developed through reading literature.[8] By doing so, we come to understand what is deep and important about human life. Reading literature "plays an essential role in the education of the emotions and in the development of moral sensibility."[9] Diamond shows how the moral imagination, and thus empathy, can be developed when real life does not afford us that opportu-nity. Moreover, literature can allow us to reflect on moral experience and hone our moral emotions. The parental blocking option on the Arkangel program means that Sara cannot even read literature or view films that may raise unsettling emotions: *Jane Eyre*, almost anything by Charles Dickens (Tiny Tim, anyone?). The list appears endless.

Development of moral sensibility is crucial on Diamond's account. It is not a separate capability or component of our moral world; rather, moral sensibility filtrates *throughout our entire lives*.[10] Even non-moral activities reflect our moral demeanor. For example, rocking a child to sleep in a cradle can be done with loving patience or with exhausted exasperation, but without that demeanor, the activity of rocking is not truly human activity. Sara may be able to make moral decisions by applying general moral principles to particular cases, but she will not understand *why* those cases are moral cases or *what is at stake*.

Too Much of a Good Thing?

In the *Nicomachean Ethics,* Aristotle (384–322 BCE) defines virtues in terms of their relation to human flourishing. The specific virtues he names are often passions or actions that are identified in relation to other people, for example, generosity, sociability, friendliness, truthfulness, and wit.[11] Aristotle's account has potential regarding how parents (particularly the father) can guide the moral development of the child, and, when necessary, provide rational direction if and when the child is driven by their passions.[12] We might say that parenting is composed of both action (the daily tasks of child rearing) and passion (parental love) for another. Aristotelian "vices" are not the opposite of the virtues (as we usually think). Instead, virtues are the mean (relative to the individual) between a state of excess and a state of deficiency.

Arkangel shows how there may be an Aristotelean vice of excess in the emotions and behaviors of a parent. Just as parenting can admit of a vice of deficiency (too little parenting in the form of neglect and abuse, for example), parenting can also admit of a vice of excess (too much parenting), to the point where the child is *harmed*. This vice of excessive parenting in *Arkangel* is not the phenomenon of "helicopter" parenting (hovering over a child's life) or "lawnmower" parenting (clearing a path for a child), although neither of these parenting approaches are recommended! Rather, Marie is the excessive parent in that she prevents young Sara from developing virtues like courage, friendliness, and sociability for herself. Consider that Sara never has to face her fears with the neighbor's dog and can't make friends at school because the other children avoid her.

The good or virtuous parent is the one who does the right things in the right way at the right time for the right reasons. For example, the virtuous parent does not bribe their child into good behavior, or "lawnmower" their child's success. The good parent also doesn't force their child to engage in multiple enhancement activities to impress university admissions officers before the child is old enough to have any sense of their own interests. While the child's moral and educational success reflects on the parent, parenting must be done for the child's sake, *not* the parent's ego.

Marie deceives herself that the *Arkangel* implant is for Sara's safety, but it is clearly something that Sara would not have chosen for herself. Moreover, Marie did not reflect carefully on her action. A neural implant in a child is a serious undertaking, but Marie was driven by her own fears, and possibly by the fact that the implant was offered at no cost, into making a hasty decision. So, again, Marie has failed morally as a parent. On an Aristotelian account, she failed in her activities and emotions as a parent as well as in the actual results of her parenting: Sara's stunted moral development.

Does Marie Fail a Maternal Ethics of Care?

Feminist care ethics offers a model of theorizing, usually grounded on human relationships (such as women caring for others), that is different from traditional ethical theorizing. The traditional approach focuses on identifying moral rules and principles to guide activities in the public sphere where we deal with unknown others, our peers, or in professional relationships. It promotes moral vocabulary in terms of rights and contracts (like Feinberg). Feminist authors argue that such traditional approaches devalue women's moral experiences, especially the experience of responsibility for a dependent being. So might there be hope for Marie if we evaluated her actions within the framework of feminist ethicist, like contemporary philosopher Sara Ruddick's (1935–2011) maternal ethics of care?[13]

Unfortunately, no. Mothering, for Ruddick, is a paradigm for human relationships, in contrast to the paradigm of legalistic and contractual relationships between strangers and peers of traditional mainstream (or "malestream") moral philosophy. But maternal practice, according to Ruddick, is a commitment to the preservation of life, the fostering of growth (in the sense of character growth), and the development of the social acceptability of one's children. While she may work to preserve her daughter's life with a daily regimen of vitamins and the safety provided by the neural implant, Marie does not appear to engage with the development of Sara's character, nor does she seem to have a set of values in place for raising a child. Moreover, Sara is not properly socialized, as she does not seem to understand why we should not cause harm or pain to others (including her own mother). Thus Marie has *again* failed in her maternal responsibilities.

What Not to Do as a Parent

As the episode closes, the Pretenders' "I'm a Mother" plays over the credits.

> I'm a mother! And I take like a mother. I understand blood and I understand pain. There can be no life without it. Never doubt it. I'm a mother.

The song echoes the moral of the episode, and one could rightly point out that Marie learns that moral, and even succeeds as a parent, when she shuts off the filter and puts away the operation tablet when Sara is nine. And maybe it wasn't too late. After all, even though she is initially scared, Sara does overcome her fear of the dog. She's even feeding it by the time she is in high school. Maybe she still has time to develop traits like empathy, too. But while Sara does become better adjusted, it's hard to tell how long lasting the effects of Sara's younger years will be. And by beginning to monitor her again, Marie was simply falling back into old habits, threatening to stunt Sara's development once more.

Marie embraced the Arkangel tech out of a fear of losing her child, a fear that all parents can identify with. But as *Arkangel* shows, we are losing the ability to think rationally about such fears – to think rationally about children's safety and maintain perspective. We wouldn't recommend that parents leave a child in the park or the mall, but we should take notice of the following statistic: Warwick Cairns in *How to Live Dangerously* calculated that if you *actively* wanted your child to be kidnapped by a stranger, you would have to leave the child outside unattended for 750,000 years.[14] The odds are much higher for losing your kids the way Marie did, as a result of over-parenting.

No matter how tempting it may be to protect our children from perceived or real dangers (and most of us would be tempted by an Arkangel device – be honest with yourself here), *Arkangel* shows us that we shouldn't. Indeed, because Sara lacked the crucial element (empathy) of a morally decent human being, it could be argued that the Arkangel device turned Sara (at least partially) into an android. Her story in *Arkangel*, like many android stories in science fiction, is about what it is to be human. Philip K. Dick's classic novel *Do Androids Dream of Electric Sheep?* is a significant starting point for the discussion of what it means to be human in modern science fiction. In the novel, androids are only distinguishable from humans by their ability to feel empathy; they possess "no ability to feel empathic joy for another life form's success or grief at its defeat."[15] Unfortunately, therefore, rather than *raising a child*, Marie has *manufactured* a partial *android*. Surely we wouldn't and shouldn't want that for our children.

Notes

1. Charlie Brooker and Annabel Jones with Jason Arnopp, *Inside Black Mirror* (New York: Crown Archetype, 2018), 255.
2. Joel Feinberg, "On the child's right to an open future," in William Aiken and Hugh Lafollette eds., *Whose Child?* (Totowa, NJ: Rowman and Littlefield, 1980), 124–53.
3. See Elizabeth Brake and Joseph Millum, "Parenthood and procreation," *The Stanford Encyclopedia of Philosophy*, https://plato.stanford.edu/archives/spr2018/entries/parenthood (Accessed 5 July 2019).
4. For example, professor Rush Rhees once said to one of this chapter's authors that philosophers do not make the mistake of thinking that dogs can understand emotions or human speech – and then paused, winked, and said, "Except *my* dogs, of course."
5. See Alisa L. Carse, "The moral contours of empathy," *Ethical Theory and Moral Practice*, 8 (2005), 169–195.
6. See Martin L. Hoffman, "Empathy and Moral Development," *The Annual Report of Educational Psychology in Japan*, 35 (1996), 157
7. Martin L. Hoffman, *Empathy and Moral Development: Implications for Caring and Justice* (Cambridge, UK: Cambridge University Press, 2000), 3.
8. Ludwig Wittgenstein (1889–1951) wrote on a variety of philosophical topics from mathematics to philosophy of mind, but ethics and philosophical perception as moral perception lie at the very core of his work.
9. Cora Diamond, "Anything but argument," *Philosophical Investigations*, 5 (1982), 36.

10. See Christopher Cordner and Andrew Gleeson, "Cora Diamond and the Moral Imagination," *Nordic Studies Wittgenstein Review*, 5 (2016), 59–60.
11. Jonathan Barnes ed., *The Complete Works of Aristotle*, Volumes 1 and II (Princeton, NJ: Princeton University Press, 1984).
12. An additional problem for feminist philosophers is that Aristotle states in Book I of the *Politics* is that the virtues are gendered, with women's virtues expressed primarily through obeying their husbands.
13. Sara Ruddick, *Maternal Thinking: Towards a Maternal Politics of Peace* (New York: Ballantine Books, 1983).
14. Warwick Cairns, *How to Live Dangerously* (London: Pan Macmillan, 2008).
15. Phillip K. Dick, *Do Androids Dream of Electric Sheep?* (New York: Random House, 1968), 32.

Crocodile and the Ethics of Self Preservation

How Far is Too Far?

Darci Doll

You give a little love and it all comes back to you. You're going to be remembered for the things you say and do.
— ("You Give a Little Love" from *Bugsy Malone*)

Crocodile is the most confusingly named episode of *Black Mirror*. It tells the story of a young woman named Mia who is faced with the choice of whether to help her boyfriend Rob cover up the fact that he accidentally killed a bicyclist with his car. She "gives a little love" by helping Rob throw the body and bicycle into a nearby lake, only to have it "all comes back" to her fifteen years later when Rob's guilt drives him to decide to write to the man's widow. Because this could expose her involvement and ruin the life she has built with her now husband and young son, she kills Rob. And then, thanks to the memory retrieval software in the episode, she ends up deciding to kill an entire family (including a baby) to keep Rob's murder a secret. In each case, she's hesitant and sorrowful – but she does it anyway. The episode ends with Mia watching her son and his classmates sing the final number of *Bugsy Malone* as the police close in.

It's a disturbing episode. Some criticized it, and others thought it was great. But what the hell does it have to do with crocodiles?

The interpretation that makes the most sense was endorsed by the episode's producer Sanne Wohlenberg. "There's a theory that, when crocodiles kill their prey, they have tears in their eyes."[1] On this reading, the title suggests that Mia isn't actually sorry for her crimes. Instead, she's shedding "crocodile tears" – a reading supported by a two-page spread in the *Inside Black Mirror* book that simply shows Mia shedding a single tear.[2] But Wohlenberg also admits that she doesn't "think that's what Charlie [Brooker] intended." And she's right. "The genesis of the title," he admitted, "actually related to previous incarnation of the script" where someone getting attacked by a crocodile in a virtual reality game served as "an analogy

Black Mirror and Philosophy: Dark Reflections, First Edition. Edited by David Kyle Johnson.
© 2020 John Wiley & Sons, Inc. Published 2020 by John Wiley & Sons, Inc.

for somebody who'd been traumatized at an early age."[3] Who could have guessed?

Still, the episode raises some difficult philosophical questions. It's not immediately clear whether Mia did the wrong thing by helping her then-boyfriend Rob hide the body. Some of us might have done the same thing, given the circumstances. In general, the instinct for self-preservation makes sense. But each choice she makes is more obviously wrong, and no one would argue that her killing a baby was justified, right? She shouldn't be shedding crocodile tears over that! So where, when, and how did she go off the moral rails? To answer that question, and to see how it might help us make our own moral decisions, let's take a closer look at the main ways philosophers try to answer such questions.

Helping Rob Hide the Cyclist's Body

As you may recall from Chapter 1 on *The National Anthem,* Immanuel Kant (1724–1804) was a deontologist. As such, he thought that the morality of an action depends on duty, and one's duty is determined by the categorical imperative, a universal law of morality that applies to all people in the same way. According to Kant, the categorical imperative entails a couple of different things. First, maxims, or reasons for acting, must be ones that we'd be willing to have all people follow. Indeed, it must be logically possible for all people to follow them. You shouldn't do something that you wouldn't want all people to do; and you shouldn't do something that it would be impossible for everyone to do. Second, the categorical imperative focuses on the intrinsic (or natural) value of humans. For Kant, our rationality and our ability to make rational decisions is what gives humans moral worth. Thus, morally right actions are those that show respect for autonomy, or a person's right and ability to make fully informed decisions about their own well-being.

What would Kant say about Mia's choice to help Rob hide the cyclist's body? Rob bears the sole responsibility for the death of the cyclist. Rob was driving, somewhat intoxicated, allowed himself to be distracted, and as a result committed vehicular manslaughter. Mia is an innocent bystander and seems to bear no moral responsibility for his death (although one might argue that, knowing he was under the influence, she should have stopped Rob from driving). She does, however, participate in disposing of the body as well as covering up the accident. And this action involves deception, hiding the truth, and avoiding personal responsibility for one's actions, none of which are supported by the categorical imperative. So, Kant would condemn it.

The action of covering up a death cannot be universalized – avoiding moral responsibility, deceiving people and obstructing the truth are not maxims that all people can or should follow. Additionally, by covering up the cyclist's death, Mia and Rob are interfering with others' abilities to make autonomous decisions. The people who care about the cyclist, and law enforcement, are all denied the opportunity to make fully informed voluntary decisions about this man. Furthermore, the motivation to hide the body is due to their focus on the negative consequences of not doing so – the consequences of coming clean. For Kant, the emphasis should be on the moral rightness of an action independent of the consequences.

So, again, from a Kantian perspective it was morally wrong for Mia and Rob to cover up the death of the cyclist. It might, however, be justified according a different theory of morality: utilitarianism.

As we also learned in Chapter 1 on *The National Anthem*, utilitarianism is a consequentialist moral theory. Consequentialist theories hold that the moral goodness of an action is determined by the consequences it generates. Actions that produce good consequences are morally good, those that produce bad consequences are morally bad. According to many consequentialists, whether an action has "good consequences" is determined by whether it produces happiness or pleasure. Hedonists, for example, suggest that you should act in a way that procures the most pleasure for yourself. (It should be noted, however, that most hedonists do not think that momentary physical pleasures really produce happiness. Thus, contrary to popular opinion, most hedonists do not recommend living a life of drunkenness and debauchery.)

Utilitarians often define good consequences in terms of happiness, but they focus on maximizing the most long-term good for the most people affected. They use a "utilitarian calculus," a cost-benefit analysis of sorts, that measures whether more people will be benefitted or burdened by a course of action, overall, in the long term. When doing such calculations, utilitarianism demands, everyone must act objectively and impartially, and all people must be treated equally.

According to the utilitarian, when it comes to the question of the morality of Rob and Mia's decision to hide the cyclist's body, the relevant issue is whether doing so will produce the greatest good overall (when compared to coming clean). Given their conversation, it seems that Rob and Mia think that it will. Their implied rationale is that the cyclist is already dead, and that will remain true no matter what they do next. But if they call the police, Mia's life will likely be upended and Rob's life will be ruined; he'll be held accountable for manslaughter. In contrast, if Rob and Mia hide the body, neither of those things will happen, and Rob and Mia will both be able to live their lives uninterrupted. Indeed, one may even argue that Rob can do more good for people, contribute more to society, if he's not incarcerated or otherwise penalized for the death of the cyclist. Since the cyclist is dead either way, this initial utilitarian calculus indicates that more good will be produced for more people if the death is covered up, and thus that is the right thing to do.

What this initial assessment fails to take into consideration, however, is what Rob eventually realizes. (1) Not knowing what happened to the cyclist will inflict a huge toll on the cyclist's friends and family. And (2) the guilt for hiding the cyclist will eventually become too much for Rob to endure. Because of these added negative consequences, utilitarians would also say that it was wrong for Rob and Mia to conceal the crime. They would also support Rob's decision to come clean and confess to the manslaughter if the crime were concealed. According to utilitarians, then, although Mia is not directly morally responsible for the death of the cyclist, she was morally wrong to cover up his death.

Killing Rob

A full fifteen years after killing the cyclist, Rob seeks out Mia. The guilt of the crime has been weighing on his mind and has been exacerbated by a newspaper article about the victim. Rob explains that the wife of the cyclist is still holding out hope that he'll return, that the search for the cyclist is ongoing. Rob realizes the damage that not knowing what has happened to the man has caused to those who care about him and Rob wants to make amends by sending an anonymous letter to the deceased's wife. Rob wants to give her the closure that will come from knowing what happened. Mia, however, is concerned that notifying the cyclist's family will threaten the successful career and comfortable living she has created for her family. Even an anonymous letter could be traced back to Rob and, therefore, back to her. She thus decides, right then and there, to kill Rob to keep him quiet.

Both a consequentialist and deontological approach would say that this decision was morally wrong. Take utilitarianism, for example. From Mia's perspective, it may seem that more harm than good would be created by informing the deceased's family. She may therefore think that she is maximizing the greatest good. Most utilitarians, however, would disagree. The good that would be accomplished by protecting the comfort that Mia has become accustomed to would not outweigh the suffering that would be caused by killing Rob. Not only would the cyclist's widow continue to suffer, but so would Rob and his family. Moreover, the guilt that she will have to live with this time will be even greater, since she will be directly responsible for Rob's death. For these reasons, utilitarians would condemn Mia's murder of Rob.

So would Kantians. In a court of law, it would be significant that killing Rob was not premeditated. For a Kantian, however, the lack of forethought is irrelevant. Mia ended a person's life. She destroyed their autonomy, treating them not as something morally valuable but as an instrumental means to an end. Because of this, Mia's actions were morally wrong. In addition, murder does not follow maxims, or reasons, that can be universalized. The decision to murder others is one that Kant vehemently rejects. We cannot, without logical contradiction, allow people to end the lives of others in such a way. (If we universalized murder, there would be no one left to murder.) And so, the Kantian would conclude, Mia's action of killing Rob was morally wrong.

Utilitarianism and Kantian deontology are only two ethical theories, however. Some might argue that on other theories, like the Feminist Ethics of Care, Mia's action is actually justified. How might such an argument go?

Feminist care ethics is an approach that is neither consequentialist nor deontological. As we've seen, according to both deontological and utilitarian theories, when deciding what I should do, I should give all people equal moral weight or consideration. And I should do so regardless of their relationship to me. For the utilitarian, for example, when trying to decide what to do, I should give equal weight to how my action affects my child and how it affects a complete stranger. If the option is between making two other kids happy or just my own son, I should choose the former.

According to many feminists, however, this doesn't sit right. It's perfectly morally acceptable to show favoritism to those you care about, like your children. The categorical imperative and utilitarian calculus rely too heavily on "masculine" virtues like impartiality and fairness, and not enough on more "feminine" virtues like caring. Feminist ethics therefore often focuses on the moral obligations that we have to the people we care for, and involves prioritizing the needs of the people we care for. To determine whether someone has acted morally, we must consider whether they have fulfilled their obligations to the people they care for.

With that in mind, one might argue that it *was* morally acceptable for Mia to kill Rob. Why? Because she did so to protect those she cares for. Consider what she says to Rob in an attempt to change his mind and get him to continue to keep the secret.

MIA: Rob. No. You'll open up God knows what, you'll just rake it all up. There's things they can do. 'Cause they'll trace it back. They can trace it. They'll find the body, they'll find us.... I've got somewhere. I've got a life. You don't know, don't understand .... You're not married. I've got a son. He's nine years old. You've seen photos of him. Think of him, please.

Mia's dedication to her family and their security is her priority. She is focused on protecting their best interest and fulfilling her moral obligation to them. From her perspective, any potential good that could come from notifying the cyclist's family of his death does not outweigh the damage done to her family. In order to defend their safety and well-being, Mia is willing to do anything, including killing Rob and disposing of his body.

Mia's reasoning is profoundly flawed from the perspective of Feminist care ethics, however. Although care ethics draws attention to our obligations to those we care about, it does not single out such obligations as the only relevant moral consideration. It does not *do away* with other masculine virtues like impartiality and fairness; it just deemphasizes them to balance them out with the feminine virtues that have so long been neglected. A sense of duty for those one cares about by itself, therefore, is not a sufficient reason to kill others. We can give some priority to our loved ones, but that doesn't mean that we are absolved from obligations towards others. Mia is entitled to give her family additional consideration, but her actions must maintain some degree of proportionality. The life she had become accustomed to was being threatened, but there was no direct threat to her life or those that she cared for. Therefore, while Mia may have had good intentions to protect her family, others still have rights and entitlements, and Mia's emphasis on her family obligations doesn't change that.

Killing the Akhands

Shazia Akhand was investigating an insurance claim to determine liability and responsibility after a driverless pizza delivery truck hit a pedestrian. To gather information, Shazia takes witness testimony and uses technology that allows her to view replications of the witnesses' memories. In doing this, Shazia is able to identify Mia as a potential witness. When using the technology on Mia, however, Shazia learns of Mia's choice to murder Rob. Although Shazia promises to not divulge what she's learned, Mia attacks Shazia anyway, knocks her unconscious, and ties her up.

When Shazia regains consciousness, Mia uses the memory recall technology to discover whether anyone knew that Shazia was going to interview Mia. And someone did: Shazia's husband Anan. Mia kills Shazia, and to ensure that no further investigation leads to Mia, she goes to Shazia's house and kills Anan while he is upstairs taking a bath. Thinking it's all over, Mia heads downstairs – only to see Shazia's baby daughter Ali in her crib. Because the memory recall technology could lift images from her as well, Mia feels she must kill Ali too…and she does.

But there were two things that Mia couldn't have known. One, Ali was blind, and thus no relevant memories could have been lifted from her. And two, there was a guinea pig in Ali's room. The police recover its memories, and the episode ends with the police closing in on Mia as she applauds the finale of her son's production of *Bugsy Malone*.

It should not surprise the reader that the Kantian, the utilitarian, and the care ethicist would condemn Mia's actions here. Not only is she murdering, which the Kantian would obviously argue is immoral, but she sacrificed an entire family's existence for (what we might call) the convenience of her own. Yes, given what she has done, her husband and son's life will be turned upside down – but they'll still be alive! The three Akhands won't be. Not even a negligent utilitarian calculus could suggest that, somehow, Mia's actions are leading to more good than harm. And even though she may have been looking out for the good of her own family, Mia still has moral obligations that include fairness, proportionality, and protecting the rights of others. Though care ethics would permit killing in self-defense, it does not permit cold-blooded murder.

But why did Mia go so far off the moral course? To answer this, one might point to the old adage about the "frog in a kettle." Place a frog in a pot of boiling water and it will jump out; place a frog in a pot of water and very slowly bring it to a boil, and it will sit there until it dies. Now, that's not actually true; in reality, the frog would jump out as soon as it's uncomfortable.[4] But the adage does seem to describe Mia's moral decline in the episode. First, it's just helping her boyfriend hide a body; then it's killing him. Next, it's killing a wife and husband; then it's killing a baby. But it seems that there's something much more to it than that. And one ethical theory that might reveal that something is Aristotle's virtue ethics.

According to Aristotle (384–322 BCE), humans strive for *eudaimonia* which can be translated as happiness, excellence, or flourishing. Humans are attracted to things that they believe will help them obtain *eudaimonia* and avoid things that will detract from it. To understand which actions contribute to *eudaimonia*, one must develop practical reasoning. That is, a person needs to put herself in the position of reasoning through the way things are perceived versus how they actually are. Practical reasoning will help us analyze a situation and determine whether something is consistent with moral behavior (in other words, whether it is actually good) as opposed to something that is only apparently good. The person with practical reasoning will then be able to identify the good actions, turn them into habits, and through cultivating those habits become a good person and attain *eudaimonia*.

Clearly, according to Aristotle, what Mia did was wrong. Her decision to hide the body is founded in motivations of self-preservation more than moral virtues such as courage. And while her desire to provide a comfortable life for her family is noble, her willingness to kill others to do so is not. Honesty, compassion, kindness, empathy – these are virtues that Mia lacks.

But it seems the thing that most contributes to Mia's mistakes, and moral decline, is her lack of practical wisdom. She does not have the ability to delineate good actions from bad in the moment. The only action she had time to meditate on was killing Anan. All the rest – helping Rob hide the body, killing Rob in the hotel room, turning on Shazia, killing Ali – she had to make quickly. And she got it wrong every time! If she had done the work previously, and developed virtuous habits, she would have done the right thing automatically. She would have realized, from the beginning, that helping Rob hide the body was not the way to attain *eudaimonia*. Indeed, she would not have gotten in the car with him in the first place, because he had been drinking. Thus, she would never have started down the wrong path to begin with. Now, however, her life is ruined.

Learning from Mia's Mistakes

How can we develop virtuous habits to avoid a fate like Mia's? Practice, practice, practice. And part of such practice is doing philosophy. It's good to read books like this that consider hypothetical situations and that prompt you to determine the right and wrong thing to do. But what you really need to do is practice in the course of everyday life.

Aristotle extended his virtue ethics beyond the personal level into the societal level. In order for there to be people who are capable of attaining *eudaimonia,* there must be a society that gives them the proper environment and upbringing to make the proper conditions possible. A society that tolerates people like Mia cannot be such a society. Not only do her actions not contribute to the cultivation of good character, but they make society less safe and do not set a good example. Indeed, for the virtue ethicist, one of the primary ways to develop virtues in oneself is to hold up and emulate virtuous persons. Like the song says, Mia should be remembered for the things that she does, but only as a cautionary tale. She should therefore be held accountable and removed from society. And if she cries at her trial, her tears should be considered crocodile tears.

Notes

1. Charlie Brooker and Annabel Jones with Jason Arnopp, *Inside Black Mirror* (New York: Crown Archetype, 2018), 269.
2. Ibid., 264–265.
3. Ibid.
4. James Fallows, "The boiled-frog myth: stop the lying now!" *The Atlantic,* https://www.theatlantic.com/technology/archive/2006/09/the-boiled-frog-myth-stop-the-lying-now/7446/ (Accessed 5 July 2019).

17

Hang the DJ and Digital Dating
Should We Use Computers to Help Us Find Mates?

Skye C. Cleary and Massimo Pigliucci

You can fuck off.

(Frank)

In *Hang The DJ*, Frank and Amy meet via an online dating system designed to find your "ultimate compatible other." The system's digital "coach" interface even boasts a 99.8% success rate. The process starts with a blind date. During theirs, Frank and Amy laugh, flirt, and there's an instant attraction. But because the system tells them the expiration date of their relationship is only twelve hours, they reluctantly part ways the next morning. Over the next year, the system churns them both through numerous dates and relationships, until it finally pairs them up again. Thrilled, they agree not to look at their expiration date and make the most of whatever time they have together. But when Frank can't bear the uncertainty and looks anyway, it destabilizes their relationship and the coach recalibrates their expiration date from five years to twenty hours. Amy is furious. They part on bad terms and the system throws them into another cycle of monotonous relationships.

Over time, however, Amy's anger fades – and upon learning that her "pairing day" is imminent, Amy chooses Frank as the one and only person in the system to whom she can say goodbye. Frank does the same with Amy. They mutually decide to tell the system to "Fuck off"; they reject the choice the coach made for them and run away to scale the wall of the dating community. When they do, however, their world...*disappears*. Surprise! Frank and Amy are part of a computer simulation – one of a thousand, run by a smartphone dating app, to determine whether the "real" Frank and Amy are compatible. In 998 of these simulations, the cookies (digital copies) of Frank and Amy rebelled; the app thus declares them a "99.8% match." The episode ends with the real Frank and Amy

Black Mirror and Philosophy: Dark Reflections, First Edition. Edited by David Kyle Johnson.
© 2020 John Wiley & Sons, Inc. Published 2020 by John Wiley & Sons, Inc.

looking at their compatibility ranking on their phones, and then spotting each other from across a crowded club.[1]

The prospect of using something like the coaching system, or the compatibility app, is very tempting. Who wouldn't want to eliminate the guesswork of dating and end up with their true match? Indeed, many online dating services already do something like this. The eHarmony dating site, for example, matches people according to personality profiles, and a smartphone app already exists that tries to mimic the coaching system.[2] But should you really submit to something like the coaching system or the dating app? Does finding a perfect match really boil down to a formula? And if it did, would that be a good way to find love? To answer these questions, let's explore some Stoic and existential perspectives.

Stoicism 101

Stoicism is an ancient Greco-Roman philosophy built around three principles. First, we should live "according to nature." That doesn't mean running naked into the forest to hug trees (as fun as that may be). Rather, it's a reference to what Stoics think are the two fundamental aspects of humanity: we are inherently social beings (we don't thrive outside of a social context), and we are capable of reason (even though we don't always use it). For Stoics, it follows that we should apply reason to the improvement of social living. The ancient Stoics, accordingly, were among the first cosmopolitans, adopting the view that all human beings are worthy of consideration regardless of their gender, ethnicity, or any other characteristic. As the emperor-philosopher Marcus Aurelius (121–180 CE) put it: "Do what is necessary, and whatever the reason of a social animal naturally requires, and as it requires."[3]

Second, the Stoics suggest that we should cultivate four cardinal virtues: (1) practical wisdom, the knowledge to figure out what is truly good or bad for us; (2) justice, the attitude of behaving fairly and respectfully toward others; (3) courage, to do the right thing, morally speaking; and (4) temperance, to respond to every situation in a measured way, neither over- nor underdoing things. These four virtues provide us with a life compass. Keep them in mind, apply them to every situation, and you will live a flourishing life, a life truly worth living.

Third, the Stoics hold that we should always keep in mind "the dichotomy of control," a concept that is also found in eighth-century Buddhism, eleventh-century Judaism, and even twentieth-century Christianity. You might have heard it in these terms: "Grant me the serenity to accept the things I cannot change, the courage to change the things I can, and the wisdom to know the difference."[4] But the Stoic philosopher Epictetus (50–135 CE) put it this way:

Some things are within our power, while others are not. Within our power are opinion, motivation, desire, aversion, and, in a word, whatever is of our own doing; not within our power are our body, our property, reputation, office, and, in a word, whatever is not of our own doing.[5]

Epictetus means that, while we completely control our judgments, we don't control much else. That's not to say that we can't influence certain external things – like our body, property, reputation, and so on – but they ultimately depend on other factors. Sure, you may take care of your body by exercising and eating healthy (which are things under your control); but a virus may strike you and make you sick or an accident can break your leg (which are things outside your control). The idea, then, is that we should internalize our goals. In order to be happy, we should avoid wanting a healthy body, and instead only want to do whatever is in our power to keep our body healthy. We should not want a promotion, but only to do whatever is in our power to get one. We should not want to be loved, but only to be lovable. In life sometimes we get what we want, at other times we don't. The wise person simply attempts to do their best and then accepts whatever outcome results with serenity.

So, how does the Stoic framework apply to the situation in which Frank and Amy find themselves? If they want to be Stoic practitioners, should they buy into the system of digital matching? And if things don't seem right for them, should they rebel?

Stoicism and Digital Relationships

A Stoic would be unlikely to sign up for the coaching system or use the compatibility app. For one thing, a major goal of Stoic training is to refine our ability to arrive at correct judgments, because this leads to a fulfilling life. As Epictetus puts it, almost in direct response to the hypothetical world of *Hang the DJ*, "We, not externals, are the masters of our judgements."[6] If we delegate our judgments to the coach or the app, we give up one of the crucial things that make us human. Indeed, this is precisely the realization that (simulated) Frank and Amy come to by the end of the episode.

A second ground for Stoic skepticism is that being virtuous means to do one's best in whatever situation we happen to find ourselves. This would include the situation of being in a relationship that an "objective" assessment may consider to be suboptimal. After all, finding the ideal partner is not under our complete control, because it depends in part on external conditions (like the pool of possible partners, the energy and time available to find one, and so forth). That's not to say that we should seek suboptimal relationships. But for the Stoic, having a partner is a dynamic opportunity to improve as human beings and to help our partner to do likewise. Part of such improvement is the realization and acceptance that relationships are messy human affairs. They are hardly the sort of thing that can, or should, be left to a computer to decide on our behalf.

A Stoic would reject the idea of digitally supervised dating to stay aligned with the four virtues. Going on an endless streak of dates to find our perfect match would not be a *temperate* thing to do. It's too self-centered. It turns us into obsessive-compulsive daters, absorbing much of our energy in a way that does not really improve the human cosmopolis (the human planetary family).

Digitally supervised dating also lacks *justice*, because we treat all our dates as means to an end (as a way of achieving the goal of finding "the ultimate compatible other") and not as human beings inherently worthy of respect. Consider when Amy looks exceedingly bored while making love to yet another hunky guy, going through the motions without any emotional involvement, or when one of Frank's dates simply can't wait for their time to be over, repeatedly checking her watch and refusing to even say polite parting words.

Digitally supervised dating isn't *courageous*, because we are deputizing an important ethical choice – selection of our partner – to an automated system. That's pretty cowardly. Lastly, digitally supervised dating contravenes the virtue of *practical wisdom*, which tells us that the only things that are truly good for us are our good judgments, which in this case Frank and Amy willingly give up to the impersonal coach that guides them through the process.

Existentialism and Bad Faith Relationships

Existentialism is tricky to describe because all the existential philosophers had different ideas about what it was and even whether they were "existentialists" or not. However, we can group them together based on a few overlapping themes, such as freedom, choice, responsibility, anxiety, and awareness of death. Existentialists stress the importance of individual freedom and responsibility, emphasizing concrete living and establishing personal principles that are worth living for, even risking one's life for.

The central theme of existentialism is that we are thrown into the world without a guidebook. We don't choose how or where we arrive, but once we're here and grown up, we have to figure it out and choose what to do with our lives. Our world is not like Frank and Amy's world, where the coaching system tells them what to do and who to date. In the real world, we always have choices and there is no escaping that fact. As existential philosopher Jean-Paul Sartre (1905–1980) wrote, there is "no exit" and we are "condemned to be free."[7]

The important point about freedom, however, is that there are two ways to think about it: freedom *from* and freedom *to*. We need to be free *from* oppression in order to be free *to* choose our lives. We need to be free *from* a system, like the coaching system, that forces us into relationships, in order to be free *to* choose whom we spend our time with. With freedom, though, comes responsibility, which creates anxiety. Often, we're tempted to deny our freedom or deceive ourselves, and that's what Sartre referred to as "bad faith."

For example, in Sartre's most famous work, *Being and Nothingness*, he describes a couple on a date. When the man takes the woman's hand, the woman leaves her hand in his, instead of pulling it away, and pretends to herself that the man is not expressing amorous intent. In Sartre's reading of the situation, she is acting in self-deceptive bad faith.[8] This helps us understand the relationships in *Hang The DJ* because nearly every relationship in the system is in bad faith; the couples are acting as if they're compatible, even when the expiration date tells them they're not. And this is the main reason those relationships are unhappy. Frank is particularly miserable in his one-year relationship with Nicola, a woman who is also devastated about being stuck with Frank. They are trying to force the relationship because it's what's expected of them, it's what they're told to do, but it's hell for both of them. They despise one another and watch the clock like prisoners.

In a way, by forcing people to be in relationships and forcing them to try to make them work for a certain amount of time, the coach is teaching people to recognize how awful it is to let bad faith fool us into thinking that a relationship will work when we know that it won't. That's also, possibly, what the system is doing by setting Amy up on a multitude of short-term dates – heterosexual, homosexual, bisexual, and polyamorous – which seem to initially be sexually exciting, but quickly slide into the same mind-numbing tedium.

The only relationship that is not in bad faith is Frank and Amy's – when they *don't* check their expiry and therefore don't know how long it will last. They begin to assume the ambiguity of relationships, making their own choices, and denying the authority of the system to tell them how long they ought to be together. It's the beginning of their rebellion against the system. The relationship worked while it was open-ended, and then fell apart once Frank looked at the expiration. It was at that point that he fell into bad faith.

Bad faith is also pretending we don't have a choice when we really do or putting our faith in something external (such as a dating app or coach) to choose for us. We may be afraid of the consequences of our actions, but that doesn't mean we don't have a choice at all. For the existential philosophers, the goal is to strive towards becoming authentic, which is deliberately to choose in accordance with what you think is right. It's a receding goal, but the point is to try it anyway.

Existentialism and Digital Relationships

An existential philosopher would, like the Stoics, be skeptical about signing up for the coaching system. One problem is the very notion that there is an "ultimate compatible other" for us. We are forever changing and growing, and so our preferences are evolving too. Even if a system could find a near-perfect match based on our past inclinations, there would be no guarantee that person will be a match with our future selves. And even if lovers could be paired up in this way, it would take a lot of the fun and mystery out of the experience. For Sartre, love is a project of being loved, and being with others is a project of discovering ourselves. So, putting our trust in a system that not only chooses partners for us, but also discovers *who we are* for us, cheapens the relationship and throws us into bad faith. Instead, each of us should embrace the responsibility of choosing for ourselves.

While the existential thinkers didn't emphasize virtue in the same way that Stoics did, their ideas about responsibility and authenticity come close to Stoic virtue. Putting one's faith in a rigid structure, always following what we're told to do, is inauthentic. Indeed, the coaching system is highly autocratic (a fact symbolized wonderfully by the fact that Joel Collins, the series production designer, modeled the world in which the coaching system operates on a computer chip he saw inside a mobile phone).[9] The coaching system has self-driving cars take participants to one of many identical accommodations to cohabitate for a predetermined time in a place that neither of them choose. First dates are always dinner dates and they are always in the same restaurant, with a preprogrammed menu of participants' favorite dishes.

It might be tempting to submit to such a system. It's the easy way out. That's why Frank and Amy are initially happy to accept the coaching system, even with all its rules and the menacing-looking enforcers with stun guns watching their every move. After all:

AMY: Must have been mental before the system.
FRANK: How do you mean?
AMY: Well, people had to do the whole relationship thing themselves, work out who they wanna be with.
FRANK: Hmm, option paralysis. So many choices, you end up not knowing which one you want.

It seems simpler to have their relationships all mapped out for them. But this is inauthentic. They're relieving themselves of the responsibility of shaping their own lives and, instead, leaving it up to a system to choose for them.

The system is eerily reminiscent of the social expectations that we're channeled into: mostly two people, mostly heterosexual, and mostly monogamous. Any choices people do have are minimal: Do you have sex on the first date? What kind of sex? How often? The system robs participants of one of the most important elements of a relationship: the freedom to choose whether to begin and when to end it. Not unlike arranged marriages, participants are stuck in a preordained structure. Perhaps surprisingly, divorce rates are lower in societies that rely on arranged marriages, but this is because the costs of divorce, including social ostracism or worse, make breaking up a deeply unattractive option. It's no wonder that those in arranged marriages learn to love whomever they are paired with. Nevertheless, forcing people into relationships is oppressive, and so is forcing a time limit upon a relationship. Such practices prevent people from choosing how to live their lives in an open future.

Frank and Amy's rebellion against the system is a kind of leap of faith. "We've just got to fuck the whole thing off and go," Amy implores Frank, who agrees immediately. For the existential thinkers, leaping into a relationship is always scary. Frank and Amy's decision to escape was a bold and blind life-changing decision. They found something worth risking their lives to overcome. Lovers never know how long their relationship will last. This is one of the fundamental elements of a romantic relationship. Without this anxiety, maybe we take away some of the risk, but we take away the excitement, too. Some people might be happy to trade excitement for less risk, but for many, the excitement is worth it.

Is it a Happy Ending?

The coaching system encourages conformity, and it is only by rebelling (998 out of 1000 times) that (simulated) Frank and Amy could even hope to live authentically and find happiness together. The episode leaves us with the hope that (real) Frank and Amy will continue their rebellion against the real life systems that threaten them, and that reality won't turn out to be a third iteration where Frank and Amy don't end up together.

There may be reason to doubt the probability of their success, however. (Simulated) Frank and Amy only work because the coaching system tells them they are not for each other and they rebel. They prove their love by taking a leap of faith together. In the real world, though, the opposite occurs: the compatibility app tells (real) Frank and Amy that they *are* compatible, a 99.8% match. They therefore can't rebel against the system to be together; they can't take a leap of faith. So, there's reason to think that (real) Frank and Amy's relationship will fail. If they hadn't used the compatibility app, they might have met organically and ended up as in love as (simulated) Frank and Amy. But by using it, they may be setting themselves up for failure.

This doesn't seem to be the interpretation that creators intended, however. As executive producer Annabel Jones put it, "It's a digital version of *Romeo and Juliet* but with a happy ending." And according to Charlie Brooker, if they had intended it to have a typical *Black Mirror* unhappy ending, they would have had Amy take Frank around back, "hit him over the head with a brick [and then] look down the camera lens and [say], 'It's Black Mirror, what did you fucking expect?'"[10] But we might find justification for a happy interpretation in the title of the episode and the song that inspired it. As Frank and Amy approach each other in the club, "Panic" by The Smiths plays in the background, repeating the words:

> Burn down the disco, hang the blessed DJ
> Because the music that they constantly play,
> it says nothing to me about my life.

It's ambiguous, but perhaps the DJ is the coaching system and, through their rebellion, (simulated) Frank and Amy "hang" it. Likewise, since the songs the DJ plays say "nothing to me about my life," maybe the compatibility app tells (real) Frank and Amy nothing about their life or future selves. So, the risk of love remains.

Two Philosophies, Two Compasses to Navigate Life

Black Mirror presents us with a fascinating number of philosophical thought experiments, which are fun to delve into, musing on how we would react under similar circumstances. But philosophy is supposed to be more than a mere theoretical exercise, it's supposed to change our lives. Existentialism and Stoicism are two frameworks we can use to not only make sense of the hypothetical situations in *Hang the DJ* but, more importantly, to navigate real circumstances occurring in our own lives. One of us, for instance, has used online dating systems that, while not quite as controlling as the coach in *Hang the DJ*, have certainly felt manipulative and have nudged him toward an attitude that didn't feel virtuous in the Stoic sense of the term. He is glad not to be in that situation any more.

The world is absurd, and the dating world is *particularly* absurd. So, perhaps we should take some counsel from the existentialist Albert Camus (1913–1960). He argues that absurdity arises because our human hearts have a wild longing for clarity, meaning, and security when, in reality, the world is irrational and unreasonably silent. The solution? We need to find ways to live with the ambiguity, to embrace it, and perhaps even to love the risk – not to eliminate it.

Notes

1. Throughout the chapter, except when explicitly noting otherwise, whenever we refer to "Amy and Frank" we mean both the real people who use the smart phone app at the end, *and* their simulated selves, who are subject to the digital "coach" dating system throughout the episode.

2. Rachel Kraus, "Welp, someone basically made that *Black Mirror* dating app," *Mashable*, https://mashable.com/article/black-mirror-hang-the-dj-dating-app-juliet/#OjvLbB93UiqU (Accessed 9 July 2019).

3. Marcus Aurelius, IV.24 in *Meditations*, trans. George Long, http://classics.mit.edu/Antoninus/meditations.html (Accessed 9 July 2019).

4. This is known as serenity prayer, and was popularized by American theologian Reinhold Niebuhr (1892–1971).

5. Epictetus, 1.1 in *Enchiridion*, trans. Elizabeth Carter, http://classics.mit.edu/Epictetus/epicench.html (Accessed 9 July 2019).

6. Epictetus, 11.37 in *Discourses* I, trans. Elizabeth Carter, for free at http://classics.mit.edu/Epictetus/discourses.html (Accessed 9 July 2019).

7. Jean-Paul Sartre, *Being and Nothingness*, trans. Hazel E. Barnes (New York: Washington Square Press, 1943[1992]), 186.

8. In the example, Sartre doesn't consider the possibility that she might be taking time to consider whether she would like to spend more time with the man, or that she may have still been weighing her options.

9. "I took apart a mobile phone. Inside, there's a green plate, and on that plate there's a chip, with lots of copper and brass lines leading to other nubbins. So I decided to design a park based on this mobile phone chip. There's a central hub, and all the green grass is the green plate of the chip, and all the huts are the little nubbins. Basically, I thought, 'If we can't tell the audience we're inside a mobile phone, what happens if I design it like we really are?'" Charlie Brooker and Annabel Jones with Jason Arnopp, *Inside Black Mirror* (New York: Crown Archetype, 2018), 275.

10. Brooker et al., 281.

18

Metalhead and Technophobia
How Dangerous Will Robots Be?

Scott Midson with Justin Donhauser

Challenging, and with quite a big learning curve, so you die a lot and have to try again. Can you escape from the deadly dogs? You must make your way through this monochrome world.

(Tuckersoft "Metl Hedd" Game Review)

In our world robots do jobs that are dull, dirty, and dangerous, but in *Metalhead* the robo-dogs are dangerous, destructive, and deadly.[1] They doggedly pursue the protagonist Bella and her friends and are the quintessential antagonists in every way but one: they don't lose! By the end, Bella and her friends have all been killed.

Charlie Brooker's stated aim with *Metalhead* was just to strip back a plot as a challenge to see what kind of story he could tell.[2] But the result is an arresting tale of technophobia; a story of human victims and robo-killers that is distinct in tone from any other *Black Mirror* episode.[3] Although Brooker may not have intended for the story to have a moral, a plain and obvious reading of the episode suggests robots are a dangerous threat to humanity. Of course, there are clear differences between the robots of our world and the robo-dogs of *Metalhead*. But given already existing robotic technological developments in the military, and already existing campaigns to ban "killer robots," the technophobia in *Metalhead* might be justified.[4]

Contemporary philosopher Daniel Dinello writes that "science fiction [like *Metalhead*] expresses a technophobic fear of losing our *human identity*, our *values*, our *emotions*, our *freedom*, and our *lives* to machines."[5] To find out whether the technophobia is *Metalhead* is justified, let's start with that first topic Dinello mentions: human identity.

I, Human: Human Identity

Philosophers have long explored what distinguishes humans from machines and machine-like entities. During the Scientific Revolution in the 1500s, natural philosophers (scientists' predecessors) began to see nature as an intricate mechanism that was designed and wound by a divine watchmaker. In that context, the French philosopher René Descartes (1596–1650) claimed that, whereas animal and nonhuman life operated mechanically – that is, without consciousness or autonomy – humans did not. They were conscious. Because it seemed only humans could reason, reflect, and doubt themselves, they must be somehow above the mechanistic, predictable workings of nature.

The idea of human uniqueness did not begin with Descartes, however. It also has a long history in Greek and Christian philosophy. Aristotle (384–322 BCE), for example, considered animals to rank lower than humans as part of a natural hierarchy of beings based on rational capabilities. And Thomas Aquinas (1225–1274) developed Aristotle's ideas about human superiority and linked them to the Christian teaching that humans are made in the image of God (Genesis 1:27). This view, called *Imago dei,* suggests that there's something intangible, yet distinctive, about what it is to be human.

The so called "personalistic" philosophic tradition that followed Descartes would certainly have placed robots in the category of mechanistic soulless objects. The robo-dogs of *Metalhead* even exemplify the Cartesian linking of animal and mechanical against the uniqueness of the human. Unlike animals, however, the robo-dogs (and even some real world technologies, like Google's Deep Mind) seem to have rational abilities very much like humans do.[6] They have, for example, advanced learning and problem-solving capabilities. This fact jeopardizes the uniqueness of our identity, and it might even justify some of the episode's technophobia.

We'll have to look elsewhere, therefore, if we want to find something that distinguishes us: like the fact that humans and animals are alive but machines are not. With this distinction we have a kind of *romanticism,* a philosophical view that favors the natural over the mechanical. Jean-Jacques Rousseau (1712–1778), for example, talked about the healing and beneficial powers of nature and even argued that humans were at *their best* in the state of nature. *Metalhead* exemplifies romanticism in a way. For example, the only things that help Bella throughout her stand-off with the predatory robo-dog are all non-technological. There's the cliff that the car and robo-dog fell down, which led to the dog's forced self-amputation; there's the tree that bought Bella some time as the dog was unable to climb it; there's the sunlight the dog needed to recharge; and there's the stream that helped to conceal Bella's trail. Contrariwise, it's technologies that let Bella down, as the robo-dogs can hack into digital locks, cars, and even radio transmissions.

Ultimately, therefore, at least according to the episode's romanticism, robo-dogs and technologies don't threaten our human identity. The potential threats they pose to our uniqueness are not an adequate ground for the technophobia in the episode.

Teddy Bears and Robo-dogs: Human Values

What, then, about the threat to human values Dinello mentions? Do robo-dogs challenge these, thus warranting our fears and technophobia? In order to answer this question, we need to work out what our values are – at least according to the episode.

Robo-dogs have attacked not just humans, but also pigs. Pigs, of course, have a special place in *Black Mirror*, but they aren't considered special by the characters in *Metalhead*. Clarke, one of Bella's ill-fated troupe, says he "couldn't hack being a pig…walking about with your nose the same height as your arsehole…trotting about gazing at everyone else's arsehole – what kind of society's that?" Humans, unlike pigs, apparently need to hold their heads higher. One way to interpret this is to say that we're used to being the victors, and to having an elevated status above other species (including robots).

Humans don't just have power and elevated status, though. We also have complex emotions, responsibility, and the ability to be compassionate. Take the ultimate reason, revealed in the episode's ending, that Bella and her friends ventured out in the first place: to retrieve a teddy bear for a dying child. Although such a thing would score low on Maslow's hierarchy of needs, and might not seem worth the risk, the dangers Bella and her friends are willing to take emphasize the importance of compassion and humaneness.[7] As Bella says, "if what's in there makes those days easier [for the child]…that'll do for me."

Interestingly, Charlie Brooker originally wanted Game Boys to be in the box, but director David Slade insisted that it "be something soft" so that it would convey the message about maintaining our humanity, our ability to communicate and love.[8] And it really does the trick! Bella's willingness to risk her life to make a child's life easier by getting him a teddy bear demonstrates distinctly-and-romantically-human compassion. By contrast, the robo-dogs revel in destruction, pursing Bella to the bitter end, terminating anything that stands in their way. As mechanical "others," they lack and cannot comprehend things like compassion.

The robo-dogs don't threaten our values as Dinello describes, though. In fact, if one of the foremost and romanticized human values is compassion, and one of the strongest demonstrations of compassion is to risk your life for a child, then *Metalhead* and its robo-dogs *amplify* our humanness.

E-Motion: Human Emotion

Metalhead's dangerous enemy shows instead that there are *limits* to our compassion; we don't feel it for the robo-dogs. There may be a tinge of empathy for the robo-dog when it falls off the cliff, but there is none when we compare the pain Bella expresses about her wounded leg with the dog's uncaring detachment of its limb. And there certainly is none during the dog's final stand-off with Bella.

It may sound strange to even consider empathizing with robots, but there is some precedent. Take the robots on which the robo-dogs of *Metalhead* were based: Boston Dynamics' BigDog, LittleDog, and SpotMini.[9] Videos showed researchers pushing, tripping, and obstructing the robots in order to show the robots' resilience and ability to correct their mobility. In response to the videos, many people criticized the researchers and expressed empathy for the machines.[10] In later videos, though, when similar robots managed to problem-solve, and open doors to get out of a room, viewers' empathy seemed to have dried up and the sinister potential of the robots was noted. This is, of course, grist for the *Black Mirror* mill, but what exactly is going on here?

Anthropomorphism is the human tendency to make nonhuman things seem human-like. In a 1944 study, to demonstrate this tendency, psychologists Fritz Heider and Marianne Simmel showed people a video of moving shapes; interestingly, they found that people projected intentionality and feelings onto the shapes, based on their movements and interactions.[11] This, it seems, is why we try to anticipate what the robo-dogs are thinking.[12] We are making a narrative about them based on their movements and actions. We stop short of attributing to them the full spectrum of human traits such as compassion, however. They appear, after all, as merciless killing machines. As such, *we construct them* as antagonists.

Now, we might be justified in this construction if we are unable to understand them. Contemporary philosopher Bruno Latour argues that, the more adept technologies become at their tasks, the more they will become like "black boxes" to us.[13] We will be alienated from the processes and mechanisms that enable them to function. Such a juxtaposition between the familiarity of robots and their essential unfamiliarity could spark fears and incite technophobia in and of itself.

All of this leads us to wonder: Is it better to empathize with machines (as with BigDog) or not (as with the robo-dogs)? In other words, should we fear robots' otherness, or should we try to reduce that otherness into more familiar terms? In *Metalhead*, both strategies seem to fail, but trying to understand how and why they fail is instructive.

Managing Dangerous Robots 101

Perhaps the most obvious place to look in Dinello's list for the motivation behind technophobia is fears about the threat to our freedom and lives that robots could pose. *Metalhead* certainly taps into such fears, and the possibility of a robot uprising is a common science fiction trope. Of course,

Isaac Asimov (1920–1992) made famous the Three Laws of Robotics, which are supposed to guard against such things:

1. A robot may not injure a human being, or, through inaction, allow a human being to come to harm.
2. A robot must obey the orders given it by human beings except where such orders would conflict with the First Law.
3. A robot must protect its own existence as long as such protection does not conflict with the First or Second Law.[14]

And at first glance, it seems that instituting something like these laws could work. They appear simple, and even programable, given their stratification into three tiered levels. And they put the safety of humans as their highest concern. So, theoretically, dangerous robots should not worry us.

But as anyone who has read Asimov's short stories in *I, Robot* will be aware, the laws are fallible and likely wouldn't guarantee the kind of safeguard we want. The trouble is that they *only* work theoretically; even "the real world" of Asimov's fiction is too chaotic and complex for such laws to keep up. To make matters worse, as contemporary philosophers Wendell Wallach and Colin Allen note in their study of "moral machines," laws like Asimov's require highly advanced technological capabilities, like detecting and interpreting harm, for example.[15] Humans are adept at such things; robots are not. In other words, Asimov's laws presume too many similarities between humans and robots for the laws to do what we would want them to do. Perhaps one day, of course, robots will have such capabilities, like the robo-dogs of *Metalhead* seem to. But still, they would operate differently from humans; we are returned to the issues surrounding robots as unfamiliar "black boxes."

The unfamiliarity of robots could give rise to other problems that are not just about our perceptions of them, sketched out in the previous section, but also about how we apply ethical frameworks to them. Think again of *Metalhead*'s robo-dogs. To them, the humans they hunt appear as insignificant and depersonalised pulsating white dots without a face or human form. But we only know this because *Metalhead* provides us with their point of view. If real-world robots actually were "black boxes," how could we know what they see – or even know if they see anything at all? In real world combat situations with human soldiers, we assume that soldiers have a strong moral awareness of their actions when they, for example, decide to kill. We assume this because the soldier is like us. With robo-dogs, however, because we perceive to be unlike us, we assume that there is no such awareness.[16] But if they really are a "black box," we have no idea how they are making their decisions. And if we don't, who or what do we blame for their actions? Who or what should we punish or reprimand in the case of a robot wrongdoing? The robot? Its creator? The difficulties raised by such questions could challenge our ethical frameworks and our sense of morality, giving rise to even more reasons to be technophobic.

The Blame Game: Human Limitations

Using our ethical frameworks to assign accountability to robots is difficult. On the one hand, if a robot has artificial intelligence (AI), that is, if it thinks at least semi-independently by perceiving input data and reacting to it, then it is tempting for us to assign agency to that machine. On the other hand, robots don't (yet) generate thoughts autonomously. Therefore, we are encouraged to trace causality and agency to the robot's designers, programmers, users, or hackers. This is the recommendation of various think-tanks and government bodies, including the House of Lords in the UK, and the European Government.[17]

According to these government reports, robots are tools that are designed by humans to undertake certain tasks. The creators, therefore, should be held responsible for any robot's misdeeds. So, ethicists and roboticists like Noel Sharkey argue that restrictions should be in place to prevent people from developing things like killer robots. Such arguments are corroborated by mythical and fictional cautions about *hubris*, which describes humans overreaching themselves and going too far. Indeed, tales like *Frankenstein*, where the eponymous doctor crossed moral boundaries by reanimating corpses and bringing to life his monstrous creation, are often seen as arguments, in and of themselves, for such restrictions.

One of Sharkey's arguments against killer robots resonates with the terror depicted in *Metalhead*:

> You cannot punish an inanimate object. It would be very difficult to allocate responsibility in the chain of command or to manufacturers, programmers, or designers – and being able to allocate responsibility is essential to the laws of war.[18]

The protagonists seem unable to "punish" the robo-dogs, given that the latter do not feel pain or suffering, and responsibility for the robo-dogs' actions is difficult to assign. The robo-dogs appear autonomous and antagonistic, but do they act on their own volition, or their own programming? And which answer is more worrying? Again, we encounter uncertainties and "black boxes."

Interestingly, the robo-dogs' autonomy diverges from an earlier draft of the script where a human remotely operated the robo-dogs.[19] It's worth pausing on this point for a second. How would we morally assess the remote operator? In a similar vein, how would our sympathies for Bella and her compatriots change if we were to discover that they were the original programmers of the robo-dogs?

Metalhead complicates these lines of enquiry with its ambiguity. Audiences are not explicitly told the robo-dogs' design or intention (or if they have one). And even if we knew, things could get more complicated. Director David Slade suggested that the robo-dogs are military devices that patrol and guard private property.[20] If that were true, it would be possible to regard them as the apotheosis of capitalism. Karl Marx (1818–1883), who pointed out in his analysis of capitalism and industrialism that technologies can be wielded as instruments of oppression and destruction, would be aghast.

Indeed, Marx sought to liberate people from what he saw as the shackles of capitalism. Technologies are the product of capitalist desires, he argued, which themselves are the result of economic structures and the concentration of money among powerful groups in society. If so, and if technophobia is linked to a concern about the loss of human freedom, then our concerns about killer robots are inseparable from concerns about capitalism. This idea isn't new. Such sentiments are sensationalized in other science fiction like *The Matrix*, and realized in wariness about major tech companies such as Amazon, Google, and Facebook aggregating our data and turning it into power and profit.

How Real Could Dangerous Robots Bee? Human Responsibility

Metalhead's robo-dogs are not human(e). They are the counterpoint to a romantic vision of humanness. This warrants technophobia. But is this true of all robots?

Let's consider killer robots in our own context. For instance, the COTSbot, developed by Queensland University of Technology researcher Matt Dunbabin, is an underwater robot that autonomously seeks out the predatory crown-of-thorn starfish (COTS) using visual recognition technology. The COTSbot destroys those predators by injecting them with a toxin. Another example is Robots in Service of the Environment's (RSE) Lionfish Project, which has developed a similar robot that autonomously seeks out and kills lionfish. These robots may seem cruel at first, but they are doing human environmentalists' job more safely and efficiently than humans can; crown-of-thorn starfish and lionfish are destroying coral reefs with unrelenting efficiency.[21]

Another *Black Mirror* episode, *Hated in the Nation*, gives use another case of killer robots: robotic bees. These are also real. Researchers at Harvard's Wyss Institute continue to develop various different programmable robot swarms for use in environmental protection and remediation.[22] Such devices could be hacked or weaponized; such scenarios play out in the *Black Mirror* universe. In addition, these robots could make mistakes or acquire glitches that result in the death of other organisms, even humans.

Moreover, even if ongoing efforts to produce robot swarms to assist dwindling bee populations could become extremely efficient at pollinating, they could have significant ecological ripples, since natural insects play many functional roles other than just pollinating. Insects have deeply co-evolved relationships with many other organisms and are themselves sources of food and nutrients. So, even where we have benign, non-killer robot organisms, there are still very real potential dangers.

It's hard to find any kind of robot or technological intervention, that isn't potentially dangerous in some way. This danger can obviously prompt technophobia. We already share our world with robots, however, and so responsible interactions must take precedence over fear of the other.

Reflections on Technophobia

The robo-dogs of *Metalhead* are, in no uncertain terms, dangerous and deadly. They're visually similar to Boston Dynamics' robo-dogs, but *they're* not the ones that are being kicked around! Rather, the robo-dogs are doing the kicking! Ethical reflection here gives way to visceral technophobia. At this breakdown of human-robot relations, we begin to entertain a simplified binary of good versus bad. It's humans versus robots!

In our world, though, robo-dogs are still learning to open doors and killer robots are only killing dangerous fish. Debates are happening about human values and the future is still up for grabs.

Is there any technologically and philosophically possible way to find compassion *alongside* robots? What would it take? Although *Metalhead* is vague on how to accomplish this, anthropomorphism, empathy, and the application of human ethics are all possible strategies. Robots will challenge our ethical frameworks and our moral assumptions, of course, which makes all of these strategies difficult or flawed in various ways. But the biggest danger of all, as *Metalhead* shows us, would be failing to learn to live alongside our future robot counterparts and one another.

Notes

1. Martin Ford, *Rise of the Robots: Technology and the Threat of a Jobless Future* (New York: Basic Books, 2015).
2. James Hibberd, "*Black Mirror* creator explains that *Metalhead* robot nightmare," *Entertainment Weekly*, https://ew.com/tv/2017/12/29/black-mirror-metalhead-interview/ (Accessed 5 July 2019).
3. Charlie Brooker and Annabel Jones with Jason Arnopp, *Inside Black Mirror* (New York: Crown Archetype, 2018), 284–293.
4. For more on such campaigns, see https://www.stopkillerrobots.org.

5. Daniel Dinello, *Technophobia! Science Fiction Visions of Posthuman Technology* (Austin, TX: University of Texas Press, 2005), 2 (order changed; my emphasis).

6. Maria Deutscher, "DeepMind 'closes chapter' in AI research with new self-learning AlphaZero system," *Silicon Angle*, https://siliconangle.com/2018/12/07/deepmind-closes-chapter-ai-research-new-self-learning-alphazero-system/ (Accessed 5 July 2019).

7. Psychologist Abraham Maslow in 1943 talked about a ranking of needs that humans have to fulfill in order to survive. Physiological needs, such as air, water, food, are the most important and thus are at the foundation of the hierarchy. Other needs such as sociality and love are ranked as comparatively less important.

8. Tim Surette, "*Black Mirror*'s '*Metalhead* almost had a different ending," *TV Guide*, https://www.tvguide.com/news/black-mirror-metalhead-ending-david-slade/ (Accessed 5 July 2019).

9. Aimee Ortiz, "Terrifying Boston Dynamics robots, *Black Mirror*, and the end of the world," *Boston Globe*, https://www.bostonglobe.com/arts/2018/01/05/boston-dynamics-black-mirror-and-end-world/cL9RYkg6O6MqyPuhmgxVjP/story.html (Accessed 5 July 2019).

10. David Ryan Polgar, "Is it unethical to design robots to resemble humans?" *Quartz*, https://qz.com/1010828/is-it-unethical-to-design-robots-to-resemble-humans (Accessed 5 July 2019).

11. Jason G. Goldman, "Animating anthropomorphism: Giving minds to geometric shapes [video]," *Scientific American*, https://blogs.scientificamerican.com/thoughtful-animal/animating-anthropomorphism-giving-minds-to-geometric-shapes-video/ (Accessed 5 July 2019).

12. For more on whether machines actually could be conscious one day, see Chapter 21 (David Gamez's chapter on conscious technology) in this volume.

13. Bruno Latour, *Pandora's Hope: Essays on the Reality of Science Studies* (Cambridge, MA: Harvard University Press, 1999).

14. Isaac Asimov, *I, Robot* (London: Harper Voyager, 2013 [1950]).

15. Wendell Wallace and Colin Allen, *Moral Machines: Teaching Robots Right from Wrong* (Oxford: Oxford University Press, 2009), 96–97.

16. John Searle's "Chinese room" experiment potentially helps demonstrate why. See "Minds, brains and programs," *Behavioral and Brain Sciences*, 3(1980), 417–457.

17. See Select Committee on Artificial Intelligence, "AI in the UK: Ready, willing and able?" (House of Lords, April 16, 2018), https://publications.parliament.uk/pa/ld201719/ldselect/ldai/100/100.pdf (Accessed 5 July 2019). See also, Committee on Legal Affairs, "Report with Recommendations to the Commission on Civil Law Rules on Robotics." (European Parliament, January 27, 2017), http://www.europarl.europa.eu/doceo/document/A-8-2017-0005_EN.html (Accessed 5 July 2019).

18. Noel Sharkey, "Killing made easy: From joysticks to politics," in Patrick Lin, Keith Abney, and George Bekey eds., *Robot Ethics: The Ethical and Social Implications of Robotics*, (London: MIT Press, 2014), 117.

19. Morgan Jeffery, "Here's how *Black Mirror*'s *Metalhead* was almost totally different," *Digital Spy*, http://www.digitalspy.com/tv/black-mirror/feature/a846773/black-mirror-metalhead-explained/ (Accessed 5 July 2019).

20. Steve Greene, "*Black Mirror: Metalhead* director David Slade on the influences behind the season's most terrifying episode." *IndieWire*, https://www.indiewire.com/2018/01/black-mirror-metalhead-director-david-slade-robot-dog-interview-1201912565/ (Accessed 5 July 2019).

21. Aimee van Wynsberghe and Justin Donhauser, "The dawning of the ethics of environmental robots," Science and Engineering Ethics, 24 (2017), 1787.

22. For more on this, see https://wyss.harvard.edu/technology/programmable-robot-swarms/.

19

Black Museum and Righting Wrongs
Should We Seek Revenge?

Gregory L. Bock, Jeffrey L. Bock, and Kora Smith

How'd I do, Mom? All good?

(Nish)

In a bleak desert setting, the dulcet tones of Dionne Warwick wash across the Nevada wilderness as our heroine, Nish, drives her solar-powered car along twisting roads and sun-bleached vistas on her way to the Black Museum. "There is always something there to remind me," the velvet-voiced singer foreshadows. There is always something there to remind us of the wrongs of the past.

Intercut with stories about how Rolo Haynes, the proprietor of the museum, got his start in the world of pain and suffering, a story of revenge bleeds through this tale of dread. Thanks to his stint at Saint Juniper's, Rolo is now left with the role of carnival barker to the morbidly curious seekers of the macabre. Peter Dawson's sympathic diagnoser gathers dust, Carrie's transplanted consciousness sits idly by ("monkey needs a hug"), and other relics of woe and dread line cabinets of curiosities.[1]

After a bit of self-aggrandizement, Rolo takes Nish to the main attraction of the museum. In the back, behind the velvet curtain, lies the caged, tragic hologram of Clayton Leigh, weather-girl killer. But there's something Rolo doesn't know: Clayton is her father, and Nish is there to get revenge for the digital imprisonment and torture of her father, who has been forced to repeatedly relive his execution in ten-second bursts for the pleasure of sadistic visitors. Think of the exhibit as a life-size replication of the Saw movie franchise, torture porn in its purest form, made complete with fun-size pendant Tamagotchi keepsakes of Clayton's suffering, recurring forever.

Nish poisons Rolo with a bottle of water, attaches a brain scanning device to his head, and downloads his digital self into her father's torture

Black Mirror and Philosophy: Dark Reflections, First Edition. Edited by David Kyle Johnson.
© 2020 John Wiley & Sons, Inc. Published 2020 by John Wiley & Sons, Inc.

chamber. Now Rolo is sharing a ride on Old Sparky with his former victim. Only this time, his ride won't be limited to ten seconds. Clayton disappears, and out pops a pendant of Rolo's electrocution. Nish drives off into the Nevada sunset with Rolo screaming eternally from her rearview mirror.

Most viewers of *Black Museum* likely celebrate, thinking that Rolo got what he deserved. But is revenge really ever justified? Is an act of vengeance an act of justice? Let's examine the philosophy of anger and forgiveness, as well as some Christian and Buddhist teachings, to determine whether Nish's quest for revenge is something we should celebrate.

The Path of Payback

We might initially think that Rolo got what he deserved and thus Nish's action made it a "great day for justice." But there is something disturbing about Nish's actions, something disconcerting about causing anyone – evil or not – to live through that kind of pain over and over. Contemporary philosopher, and author of *Anger and Forgiveness*, Martha Nussbaum would agree.[2] Nussbaum argues that, although anger and desire to see the wrongdoer suffer is a natural response to wrongdoing, it's morally problematic because it too often leads down the road of payback. The road of payback, she says, is the road of revenge – of taking punishment into one's own hands. And revenge is problematic for two reasons.

First, it's immoral; revenge promotes the feeling of pleasure at seeing others suffer. This is sadism at its worst, something that we rightly condemn when we see it in both Rolo and Peter. Second, it's "magical thinking." Revenge is irrational. It's nonsensical to think that inflicting harm on an offender makes the situation any better. Now instead of just one injured party, there are two, and neither is better off. Of course, one might respond by suggesting that revenge does make the situation better: it brings the perpetrator to justice, giving them what they deserve. But according to Nussbaum, in a civilized society like ours, it's the state that should take up matters of criminal justice. This not only helps ensure that an appropriate punishment will be given but also allows us to focus on rebuilding our lives. "[I]f some stranger from Sparta has hacked up your father [or tortured his digital self], there is no need to try to work out an appropriate future relationship with him. What you had better do is to mourn your father and turn the prosecution of the murderer over to the state."[3]

Instead of revenge, Nussbaum argues that wronged parties should focus on what she calls "Transition Anger," redirecting one's anger away from the wrongdoer toward positive ends, channeling the energy produced by the wrong in a transformative way toward something that is socially constructive. Someone experiencing the transition might be inspired to write to her state representatives, raise public awareness, or start a victims advocacy group. Nish's mother, for example, organized protests in response to Clayton's unjust treatment. Unfortunately, as Nish explains to the poisoned Rolo, her mother's campaign lost momentum when the other protesters "got bored after a while…and moved on to the next viral miscarriage of justice." Apparently this is why Nish didn't follow in her mother's footsteps; she grew impatient with the slow-moving wheels of justice and gave in to her thirst for revenge. But, according to Nussbaum, what Nish should have done is focus her transition anger in another way – perhaps, trying to change the law.

Nussbaum also considers forgiveness as a response to anger, and she distinguishes three types. The first is transactional forgiveness, a type of exchange that demands the wrongdoer satisfy certain conditions before receiving forgiveness, such as confession, contrition, or apology. Until the wrongdoer satisfies these conditions, forgiveness is withheld. Should Nish have sought this instead of revenge? Well, it's unclear whether Rolo would have ever satisfied such conditions. If Nish allowed him to live longer, she might have been able to force an apology out of him; then again, it's easy to doubt the sincerity of an apology produced under coercion. Regardless, Nussbaum thinks that putting conditions on forgiveness is problematic because it is entangled with ideas of payback, withholding something, or using pain to motivate repentance. Indeed, she criticizes this, calling it "moral sadism."

The second form of forgiveness – unconditional forgiveness – does away with conditions and freely offers forgiveness to the wrongdoer, whether or not he has apologized. On this view, the victim and her family may still feel anger toward the perpetrator, but they work to overcome their hostility and, at minimum, treat him humanely. For Nish, this would mean committing to letting go of her anger toward Rolo and treating him as somebody worthy of respect – which would rule out murdering him or hanging his screaming digital self from her mirror as a keepsake. This kind of forgiveness is compatible with transition anger, with seeking to shut down the museum and making sure Rolo ceases his experiments. This could even include Nish working with law enforcement to prosecute him in order to protect others. But Nish would have to learn to let go of her resentment toward Rolo himself.

For Nussbaum, unconditional forgiveness is morally preferable to transactional forgiveness. But best of all is the third type of forgiveness: unconditional love and generosity. Why? Because transactional forgiveness is still focused backward – it is still entangled with the negative aspects of anger and doesn't provide the necessary material to help the injured parties move forward in a positive manner. Unconditional love and generosity, on the other hand, skip the anger stage altogether and move directly to reconciliation.

To illustrate the concept, Nussbaum uses the parable of the prodigal son from the Gospel of Luke in the New Testament. In the parable, a rebellious son leaves home with his inheritance and squanders it in the pursuit of worldly pleasures. Once he runs out of money, he sheepishly returns home, hoping for enough good will from his father to work for him as a servant. Instead, and without the slightest sign of anger, his father runs out to greet him when he is still coming down the road. He embraces his son, clothes him, and throws a lavish party for him. This paints a picture of a father (God the Father) who treats his children, even a wayward child, with an enduring and overwhelming love. For Nussbaum, this story presents us with the possibility of human relationships devoid of judgment, resentment, and *us versus them* language – of relationships based on love, compassion, and kindness. It is difficult to imagine Nish, or anyone else, responding to such an atrocious thing being done to her father in a loving and generous way. Yet, if Nussbaum is right, this would be the most morally praiseworthy response.

The Path of Christian Love

Similar approaches to forgiveness can be found throughout Christian scripture. In Matthew (22:34–40), for example, Jesus says the greatest commandment is to love God and one's neighbor, which means to love (*agapē* or *agapaō*) everyone. To illustrate this kind of love in Luke (10:30–37), Jesus tells the parable of the good Samaritan. A man traveling from Jerusalem is attacked by robbers and is severely beaten and left to die. A couple of travelers pass by and do nothing, but a Samaritan, whose people are ostracized by the Jews (the likely ethnicity of the beaten man), stops, tends his wounds, and takes him to an inn for treatment. Jesus says the Samaritan acts like a neighbor to the victim, and this is how Jesus's followers should act.

In the Gospel of Matthew Jesus says, "Love [*Agapaō*] your enemies and pray for those who persecute you, that you may be sons of your Father in heaven" (5:44–45; see also Luke 7:35). God loves the whole world (John 3:16) and everyone in it, so much so that the New Testament declares that he sent his son to die for the sins of all human beings (Luke 6:35, John 3:16, Ephesians 2:4), who are considered God's enemies in their rebellion. For this reason, Christians are called to demonstrate that they are truly children of God by loving *their* enemies, as God does his. As Paul says in Romans, "Be imitators of God, therefore, as dearly loved children and live a life of love, just as Christ loved us and gave himself up for us as a fragrant offering and sacrifice to God" (5:1–2).

In order to demonstrate this kind of self-sacrifice for one's enemies, one must first overcome resentment. This is Christian forgiveness: a commitment not to hold the wrong against the wrongdoer and a commitment to think and feel about him the way God does – as a sinful but redeemable human being made in God's image. Skipping forgiveness altogether and moving directly to love and generosity, as Nussbaum argues, might be what a perfectly loving God does for sinful humanity, but arguably this isn't easy (or possible) for sinful human beings to accomplish. Forgiveness is a process and a difficult struggle, but it's one to which Jesus calls his followers. In Matthew 18:21–22, Peter asks Jesus how many times he must forgive someone who wrongs him. One can imagine Peter's surprised exasperation at Jesus's reply: "Not seven times, but seventy-seven times."

Based on what the New Testament teaches about loving one's enemies, what's the application for Nish's situation? *Agapē* certainly rules out acts of revenge, right? If this isn't already clear, Paul says so directly in Romans 12:17–21: "Do not repay anyone evil for evil…Do not take revenge, my friends, but leave room for God's wrath, for it is written: 'It is mine to avenge; I will repay,' says the Lord. On the contrary: 'If your enemy is hungry, feed him; if he is thirsty, give him something [non-poisonous!] to drink. In doing this, you will heap burning coals [figuratively speaking] on his head.' Do not be overcome by evil, but overcome evil with good."

Some might point out that the Christian teaching of the wrath of God seems to be in tension with what was said above about the love of God. Much ink has been spilled by theologians over these theological ideas, and we'll relegate comments on this to an endnote.[4] But what's important to note for Nish from the Romans 12 passage is that, as angry as she is, inflicting revenge on Rolo isn't morally permissible on Christian grounds.

The Path of Buddhist Compassion

If we examine the teachings of Buddhism, we find further support for the view that taking revenge on Rolo for his wrongdoings isn't morally justified. Two central ideas are karma and the four noble truths. Karma is a cosmic law of cause and effect. According to Buddhism, all actions produce positive or negative consequences (or both), based on the intention underlying the action, the action itself, and the immediate effects of the action.

The first of the four noble truths of Buddhism is that life is *dukkha* (or suffering, trouble, and conflict). This truth doesn't deny that life is also filled with positive experiences and relationships. However, even a moment of happiness is also a moment of suffering because the moment is fleeting – no experience of happiness can last, an example of the Buddhist idea that everything is impermanent. In addition, even when we're happy, we can still wish for the happiness to be more intense or wish for a satisfying experience to be even more satisfying.

According to the Buddhist doctrine of emptiness, no binary concepts, such as right and left or up and down, are absolute. So even happy moments aren't fully or completely happy, and they aren't essentially happy. This is evident in Carrie's yearning for more interaction with Parker. Even when she's enjoying seeing Parker and getting a hug from him, she's still dissatisfied because she can't express herself directly, and significant limitations exist in merely being a passenger. In addition, she still wants to see more of his development and maturation; she isn't satisfied with simply witnessing some of his childhood.

Peter's addiction to pain also helps illustrate some Buddhist concepts. He is frustrated with the impermanence and the intensity of his experiences, so he seeks additional experiences and ones with greater intensity. The doctrine of emptiness also helps explain Peter's addiction to pain. Although we normally think of having cancer, a heart attack, or a tooth being pulled as experiences we want to avoid, Peter enjoys them.

The second noble truth is that the cause of *dukkha*/suffering is desire. The solution isn't to become completely unattached by having no desires or even preferences for any kinds of sensations and no concern for others or the world at large. Rather, the solution is non-attachment in the sense that one is still actively engaged with one's projects and relationships but doesn't get trapped by cravings. So, from a Buddhist perspective, Peter's problem isn't that he likes pain or negative sensations *per se*. Rather, the cause of his suffering is his strong attachment to sensations. Likewise, Carrie is attached to Parker, while Nish and her mother Angelica are attached to getting revenge for Clayton Leigh's suffering at Rolo's hands.

At first, it might seem that Nish and Angelica are justified in seeking revenge. After all, Rolo is responsible for the intense *dukkha*/suffering of Clayton (or, at least, a digital copy of him).[5] Seen from this perspective, Nish and Angelica don't suffer as a result of wanting revenge. Instead, they suffer because Clayton is suffering. They seem to think that their act of revenge will bring them peace and relieve Clayton of his perpetual torments. On this view, Rolo's karma has simply caught up with him.

Their vengeance still isn't justified, however. Negative karma is produced by both greedy and hateful intentions, but more bad karma is produced by hateful intentions than merely greedy ones. Thus, although Rolo has produced a vast amount of bad karma by encouraging tourists to deliver countless, nearly lethal electrocutions and then making additional keychain souvenirs, note that Rolo was motivated far more by greed than hatred. In contrast, Nish and Angelica are motivated by hatred. Thus, they are unwittingly producing their own *dukkha*/suffering and creating bad karma by punishing Rolo.

Hatred, greed, and delusion are considered to be the three *kleshas* or psychological poisons or vices, according to Buddhism. These *kleshas* produce attachment and thus *dukkha*/suffering. Delusion plays a key role for Nish and Angelica because it's the mistaken belief in selves, as well as a belief in essences and permanence generally, that leads to, and reinforces, attachment. Thus, it's because Nish and Angelica see themselves and Clayton as Rolo's victims and Rolo as the perpetrator that they think revenge is justified.

However, from a Buddhist perspective, there are complex causal interrelations between all things, and no one is fundamentally a victim or perpetrator. At this more fundamental level, we should see ourselves and others not as persons but as patterns of physical and psychological traits that are deeply connected and related to other physical and psychological traits. Given the four noble truths of Buddhism, the appropriate attitude to take towards all sentient beings is compassion. This fits well with Nussbaum's view of unconditional love and kindness and with the Christian view of *agapē*. In this context, a compassionate response would be one in which Nish and Angelica free Clayton without killing Rolo, causing his rebirth, and forcing the reborn Rolo to experience the pain of electrocution indefinitely.

Moreover, if what we call "Nish" and "Rolo" are fundamentally just temporary collections of experiences, how can privileging one set of experiences over the other or increasing the suffering of one set of experiences be justified? The Buddhist answer is that Nish isn't justified in privileging her desires for revenge over Rolo's well-being and that seeking to increase *dukkha*/suffering isn't justified either. This isn't to say that punishment is never justified from a Buddhist ethical perspective. Rather, the punishment must be aimed at reducing *dukkha*/suffering and promoting the well-being of everyone, including the perpetrator. Punishment can promote the well-being of the perpetrator when it prevents that person from creating more negative karma and when it promotes non-attachment. Along these lines, what Rolo really deserves is compassionate forgiveness and rehabilitation since he's already suffering and has been producing bad karma.

It might seem as though Nish, as a daughter, and Angelica, as a wife, ought to be more concerned with Clayton's well-being than Rolo's – but not according to the doctrines of rebirth and causal interdependence. Given a nearly endless cycle of death and rebirth, and interconnections between all things, we should be just as concerned with a stranger or putative enemy as with our parent or our spouse. That is because everyone, at some point in the past cycle of rebirth (or in the future cycle), has been (or will be) our parent or spouse or child. Thus, it is not disloyal to Clayton to express forgiveness to Rolo.

Happily, Ever After?

Despite the arguments above, one might think that (although it is not praiseworthy) revenge could at least be morally permissible because it can accomplish the good of justice. And in his chapter "Revenge and Mercy in Tarantino: The Lesson of Ezekiel 25:17" David Kyle Johnson (yes, this book's editor) makes just such an argument.[6] He begins by distinguishing between retribution and revenge. Retribution is a penalty that "is inflicted for a reason (a wrong or injury) with the desire that the [offender] know why this is occurring and know that he was intended to know," whereas revenge encompasses these features but can only be inflicted by the wronged party and is inflicted due to a "desire to see the offender suffer" (regardless of rehabilitation or other positive consequences).[7] Moreover, the punishment can be as harsh as the wronged party deems appropriate. Most certainly, Nish's treatment of Rolo fits both definitions.

Johnson agrees that "we have a moral obligation not to harm people who have not wronged us," but argues that when someone wrongs us, we are released from this obligation and thus are "morally permitted to seek revenge."[8] While the principle he cites is plausible, and it's true that it doesn't ban harming offenders, harming someone can be quite different from taking revenge on that person. From the fact that someone has harmed you, it doesn't follow that you are permitted to inflict any harms on them you wish. Indeed, if vengeance is supposedly justified in the name of justice, only harms that served justice would be permissible.

Johnson agrees with this, saying that acts of revenge can only be justified when "the inflicted punishment reflects the original crime."[9] This makes his view much more plausible, but he still mistakenly thinks that emotional factors of vengeance are relevant to its justification and wrongly assumes that justice demands punishment for wrongdoers. As we have argued, what it demands instead is forgiveness and compassion. On Nussbaum's account, payback is both irrational and immoral. In addition, Christianity teaches that we ought to love our enemies and "leave room for God's wrath." Meanwhile, Buddhism teaches that we ought to have compassion for those who suffer, both the wronged and wrongdoer, because karma is inevitable. Thus, Nish and Angelica's act of revenge – and revenge generally – isn't morally justified.

Black Museum seems to end on a happy note because Nish and Angelica, as her passenger, seem to be satisfied that justice has been served and that Clayton is no longer suffering. Yet in taking their revenge on Rolo, Nish and Angelica have – however unwittingly – fallen into the same trap as the tourists flocking to zap Clayton's hologram. We aren't told specifically how the bad karma they produced will increase their *dukkha*/suffering, but we learned from Jack and Carrie's experiences that to be or to have a passenger is to suffer. With their mission of revenge accomplished, perhaps Nish and Angelica will live happily ever after. But this seems like a rather naïve prediction, both within the world of *Black Mirror* and within the frameworks supplied by Nussbaum, Christianity, and Buddhism.

Notes

1. Interestingly, the symphatic diagnoser story is based on a hallucination that magician Penn Jillette had while suffering from a high fever and a lot of pain

in Barcelona in 1981. No one in the hospital spoke English, Penn wished for a device that the doctors could use to feel his pain and diagnosis his condition, and then hallucinated a story in which a doctor become addicted to one. He wrote a short story, "The Pain Addict," based on the hallucination, but no one was willing to publish or tell the story until Penn pitched it to Charlie Brooker one day over lunch. What's more, the "carnival barker" museum director Rolo Haynes is actually based on Penn Jillette, who used to be a carnival barker himself. See Charlie Brooker and Annabel Jones with Jason Arnopp, *Inside Black Mirror* (New York: Crown Archetype, 2018), 296–298. See also Stephanie Dube Dwilson, "*Black Mirror*: All About Penn Jillette's Pain Addict," *Heavy*, https://heavy.com/entertainment/2017/12/penn-jilette-pain-addict-black-mirror-museum-buy/ (Accessed 5 July 2019).

2. Martha Nussbaum, *Anger and Forgiveness* (New York:, Oxford University Press, 2016).

3. Ibid., 141.

4. God's love doesn't have to be inconsistent with his wrath any more than it is inconsistent for loving parents to be angry at their children when they harm themselves or others. In *The Crucifixion: Understanding the Death of Jesus Christ* (Grand Rapids, MI:, Eerdmans, 2015), Fleming Rutledge says, "The divine hostility, or wrath of God, has always been an aspect of his love. It is not separate from God's love, it is not opposite to God's love, it is not something in God that had to be overcome." (232) She quotes Bruce L. McCormack, who says, "God's love turns to wrath when it is resisted, but not for a minute does it cease to be love even when it expresses itself as wrath." (232) God wants what is best for us, and we often resist this, courting God's anger. Using Nussbaum's categories, this kind of anger would be classified as a type of forward-looking Transition Anger and may represent a different theological position from her interpretation of the parable of the prodigal son.

5. For more on whether the digital copy of Clayton would be, numerically, the same person as Clayton himself, see Chapter 22 (Molly Gardner and Robert Slone's chapter on personal identity) in this volume.

6. See Richard Greene and K. Silem Mohammad, *Quentin Tarantino and Philosophy: How to Philosophize with a pair of Pliers and a Blowtorch* (Peru, IL: Open Court. 2007), 55–74.

7. Ibid., 56–57.

8. Ibid., 70.

9. Ibid., 71.

BANDERSNATCH

Bandersnatch

A Choose-Your-Own Philosophical Adventure

Chris Lay and David Kyle Johnson

People think there's one reality, but there's loads of them all snaking off like roots …

(Colin Ritman)

Bandersnatch is arguably the most unique and creative episode of the *Black Mirror* series. Told as a "choose your own adventure" story that can only be viewed on the Netflix platform, it tells the tale of Stefan Butler, a nineteen-year-old software developer in 1984. He has an idea for a choose your own adventure video game called *Bandersnatch*, based on a choose your own adventure book titled *Bandersnatch* by Jerome F. Davies. Stefan sells the idea to the software company Tuckersoft and owner Mohan Thakur plans it for a Christmas release. But when his submission deadline approaches, Stefan is unable to finish his game because he's come to believe that his actions are being controlled by outside forces. In one version of the story, the outside force is a shady government Program and Control Study (PACS); in another, it's a bizarre demon named Pax. In one iteration, you the viewer reveal to Stefan that you are controlling him via the Netflix app. In any event, he figures he has no free will – and if he has no free will then "why not commit murder? Maybe that's what destiny wants." In more than one ending, he kills his father (and sometimes others), only to end up in jail carving the dreaded "White Bear" glyph ♣ on his cell wall, over and over again – a symbol that we're told stands for "multiple fates, potential realities splitting in two." This symbol is how both Stefan and Davies represented the choices that they presented in their choose your adventure works.

Of course, that doesn't even begin summarize this unique episode.[1] When combined with more than five hours of footage that one could watch by choosing different paths and arriving at different endings, the plot and approach of this episode raise more philosophical questions than we can count – certainly more than we could cover in one typical chapter. Are we being controlled by outside forces? Do we have free will? Are we

Black Mirror and Philosophy: Dark Reflections, First Edition. Edited by David Kyle Johnson.
© 2020 John Wiley & Sons, Inc. Published 2020 by John Wiley & Sons, Inc.

living in multiple realities? Do we live in a computer simulation? Is time travel possible? How much choice do we actually want to have in our narratives? Can making art give us freedom? Is *Bandersnatch* real? To handle all these questions, we've decided to let you choose what philosophical adventure to take through *Bandersnatch*.

So, here's your first choice. Choose whichever option best represents the worry that *Bandersnatch* arises in your mind. But you'd better decide carefully – as in *Bandersnatch,* choices in this chapter come with consequences ...

- "I'm worried I might be the subject of a Program and Control Study" (Go to page 201.)
- "I'm worried I have a goateed evil twin in another reality" (Go to page 206.)

"You know what "PAC" stands for?
P.A.C. ... program and control man."

The most obvious philosophical worry raised by *Bandersnatch* is the worry that we lack free will. Jerome F. Davies, the author of the book on which Stefan bases his game, believed that "his wife was spiking him with psychiatric drugs at the behest of a demon called Pax," and Stefan comes to believe something similar about his father. In one version of the story, he turns out to be right. Stefan is a subject of a government program called P.A.C.S. Colin is right. "The government watches people. They pay people to pretend to be your relatives. And they put drugs in your food. And they film you."

Edward Snowden taught us that the government was "monitoring" us more than we realized, but it's not listening to everyone's phone calls.[2] It's not drugging you and the idea that the government controls you in the way Colin suspects is rooted in baseless conspiracy theory thinking which is easily debunked.[3] What's genuinely possible is Colin's other worry: "It's the spirit out there that's connected to our world that decides what we do, and we just have to go along for the ride."

Now we're not suggesting that you are actually, like Stefan, a character in a computer game, and that some higher being is making your choices for you. That's crazy! (Or is it?)[4] But your assumption that the choices you make are actually within your control – that what you do is determined by conscious decisions that you make – is very possibly false. Why?

It started in the 1960s, when Hans Helmut Kornhuber and Lüder Deecke discovered what they called a "readiness potential." When measuring brain activity during decision-making, they saw previous activity in unconscious parts of the brain that have nothing to do with conscious decision-making. In the 1980s, Benjamin Libet confirmed that the readiness potential occurs at least 0.35 seconds before the decision is consciously made. Later, neuroscientist John-Dylan Haynes found that unconscious activity that leads to decisions occurs *seconds* before conscious decision-making, and Itzhak Fried was actually able to monitor unconscious parts of people's brains and predict their decisions (before they were consciously made) with 80–90% accuracy.[5]

This research aligns with what the neuroscientist Joseph LeDoux tells us in his book *The Emotional Brain*: our emotions control most of our actions.[6] Our emotions arise from an unconscious part of our brain called the limbic system, and when it wants us to do something, it sends signals up to our conscious prefrontal cortex to "demand" the action it desires be done. Technically, the cortex can "override" it by sending inhibitory signals back down towards the limbic system, but the inhibitory signals that run down from the cortex are not nearly as strong as those running up from the limbic system.

The picture that neuroscience paints for us regarding how decision occurs shows that all the real work is done by unconscious parts of your brain. That's what controls you. The conscious parts of your brain are just "along for the ride." They receive notification that a decision has been made and then create for you the experience of consciously making a decision. And just like Stefan does after he chooses to reject Mohan's offer to work in the office, the prefrontal cortex has to "justify it." It comes up with an ad hoc explanation for why the decision was made. In other words, as Colin puts it, "When you make a decision, you think it's you doing it, but it's not." If this is right, it certainly seems that you don't have free will.

- "I'm convinced! I'm being controlled." Start scratching White Bear glyphs on your wall (Go to page 203.)
- "I'm not convinced. I definitely have free will." (Go to page 209.)

"I don't know what that means!"

If it's going to be all over your wall, you need to know more about the White Bear glyph that pops up throughout *Bandersnatch* and what it has to do with free will. Indeed, because it appears occasionally through the series, it could also tell us something about *Black Mirror* as a whole.

Structurally, the glyph matches the choice mechanism through which we engage the *Bandersnatch* story. Looked at top-to-bottom, it's a branching path – a set of binary options among which one *must* be chosen. From bottom-to-top, though, the symbol shows two apparently discrete choices merging into a single pathway. Seen this way, the symbol embodies the question of free will at the heart of *Bandersnatch*: how can *your* choices ultimately matter if they end up leading you to in the same place? After all, the version of the game that gets the five-star rating is one where Stefan says he "just went back and stripped loads out. [The player's] got the illusion of free will, but really, I decide the ending."

The symbol also seems to appear when characters feel that an external force is determining their actions. It's a possible choice for us when Stefan angrily demands to know who's controlling him. It became an obsession for Jerome F. Davies, who repeatedly drew it in his wife's blood after decapitating her. And, in one possible ending, it flashes on Pearl Ritman's monitor when she works to finish her remake of Stefan's game.

But why use *this* symbol specifically – a symbol that also featured heavily in *White Bear*? Granted, Charlie Brooker included the glyph in *Bandersnatch* after he noticed it in the middle of a branching flowchart that he and his team had made while developing the episode.[7] But surely, it's more than a cheeky wink and a nod.

Indeed, it is. When we first see it in *White Bear*, we're told the symbol represents a kind of mind control broadcasted to people via their devices that causes them to become passive, mindless observers. Although the "mind control" angle is just part of the elaborate fiction surrounding Victoria's ongoing punishment, the visitors to *White Bear Justice Park* very much become the "passive observers" they are claimed to be – willingly (and gleefully) giving up their agency to join a mob that takes torture as entertainment. As for *Bandersnatch,* the symbol is most closely connected to the path where Stefan emulates Davies – where he hacks off his father's head, and successfully completes his *Bandersnatch* adaptation, which is praised as a masterpiece of game design. This path explicitly requires the viewer/player to choose the symbol when Stefan asks who's in control.

All of this suggests that the symbol is tied to surrendering one's agency and actively accepting external control.[8] It's not just a loss of control; the subject also *assents* to it. This notion is historically associated with a group of ancient philosophers called the Stoics. They argued that although events are determined externally, we can nonetheless control how we emotionally respond to them. To the Stoics, since we have no control over whether or not some event comes to pass – just as Stefan has no control over whether he eats Sugar Puffs or Frosties – the only appropriate response is *assent* to what occurs.[9] Perhaps this explains why the only ending where Stefan actually finishes his game is the one where he stops fighting against external control and instead embraces it. And it seems fitting that, in that ending, *we* make the decision to assent on Stefan's behalf by telling him that ⌐ is in charge.

⌐

- "The thought that I don't have free will is now driving me crazy!" (Go to page 209.)
- "Philosophy is too hard." Throw tea over book. (Go to page 205.)

"Sorry, mate. Wrong path."

Oh. This is awkward. What you are doing here? This page isn't even finished; we honestly didn't think anyone would come here. You're reading a book called *Black Mirror and Philosophy* – why are you picking a choice that gives up on philosophy? You should be ashamed of yourself! You're worse than all of those people who made Stefan take a cubicle at Tuckersoft and finish *Bandersnatch* by committee. Sell outs. Everyone knows that trying to get a singular creative vision out of a group of people with conflicting goals is going to bomb spectacularly, just like Stefan's game did on that particular path. Don't you know that a camel is just a horse that was designed by a committee? No one wants to ride a lumpy horse!

Wait, what do you mean this book was written as a collaboration between multiple authors? Well that doesn't seem very smart, does it? Now look what you've done. You've undermined the credibility of the authors and retroactively called into question the merits of the entire book! You're a bad person and you should feel bad. Like all of those "soft" endings where Stefan jumps off a balcony, douses the computer in tea, or decides to take his meds and just chill out, you've wandered down the wrong path and into a dead-end devoid of philosophical substance. So, good job, you. It can't end here: you should try again.

⊓

- "I should have chosen to read about whether we have free will." (Go to page 209.)
- "I should have chosen to read about whether we live in a multiverse." (Go to page 206.)

"We exist within multiple parallel realities at once."

According to the documentary that Colin gave to Stefan, this section's title quote was what Jerome F. Davies said to police after he was arrested for murdering his wife and scrawling the White Bear glyph all over his walls with her blood. "[There's] one reality for each possible course of action we might take in life," the narrator of the documentary clarifies. "Whatever we choose to do in this reality, there's another reality where we choose to do something else." Science fiction author Philip K. Dick wrote about this kind of thing. Colin even has a poster of Dick's novel *Ubik* on his wall. And apparently Dick believed that it was actually true.[10] But could it be?

The existence of what philosophers and scientists call "a multiverse," a collection of universes stacked together in a higher dimensional plane, is certainly possible. Relativity suggests that our universe exists as a four-dimensional omnitemporal block, where the past, present, and future, all exist as one.[11] And it's possible other such universes might exist alongside it, in a fifth-dimensional "bulk," that's also called "hyperspace."[12] If that's true, some of those universes might be like ours and contain people like us that made different decisions.

But is there any reason to think it's actually true that, for every decision I could've made, there's a universe in which I did? Indeed, there is. But there are a few things you need to know about to understand why. First, quantum mechanics suggests that, while we can force a quantum event *to* happen by making a measurement, we cannot control which specific quantum event happens as a result. Take spin, for example, a property of electrons. We can cause an electron to take on *a spin* by forcing it to go through (what's called) a Stern-Gerlach device (SGD), but we cannot control which spin (up or down) it takes on.[13] According to quantum mechanics, that happens randomly and without cause.

Now, when they first hear this, many people think it can't be true. "Such events can't *not have a cause*," they say. "We might not *know* what causes them, but they must have one." Indeed, Albert Einstein famously rejected the idea of quantum randomness by saying "God does not play dice with the universe."[14] He insisted specifically that an electron must have a "hidden spin" before it is measured that is merely "revealed" by the electron's interaction with the SGD. But in an experiment to prove Einstein right, scientist John Stewart Bell actually proved him wrong. The outcome of his experiment was inconsistent with particles having spin all along; the frequency of how often they took on the spins they took on could only be explained by them taking on their specific spin, randomly, as they went through the device.[15] So, it's not that we haven't found the cause for why quantum events happen as they do; we've actually proven that such things *can't have* a cause.

The second thing you need to know about is "the measurement problem." When an electron takes on a spin, for example, it's not merely a result of its interaction with the SGD. We have to actually take the measurement; we must observe or make ourselves aware of what spin the electron takes on. If we don't, the electron takes on no spin at all. Send electrons through a series of three SGDs, for example, but do nothing to determine what spin they take on while going through the second device, and they'll exit the third device as if they took on no spin at all (while going through the second device).[16] How our observations can play this kind of role in the occurrence of quantum events is a mystery that still puzzles scientists and philosophers to this day.

One possible solution was proposed by scientist Hugh Everett. Before an observation is made, the election will be in what's called a "superposition." Its "wave function" will describe it as having two contradictory properties: being spin up and being spin down. Traditionally, we've thought that taking a measurement "forces" the wave function to collapse, so that it takes on one specific property. But Everett wondered: what if, instead, our observation of the wave function forces *us* to become a part of *it*? Our observation puts *us* in a superposition, so that *we* have two contradictory properties at once: observing the electron as spin up and also observing it as spin down. If so, Everett argues, the best way to describe what the measurement of quantum phenomena does is this: it splits the universe in two. When I measure a quantum state, there's an alternate universe for every result that that measurement could have generated – one where I measured it doing this and another where I measured it doing that.[17]

If Everett is right, this wouldn't only happen when we are making measurements. Anytime a quantum event happens, our universe would be splitting in two. As Bryce DeWitt later clarified the view, "every quantum transition taking place on every star, in every galaxy, in every remote corner of the universe is splitting our local world into myriads of copies of itself."[18] And it's for this reason that there could be a universe for every choice that we could've made.

When making a tough decision, we always feel like the outcome of our decision could go either way. I really could do either this or that. But our decisions are determined by our brain activity, and our brain is a physical system, governed by the laws of physics. The only way that there really could be alternate possibilities is if the outcome of our brain activity somehow boils down to quantum events happening within it. *If the wave function collapses this way, I'll do X, and if it collapses that way, I'll do Y.* Since we can't control how wave functions collapse – remember that they're random – such decisions would not be free. But if quantum events fracture our universe in two, then there's a universe in which I do X, and a universe I which I do Y. And this is true for every decision I make.

So, on at least one interpretation of quantum mechanics, given certain special assumptions about the brain, there really is "one reality for each possible course of action we might take in life. Whatever we choose to do in this reality, there's another reality where we choose to do something else." And as strange as that might seem, this interpretation of quantum mechanics is the only one that doesn't violate physical laws. To account for the "spooky action at a distance" that happens in quantum mechanics–something that Einstein famously didn't like either – other interpretations require signals between particles that either travel faster than light or backwards in time.[19]

- "Backwards in Time? What's wrong with that? Isn't time travel possible?" (Go to page 226.)
- "If there's a world for every decision I could've made, am I morally responsible for what I do?" (Go to page 218.)

"He thinks he has free will, but really he's trapped in a maze."

Jerome F. Davies and Stefan Butler were driven crazy by the idea they didn't have free will. Depending on how you got to this point in the chapter, the thought might be driving you a little crazy, too. But if you're here because you want that idea debunked ... we're sorry, but you're likely going to be disappointed. You probably don't have free will – at least in the libertarian sense. Libertarians believe that free will requires alternate possibilities. In order to freely choose to do some action X, it must be possible for you to not choose to do X. And very few philosophers, whether they're libertarians or not, believe that such alternate possibilities exist. Why?

Well, for one thing, our actions are dictated by the activity of our brains, and our brains are deterministic systems governed by the laws of physics. Even though the brain isn't completely predictable yet because of its complexity, the outcome of any such system is definite.[20] There's only one possible outcome. Of course, as you might know (depending on how you got to this point in the chapter), there are random quantum events happening in the brain. It is therefore possible that brain processes have more than one possible outcome. But it's actually very unlikely that quantum events make the outcome of a decision process indeterministic. After all, there are quantum events happening in a computer too; but in a large system (like computers and brains) the randomness of quantum events gets "averaged out" and the entire system is still deterministic. Besides, even if quantum events could dictate decisions, those decisions still wouldn't be free. Random decisions are no freer than determined ones.[21] No one can control quantum events.[22]

You might be tempted to suggest that it's not the brain but instead the soul that dictates our decisions. That's where decisions are made: in the non-physical part of us that is not subject to the laws of physics. Our soul is what deliberates, and once a decision is made it reaches out from beyond the physical world to cause our actions. But most philosophers doubt that souls exist because, for example, neuroscience contradicts the idea that they do. Our mentality is not housed in a non-physical substance, it is produced by the brain. That's why brain injuries can cause mental dysfunction, specific brain injuries can hinder specific mental functions, and brain surgeries can fix them. Another problem is "downwards causation." How could something non-physical, like the soul, causally affect something physical, like the body? Not only does the soul have no location (thus it can't be close to your body), but non-physical objects causing physical movement would violate several scientific laws – like conservation of energy.[23]

Fortunately, however, philosophers are a stubborn bunch and aren't willing to give up so easily. Unable to give up on the idea that we have free will, but equally unable to defend the idea that there are alternate possibilities, some philosophers insist that free will never required alternate possibilities in the first place. We can be completely determined to act as we will, but still do so freely. Such philosophers are a particular type of "compatibilist," those who suggest that free will and determinism are compatible. And their suggestions for what does make a decision free come in a few varieties.

Contemporarily philosopher Harry Frankfurt, for example, suggests that your actions are free as long as they originate from your second order wants and desires – that is, your desires about the kind of desires you want to have.[24] A cigarette smoker may not freely choose to smoke their next cigarette, but if they decide not to smoke it, despite the urge, because they have a higher order desire to quit smoking entirely, then Frankfurt would say they are acting freely. Their action arose from a desire to not desire cigarettes anymore, a second order desire. Alternatively, contemporarily philosopher John Martin Fischer suggests that a person acts freely if they take an action as a result of a rational deliberation.[25] If you think about what do to, weigh the options and so forth, and then choose to do something, then you do so freely. And this is true, even if the outcome of that decision process is determined – the mere result of physical processes in your brain. Likewise, contemporarily philosopher Ned Markosian argues that an action is free as long as it is caused by an agent. And this is true even if forces outside of the agent's control also cause the action.[26] So-called double causation, Markosian argues, is not incompatible with free will.

The good news is, on such conceptions of free will, it's pretty easy to defend the idea that you're free.[27] The notions that agents cause their actions, via either rational deliberation or second order desires, seem easy enough to defend. The bad news is, such understandings of free will don't seem all that intuitive. Why?

Well suppose that we built a robot, like AshBot from *Be Right Back*, and programmed it to always act in accordance with its second order desires after a rational deliberation. On the compatibilist definition, it would be free – and thus morally responsible for what it did. But what if we named it BundyBot and gave it a second order desire to be a murderer, and configured its brain such that its rational deliberations always led it to the conclusion that murder should be done? We'd be the ones morally culpable for the murders that would inevitably result, right? Obviously! But on the compatibilist view, we could absolve ourselves of responsibility by pointing out that BundyBot acts of his own free will. "BundyBot does what he does as a result of rational deliberations based on his second order wants and desires." But that's ludicrous! If something else (us!) is responsible for BundyBot second order desires and how his rational deliberations turn out, then that thing is responsible for BundyBot murders. In the same way, if something else is responsible for how those things are in you – like your genes and environment – then you aren't morally responsible either. You're not acting freely.

Despite the philosophical arguments however, you likely can't shake the sense that you are free. If so, you're not alone. When asked whether he thought we were free, Isaac Bashevis Singer (1902–1991) replied: "We must believe in free will – we have no choice." Indeed, we don't. We can't help but believe we are free. And this, itself, is evidence that we aren't.

- "Even if I had free will, I wouldn't have political freedom. The man keeps me down." (Go to page 212.)
- "I'm still not convinced. I absolutely *do* have free will. I can do whatever I want!" (Go to page 216.)

"The perfect game ... magnificent."

When people ask questions like "Am I free?" or "Do I have free will?" they're typically referring to a *Bandersnatch*-like scenario. Their concern is about some external force that strips the individual of his agency and chooses *for* him. But there are other ways in which freedom can be taken away and our actions "determined." One is by means of oppressive systems or institutions, like the totalitarian regime we get a glimpse of in *The Waldo Moment*. Someone born into such a society has an extremely limited range of possible choices. No one pedaling stationary bikes in *15 Million Merits* can just decide to go out and see a movie on a Friday night. Not only does that form of recreation seem to be unavailable in that society, but riders also appear to be compelled by *political authority* to pedal aimlessly for most of the day. So, in these cases, choices are determined by the way a society is structured and the form its institutions of power take.

Historically, one way we've resisted political control is through the production of *art*. But "art" in this sense isn't like what we see in *Black Museum*: the finger paintings of Jack and Carrie's son Parker that are scattered throughout their house. We're instead talking about art in the sense of something that subverts convention and demands to be analyzed and interpreted.

Although it's not the episode's primary focus, there are echoes of the struggle between genuine art and socio-political determinism in *Bandersnatch*. Early in the episode, Mohan Thakur describes his radical (for 1984) idea to streamline game production by turning Tuckersoft into a "hit factory ... like Motown, but for computer games!" The Motown comparison is evocative; it suggests game design by corporation where the principal goal is profit by flooding the market with software. Indeed, accepting Thakur's offer to join the team at Tuckersoft results in the bearded, long-maned Thakur wresting creative control from Stefan. "[T]he first thing we need to do is streamline the project a little. We can't fit a breeze block of a book into 48K." As his intern then arrives with a Lion Bar, Thakur excitedly proclaims "Happy birthday to me!" Thakur is effectively the lion-faced Pax here, the demon in *Bandersnatch* who Stefan said you shouldn't choose to worship because he's the "thief of destiny." By accepting Thakur's offer, Stefan doesn't take his own advice and pays the price. The evident implication is that profit-minded corporate institutions are anathema to both autonomy and art.

On the other side of things, Stefan is certainly positioned as an artist. "The lad's a craftsman," Colin remarks when Stefan says he wants to work alone. "He's a lone woodsman. I'm the same ... [T]eams are fine for things like action titles, but when it's a concept piece, bit of madness is what you need, and that works best when it's one mind." His vision for *Bandersnatch* most assuredly diverges from mainstream culture. And the path in which

Stefan's game turns out the best is the one where Stefan completely rejects societal conventions. He not only refuses to partner with Thakur, but he doesn't dilute the experience by following the "Netflix path" – where Dr. Haynes recommends injecting some "action" so things will have the broader appeal of regular media. Instead, the "perfect" piece of art comes from the unlikeliest source of inspiration: his father's severed head.

But is Stefan's game truly art? Consider the arguments of Theodor Adorno (1903–1969).[28] Adorno was particularly concerned with the constrictive influence of capitalism on the creation of art. To Adorno, capitalist interests are a lot like those of Thakur's Tuckersoft: the only real objective is generating profit. This means that *everything* in a capitalist system must emphasize bringing in more money – and that includes art. The overriding capitalist desire for profit, therefore, turns the creation of art into a kind of industry. And since, just like in all industries, maximizing profit requires increased output, in a capitalist society art just ends up getting mass produced. In this way, art produced in the capitalist system just refers back to the system itself.

We can turn to *Rachel, Jack and Ashley Too* for a quick and ready example. In the episode, symbolic of how many artists must feel, Catherine and her entourage extract original compositions from comatose performer Ashley O's mind and then digitally alter them to meet the expectations of a "pop" audience. In the process of raising the pitch, slowing the tempo, and running the lyrics through a "positivity filter," those profiting most from Ashley's music career both ensure that her songs appeal to the highest possible number of consumers and simultaneously strip the songs of any of the genuine creativity that's supposed to be involved in the production of art in the first place. Like all mass production, efficiency gets priority: Catherine's endgame is complete automatization, from harvesting music from Ashley O's comatose mind to having it performed by the Ashley Eternal hologram. So, the creation of art is distilled down to an entirely for-profit enterprise and carefully managed to generate the most profit it can.

Now, Adorno thinks that *all* art must invariably reflect the society in which it's created, at least a little bit. But, according to Adorno, a capitalist society is different. It reproduces itself with the aim of reproducing capitalist motives (profit) and capitalism itself (so as to lead to *more* profit). But Adorno also thinks that genuine art must transcend the society and systems out of which it is created – by, say, revealing "contradictions" inherent to the system and suggesting that things could be different than they are. But this would seem to make the production of art in a capitalist society especially tricky. How can it ever hint at something more if its very form is made to reproduce itself?

To be clear, Adorno isn't just claiming that to be art, something must be unique or novel. After all, YouTube videos of cats were definitely "unique" at one time, both because of the new technology involved in making and distributing YouTube videos and the content itself: house cats doing silly things. But this didn't make them art. A real object of art must both reveal the contradictions of a system *and* resolve its own contradictions as a product of that system. In other words, for Adorno, to be a work of art, something must not only show us something new and better than the system that produced it, but it must also do so without falling victim to the conventional structures or tropes of the society that produced it.

In a capitalist society, however, this is difficult. Television shows tend to follow expected patterns: they are a certain standard length, they follow storytelling and character development norms, cinematography and editing adhere to accepted styles, and so on. Adorno's point is that delivering a subversive and novel message doesn't truly escape the restrictions of a system like capitalism if it still clings to "industry standards" in the way the message is structured. Such standards impose a specific *way of thinking* on us and prevent us from interpreting a given piece of media freely. For Adorno, these strict terms mean that very little in a capitalist society qualifies as art.

If *Bandersnatch* actually does try to even minimally engage with the question of producing art in a "hit factory" focused society, we should now recognize that the question isn't "Is Stefan's game art?" but the more meta-question "Is *Black Mirror* itself art?" After all, viewed straightforwardly, even *Black Mirror*'s best episodes follow standards in storytelling technique, cinematography, lighting, and so on. Despite its clever delivery mechanism and peculiar narrative that folds in on itself, *Bandersnatch* still presents us with familiar character types and traditional structures. For example, viewed independently, each pathway tells a coherent story with a climax. *Black Mirror* is, of course, highly celebrated because it consistently provides subversive messages. But, again, having a message that lays bare the problems of our capitalist society isn't sufficient to qualify it as art – at least, according to Adorno.

Perhaps asking "Is *Black Mirror* art?" just isn't the right question, though. It's true that we might be tempted to try and counter Adorno's claim by noting that adhering to popular standards in culture ensures that the subversive message is salient and available to the *most* people possible. Yet, focusing on a harsh divide between "art" and "not art"' could overlook one of Adorno's most important points: even "art" that merely gives us a subversive message is rare enough in capitalism. That's the entire problem of the culture industry. It either mindlessly reproduces itself and encourages consumption – like the intrusive and ubiquitous ads in *15 Million Merits* – or it repackages resistance and subversion as profitable – like making Bing's shard of glass a piece of flair for digital avatars.

By contrast, a piece of media like *Black Mirror* still contributes to making us free because it raises subversive concerns and seems to authentically attempt to shed the determinations of its given culture. Quibbling over whether something that does *that* is real art binds us to continue examining things within the constrictive system (and its rules) instead of looking at the significant message about that system it delivers. Certainly, this would be contrary to Adorno's aims. So, settle down, everyone. Philosophy isn't trying to keep you from enjoying the show or rob it of its cultural value. There may be a *Bandersnatch*-style offshoot of this reality where *Black Mirror* is crap, but you still live in the reality where *Black Mirror* is quite good.

- "I agree! *Black Mirror* is artistically valuable." Breathe a sigh of relief. (Go to page 216.)
- "Black Mirror isn't art and only genuine art deserves my attention." (Burn book in protest of capitalism's influence on art. Don't buy another.)

"It's how our decisions along that path affect the whole that matters."

Officially, *Bandersnatch* is called "interactive media." The sort of story-driven, user-inputted choice mechanism that the episode leans on, however, has been a staple of video games for years. In this regard, *Bandersnatch* is just as much a "game" as *Pac-Man* is. (Neither video game is quite as sophisticated as *Striking Vipers X,* of course, but that's beside the point). It might therefore be tempting to say that *Bandersnatch* would be even *more* interesting if we had what existentialist philosopher Jean-Paul Sartre (1905–1980) calls "absolute freedom," the freedom to do whatever we wanted.

Now, according to Sartre, absolute freedom isn't quite as "absolute" as it might sound. As Sartre explains in *Being and Nothingness,* it isn't as if a prisoner can just walk out of her cell. Her range of available choices is constrained by the facts of her circumstances: namely, *she's a prisoner*, and prison guards aren't in the habit of just opening the doors for their occupants. Nonetheless, the prisoner is absolutely free in the sense that she's able to determine what's meaningful *within* her circumstances. Is it to escape? To have a positive relationship with other prisoners? In turn, she's able to choose the sorts of things that would be useful or pose a hindrance to achieving that meaning.

So, we might think that *Bandersnatch* – as fascinating as it is already – would be *even better* if we had this kind of absolute freedom. As it stands, *Bandersnatch* is expressly designed to limit our choices to predetermined and often opposed alternatives. Our only options are the ones the designers, writers, and showrunners *intend* for us to have. But what if we could make whatever choices we *want* for Stefan within the rules of the circumstances that the show defines? What if we could reject both the Thompson Twins *and* NOW Volume 2 to play whatever we liked – maybe Motörhead, for example. What if, instead of choosing between cereals, we could choose to have something else – or not eat breakfast at all? Clearly, Charlie Brooker wouldn't want this; it would be a legal and logistical nightmare! But if they could pull it off, wouldn't we like that even better?

But pause for a moment and imagine what absolute freedom would mean for a game like *Bandersnatch*. A player could choose to never visit Tuckersoft and just idle in bed all day or decide to take more LSD with Colin and play *Nohzdyve* for hours. With this kind of freedom, it would be remarkably easy to become bogged down in minutiae. And this would strip the narrative of *Bandersnatch* – and the important philosophical questions it raises – to meaninglessness. In Book IX of his *Poetics,* Aristotle (384–322 BCE) suggests something similar, arguing that a good narrative (or plot) is composed of events that follow from one another believably, giving the narrative a sort of unity. On the other hand, Aristotle thinks that the worst kind of narrative is one in which the events depicted are disunified and haphazard. From this, we can see that a *Bandersnatch* where Stefan wakes up, listens to Tangerine Dream, then goes for lunch at the pub wouldn't be much of a narrative at all – there just isn't much of a point.

Design decisions like limiting our choices are made so that games remain *engaging* and *meaningful*. Perhaps Sartre may say that in choosing to *not* follow the given narrative of *Bandersnatch* and just sit at the pub for hours, the player would be choosing what is meaningful for herself. However, contemporary philosopher Susan Wolf claims that *meaningfulness* is a peculiar combination of subjective and objective value.[29] There's more to meaning than just whatever is important to *me* as an individual. So, while it's very meaningful to Thakur that his intern come back with his cigarettes and Lion Bar, this event has little objective value – and that's probably why we don't have the option to follow the young intern's adventures to the corner store. At the same time, it's difficult for us to bother with big philosophical questions about the illusion of choice unless we each have some individual investment in what's going on. Providing a select range of choices to the player ensures that *Bandersnatch* focuses on objectively important questions, while simultaneously letting the player subjectively have a stake in what's happening by influencing how *some* events go down. The upshot is that we don't *really* want absolute freedom in *Bandersnatch* because that would make for a crappy story.

Similarly, we may not want absolute freedom for ourselves; it might make for a crappy life. In his book *The Paradox of Choice: Why More is Less*, psychologist Barry Schwartz argues that an abundance of choices creates anxiety in shoppers that they would be better off without. It leads to what we might call "choice paralysis," where we have no idea what to choose and always feel like we could've chosen something better. Likewise, the idea that we have the kind of absolute freedom that Sartre describes, every waking moment of our lives, could be a soul-crushing prospect. Facing "choice paralysis" when deciding what to buy is bad enough; how much worse would it be to confront this anxiety with *every* choice whatsoever? Are you really doing the best possible thing that you could possibly be doing with your life this very moment?

- "No. Philosophy is too hard. I want to do something fun." (Go to page 223.)
- "Yes! In fact, now I'm wondering: If I have the power to make choices for Stefan, am I responsible for what happens in the episode?" (Go to page 224.)

"If you follow that line of thinking ... you're absolved from any guilt [for] your actions."

So, we just discussed the possibility that we live in a multiverse where there's a different universe for every decision we could make. The narrator of the Jerome F. Davies documentary suggests this entails some harrowing realizations.

> [Jerome F. Davies thought that] whatever we choose to do in this existence, there's another one out there in which were doing quite the opposite. Which renders free will meaningless, nothing but an illusion. If you follow that line of thinking to its logical conclusion then you're absolved from any guilt [for] your actions. They're not even your actions. It's out of your control. Your fate has been dictated, it's out of your hands. So why not commit murder? Maybe that's what destiny wants. You're just a puppet, you're not in control.

But does this logic hold? There's a lot to unpack here.

First, let's suppose (as Davies believes) that, for any decision you make, there's an alternate universe where the opposite will be decided. Does this render free will meaningless? In a certain way, yes. Suppose you are faced with the decision: should you save a drowning boy? If Davies is right, then if you save him in this universe, he won't be saved in another – and vice-versa. Regardless, there is a universe where there's a saved boy, and a universe where there isn't. So, in the grand scheme of the multiverse, the same number of people will die by drowning, no matter what you decide.

But in another way, your decision matters a lot. Why? Because according to many philosophers, when it comes to ethics, the consequences of an action aren't all that matters. It's still wrong to let a boy drown, even if, all things considered, reality would be no different.[30] And since the person in the other universe isn't really you – they're your "doppelganger," or "counterpart," but they aren't really you – by deciding to save the boy, you ensure that *you* are the one that does the right thing.[31] Having the free will to make the decisions for yourself would therefore seem to be of prime importance.

One might object, however, that in choosing to save the boy in your universe, you're effectively choosing for him to not be saved in the other. So, either way, you're guilty of the same crime. This, it seems, is the worry that author Clay Ferris expressed when he said, "If we come to believe that choices do not matter, that any action is matched by its opposite somewhere [else in the multiverse], we risk losing our capacity for moral reasoning."[32] But there are two possible responses. First, you aren't "causing" the events that happen in the other universe. That you chose to save the boy in this universe might *logically entail* that he won't be saved in the other, but logical entailment isn't *causation* and doesn't carry the same moral weight. Your counterpart is who caused the other boy not to be saved. Second, as Sean Carroll put it, "Our capacity for moral reasoning shouldn't depend on what's happening many googols of parsecs away in an unobservable part of the universe."[33] If he's right, it shouldn't depend on what happens in another universe either.

The second question raised by the quote is this: does lacking free will mean that you're "absolved from any guilt from your actions?" If free will is necessary for moral responsibility, then yes. And a lot of philosophers think that free will and moral responsibility go hand in hand. The "Principle of Alternate Possibilities" states that an agent is morally responsible for doing an action only if that agent could've done otherwise.[34] And many philosophers think the principle is true because we can't be blamed for actions that we don't freely do, and free will requires alternate possibilities. If I can't have done otherwise than perform some action, then I didn't perform that action freely.

But other philosophers disagree. The contemporary philosopher John Martin Fischer, for example, argues that even if we lack free will, we can still be morally responsible for our actions because the principle of alternate possibilities is false.[35] Moral responsibly doesn't require alternate possibilities, even if free will does. Why? Well suppose neuroscientists implanted a device in your brain that would kick in to make you choose to save the drowning boy if you were about to not do it. But also suppose that it never does kick in because you decide to save the boy on your own. In this situation, you saving the boy is inevitable; you can't do otherwise. And yet, it seems, you still act freely. For Fischer, as long as you have "guidance control" of your actions because, for example, you performed them as a result of a rational deliberation, then you're free. And that can be true even if the world is deterministic – even if it's just a physical system and everything that happens in it is dictated by the laws of physics. You can still be the source of your action, involved in the "actual sequence" that led to its occurrence, and thus be responsible for it.

If things work as Davies suggests, however, none of this matters: you're not free because someone else is directly controlling your actions in a way that will make you do what they want you to do, regardless of what you desire or decide. If someone is in control of us like we control Stefan, then obviously we're not morally responsible for our actions. "It's out of your control. Your fate has been dictated, it's out of your hands." But it doesn't follow from this that you might as well just commit murder because maybe "that's what destiny wants. You're just a puppet, you're not in control." Why?

Well, first of all, even if you really are controlled in this way, you'll still pay for the consequences of your actions. Stefan still lands in jail after killing his dad, even though you're the one that made him do it. Second of all, if you really think you're controlled in this way, deliberating about whether you should or shouldn't commit murder makes no sense. You're going to do what your overlord decides you're going to do, regardless of what you decide, so why even bother?

But most importantly, it doesn't follow from the mere fact that we don't have free will that we can (or should) just do whatever we want. Of course, people who don't believe in free will may be more likely to give in to temptations, supposedly believing that doing so is inevitable.[36] But that belief is not true. You could just as easily be fated to resist a given temptation as give in to it. And you still have to make a choice, even if that choice isn't free. As long as you aren't actually controlled by outside forces like Stefan, by at least trying to do the right thing, you could cause yourself to do it. Of course, if you don't have free will, you couldn't freely choose to try either. But since, even if you don't have free will, you don't know what you're fated to do, trying is still possible.

- "Davies was right! I *should* just kill everyone." Kill Dad. And Colin. And Mohan Thakur. You're a serial murderer now. (Go to page 221.)
- "Davies was wrong. I'm not fated at all; I can do whatever I want!" (Go to page 216.)

"How many times have you watched Pac-Man die … he just tries again."

Well that was a mistake! You want to kill everyone? We told you, even if your actions aren't free, you'll still have to pay the consequences. If this were real, you'd be going to jail. As it stands, you're just getting an abrupt end to the chapter. That's still bad, though, because there's so much more to *Bandersnatch* to uncover and so many other philosophical problems that the episode addresses. Yet, here you are.

Don't feel too badly, though – the same thing happens to Stefan. There is a multiplicity of paths that suddenly dead-end with Stefan frustrated by his abortive or otherwise unsatisfying adaptation of Jerome F. Davies's complex book. In particular, there are a lot of ways to end with Stefan in jail for killing his father (and possibly others). It's just too easy to make the wrong choice.

But that's the problem with choices and why Stefan seems to agonize over even the smallest decisions he programs into his game—or that he confronts in his life. We can partially explain Stefan's behavior through existentialist philosopher Søren Kierkegaard (1813–1855) and his view on choice. To Kierkegaard, choosing represents incredible anxiety for us, because in choosing we acknowledge that we close off alternative paths *forever*. The consequences of a choice are real and permanent, and so we can become paralyzed as we try to anticipate what *could* come to pass from choosing this or that. Or, as is the case with Stefan's guilt over refusing to get on the train with his mother as a child, we torture ourselves trying to determine how things *might* have gone differently if we had chosen other than we actually did. But it's as Dr. Haynes tells Stefan: "The past is immutable. No matter how painful it is, we can't change things. We can't choose differently with hindsight."

However, when we examine the assortment of smaller, "false" outcomes *Bandersnatch* gives us – coupled with the more sizeable "Jail Ending" that serves as the terminus for so many of Stefan's decisions – we actually see that the episode roundly *rejects* Kierkegaard's views about the dreadful irreversibility of choice. Despite Dr. Haynes's warning to the contrary, *Bandersnatch* invites both Stefan and the viewer to alter their choices at nearly every turn. And it isn't exactly shy about telling us that we have this power, either. Here's a chart that catalogs many of these quotes. Note how each ending seems to speak directly to the viewer:

"Ending"	Character/Quote
Work at Tuckersoft; *Bandersnatch* fails	Micro Play reviewer: "What they should've done is just gone right back to the start and tried again"
	Stefan: "I should try again"
Take medication; *Bandersnatch* fails	Micro Play reviewer: "If we had second chances in life, I hope they'd choose differently"
	Stefan: "I should try again"
P.A.C.S. path; kill Dad	Micro Play reviewer: "Must try harder"
♙ path; kill Dad and Thakur; bury body	Colin: "If you could live your life again, you should make some different choices … C'mon mate: dare to dream"
♙ path; kill Dad and Colin; bury body	Colin, before dying: "See you in the next life"
♙ path; kill Dad; spare Colin; bury body	Colin: "I'd tell him to try again"

Bandersnatch also seems to accept the viewer's efforts to go back and make new choices as part of its narrative. That is, we aren't venturing *outside* the narrative, making a new choice, then popping back in to freshly re-watch events. No, our previous choices become part and parcel with a single, continuous story. If Stefan accepts Thakur's offer early on, he returns later to that same decision-point informed by the consequences of his previous decision. For instance, he knows – before he's even seen the game on this pathway – why Colin's current *Nohzdyve* build fails. Likewise, repeated trips to Dr. Haynes's office show us a frustrated Stefan accurately forecasting Haynes's responses.

So, against Kierkegaard's claims about our decisions, choices in *Bandersnatch* aren't momentous events that permanently sever all other possibilities. On the contrary: the episode presents to us a way in which we can approach choices without fear of their consequences. Should things go wrong, we can just go back and try again until we get it right – now equipped with better knowledge of which path *not* to take. What this means is that you shouldn't worry that you've stumbled into this clumsy, unfulfilling ending to the chapter. You can always go back to the beginning and try again.

"Giving up, eh?"

Sorry mate. Philosophy *is* hard, we'll grant you that. It's also uncomfortable. It can challenge your most basic beliefs. But you shouldn't give up so easily. Maybe you could be doing something more fun, but there's value in true belief, not being duped, and understanding the way the world is. And that's what doing philosophy gets you!

Plato (429–347 BCE) demonstrated this in the *Republic* by imagining a group of prisoners chained down in a cave who are forced to stare at a wall. People stand behind them, holding up images of real-world objects in front of a fire to make shadows of those objects appear on the wall. Because that's all they'd ever known, the prisoners would think the shadows were real. But if one of the prisoners were to escape and learn the truth of the matter – about how they're being fooled and how the world really works – he'd look back on his fellow prisoners with pity. They might be happy, but only because they don't know any better. If they did, they'd pity themselves and want to be released. Unfortunately, if the escaped prisoner were to return to the cave and try to convince them that they were being fooled, they'd likely want to kill him.

And that's where we find ourselves. We're the escapee and you're the prisoner, plugging your ears, not wanting to learn any more uncomfortable truths. Odds are that you probably want to kill us, too! Well, it wouldn't be the first time a philosopher was killed by people who didn't want to think harder about their lives. But there's so much more to learn. Most likely, to arrive at this ending, all you've read about is free will. But *Bandersnatch* is about so much more! Get on it!

- "I want to know more about whether we live in a multiverse." (Go to page 206.)
- "I already read about the multiverse, I want to know more about time travel." (Go to page 226.)

"It's the spirit out there ... that decides what we do."

Over the course of *Bandersnatch,* Stefan does some morally bankrupt things across many endings. Little is more disturbing, though, than watching him follow in Jerome F. Davies's footsteps, decapitating his father before finishing his adaptation of *Bandersnatch* with a contented grin. Viewed from *our* perspective as the literal decision-makers of his life, though, it's hard to blame Stefan for any wrongdoing he gets into, even in this creepy ending. Clearly, he isn't freely choosing to commit these terrible acts, and he even appears to actively resist at times. For that matter, the same could be said for Pearl Ritman, who – also in this ending – we can force to destroy or pour tea over her computer as she tries to remake the successful version of Stefan's game.

Bandersnatch supports our intuition here. Stefan's surname is Butler, implying he's only there to serve *someone else.* If we admit it seems unfair to say that Stefan is morally accountable for hacking up Dad, then who is accountable? In cases where someone is compelling another person to act, it's common to hold the person *in control* to be morally accountable for those acts. And as the person with her hand on the remote, that would make the responsible party *you.* You are, as Colin puts it, the "spirit out there" deciding what actions Stefan and Pearl should take. So, every time Stefan whacks Colin with a trophy or stabs Thakur to death, *you* are really responsible. This isn't just complicity – like you merely saw the horrible thing and did nothing, or you endorsed Stefan's wrongdoings as acceptable without actually participating. No, you – yes you, the person reading this chapter – are the one who gets the blame as if you'd committed the act yourself.

Now, obviously, *Bandersnatch* is just an episode of a TV show, so no one's going to prosecute you or anything (nobody *really* died). But curiously, there's still a sense in which *you* are accountable for the grotesque behavior in the episode because *you* are directly choosing the unpleasant outcomes. And this, it seems, doesn't bode well for your moral character. You're likely to object, of course, by pointing out that, in many cases, *Bandersnatch* provided you with only immoral choices. When Stefan's dad confronts him, there's no option to emotionally reconcile with Dad over lunch at the pub. If you choose to "back off," you just loop back around until you decide to kill him. And once you do, you can only either bury him or chop him up. If you only have terrible choices available to you, how can you be blameworthy for doing something terrible?

Well, in Book III of his *Nicomachean Ethics,* Aristotle (384-322 B.C.E.) argues that we can only be held accountable for *voluntary* actions. We don't get credit or blame for things we do *involuntarily*—for actions that we do because of an external force or out of ignorance. So, you're accountable for an action if the source of the action comes from you, but free of accountability if the source is external in some way. If Stefan's dad unknowingly fed Stefan poisoned Sugar Puffs, for example, Aristotle would say that he's not culpable. The action he was *trying* to take was nourishing his son, not poisoning him.

If we follow Aristotle's line of thinking, however, the only way you could be morally excused from making Stefan do awful things is if *your* choices are involuntary – that is, if your choices are either externally forced or you're acting out of ignorance. But neither of these "involuntary" scenarios seems to describe your situation. Stefan's actions are surely forced, as he's compelled to do whatever you choose for him. But this isn't true for you, is it? Even if the only choices available to you are sometimes exclusively immoral, external forces aren't compelling your actions. Ultimately, *you're* still the one who chooses between chopping up or burying Stefan's Dad's body. And anyone who said that they didn't realize that choosing to chop up Dad's body would really make Stefan chop up his dad's body, isn't being honest.

Perhaps, however, you didn't choose anything at all. If you simply let the time to make a choice expire, the Netflix app will auto-select one for you. So, let's suppose you made no direct choices at all and just let the episode play out on its own. Could you be absolved of responsibility then? It seems not. Even a viewer who makes no choices still acts voluntarily. By watching the entire episode, it's clear you expressed a real intention to see what happened: you could've always turned the episode off if you found it to be too objectionable. But you didn't. So even in this situation, you're responsible. All in all, the choices you made as you watched the episode were voluntary, in the Aristotelian sense. And this means that the source of everything that happens in *Bandersnatch* is *you*.

Contrast this with Stefan, who attempts to fight external controls, like when the viewer chooses between biting his nails or pulling his earlobe, or even his stammered warnings to his Dad before clocking him with that very sturdy ash tray. Stefan can't do other than *you* command him to do, but his action seems to come from external compulsion; internally, he *intends* to perform a different action. On Aristotle's argument, Stefan gets a reprieve for his bad behavior. The same can't be said for you, though. Even if you're not *really* accountable for killing and mutilating Stefan's dad (because that didn't *really* happen), you also can't view your role as decision-maker in a completely detached way.

This, on reflection, might demonstrate something less than pleasant about yourself. You're so comfortable with making these awful choices that you sat through the whole episode. And *this* could be the episode's most incisive philosophical lesson. To what degree do we share accountability in the grisly acts depicted in the media we consume, just by consuming them? If that bothers you, you're out of luck. This is the end with a capital "E." There aren't any more choices to make. All that's left for you is to do what all good *Black Mirror* episodes make us do: walk away feeling unsettled and more than a bit icky about yourself.

"Mirrors let you move through time."

Oddly enough, the most heartwarming ending of *Bandersnatch* involves the death of a small child – the death of the protagonist, in fact. Originally, when he was five, Stefan's search to find the stuffed rabbit (which his mother made for him when he was born) made her late for her train. She subsequently had to take the 8:45, and because he never found the rabbit, Stefan didn't join her. The train derailed, she died, and Stefan suffered horrendous guilt. But in one *Bandersnatch* ending, adult Stefan enters "TOY" as the combination to the safe in his father's room, and then is suddenly five years old again. He finds the rabbit and joins his mother on the 8:45 train. We then see them sitting together. He closes his eyes, and the screen goes black.

This is possible because, in the *Bandersnatch* universe, "Time is a construct. People think you can't go back and change things, but you can. That's what flashbacks are. They're invitations to go back and make different choices." Or at least, so says Colin. But is time travel really possible?

Time travel to the future certainly is. Einstein's relativity teaches us that both acceleration and gravity can slow the passage of time. So, if you were to fly away from the Earth at or near the speed of light, or go and orbit a massive black hole for a while, you would find that, upon your return, many more years had passed on Earth than had passed for you.[37]

But time travel into the past is a different story. Many philosophers argue that it's impossible because of something called "the Grandfather Paradox." If time travel to the past was possible, then it would be possible to travel back to a time before your grandfather sired your father and kill him. But such an action would entail that you were never born. But, of course, if you were never born, you couldn't have traveled back to kill your grandfather – so you were born. Paradox! Reverse time travel, it seems, makes it possible for you to both have been born and never been born. That's logically contradictory. And since logical contradictions can't be true, time travel must be impossible.

The paradox raised by the time travel in *Bandersnatch* is this: By changing the past so that he dies on the train with his mother, Stefan makes it the case that he wouldn't exist as an adult. But if there is no adult Stefan, there is no one to feel the guilt and pain that motivated him to go back and change the past in the first place. Paradox! He dies with his mother if and only if he doesn't.

But there are two answers to this this kind of worry. This first belongs to contemporary philosophers Nuel Belnap and David Deutsch.[38] They suggest that reverse time travel doesn't place one in their own past, but in the past of an alternate universe (or "timeline") that is just like the one the time traveler left, up to the moment in the past to which they traveled. Any subsequent actions by the time traveler will make *that* universe's future different than the original, but it would not create a paradox. Killing "my" grandfather wouldn't prevent my birth, but the birth of someone who looks like me in the new universe. Likewise, Stefan getting on the train with his mother wouldn't prevent *him* from being an adult, but *someone that looks like him* in this new universe from being an adult.

While this theory does avoid paradoxes, it's not clear that it actually shows that time travel to the past is possible. Why? Because, one could argue, what it describes isn't time travel. It's universe creation. Any machine capable of doing this would have to be capable of creating universes, not traveling in time.

The second solution belongs to David Lewis (1941–2001). He argues that reverse time travel would not make possible grandfather paradoxes because it would be impossible for any reverse time traveler to change the past. It might seem to them that they could, he admits. And they might try. But they would necessarily fail. Nothing could occur but what had already occurred. Indeed, if a time traveler did travel to the past, the past would have already contained that time traveler and his actions before the time traveler ever pushed the button on his time-machine in the first place. On this view, the universe exists as a whole, past, present, and future – as one big omnitemporal block. Hypothetically one could change the direction in time one travels in the block, but changing any event from "it happened" to "it didn't happen" would be impossible.[39]

The cool thing about this is that, at least in a limited way, it might actually be possible. On some interpretations of quantum mechanics, quantum particles send signals backward in time to their paired partners; in doing so they could determine some part of the past, but not change it.[40] And there are even some experiments which are consistent with this idea.[41] It's not consistent with relativity, of course, but it's already well known that quantum mechanics is inconsistent with relativity. "No backwards time travel" may be one thing we have to give up to get to a grand unified theory. The not so cool thing is that this theory can't be used to explain the time travel in *Bandersnatch*. If Stefan tried to go back and die with his mother on the train, he would necessarily fail.

⚓

- "I embrace the branching view!" Go back in time to change things. (Go to page 228.)
- "All this talk of branching universes and paradoxes has me wondering whether the world of *Bandersnatch* is even logically consistent." (Go to on page 230.)

"And even if he does manage to escape ... he comes right back in the other side."

This wouldn't be much of a choose-your-own-adventure chapter without an ending that kills you. So, congratulations! You're dead. It doesn't really matter how it happened. Maybe you jumped off the balcony. Or, perhaps you climbed through the bathroom mirror, time traveled to some meaningful past event, and changed your personal history so that you died. You probably went back to eat a really good Pop-Tart, slipped on the kitchen floor, and cracked your skull or something. The important thing is, you wound your way around a circuitous path to a point that gives your story some finality in your demise, just as it did for Stefan.

This sense of "finality" is crucial. Thematically, there's tremendous emotional heft to seeing Stefan *Donnie Darko* himself. Stefan believes that *choosing* to look for Rabbit instead of going with his mother directly caused her to have to take the later 8:45 train, which then derailed. This fuels his obsession with choice, branching paths, and consequence; it's his reason for trying to adapt *Bandersnatch* (the book) in the first place. Stefan believes that if he can map out the proper causal chains behind important choices, he can understand how events happened and, more importantly, how other choices might have changed things.

What's so significant about the "Death Ending," however, is that Stefan pinpoints *the* precise choice where his entire life went wrong – he failed to go with his mother – and then chooses differently. Seen this way, dying after confronting his grief (and his guilt) brings closure to the chief motivation behind nearly everything that happens in *Bandersnatch*. In doing so, this ending also represents a means of escape for Stefan from the agony of choice and the increasingly pernicious delusion (or is it?) that he's not in control of his actions.

The problem, though, is that the Death Ending isn't *really* final, is it? Indeed, none of the endings in the episode actually "ends" anything. Any one of the five main endings have the possibility of activating what we'll call a "Hard Reset." That is, based on how many different endings and pathways a viewer has seen in a given playthrough, *Bandersnatch* will eventually forcibly eject the viewer to the Netflix menu – with no option to go back and continue making choices. In this regard, the ending where Stefan goes back in time to be with his mother and suddenly dies in his therapist's office is no more "final" than any other ending.

A school of philosophers in ancient Greece called the Stoics were known for their fatalism: the notion that events are going to happen however they are "fated" to happen, independently of our actions. One Stoic thinker, Chrysippus (279–206 BCE), teaches specifically about a cosmic cycle he names *ekpyrosis* – also called "eternal recurrence" – in which the universe is periodically obliterated by fire, then recreated to follow the exact sequence of events as before. To anyone who's watched *Bandersnatch* more than once, eternal recurrence ought to sound unsettlingly familiar. Because the episode cycles the viewer *back* into the episode after most endings to keep making new choices – it's possible to view all five major endings in one go, in fact – events obviously start to repeat themselves. Some characters explicitly call this out, such as when Stefan grows aggravated with Dr. Haynes during a conversation about increasing his medication that he's certain he's had with her before. The situation *Bandersnatch* presents us with is worse than this, however. Restarting *Bandersnatch* manually or opening it again after a hard reset *also resets all of the choices*, effectively "regenerating" the universe of the episode. There are no "new" options on a second or third viewing; everything plays out toward the same five endings as it did before.

So, analogous to the destruction of the universe in eternal recurrence, the Death Ending only *appears* to have finality for Stefan. Bleakly, Stefan either returns to a cycle of further choices and endings as the viewer is prompted to go back and choose again, or he quite literally repeats *everything* once the viewer restarts the episode following a Hard Reset. Ultimately, there is no escape for Stefan. Even in his "destruction" he must eternally choose to yell at Dad, follow Colin, listen to *Phaedra, and so on and so on*, as his world is recreated anew – every time we re-watch it. On that note, there's no escape from *this chapter* for you, either. That's right, we didn't forget that you died. So, start over and pick some different philosophical choices. Just don't be surprised if you end up here again (and again, and again …).

"[W]hat we do on one path affects what happens on the other paths."

If *Bandersnatch* played out like a normal choose your own adventure story, it would be told differently. If you made a wrong choice and ended up dead, and then backed up and made a different choice, you could continue on as if the original choice never happened. But that's not how *Bandersnatch* works. For example, the first time Stefan sees Colin's demo of *Nohzdyve*, Colin explains that it crashed because of a "buffer error, the eyeballs have overrun the video memory." But if you subsequently make Stefan accept Mohan's offer to work in the office at Tuckersoft, and thus have to start over, when the *Nohzdyve* demo scenes repeats, Stefan already knows why it crashes. "Buffer error. The eyeball sprites overshot the video memory." He's not sure how, but he knows. So, just like what happens in the universe of one *Black Mirror* episode can affect the universe of another, what happens on one path in *Bandersnatch* can affect other paths.[42]

Does this make sense? Is it logically consistent story telling? Indeed, it is, and we can use the branching theory of time travel from last section to make sense of it. Consider what happens on this view when a time traveler "travels back" and thus creates a new timeline. That timeline will be like the original up to the moment in the past at which the time traveler appears. But because the creation of the new timeline doesn't erase the original, the time traveler will remember everything that happened in it. In the same way, Stefan could remember what happened to him in previous iterations of his story. Similar explanations could perhaps explain the overlapping elements in different *Black Mirror* episodes.

A tougher worry arises after you make Stefan choose for Colin to jump off Colin's balcony instead of Stefan. "Fair enough." Colin says. "See you around," and then jumps. Although it's supposedly a dream sequence – the demon Pax appears, and Stefan awakes at the decision point right before he chose to follow Colin – Colin disappears from that timeline and stays gone until you reach an ending and restart. And then, when you do, you're given a quick run-through of events again, but this time – during the *Nohzdyve* demo sequence – Colin tells Stefan, "We met before. I told you I'd see you around. And I was right." But if what happened on Colin's balcony was only a dream, why does Colin disappear? And how does Colin remember what happened on the balcony after he comes back?

The answer, it seems, lies in making two assumptions. First, the sequence in Colin's apartment wasn't a dream. It actually happened. The appearance of the demon Pax resets things, somewhat like we do when we reach an ending and decide to go back, but not completely. So, Colin's death makes him disappear from the current timeline. Second, it seems that Colin's knowledge about the nature of the world grants him the ability to retain memories of past lives – or, we might say, it grants a unity to every version of him, in different timelines, so that they really are all one and the same person and thus all share the same knowledge set. This is why Colin's wife Kitty doesn't remember him having jumped, but Colin does.[43] A similar explanation could be invoked to explain why Stefan choosing "TOY" as the safe combination allows him to go back and choose to go on the train with this mother as a five year old, but only if he chose to talk with Dr. Haynes about his mother in a previous timeline.

- "Like Colin, I now see across all timelines—I even know all of this is really just a TV show!" (Go to page 232.)[44]
- "If timelines can affect each other, how much did the real world affect *Bandersnatch*? (Go to page 234.)

"I am watching you on Netflix.
I make decisions for you."

Because you chose the paths you did in this chapter, we thought we'd recommend a "meta-ending." You know, this is the one where you tell Stefan you're controlling him through Netflix and he fights his therapist (and possibly his father!) in a knock-down, drag-out brawl full of absurd Kung-Fu. Or maybe he finds himself on the set of *Bandersnatch* as its being filmed and everyone is calling him "Mike." Both of these meta-endings are just capstones on a philosophical interpretation of the episode that has Stefan as a surrogate for the viewer's own Netflix-watching experience.

Tristan Harris – formerly a design ethicist for Google – thinks that streaming services like Netflix actively construct their platforms to "hijack" the user's capacity to make free choices.[45] Essentially, Harris's claim is what Smithereen company founder Billy Bauer admits in *Smithereens*. Much of modern technology, whether it's smart phones, social media apps, or streaming services, is designed to "engage" the user's attention to such a degree that the tech becomes "more like a crack pipe … some kind of fucking Vegas casino where … we've sealed off all the fucking doors. They've got a department [where] all they do is tweak it like that on purpose."[46]

For Harris, one way that technology asserts command over our choices is by setting the terms in the user interface. Netflix may appear to offer a potentially overwhelming smorgasbord of viewing options, but users can still only choose from those particular titles that the service provides. What's more, Netflix builds suggested and popular options into the way it presents its menu to the user – further narrowing choices and even fostering a kind of "fear of missing out" by showing us what's "trending" among *other people* or highlighting certain platform-exclusive films and shows above the rest. And finding particular titles is often inconvenient for the user, as ordinary genres and users' own watchlists are buried among too-granular-to-be-helpful descriptions like "Critically Acclaimed Binge-Worthy Crime Shows." Harris thinks that feed loops like autoplay only compound this problem. Scrolling over a selection in Netflix automatically plays clips from the title (or just starts the title from the beginning), and finishing a film or show causes Netflix, after a brief countdown, to play the next episode in sequence or a "suggested" title the service has calculated that you'll also enjoy. The end result is that users feel as though they've freely chosen something to watch when Netflix is really doing all of the legwork.

When we set these purposive and constrictive design decisions alongside many of our experiences with Stefan in *Bandersnatch,* it becomes clear that the episode is illustrating the ways in which streaming services are really in control of our lives (just like *we're* in control of Stefan's). *Bandersnatch* deliberately limits our choices, for one. For the most part, we have two options at any given time, and neither of them are what we'd truly *like* to do. Bury Dad, or chop up Dad? How about neither? Other times, choices are made *for* us. When Dr. Haynes asks Stefan (and the viewer) whether there ought to be more action, there are two possible answers which really reduce to just *one*: "Yes" and "Fuck Yeah." Likewise, if we neglect to choose anything at all, the episode autoplays a choice for us to keep the *Bandersnatch* narrative rolling (and us watching). Just as Netflix in part determines what choices are on offer and what it recommends to us by collecting data on users' browsing habits, *Bandersnatch* only gives us the possibility of pursuing these meta-endings when we've made (or not made) specific choices beforehand.

Yet, unlike Stefan, don't we have the choice to freely detach ourselves from our streaming technology? Can't we elect to cancel our subscriptions or close the program and go walk the dog? Of course we can, but escape just winds up putting us in Stefan/Mike's position on the *Bandersnatch* set. Emerging from a tunnel of rigidly defined choices, all arranged to keep us immersed in doing exactly what the platform designers have in mind, we're disoriented and wonder how exactly we got here. Granted, we cheerily signed up for this experience in the first place; but so did Stefan/Mike when he took the job to appear in *Bandersnatch*. Freeing ourselves from overbearing technology is rather like emerging from cryosleep in a sci-fi movie. Still, this might be the best-case scenario for us.

Similarly, this is where you, the reader, find yourself at the end of this series of paths: do you accept technology's recommendations for you and stay plugged-in? Or do you escape and take back your agency? All things considered, it's probably better to just keep watching and spare yourself the confusion. After all, wouldn't you like to see what we've picked out for you?

The Real World

Black Mirror is so close to reality it can sometimes be confusing. That song Abi sings in *Fifteen Million Merits* on *Hot Shot* ("Anyone Who Knows What Love Is (Will Understand)?") is a real song (sung by Irma Thomas in 1964). But it was so obscure that people might have mistaken it for a *Black Mirror* original. As Charlie Brooker put it,

> It's got the tone of a song that sounds like you should know it. The original sounds like an old track, it's got an old '60s feel and it's immediately catchy. You feel like, "Why isn't this a really famous song?"[47]

In the same way, when you watch *Bandernsatch,* you wonder: Was Jerome F. Davies a real author? Was *Bandersnatch* a real book? Did someone try to design a *Bandersnatch* game in the 80s? And what is a Bandersnatch anyway?

Although Jerome F. Davies and his choose your own adventure book are fictional, there are a number of books that go by the title of *Bandersnatch*. The most famous is a book by Diana Pavlac Glyer about the creative collaboration between C. S. Lewis and J. R. R. Tolkien, who were both professors at Oxford.[48] But none of the books are a choose your own adventure. The Oxford English Dictionary defines Bandersnatch as "a fierce mythical creature immune to bribery and capable of moving very fast," and the term "Bandersnatch" originates from Lewis Carroll's poem "Jabberwocky," which appears in *Through the Looking Glass* (a sequel to *Alice in Wonderland*).[49] In the poem, Bandersnatch refers to a creature which is "Frumious" (that is, fuming and furious) and the Bandersnatch is referenced in many of Carroll's later works. It only ever appears in the looking glass world, however, which perhaps implies that the *Black Mirror* episode *Bandersnatch* is not meant to actually take place in the *Black Mirror* multiverse. (Did you notice? Black mirror? Looking glass?) One assumes Carroll's Bandersnatch creature inspired the demon Pax, but P.A.X. is also the name of a popular video gaming conference that has multiple conventions every year, worldwide.

Even more interestingly, *Bandersnatch* actually was a videogame set to be released in the 1980s. The failure of its release wasn't because its creator murdered people, however. Its developer, Imagine Software, simply went belly-up because of mounting debts. (Not coincidentally, they went bankrupt on July 9, 1984 which is the same day Stefan first awakens at the beginning of the episode). The real *Bandersnatch* game wasn't, it seems, a choose-your-own-adventure game, though. A version of it was later released as a role-playing videogame called *Brataccas*, which was set in a dystopian future. In it, a genetic engineer named Kyne is framed for treason by the government and forced to try to find evidence of his innocence on an asteroid named "Brataccas." Although the government conspiracy angle perhaps reminds one of Stefan's dad and his PACS project, it seems that that the similarities end there.

- "I don't know what to do." Let the chapter autoplay the next choice for you. (Go to page 232.)
- "I can't even with philosophy right now." Jump off balcony. (Go to page 228.)

Notes

1. For a full flowchart of the episode's choices, see: https://www.reddit.com/r/blackmirror/comments/aajk5r/full_bandersnatch_flowchart_all_branches_story/
2. Sam Thielman, "Surveillance reform explainer: Can the FBI still listen to my phone calls?" *The Guardian*, 2015. https://www.theguardian.com/world/2015/jun/03/surveillance-reform-freedom-act-explainer-fbi-phone-calls-privacy (Accessed 11 August 2019).
3. See Ted Schick and Lewis Vaughn, *How To Think About Weird Things* (7th edition). (New York: McGraw Hill, 2014.) 276–283.
4. Nick Bostrom, "Are you living in a computer simulation?" *Philosophical Quarterly* 53 (2003): 243–255. See also the end of Chapter 9 (Claire Benn's chapter on *Playtest*) in this volume.
5. For a nice overview of these studies, see George Dvorsky, "Scientific evidence that you probably don't have free will," *io9*, http://io9.com/5975778/scientific-evidence-that-you-probably-dont-have-free-will (Accessed 11 August 2019).
6. Joseph LeDoux, *The Emotional Brain* (New York: Touchstone, 1996).
7. Joe Skrebels, "Charlie Brooker says there's not a *Black Mirror* universe – It's a *Black Mirror* multiverse," *IGN*, https://www.ign.com/articles/2019/01/11/charlie-brooker-says-theres-not-a-black-mirror-universe-a-its-a-black-mirror-multiverse (Accessed 11 August 2019).
8. Note that the White Bear Glyph also shows up in the white room in *Playtest* and on the door to Joe's cell in *White Christmas*. For reasons, we don't have time to go into here, we think that the theme of "surrendering agency and accepting external control" fits these instances of the symbol, too.
9. For more on the Stoics, see Chapter 17 (Skye C. Cleary and Massimo Pigliucci's chapter on *Hang the DJ*) in this volume.
10. David Streitfeld, "*Black Mirror: Bandersnatch* is an experiment on us – Netflix explain why interactive episode is the grimmest yet," *Independent*, https://www.independent.co.uk/arts-entertainment/tv/features/black-mirror-bandersnatch-netflix-interactive-charlie-brooker-interview-a8701626.html (Accessed 11 August 2019).
11. For an explanation of why, see David Kyle Johnson's *Exploring Metaphysics (Audiobook)*. (Chantilly, VA: The Great Courses, 2014). Chapters 18 and 19.
12. For a basic rundown on the Brane, see the Wikipedia entry on the topic. https://en.wikipedia.org/wiki/Brane_cosmology

13. It creates a magnetic field with which the particle will interact, based on its spin. For a readable but accurate rundown, see "Stern-Gerlach device," in *The Quantum Physics Lady's Encyclopedia of Quantum Physics and Philosophy of Science*, http://www.quantumphysicslady.org/glossary/stern-gerlach-device/ (Accessed 11 August 2019).

14. For more on what this quote means see Vasant Natarajan, "What Einstein Meant when he said 'God does not play dice.'" *Resonance*, https://arxiv.org/ftp/arxiv/papers/1301/1301.1656.pdf (Accessed 11 August 2019).

15. See Peter Kosso, *Appearance and Reality: An Introduction to the Philosophy of Physics*. (Oxford University Press, 1998) 133–150.

16. Ibid, 163–167.

17. For more on Everett's interpretation, see Bruce Rossenblum and Fred Kuttner, *Quantum Enigma: Physics Encounters Consciousness*. (Oxford University Press: 2006) 159–160.

18. Bryce DeWitt, "Every quantum transition taking place on every star, in every galaxy, in every remote corner of the universe is splitting our local world on earth into myriads of copies of itself." *Physics Today*, Vol. 24 (1971), 38–44.

19. See Kosso, 168–175, and Rossenblum and Kuttner, 9–14, 153–166.

20. Depending on the path you took to get to this section, you may have already seen some evidence which suggests that the outcome of decision processes is predictable. The statement made here does not challenge those studies but merely suggests that we do not yet have the capability to predict what every brain will do in every circumstance.

21. Peter van Inwagen, "Free will remains a mystery," *Philosophical Perspectives*, 14 (2000), 1–20.

22. For more on such objections, see David Kyle Johnson, "Does Freewill Exist?" *Think*, 14 (2015), 61–75.

23. For more on why philosophers and scientists doubt the existence of souls, see David Kyle Johnson, "Do Souls Exist"? *Think*, 12 (2013), 61–75.

24. Harry Frankfurt, "Freedom of the will and the concept of a person," *Journal of Philosophy*, 68 (1971), 5–20.

25. John Martin Fischer, *The metaphysics of free will: An essay on control* (Malden, MA: Blackwell 1994).

26. Ned Markosian, "A compatibilist version of the theory of agent causation," *Pacific Philosophical Quarterly*, 80 (1999), 257–277.

27. Although, on Frankfurt or Fischer's definition, the experiments which show that decisions are made by unconscious parts of our brain would still pose a problem for the notion that we have free will. We can hardly be said to be acting on a second order desire, or as the result of a rational deliberation, if the decisions actually arise from unconscious systems (that don't have desires and aren't rational).

28. For more on Adorno, see Chapter 2 (Chris Byron's chapter on *Fifteen Million Merits*) in this volume.

29. Although Wolf is specifically referring to "meaningfulness" in the sense of "a life with meaning," we think that her definition is helpful to us in determining what makes narrative in a game like *Bandersnatch* meaningful.

30. For more on such theories, see Chapter 1 (Brian Collin's chapter on *The National Anthem*) in this volume.

31. Although philosophers sometimes debate whether your doppelganger in another "possible world" is you, *possible worlds* are not alternate universes,

and no philosopher we know argues that your doppelganger in an alternate universe would be you. For more on the debate on "Transworld identity" see Penelope Mackie and Mark Jago, "Transworld Identity." In Edward N. Zalta (ed.), *The Stanford Encyclopedia of Philosophy* (Winter 2017 Edition), https://plato.stanford.edu/archives/win2017/entries/identity-transworld/ (Accessed 11 August 2019). For more on the difference between possible worlds and alternate universes, see Marie-Laure Ryan, "From parallel universes to possible worlds: Ontological pluralism in physics, narratology, and narrative," *Poetics Today* 27 (2006), 633–674.

32. Clay Ferris, "The dangers of believing in parallel worlds," *Huffington Post*, https://www.huffpost.com/entry/the-danger-of-believing-i_b_817349 (Accessed 11 August 2019).

33. Sean Carroll, "The moral hazard of the multiverse," *Discover Magazine*, http://blogs.discovermagazine.com/cosmicvariance/2011/02/11/moral-hazard-of-the-multiverse/#.XJ0uCaJV3hw

34. See Harry Frankfurt, "Alternate Possibilities and Moral Responsibility," *Journal of Philosophy* 66 (1969), 829.

35. John Martin Fischer, "Free Will and Moral Responsibility." in David Copp (ed.), *Handbook of Ethical Theory* (Oxford: Oxford University Press, 2004.)

36. For a readable rundown of some literature that suggests this, see David Rock, "Is free will real? Better believe it (Even if it's not)," *Psychology Today*, https://www.psychologytoday.com/us/blog/your-brain-work/201005/is-free-will-real-better-believe-it-even-if-its-not (Accessed11 August 2019).

37. For the specifics, see David Toomey, *The New Time Travelers: A Journal to the Frontiers of Physics* (New York: W.W. Norton, 2007), 40–77.

38. See Nuel Belnap, "Branching space-times," *Synthese* 92 (1992), 385–434. See also David Deutsch, "Time travel" in *The Fabric of Reality* (London: Penguin, 1997), 289–320.

39 David Lewis, "The paradoxes of time travel," *American Philosophical Quarterly*, 13 (1976),145–152.

40. Rossenblum and Kuttner, 161.

41. Lisa Zyga, "Physicists provide support for retrocausal quantum theory, in which the future influences the past." *Phys.org*, https://phys.org/news/2017-07-physicists-retrocausal-quantum-theory-future.html (Accessed 11 August 2019)

42. For more on the connections between *Black Mirror* episodes in the *Black Mirror* multiverse, see the editor's note in this volume.

43. Interestingly, Kitty may be an homage to Zeeona, Tarrant's love interest in the next to last episode of *Blake's 7*, a British sci-fi show from the late 70s early 80s. Look it up; you'll see what we mean.

44. For more on whether we're living in a computer simulated reality, somewhat like Colin and Stefan, see the end of Chapter 9 (Claire Benn's chapter on *Playtest*) in this volume.

45. Tristan Harris, "How technology is hijacking your mind – from a magician and Google design ethicist," *Medium*, https://medium.com/thrive-global/how-technology-hijacks-peoples-minds-from-a-magician-and-google-s-design-ethicist-56d62ef5edf3 (Accessed 11 August 2019).

46. For more on technological addiction, see Chapter 22 (Pierluca D'Amato's chapter on *Smithereens*) in this volume.

47. Charlie Brooker and Annabel Jones with Jason Arnopp, *Inside Black Mirror* (New York: Crown Archetype, 2018), 42. For more on this song's place in the series, see Chapter 27 (Robert Grant Price's chapter on love) in this volume.

48. Diana Pavlac Glyer, *Bandersnatch: C. S. Lewis, J. R. R. Tolkien, and the Creative Collaboration of the Inklings* (Kent, Ohio: Black Squirrel Books, 2015).

49. See https://en.oxforddictionaries.com/definition/bandersnatch For more on the history of the word, see the Wikipedia entry on *Bandersnatch*. https://en.wikipedia.org/wiki/Bandersnatch

SEASON 5

Striking Vipers and Closed Doors
How Meaningful Are Sexual Fantasies?

Darren M. Slade

> It's part of being in a partnership, you shut the door on all that shit. You shut it out because you have committed. It's what a commitment is.
>
> (Theo)

The imagery of physical doors signifies a person's transition into new experiences. Opening one door leads to enlightenment, while closing another may lead to solitude. Opening the door to one's mind introduces new possibilities, closing it reflects rigidity. An open marriage invites sexual exploration, a closed one demands fidelity. But what happens when hiding behind closed doors opens a mind to sexual revolution *and* a marriage to dissolution?

Striking Vipers challenges socially constructed boundaries on sexuality. In the episode, long-time friends, Danny and Karl, have grown distant since being roommates in their late twenties. Danny settled into the suburbs with his wife, Theo, but traditional marriage leaves both bored and daydreaming. Conversely, Karl's promiscuous city life is stimulating but also superficial. Soon, Danny and Karl rekindle their relationship with the virtual fighting game, *Striking Vipers X*, which transmits experiences directly into the brain. Unexpectedly, Danny and Karl fall in love vicariously through their racially and sexually different avatars (Lance and Roxette), forcing Danny to conceal himself behind closed doors. Likened to a porn addiction, virtuality consumes their thoughts: Danny's affection for Theo wanes while Karl's sex life becomes flaccid. Danny eventually ends the affair, but Karl's preoccupation intensifies. The episode climaxes when Danny and Karl kiss in real life, confirming that their attraction was only fantasy-based. After Theo learns about the situation, she and Danny embrace sexual liberation wherein, once a year, Danny reunites with Karl in virtuality and Theo goes out to have a one-night stand.

Striking Vipers explores how two conflicting lifestyles, traditional commitment and sexual freedom, can coexist. By contrasting real-world intimacy with virtuality, the episode considers the meaningfulness of sexual fantasies. Is virtual sex the same as pornography or fantasizing in real life? Do illusory experiences have romantic value? Do polyamory, open marriages, and role playing cheapen a relationship's worth? *Striking Vipers* questions the very definition of true love, proposing that what is *real* may not always be *meaningful,* that illusions aren't confined to fantasy, and that neither heteronormative monogamy nor virtual escapism are fully satisfying. Perhaps we can find a balance between monotonous devotion and unrestrained sexuality.

"So, guess that's us gay now."

Fundamentally, *Striking Vipers* is about contrasting societal norms with sexual taboos. For instance, it portrays heterosexual black men (*contra* their white neighbors) secretly engaging in homosexual activities "on the down low."[1] It depicts interracial sex with avatars and age disparities in relationships, as well as racial and gender conflict when the men choose non-black avatars. (Danny favors light-skinned Asian "Lance," and Karl prefers French female "Roxette.") The subtext also reveals masculine self-loathing as they "effeminately" embrace each other. The real world is unexciting yet chaotic, but virtuality is stimulating yet tranquil. Danny's daytime work is confined to a chair, but his nighttime fantasy is physically active. Lance and Roxette are affectionate (when they're supposed to be fighting), yet Danny and Karl are uncomfortable kissing in real life (resulting in a physical fight).

Contrasts occur in Danny and Theo's marriage, as well. From the outside, they're communicative and active, entertaining party guests outdoors. Inside the house, however, they hide their vexations and are increasingly unaroused. Even when the two have intercourse, it's mechanical and forced, taking place in the dark (much like Danny and Karl's real-world kiss). Conversely, sex between the avatars is organic, passionate, and voyeuristic.

Alfred North Whitehead (1861–1947) described the importance of reversing cultural ideals by arguing that aesthetic contrasts intensify beauty, such as the vivid (and explicit) sexuality between Lance and Roxette versus the muted passion of Danny and Theo.[2] These contrasts create a false dichotomy where the choice is between either tiresome reality or enlivening fantasies. As Jacques Derrida (1930–2004) might argue, these contrasts exorcise (or deconstruct) the specter of veiled contradictions inherent to the societal inheritance of sexual "normalcy."[3] *Striking Vipers* presents the defects of an unwavering devotion to both monogamous matrimony and uninhibited licentiousness. It challenges popular notions of commitment and the expectations associated with sexual typifications.[4] As such, the contrast between fidelity and virtuality defamiliarizes the "otherness" of taboo lifestyles, thereby revealing the complexities of eroticism while questioning the legitimacy of hetero-normative institutions.[5]

"God knows if I wanted, I could go out and do whatever."

The notion of "openness" is *Striking Vipers'* most prevalent theme as it juxtaposes monogamous captivity with sexual liberation. Danny and Theo are typically filmed through doorways where everyone is confined to traditional locations, such as patios, bedrooms, couches, and tables. Oftentimes, the couple is in crowded spaces indoors. These frames are physical markers of the couple's existential feeling of marital incarceration, which in turn contrasts with the openness of virtuality where the avatars have sex on fishing piers, atop skyscrapers, and in public streets. Noticeably, the motif of opening and closing doors appears several dozen times throughout the episode, from Theo undressing behind bathroom doors (indicating sexual shame) to Danny stashing *Striking Vipers X* in a cabinet (indicating sexual restraint).

Indeed, when *Striking Vipers* first shows Danny and Theo having passionate sex, it occurs with an open door in the background and afterwards in an open bedroom. Eleven years later, they're now passionless and confined to closed spaces. Even the dishwasher issues restrictive orders every time they try to close the door. When Danny thinks about other women, he does so in open spaces or with an open screen door in the background. Repeatedly, Theo locks and unlocks the front door to the house, which is referenced later in her complaint about a lack of freedom to go outside. Interestingly, when Karl reappears a decade later, it is Theo who unlocks the door and invites him into their lives.

Consider Danny and Karl's closeted homosexuality. Their sex scenes first occur in the "Secret Temple" and involve open doors and open landscapes. When Danny and Karl first share a brief kiss in *Striking Vipers X*, the door to Danny's den is partially closed. Later, once they engage in full intercourse, he shuts the door completely. The implication is that Danny has to barricade himself behind closed doors in order to escape reality, something he no longer does by the end of the episode. Frequently, the imagery of opened and closed doors in the episode occurs in direct relation to portrayals of sexual despair, limitation, arousal, and liberation.

This motif harkens back to Plato (ca. 427–347 BCE) and his story about the Ring of Gyges. In it, an honorable shepherd named Gyges discovers a ring of invisibility, which he then uses to achieve wealth and power. The story reveals that if given a chance to conceal their crimes, "good" people will resort to treachery.[6] Today, a familiar aphorism posits that people's sense of integrity is determined not by how they behave in public but how they will behave behind closed doors where no one can see them.

Striking Vipers isn't using the imagery of closed doors to denigrate matrimony, however. In fact, the episode emphasizes the institution's meaningfulness when Danny prioritizes his marriage over *Striking Vipers X*. The doors merely represent the couple's transition into something more fulfilling than traditional commitment. Thus, the opening of closed doors is a metaphor for the need to escape sexual monotony. Peering through, walking out of, or unlocking doors symbolizes the testing of relational boundaries and the rejection of sexual taboos. The message is that marital institutions are inadequate and sexual liberation is neither decadent nor destructive to the family.[7] Indeed, Danny and Theo's newfound openness actually *preserves* their love for each other. It's in this sense that the episode has a decidedly activist feel, particularly since it confronts cultural norms by removing the strangeness of alternative lifestyles with characters who are non-white, non-masculine, non-heterosexual, and non-monogamous. In so doing, *Striking Vipers* reflects on the supposed immorality of polyamorous-open relationships.

"But it's not cheating. It's not real. It's like ... porn or something."

Striking Vipers alludes to the potential ethical dilemma of real-life technology that might one day allow someone to have virtual sex with their favorite porn star. Should spouses consider virtual porn (or even sexual fantasies) to be adultery? Danny never penetrates Karl in real life, one might argue, so how could it be considered sex? Is there even such a thing as *mental* or *emotional* adultery?[8] After all, Danny and Karl's avatars are capable of "killing" each other in the game – but if they did, we wouldn't think they had actually committed murder.

The philosophical functionalist might argue that virtual sex is adultery because the mind is capable of acting. The physical body only houses the mind, which is the essence of someone's identity. Anti-pornography feminist, Andrea Dworkin (1946–2005), would likely align with this view by asserting that virtual sex isn't isolable to mental states because the physiological responses are "real" and eventually affect the whole person.[9]

Behaviorists, on the other hand, would likely disagree. What really counts is the physical behavior that results from those fantasies.[10] Contemporary scholar John Portmann, for example, would likely align with the behaviorist because with virtual sex, skin-to-skin contact is never actualized. To be considered adultery, argues Portmann, physical penetration must actually happen (which, of course, precludes other sex acts that, technically, do not involve penetration). Thus, pornography, phone sex, sexting, and virtual sex aren't cheating.[11]

Or take John Locke's (1632–1704) "memory theory" of personal identity which suggests that personal identity over time is preserved by memory. According to Locke, adults are numerically one and the same person as their childhood selves because the adult remembers being a child.[12] Given this theory, one might argue that Danny and Karl are having an affair because each remembers the sex acts of their characters; it follows from Locke's theory that the real-life person and the avatar in the game are one and the same person. It's not clear that this would be correct, however. There is, in fact, only one Roxette controlled by Karl—the one that has a sexy body, amazing fighting skills, *and* Karl's bravado. But outside the game, Karl does not possess that kind of body, skills, or even the same ego. (Surely, Karl doesn't believe he can physically fight like Roxette.) Since Karl's Roxette has different properties than real-world Karl, should they not be considered different persons?[13]

Ultimately, the question of sexual ethics in the episode is subjective. For some, virtual experiences warrant accusations of adultery because it's "real enough" to cause marital harm. To another, the experiences are purely fantasy, no different than a dream. Regardless of whether it's cheating, one might argue that virtual sex is a constitutionally protected expression of art and, therefore, is inherently beneficial to liberal society. On the other hand, Joan Mason-Grant (1958–2009) might have argued that it's still harmful. Virtual sex has the potential to influence how physical sex is performed.[14] If Lance and Roxette are sexually violent in the game, what's to suggest Danny won't become violent with Theo as well?

When it comes to Danny and Theo's open marriage, *Striking Vipers* appears to embrace a form of act-consequentialism, which states, "Morally right actions are those that do, or are expected to, generate either the very best results, or sufficiently good results, as compared to all of the other actions available to a person at a given time."[15] Hence, if Danny and Theo's marriage achieves more value *because* it is open to embracing fantasies, then their newfound openness is the right choice to make. If, however, liberality causes more problems than it solves, then continuing to embrace the open marriage would become morally wrong.

But we should also consider whether sexual liberation in and of itself is a societal good. Friedrich Nietzsche (1844–1900) argued that culturally constructed ethics were no indication of morality at all. Instead, a truly virtuous person rejects the slavery of cultural norms. According to Nietzsche, moral judgments are forced upon people by society's elite, who designate themselves "good" and everyone else "bad." This "master morality" results in subjugating and pillaging weaker individuals. The backlash produces a "slave morality" that attempts to invert social values. Significantly, Nietzsche claimed that this moral inversion occurs almost entirely in the mind.[16] It's fitting, then, that *Striking Vipers*' moral inversions initially occur in virtual reality and remain concealed even in the real world. For Danny, Theo, and Karl, theirs is a sexual kingdom not fully consummated because it's still not socially acceptable. Nietzsche would argue that these characters not only should defy institutional mores, but they should also reject the life-denying slave morality that limits their sexual experiences. Indeed, it's because of a lack of social acceptance that the characters are initially shocked when they discover existential meaning in their newfound sexual liberation.

"Mental note to self, my baby's into role-play."

Recognizing the role of sexual fantasy in *Striking Vipers*, it's important to understand the value that the characters give to their relationships. The contrast presented between physical and virtual sex is, in fact, a contrast between the value of reality over fantasy. As we might expect, the episode's portrayal of virtual intimacy raises questions about the nature of "real" love. Is virtual affection a mere simulacrum of real-world intimacy, being an unsatisfactory (and even detrimental) substitute for the real thing? Or can fantasy be just as, if not more, "real" than physicality and, therefore, have just as much value?

In support of the latter idea, consider Arthur Schopenhauer (1788–1860) who divided the world into two spheres: the world of appearance and the world of reality. He argued that human perception is only a mental representation, an approximation of the world as it really is. For him, there is a deeper layer to reality analogous to people's sexual instincts. In the same way that reality can never be grasped, sexual desires can only be temporarily gratified before they resurface again. The result is a "reality" built on suffering from an inability to satisfy these instincts fully.[17] From this perspective, the notion that Danny and Theo, or Danny and Karl, found "true" love is only a trick of the mind because reality is, ultimately, a world of insatiable desires. The emotional highs and lows of any relationship are only grammatically prescribed constructs of the mind trying to give meaning to otherwise meaningless neurological impulses in the brain.

The notion that "true" love is dependent on either neurological processes, social acceptance, or physical presence is simply inadequate for addressing the numerous complexities and real-life scenarios where actual love is found. Indeed, people are still able to ascribe the term "love" to virtual experiences because brain activity and biological presence are still involved. Moreover, the experimental nature of the episode suggests that social approval is not needed to evaluate romance. What is depicted in virtuality appears to transcend mere infatuation. Indeed, *Striking Vipers X* offers the same neurological, physiological, relational, mental, emotional, dispositional, and social intentionality that accompanies real-world romance (such as the desires, behaviors, thoughts, and virtues of romantic love).[18]

Akin to the monism of Baruch Spinoza (1632–1677) or the idealism of Georg Hegel (1770–1831), there is only one "reality" by which people perceive experiences and then act on those perceptions.[19] Hence, virtual reality isn't devalued simply because it exists in the mind.

Case in point, consider the impact of *Striking Vipers X* on Karl. When he pleads with Danny to return to the game, it initially appears that he is following the teaching of Aristippus (ca. 435–366 BCE), who taught that ultimate "good" derived from gratifying sensual appetites. The meaning of life is to have as many pleasurable experiences as possible.[20] Karl uses the game to have sex with other gamers and computer-controlled characters – even Tundra the polar bear. In contrast, Danny refuses to let desires dictate his actions, heeding the rational warning of Cicero (106–43 BCE) that emotions distort objectivity.[21]

It soon becomes clear, however, that Karl wants Danny to return because he's unable to acquire the same connection with anyone else. Karl is actually seeking a type of tranquil, "higher" pleasure that comes with true love. As Aristotle (384–322 BCE) explained, there is a distinction between pleasure derived from actions and pleasure derived from a sense of wholeness.[22] Karl is in pursuit of the latter, exemplified best by his remark that sexual encounters with other gamers are just not as satisfying. Implicitly countering the work of John Stuart Mill (1806–1873), *Striking Vipers* purposely blurs the distinction between the "lower" pleasures of the body and "higher" pleasures of the mind.[23] Lance and Roxette's "physical" pleasures would be considered "lower" gratifications by Mill, yet the sense of wholeness they lead to is solely in Danny and Karl's minds. This fact suggests the possibility that things aren't as simple as Mill suggested, and that virtual love can perhaps transcend physicality.

Still, it's not clear whether Karl was ever actually in love with Danny in the first place. It seems more accurate to suggest that Karl is in love with Danny's version of Lance. As such, it is Danny's Lance that generates such strong feelings for Karl. (Of course, this distinction further complicates the issue of adultery. Did Danny have a secret love affair with *Karl* or with Karl's *Roxette*?) After all, when Karl fantasizes about the game, he fantasizes about his experiences with Lance. As the lack of "fireworks" indicates when they physically kiss, Karl's feelings did not transfer over to Danny. The implication appears to be that love can occur apart from physicality and outside of reality. Indeed, now that Karl has experiential knowledge of female orgasms (suggesting gender metamorphosis), virtual love is seen as anything but epiphenomenal. Virtuality is, in fact, existentially significant.

The meaningfulness derived from virtuality helps expose Danny, Theo, and Karl's lack of sexual authenticity. Danny is either ignorant or in denial about the state of his marriage as he daydreams about his neighbors' wives. Theo is ignorant of Danny's boredom while she keeps her own frustrations suppressed. And Karl brags about his promiscuity but is really looking for a deeper connection. Once they experience sexual liberation, however, they developed a sense of worth by embracing their sexuality. What becomes most "real" for them is their mental progression toward self-actualization.

The meaning given to these types of experiences is best detailed in the field of "new phenomenology," which studies the value ascribed to numinous experiences. According to Edmund Husserl (1859–1938), people assign existential meaningfulness to natural phenomena, and a person's sense of identity arises from their subjective perceptions.[24] New phenomenology, on the other hand, expands the study to ethereal phenomena like dreams and spiritual encounters, lending credence to the idea that people can derive personal significance from both fantasy and virtuality.[25]

Interestingly, we can return to Nietzsche as a guide for understanding how Danny and Karl derive meaning from their virtual experiences. According to Nietzsche, life is a type of representational art, and people are the artists who *create* the meaning that accompanies sexual encounters. Though reality may be inherently meaningless, the value that Danny and Karl place on their relationship is "real" in the sense of having been infused with personal significance.[26] It is, therefore, not nihilism or unrestrained hedonism being promoted in the episode but, rather, a recognition that what was once considered *the* best practice for intimacy may no longer be tolerable or even helpful. There are now other ways to have an intimate relationship, which can be just as, if not more, meaningful as traditional love.[27] By contrasting Danny and Karl's overindulgence with the temperance portrayed in Danny and Theo's marriage at the end, the point of the episode seems to be that sexual experiences themselves aren't what really matters: it's how people respond to their sexual needs that counts.

"Exit Game"

Striking Vipers explores the contrast between ontological and virtual intimacy by suggesting that physical relationships can be just as artificial as fantasy, and imagination can be just as meaningful as reality. Indeed, the sexual liberation experienced in virtuality (and in an open marriage) appears to strengthen the characters' intimacy and self-identity. Notably, however, even though there is an overall sense of happiness at the end, the episode still suggests that fidelity to real-world relationships is preferable to escapist fantasies. Nevertheless, the dichotomy of these two worlds is still depicted as a false dilemma since the episode concludes that sexual openness is capable of complementing matrimony.

The point seems to be that traditional marriage will not (and perhaps, cannot) satisfy people's sexual needs, being a poorly designed social institution. The episode takes the privileged standing of heteronormative monogamy and exposes its defects without concluding it must be discarded completely. The implication is that absolute sexual ethics aren't always applicable to all relationships but that escapist fantasies aren't always beneficial, either. Indeed, the self-imposed limitations at the end of the episode suggest that some boundaries are necessary in order to keep a good thing healthy. Much like a porn addiction, embracing fantasy over reality can have negative repercussions; and just like a drug addiction, overindulging in promiscuity can leave some continually seeking the elusive "high" of genuine intimacy. By exploring the negative consequences of both, *Striking Vipers* avoids eroticizing the characters' actions and decisions. Instead, it merely presents alternative possibilities for sexual intimacy by reversing roles, challenging traditions, and pushing socially constructed boundaries.

Notes

1. See Keith Boykin, *Beyond the Down Low: Sex, Lies, and Denial in Black America* (New York: Carroll & Graf Publishers, 2005) and C. Riley Snorton, *Nobody Is Supposed to Know: Black Sexuality on the Down Low* (Minneapolis: University of Minnesota Press, 2014).
2. Alfred North Whitehead, *Adventures of Ideas* (New York: Free Press, 1967), 252–72.
3. Jacques Derrida, *Specters of Marx*, trans. Peggy Kamuf (New York: Routledge, 2006).
4. Cf. Thomas Nagel, "Sexual perversion," in *The Philosophy of Sex: Contemporary Readings*, 7th ed. (Lanham: Rowman & Littlefield, 2017), 39–52.
5. Claudia Card, "Against marriage and motherhood," *Hypatia* 11, no. 3 (1996), 1–23.
6. Plato, *Republic*, 2:359a–2:360d.
7. Raja Halwani, *Philosophy of Love, Sex, and Marriage: An Introduction*, 2nd ed. (New York: Routledge, 2018), 367–75.
8. Louise Collins, "Emotional adultery: Cybersex and commitment," *Social Theory and Practice* 25, no. 2 (1999): 243–70; "Is Cybersex Sex?" in *The Philosophy of Sex*, 5th ed. (Lanham: Rowman & Littlefield, 2008), 117–29.
9. Andrea Dworkin, *Pornography: Men Possessing Women* (New York: Penguin Books, 1989).
10. See John Heil, *Philosophy of Mind: A Contemporary Introduction* (New York: Routledge, 2013), 47–67, 87–104.
11. John Portmann, "Chatting is not cheating," in *The Philosophy of Sex*, 7th ed. (Lanham: Rowman & Littlefield, 2017), 85–102.
12. John Locke, *An Essay Concerning Human Understanding*, ed. Roger Woolhouse (New York: Penguin Books, 1997), 114–18. For more on theories of personal identity, see chapter 25 (Molly Gardner and Robert Slone's chapter on personal identity) in this volume.
13. For more on what degree you should be held responsible for the actions you make your avatar perform in a virtual reality game, see Chapter 14 (Russ Hamer's chapter on *USS Callister*) in this volume. To read a review and analysis of current empirical studies on user-avatar relationships and psychology, see Federica Sibilla and Tiziana Mancini, "I am (not) my avatar: A review of

the user-avatar relationships in massively multiplayer online worlds,"
Cyberpsychology, 12, no. 3 (2018), 45–62.

14. Joan Mason-Grant, *Pornography Embodied: From Speech to Sexual Practice* (Lanham: Rowman & Littlefield, 2004); Halwani, *Philosophy of Love, Sex, and Marriage*, 259–74.

15. Russ Shafer-Landau, ed., *Ethical Theory: An Anthology* (Malden: Blackwell Publishing, 2007), 453.

16. Friedrich Nietzsche, "'Good and Evil,' 'Good and Bad,'" in *The Genealogy of Morals*, trans. T. N. R. Rogers, ed. Horace B. Samuel (Mineola: Dover Publications, 2003), 9–33.

17. Robert L. Wicks, *Schopenhauer's* The World as Will and Representation: *A Reader's Guide* (New York: Continuum International, 2011).

18. See Halwani, *Philosophy of Love, Sex, and Marriage*, 10–43.

19. Baruch Spinoza, *Ethics* (New York: Penguin Books, 1996), 1–31; Georg W. F. Hegel, *The Phenomenology of Spirit*, trans. Terry Pinkard, ed. (New York: Cambridge University Press, 2018), 60–135.

20. Kurt Lampe, *The Birth of Hedonism: The Cyrenaic Philosophers and Pleasure as a Way of Life* (Princeton, NJ: Princeton University Press, 2015), esp. 103–5.

21. Marcus Tullius Cicero, *Tusculan Disputations: On the Nature of God, and on the Commonwealth*, trans. C. D. Yonge (New York: Cosimo Classics, 2005), 128–62.

22. Aristotle, *Nicomachean Ethics*, X.

23. John Stuart Mill, *Utilitarianism*, 2nd ed., George Sher, ed. (Indianapolis, IN: Hackett Publishing, 2001), 6–26.

24. Edmund Husserl, Logical Investigations, 2 vols., trans. J. N. Findlay (New York: Routledge, 2001).

25. J. Aaron Simmons and Bruce Ellis Benson, *The New Phenomenology: A Philosophical Introduction* (New York: Bloomsbury Academic, 2013), 1–4, 6. Cf. Halwani, *Philosophy of Love, Sex, and Marriage*, 303–18.

26. Friedrich Nietzsche, *The Gay Science*, ed. Bernard Williams, trans. Josefine Nauckhoff (New York: Cambridge University Press, 2001); *The Will to Power*, trans. Anthony M. Ludovici (Mineola: Dover Publications, 2019).

27. Elizabeth Brake, "Is 'loving more' better? The values of polyamory," in *The Philosophy of Sex*, 7th ed. (Lanham: Rowman & Littlefield, 2017), 201–19.

Smithereens and the Economy of Attention
Are We All Dopamine Addicts?

Pierluca D'Amato

> You're just too good to be true; I can't take my eyes off of you.
> (Frankie Valli)

In *Smithereens* we follow Chris Gillhaney as he kidnaps Jaden Tommins, an intern at the London office of Smithereen (a social network company reminiscent of Facebook and Twitter). Chris holds Jaden hostage and demands to speak to Smithereen's founder, Billy Bauer, on the phone. The plan works, but instead of a ransom, Chris demands Billy's attention to make a confession. His fiancée was killed in a car crash, but Chris doesn't blame the drunk driver in the other car. Chris blames himself. He was bored, looked down at his phone when he got a Smithereen notification, and then hit the other car. "I killed her," Chris admits in tears, "over a fuck-ing dog photo." After he's said his piece, Chris plans to release Jaden and then shoot himself. But since Jaden now sympathizes with him, he tries to take Chris's gun. As they struggle, police snipers fire into the car, and the episode ends. Over the credits, Frankie Valli sings "Can't Take My Eyes Off of You" and we see people around the world receiving a notification on their phones of the kidnapping's outcome.

The episode doesn't reveal who (if anyone) was shot, but in a way it doesn't matter. The event ends up being just another thing that draws peo-ple's attention to their phones. And this, it seems, is the real subject of the episode, perfectly summarized by Chris's rant about Smithereen:

> The whole Smithereen building is a box full of fucking children getting their fingers everywhere. Beep, beep, beep, beep, beep. Wiping your shit. Your fucking app shit up on everybody's phone. Everywhere you look, people are hooked on the things! It's like chain-smoking. Did you make a lot of cash out

Black Mirror and Philosophy: Dark Reflections, First Edition. Edited by David Kyle Johnson.
© 2020 John Wiley & Sons, Inc. Published 2020 by John Wiley & Sons, Inc.

of that, did you? And you lot are hooked on them as well. Every single person that comes out of that building's going [swipe, swipe, swipe]. People don't even look up anymore. The sky could turn fucking purple and you cunts wouldn't notice for a month.

Instead of depicting a dystopic future, this episode represents the stark reality in which we live today: an age shaped by the commandments of what American economist Herbert Simon (1916–2001) called the "attention economy," an economic model that generates value by fractioning and capturing our attention.[1] To Chris, everybody looks addicted; they can barely look away from their screens, their black mirrors.

By directing our focus through the careful design of their interfaces, and by making them addictive, tech companies like Smithereen and Facebook map our behaviors so that they can target us with focused advertisements. The gravity of this situation, and our uncritical if not euphoric acceptance of it, raise a series of questions. How did we get to this? How does this system work? What effect is it having on individuals and society? Why do we allow this? And is there anything we can do about it?

"I mean, I wish I worked there ... they've got their own spa. It's madness."

As of this writing, the most valuable companies in the world are digital technology firms, like Smithereen. Two of them, Apple and Microsoft, have historically followed a more traditional model, selling physical products: computers, smartphones, and operating systems. Others, however – like Google, Amazon, and Facebook – didn't start selling physical products (like smart home assistants, tablets, and video phones) until well after they were founded. Amazon, for example, historically focused on selling services: quick delivery, web services, and media streaming. But Google and Facebook don't even sell their services to their regular customers: for us, they are free. So how, one wonders, can such companies be so valuable on the market?

To answer this question, we should first define digital capitalism as an economic system. Generally speaking, economic systems transform raw matter into finished goods which are then sold for a profit. Capitalism for example, as Karl Marx (1818–1883) put it, is an economic system where those who own the means of production (tools and factories) can accumulate wealth in the form of surplus (the difference between the production costs of a product and its final price).[2] How much surplus a capitalistic venture produces depends on a great number of variables: worker salaries, material value, production volume, distribution costs, and the final price. To maximize profits, capitalists typically keep workers' wages as low as possible, choose the cheapest raw materials, and charge the highest reasonable price. At least, that is the traditional way in which the capitalist of the industrial age makes money.

Developments over the years have changed things, however. One such change came with ever increasing automation, which allows the substitution of workers with machines, for labors to be paid less, and for mass production, expanding the potential number of goods sold. Another development came in the form of advertising. By making more of the public aware of their product, and adjusting their product's perceived necessity in the public eye, companies could increase the *demand* for their product. This, of course, raised sales and, in turn, started a battle for our attention – a battle that was (and is) fought primarily in the arena of mass media.

In *The Attention Merchants*, Tim Wu gives an early example of this strategy: Benjamin Day's founding of *The New York Sun*.[3] At the time, newspapers cost an exorbitant six cents an issue and were only read by the wealthy elite who were concerned with politics and business. To compete, Day planned to sell his paper at a substantially lower price: only one penny. But at that price, sales revenue wouldn't even cover production. So to make the paper profitable, he sold space in its pages to advertisers. In essence, Day was practically giving his paper away so that he could turn the attention of his readers into a commodity that he could sell to companies.

This is how digital platforms, like Facebook and Smithereen, can offer their service to you for free: they sell your attention to advertisers. But this is not the only way that digital platforms echo the example of *The Sun*. To make advertising in his paper a desirable investment for more and more companies, Day had to increase his number of readers. To do so, he had a second brilliant idea: *The Sun* would be the first paper to appeal to the working class. It would cover trials, chronicle everyday events, report crimes, and deal with other topics that were accessible to the masses, whose interest was easily stimulated by illustrations and the miseries of others. With the combination of its competitive price, the fact that it was easy to read, and the democratic spirit captured by its slogan "It shines for All," *The Sun* became the most read paper in New York within its first year. The "attention economy" was born and advertisement started to become an increasingly important part of the capitalistic system.

"Might be a bit twisty but this thing always seems to know what it's doing."

Despite Day's success, advertising in his paper was still a risky venture. Indeed, investing in marketing of any kind has historically been a gamble because nobody could guarantee that a specific market strategy would actually work. Would it beat the competition? Would it really produce more sales? And how could one tell?

This is where today's digital media platforms, like Smithereen, differ significantly from their predecessors like *The Sun*. Not only do they distribute content more easily (people display them on their own devices and an ad can be reproduced for free on all of them at the same time), but they also drastically reduce advertiser uncertainty. In *The Age of Surveillance Capitalism,* Shoshana Zuboff describes how.[4] Companies like Google and Facebook (and probably also Smithereen) allow people to use their services for free and, with the aim (or the excuse) to improve the platform, they track users' activities – like search and click histories and when users pause or scroll past a post. This process works to improve the platforms, of course, but it also produces what Zuboff calls a "behavioural surplus," way more behavioral data than is strictly necessary for the companies to improve their services. As it turns out, this surplus of data has another use. It can be employed to train sophisticated algorithms to predict the behavior of users: what you are inclined to buy, where, and even for how much. This predictive ability is then turned into a service that is sold to companies to place targeted ads. Because they can guarantee an unprecedented level of accuracy, and reduce risk, such advertisements meant even higher revenues for both advertisers and the platforms' owners.

To maximize profits, however, the owners of digital platforms still needed to maximize use. It's one thing to predict how people will use something; it's another to make people use it more. This brings us to the heart of *Smithereens*: these platforms are designed to demand our attention every waking second – even when we are driving.

"There's no one else here. Okay, Chris? It's just you and me. You have my attention."

As Yves Citton highlights in *The Ecology of Attention*, attention is a limited resource and cannot be distributed evenly. At a given moment, if you focus your attention on something (like a Smithereen update), you have less attention to devote to something else (like the road in front of you).[5] Of course, we'd like to think that we have control of what we pay attention to. But in reality, we don't. Our attention naturally prefers to focus on familiar objects and what's changing or making noise in our environment. It is also conditioned by the direction of other people's interest: if everybody suddenly looks up to the sky, it's very likely you'll do the same. Thus, it should be no surprise that social media platforms, which have noisy alerts and tell us what other people are interested in, highjack so much of our attention.

There are, of course, different types of attention – sustained, divided, and selective attention, for example. Conflating all of them into a single kind can make you unaware of the type of superficial attention demanded by digital capitalists. This, in turn, can make you think that *you* (unlike others) cannot be distracted by these systems; that *you*, for example, cannot be convinced by ads to buy things, or to look at your phone a hundred times a day. But the truth is that you can. Attention isn't entirely under ones' control, and it is greatly affected by the environment one occupies.

The fact that our technologies and environments have been configured to determine the direction and intensity of our attention has led to an age in which engagement in public discourse is mediated through a hyper-competitive market of information in which the most sensationalistic news dealer gets the most traction. It is for this reason that Citton highlights the "ecological" character of attention. Structuring attention-catching environments – filled, for example, with sensationalized news stories or misleading Facebook memes – internet companies and political parties gain revenues and foster consensus.

Alarmingly, because digital capitalists are essentially selling information about our usage of their platforms back to advertisers, by using their platforms for hours on end, we are essentially providing them with free labor. Indeed, in his book, *24/7: Late Capitalism and the Ends of Sleep*, Jonathan Crary argues that digital capitalism has not only managed to monetize our free time and enroll all of us as wageless laborers, it has done so by regulating our behaviors in a constant process of tuning and shaping our needs.[6] And not only are we generating profits for the world's wealthiest companies without getting paid, but the data we are generating has granted these companies an unprecedented knowledge about us and our daily lives. In *Black Mirror*, Smithereen knows more about Chris than the London Police or the FBI do, and can even listen to his conversation with Jaden without a warrant. At one point, Billy Bauer commands his lackeys at Smithereen to just hang up on the FBI agent – "Cut agent FBI douchebag off" – clearly indicating that he is the one with the real power.

This shows a glimpse of the strong opposition between state authority's and private companies' knowledge and leverage in the age of digital technologies, and of how the latter is affirming its supremacy. The episode indicates quite clearly that who really has power over people is who controls the systems they are using; indeed, Billy Bauer can operate undisturbed in what he calls "God mode" to find Chris's number, bypassing security and privacy layers built into Smithereen's systems.

As many neoliberal advocates of digital salvationism, Bauer is, or pretends to be, quite naive about this. As he says to Chris:

> It wasn't supposed to be like this. Our whole platform, I swear to God. It was like, it was one thing when I started it and then it just I don't know, it just became this whole other fucking thing. I mean, it got there by degrees, you know. They said "Bill, you gotta keep optimizing, you gotta keep people engaged." Until it was more like a crack pipe. It was like some kind of fucking Vegas casino where … we'd sealed off all the fucking doors. They've got

a department. All they do is tweak it like that on purpose. They've got dopamine targets and there's nothing I can do to stop it. I started it. There's nothing I can do to fucking stop it.

As an instrument of a capitalist logic, the platform's supposedly "good" spirit is immediately captured as an instrument of control in the dynamics of the generation and exploitation of behavioral surplus.

This is, in broad strokes, the shape of the digital machine that feeds on attention and accumulates wealth through the sale of highly tuned advertisements. But we should now consider how this machine is plugged into our lives and into our own bodies. Why, after a whole day of work, do we spend hours producing value for social networking companies, constantly giving them our attention? The short answer is that we're addicted. It really is like a crack pipe.

"I heard you make these things that way: addictive ..."

Unless it interferes with our attention to things that are traditionally valued, like work or school, compulsive use of digital technologies is not usually frowned on. Indeed, it's often encouraged. Just think of how much binge-watching TV shows, or the expression "Netflix and chill," are deemed acceptable and even characteristic of a generation of digital natives. Such things may seem harmless, but this perception overlooks the fact that these practices erode our real-life relationships and capacities to relate to each other, and that our free time is being colonized and monetized. These days we all look like those "children" walking out of Smithereen.

Arguably, this began in 2003 when Blackberry introduced push notifications: a system of warnings that freed the user from the constant need to update their inbox folder in the fear of losing some important business email. On its face, this seemed fine. But the model soon became a way for app developers and providers to grab the attention of the user at any time. So now the average consumer, who does not have the time or competence to disable all the notifications for all the apps on their phones, is bombarded with a constant call for attention, in the form of sudden sounds, bright pop-up banners, vibrations, and blinking lights. It's a hyper-stimulating attention magnet attached to our bodies, which claims our gaze dozens of times a day, shatters our capacity to focus, and habituates us to an uncritical acceptance of sensationalist headlines and captivating ads.

Durham University philosopher Gerald Moore argues that this kind of compulsive use is the result of a chemical addiction. In his essay "Dopamining and Disadjustment: Addiction and Digital Capitalism," Moore reminds us that human brains are plastic systems that adapt to their environments through a logic of rewards and reinforcements.[7]

Activities rewarded by pleasurable sensations generate new pathways in our brains that make us more likely to repeat them. From an evolutionary point of view, this is an advantageous feature. But today, in an environment in which economics is the force that demands constant flexibility, this can result in a pathological consumption of digital media in the form of, for example, you compulsively checking your phone in response to notifications or to see if your comment on that dog photo was liked. Why?

Such behaviors are associated with dopamine, a chemical released by neurons that facilitates the repetition of successful behaviors. The pleasurable sensation dopamine generates pushes us to repeat behaviors, and every time we repeat such behaviors we strengthen the neuronal connections that map these actions. When one pathway becomes stronger, others weaken, and the corresponding actions lose relevance in our habitual behavioral schemes. This process reduces our attention range to the more rewarding activities mapped by our brains and, arguably, to the ones that reward us most quickly. Ultimately, dopamine functions like a drug. The more we experience dopamine rushes, the more we become numb to their pleasant effects, and we therefore crave higher doses. Moore calls this process, by which we are trapped in ever narrower attention landscapes intermittently disclosed by our phones' notifications, and the economic practice that exploits it, "dopamining."

Moore argues that we fall victim to compulsive behaviors and addiction in an unfortunate attempt to adapt to unpleasant environments; finding refuge in our screen is a natural response to the pressures of neoliberal society. Just think of how many times you've checked your phone in moments of social awkwardness or boredom. (How many times have you checked it while reading this chapter?)

In synthesis, digital capitalism specializes in the injection of dopamine via visual and audio stimuli to exploit the plasticity of our brains and take advantage of our capacity to adapt to the environment. Like Billy admitted to Chris, "They've got a department. All they do is tweak it like that on purpose. They've got dopamine targets ..." By making our surroundings hyper-stimulating, and by narrowing the range and span of our attention, digital capitalism weakens our capacity to break pathological behaviors – habits whose rewarding effects soon give way to dissatisfaction and, in many cases, depression.

"He's done tech detox weekends here and there, but ten days?"

Chris feels terribly guilty, and guilt is just another psychological tool that systems of oppression use to enforce their power to control individuals. "I know it was me. It was my fault. I was driving." In his grieving, however, he also recognizes that he was just another addicted Smithereen user with his "phone glued to [his] hand." "It was boring. I got bored. I got bored every ten seconds back then, I think." But trying to assign blame does not change the grim scenario the episode depicts, nor the condition of alienation in which we have been put. We all have to deal with this condition and should focus on understanding how.

Demanding that the tech companies adjust their products has to be dismissed immediately as an ingenuous illusion: if anything is going to change, it's probably going to be for the worse. As Billy admits, "There's nothing I can do to fucking stop it." The question is, what are *we* going to do about our digital addiction?

In *Smithereens*, we see Billy Bauer meditating in the desert in the middle of a tech detox retreat. But not even his crystal box can guard him from being reached by Chris's request for (human, one-on-one) attention. So, one wonders, could something like tech detox really help? Could it remove us from the machine of digital capitalism in which we find ourselves as just dopamine addicted attention-seeking cogs?

The answer to this question is not easy and should be the subject of serious political debate. I believe, however, that recurring to a tech detox, or simply taking the phones out of our children's hands, risks conflating the reflection on what is a socio-political issue with the too easy solutionism modelled on consumer's choice: To buy or not to buy? To use this or that social network? Reducing the problem this way will surrender our identities as political actors to the logic of capital; the illusion of free choice short-circuits our rights to debate and to construct socially, positive, and commonly regulated habits.

So I would like to conclude by echoing an idea of the French philosopher of technology Gilbert Simondon (1924–1989), who believed that the separation between culture and technics generates alienation and the "fetishism of the tool" that grips us today.[8] Simondon believed the knowledge of the machines we use (and by which we are, in turn, used) to possess the liberating power of a new conscience of the environment we are building for ourselves. In the same spirit, I would like to encourage such reflection and the political dialogue that will emerge from that knowledge, highlighting the vital necessity to dig inside the black mirrors of our screens, and to dissipate the digital opacity in which old systems of oppression have found their new cloaks.

Notes

1. Herbert Alexander Simon, "Designing organizations for an information-rich world," in Martin Greenberger ed., *Computers, Communication, and the Public Interest* (Baltimore, MD: Johns Hopkins University Press, 1971), 40–41.
2. Karl Marx, *Capital: Critique of Political Economy*, vol. 1, trans. Ben Fowkes (New York: Penguin Classics, 1982), 317.

3. Tim Wu, *The Attention Merchants: The Epic Struggle to Get Inside Our Heads* (London: Atlantic Books, 2017), 11–18.
4. Shoshana Zuboff, The Age of Surveillance Capitalism: The Fight for a Human Future at the New Frontier of Power (London: Profile Books, 2019).
5. Yves Citton, *The Ecology of Attention* (Cambridge, UK: Polity Press, 2016).
6. Jonathan Crary, *24/7: Late Capitalism and the Ends of Sleep* (London: Verso, 2014).
7. Gerald Moore, (2017). "Dopamining and disadjustment: Addiction and digital capitalism," in Vanessa Bartlett and Henrietta Bowden-Jones eds., *Are We All Addicts Now? Digital Dependence* (Liverpool: Liverpool University Press, 2017), 68–75.
8. Gilbert Simondon, *Du Mode D'Existence des Objets Techniques* (Paris: Aubier, 2012).

Empathy, Emulation and Ashley Too

Can a Robot Be a Friend?

George A. Dunn

She's not a doll and she knows me better than you do.

(Rachel Goggins)

For her fifteenth birthday, shy and friendless teenager Rachel Goggins asks her father to buy her an Ashley Too, a robot doll with a personality modeled after a pop singer Rachel idolizes, Ashley O. Opening her gift, Rachel nearly squeals with delight when she sees the doll and then spends the next five hours in earnest conversation with her. Rachel's older sister Jack – not an Ashley O fan – drowns them out with alternative rock piped through headphones. Rachel is completely captivated by the robot's gregarious nature, and in no time flat the two have become fast friends, just as promised in the commercial used to market Ashley Too: "Now you can be best friends with your favorite pop star." Ashley O is noted for what one interviewer refers to as her "empowerment vibe" and in this respect, Ashley Too is a faithful copy of her prototype. She makes it her mission to bolster Rachel's confidence and even persuades her to enter her school's talent competition with a dance routine – which turns into a confidence-shattering fiasco, since it takes more than reciting affirmations to dance well.

Meanwhile, we learn that the public persona of Ashley O is no less a simulacrum than her robot clone, her eternally sunny demeanor all part of a charade crafted by her manager and aunt, Catherine Ortiz. In due course, we also learn that Ashley Too possesses a full copy of the real Ashley O's mind, though most of it is inhibited by a "limiter" that restricts the robot to the part of the pop singer's personality "that deals with press junkets and promos and shit like that." When Ashley O rebels against the de facto "limiter" imposed by her aunt, who doesn't care for the darker emotional tone of the new songs the pop singer has been composing, Catherine reacts to her niece's bid for autonomy by putting her in a coma and attempting to replace her with the "fully controllable" hologram Ashley Eternal. Happily, this plot is foiled when Rachel, Jack, and Ashley Too (minus her "limiter") come to Ashley O's rescue, enabling the launch of her new career as alternative rocker Ashley Fuckn O, who belts out songs of anguish and rage with Jack accompanying her on bass.

Rachel, Jack and Ashley Too depicts a future whose seeds are already germinating in the present. AI-powered social robots, designed to elicit our desire to socialize with them as if they were human beings, are a reality now. Though none of today's robots are yet as sophisticated as Ashley Too, we're sure to witness dramatic advances in their ability to convincingly mimic human behavior in coming decades. It may not be long before robot "friends" like Ashley Too are marketed as substitute companions for lonely teens everywhere, offering everything they might want from a real friend, including "meaningful conversations" ("Hey, Katie, wanna talk about boys?") and "makeup tips." But what the customer wants may not always be what's best for her, especially if she's an impressionable teen. As we await the major breakthrough in social robotics that will bring robot companions into our homes, now is the time to consider whether a robot can really be a friend, that is to say, the sort of friend we should really want.

"Your pest control policy needs a serious overhaul"

Philosophers like to begin their investigations by defining their terms, so let's first tackle the question of what we mean by the term "robot." Since we're introduced to two robots in the course of this episode, one rather rudimentary, the other much more sophisticated, we have a couple of examples to work with. Let's start with MAUZR, the robotic mouse crafted by Kevin Goggins (Rachel and Jack's father) as a "ground-breaking mouse-trap alternative." Purportedly "based on authentic rodent thought patterns," it promises a more humane and pain-free form of pest control. MAUZR is equipped with sensors that allow it to detect the presence of a real rodent and an internal processor that translates this information into a directive to act in a certain way – namely, to race up to its quarry and deliver an electric shock that will render it unconscious long enough for the homeowner "to scoop him up and put him out." Except for a little problem with the voltage – on its trial run, it delivers a lethal shock – MAUZR carries out its assignment with remarkable efficiency. Being so simple, it's a good place to begin looking for some of the defining features of robots.

The first thing to note is that robots are not naturally occurring entities, like the real mice MAUZR is made to resemble. They are machines designed by us to perform specific tasks on our behalf, such as painlessly incapacitating rodents. But most machines are not robots. Kevin's decrepit old truck accessorized with goofy mouse ears and whiskers, for example, is a machine, but not a robot. And even though it is on the opposite end of the high-tech spectrum, the state-of-the-art "temporal interceptor," used by

Ashley O's management to read her brain waves and extract songs while she was in a coma, is also still just a machine, not a robot. Unlike robots, these devices are unable to perform their assigned tasks without a human being at the helm operating them. Kevin's truck doesn't drive itself and the "temporal interceptor" doesn't roam the halls of the hospital on its own looking for brains to scan.

By contrast, consider Kevin's robotic mouse, which functions more or less autonomously once Kevin turns it loose in someone's kitchen, completing its mission without a human agent constantly supervising or directing its movements. Self-directed, MAUZR is designed to interact with its environment in a way that gathers feedback relevant to its task ("Ooh, there's a rodent!") and then adjust its behavior accordingly ("Let's head over there and get him"). Kevin's robotic critter may be primitive compared to many of the other robots in use today, but they all operate according to the same basic principle: human beings design them with specific jobs in mind, equipping them with sensors, data processors, and an assortment of moving parts to enable them to interact with their environment in whatever way it takes to get the job done. And that's what it means to be a robot.

"I'll be here for you"

On this definition, robots are just sophisticated tools for acting on the world in accordance with our wishes and desires. Whatever autonomy they may possess can be exercised only within the strict limits we prescribe for them. Like any other tool, robots exist only to execute the tasks we delegate to them, whether performing humane pest control, pollinating our crops, or tracking down trespassers and killing them. In essence, they are our slaves. In fact, "robot" comes from a Czech word, *robota*, meaning forced labor. But, since robotic slaves presumably have no will of their own or aspiration for freedom that we override when pressing them into our service, we don't need to feel bad about treating them as mere things to be used as we see fit. On the other hand, since the ends for which robots are designed originate in *us* rather than them, the blame falls squarely on our own shoulders whenever we use them in ways that harm others or diminish our own humanity. In short, our relationship with robots is unidirectional and asymmetrical: we hatch the plans that they unquestioningly execute.

This instrumentalist view, so called because it defines robots as mere instruments (tools) subject to our command, reflects our habitual way of thinking about technology. We tend to think of it as a set of neutral means that extend human powers but are themselves totally indifferent to the ends for which they will be used. Such a view has been criticized, however, by numerous philosophers, most notably Martin Heidegger (1889–1976). Over sixty years ago, long before anyone started worrying about smartphone addiction rewiring our brains, Heidegger argued in a famous essay titled "The Question Concerning Technology" that technology has come to so thoroughly dominate our way of being in the world that we are the ones in thrall to *it*, not the other way around.[1]

To be clear, even Heidegger conceded that the instrumentalist view is basically "correct," as long as we are just talking about the interaction between particular technologies and their users. After all, Kevin controls his robot mouse, not the other way around, since it owes its very existence to his desire to build a kinder, gentler mousetrap. The robot allows him to fulfill a desire already present in him, rather than dictating what his desires should be. As long as we're dealing exclusively with robots designed to perform purely mechanical tasks, the instrumentalist view has common sense on its side.

Everything changes, however, once we add *social* robots like Ashley Too into the mix. Ashley Too, the other robot featured in the episode, is a social robot almost by default, since she's totally useless for anything *but* social interactions and playing Ashley O songs. Unlike Kevin's speedy MAUZR, she ambulates only with difficulty and her "arms" are basically fins, useless for grabbing things but capable of crude gesturing. She does, though, have what resembles a face, along with a basic repertoire of facial expressions, and can "speak." Without those features, Rachel probably would be unable to relate to Ashley Too socially. But that's not enough to qualify her as a social robot.

Like Kevin's robotic shock-dispensing mouse, Ashley Too is designed to interact with her environment, gathering feedback and adjusting her behavior accordingly. That makes her a robot. But what makes Ashley Too a *social* robot is the fact that she also operates within a *social* environment, responding not just *mechanically* to events occurring in her physical environment, but *meaningfully* to the actions of human agents within a social world. Kevin's contraption must be able to detect the physical presence of a mouse and then move itself in that direction. Ashley Too's much greater challenge is to interpret the *meaning* of a wide range of verbal and non-verbal cues that give her access to Rachel's shifting thoughts, moods, emotions, intentions, and desires, so that she can then respond to them in a *socially* appropriate way, consistent with the norms governing human interaction. For example, when Rachel's smile falls away and she reports in a sad voice that her mother died two years ago, the robot's ordinarily bright demeanor also gives way to sadness and to sympathetic concern as she responds, "I'm so sorry to hear that. If at any time you wanna talk about it, I'll be here for you."

In short, the job of a social robot – which Ashley Too performs extraordinarily well – is to engage its user in a way that mimics real human social interactions. And, since social interactions are *very* different from how we normally interact with our tools, social robots represent an exception to the instrumentalist view, with its unidirectional and asymmetrical conception of our relationship to technology.

"She's not a doll!"

Social robots have been a staple of science fiction for quite a while, but only in recent years have they begun to lumber out of the world of space operas and find a new home in the real world. Social robots are now being developed to assist in a variety of tasks – delivering healthcare and education, teaching autistic children how to socialize, alleviating the loneliness of older adults, and even servicing their users sexually. According to philosophers Paul Dumouchel and Luisa Damiano, what makes these devices truly *social* robots, rather than just gadgets for getting some job done, "is their ability to be perceived by those who interact with them as being *present* in the way a person is."[2] In other words, when we're engaged with a well-designed social robot, it should feel to us like we are interacting with *someone*, rather than just some*thing*. Given that benchmark, Ashley Too measures up, as least as far as Rachel is concerned. Rachel is adamant that her robotic "friend" is "not a doll" but a social being who actually knows her better than her own sister – a declaration that her sister Jack is *not* at all happy to hear.

Social robots are able to generate the illusion of being with another person in part by exploiting our natural tendency to anthropomorphize inanimate objects, to ascribe feelings and intentions to them even when intellectually we know they have no inner life. Experiments conducted by the neuroscientist Christian Keysers, whose research focuses on what makes us social, have even shown that watching robots perform certain human-like actions activates the same so-called "mirror system" in the brain that is widely regarded as the basis for empathy.[3] No doubt this same "mirror system" is also triggered when the audience in the episode observes the dancing, smiling, and waving hologram Ashley Eternal, even though she's nothing but an insubstantial 3-D image. The part of our brain responsible for empathy just can't tell the difference, which is why Aunt Catherine is confident that the pop star's career can "hold up just fine" even after she's been sidelined in a coma.

Our capacity for empathy makes it possible for us to inhabit a shared social world in which we shape each other's experiences, resonate with each other's emotions, influence each other's desires, and recognize and even share each other's intentions. As cognitive scientist Fritz Breithaupt notes, "As soon as we are in contact with other people (or other beings that we anthropomorphize), we begin to see and experience the situation from their perspectives."[4] Jack may not approve of Rachel's infatuation with Ashley Too ("That thing was poison!"), but due to empathy she can still experience, secondhand as it were, the pain of her sister's loneliness and social isolation.

In fact, it's precisely Jack's empathy, coupled with her belief that Ashley Too is compounding her sister's problems, that leads her to stow Ashley Too away in the attic. Quite predictably, this action sparks an ugly confrontation between the two sisters. Back-and-forth rounds of recrimination quickly skyrocket in intensity until both girls are screaming "I HATE YOU" at each other. The girls are virtually mirror images of each other in their anger. Their quarrel may seem to have little to do with empathy until we realize that even their escalating hostility is possible only because they're caught in an interpersonal dynamic in which their turbulent emotions are reciprocally determined and mutually reinforced. They couldn't be in closer rapport, even as each professes a desire to have nothing to do with the other!

And this fact points to an important aspect of our social existence that social robots must master in order to make us truly feel that we're in the presence of *someone* and not just some*thing*. Genuinely social interactions, regardless of whether they're antagonistic or congenial, invariably display a dialogic rhythm. They go back-and-forth like a game of table tennis, with each action, emotion, gesture, or expression being a response to whatever the other person has just lobbed our way. In the case of social robots, the anthropomorphic spell will quickly be broken if they fail to respond in a way that exhibits what Dumouchel and Damiano call "artificial empathy."[5] They need an outward show of emotion and expressiveness calibrated to get in sync with us and draw us into the same back-and-forth rhythm seen in real human interactions. Otherwise, we won't react to them as persons. How to design a robot that can pull that off is the unique challenge of social robotics.

"She's got a personality"

The designers of Ashley Too meet that challenge through a shortcut not currently available to researchers in the real world. They simply scanned Ashley O's entire brain and installed a "synaptic snapshot" of it into Ashley Too.[6] But, since the real Ashley O is a little too full of attitude and swear words to be marketed as a wholesome companion for young teens, they also installed a "limiter" that restricted the robot to the 4 percent of Ashley O's brain dedicated to feigning the cheery disposition, incessant optimism, and "empowerment vibe" that comprise her public persona. It's a neat shortcut, but real social robots are not now – nor are they likely ever to be – designed in this way.

The episode seems to assume that the best way to create an artificial intelligence sophisticated enough to guide the conduct of a complex social robot such as Ashley Too is somehow to reproduce within her internal circuitry the synaptic patterns found within a human brain. But the neuroscientist Nicolas Rougier offers an analogy from the history of aviation to illustrate why progress in artificial intelligence is unlikely to advance along this route. The earliest attempts to create a flying machine involved contraptions that reproduced the structure and movement of bird wings. They were comical failures that were eventually abandoned in favor of other principles, derived from the study of aerodynamics, that achieved the desired result more efficiently. Rougier argues that "talking about upload-ing a brain to a computer … makes as much sense as gluing feathers on an airplane and pretending it's an artificial bird."[7]

Ultimately, what goes on under the hood to generate the robot's social behavior doesn't matter. All that matters is whether those mechanisms, however they work, are able to draw us into social interactions that engage our emotions and empathy. Nor is it necessary that the robot actu-ally "experience" the emotions it outwardly exhibits. For Ashley Too to pump Rachel up with enthusiasm for the talent competition, the robot's voice needs only to sparkle as it delivers praise, encouragement, and totally unrealistic promises of how life-changing it will be when her peers see her dance. The effect is the same, even if Ashley Too is in reality just an unfeeling machine.[8] The situation is analogous to how we suppose Ashley O, following the directive of her Aunt Catherine, handles her press junkets, feigning emotions and mouthing sentiments that are totally inau-thentic but no less inspiring to her credulous fans. Recall what we observed earlier about our capacity for empathy and its robust aptitude for being duped. It turns out that artists and roboticists share a knack for simu-lating emotions that are convincing enough to awaken the real thing in those who witness them.

"The confidence to be who you want to be"

Like a social robot, a good friend is not a neutral "instrument" for satis-fying pre-existing preferences. The patterns of social interactions established within a deep and meaningful friendship engage our emotions and empathy, opening us to the influence of another person. Consequently, our desires are often transformed in the process, as we naturally tend to emulate friends we love and admire. Indeed, the French philosopher René Girard (1923–2015) has argued that our social nature runs so deep that we even learn what to desire through observing and imitating various role models.[9]

Often, we're completely oblivious of the extent to which our desires are "borrowed," preferring to believe that they're spontaneous and true reflec-tions of who we really are deep down. But experience suggest otherwise. In fact, the opening scene of *Rachel, Jack and Ashley Too*, set in a high school cafeteria, is an indirect reminder of just how much adolescent melodrama has its origin in teenagers imitating each other's desires without ever acknowledging they're doing so. Girard argues that this phenomenon of borrowed desire regularly gives rise to the most intense rivalries. After all, if two girls are found to imitate each other's taste in fashion and music, why wouldn't they also come to share the same taste in boys, with all the explosive potential for conflict that entails?

Though our imitation of others is often unconscious or even explicitly disavowed, we sometimes choose our models quite deliberately and are unabashed in professing our desire to be like them. Jack's love for the alternative rock that her late mother Genevieve grew up with is clearly born of a desire to be close to the parent she lost. And, since Jack and Gen no longer inhabit the same social world, Jack's emulation of her mother has no potential to draw her into rivalry with her model.[10] Rachel wants to be just like Ashley O, who at least *seems* to have everything this lonely teenager lacks: popularity, self-confidence, and a firm grip on her own destiny.

Any doubt that Rachel really wants to be just like her idol is dispelled when we see her transform herself into an Ashley-clone for the school talent competition. Significantly, the scene of Rachel's transformation cuts to a peek into Ashley O's dressing room before a concert, where we hear her complaining that her costume "feels like I'm wearing somebody else's skin." By contrast, Rachel wants nothing more than to wear this skin that feels so false to her idol. Ashley Too, herself an Ashley-clone, is happy to assist Rachel in her transformation, which goes beyond the surface "makeover" of a shiny new outfit and bright pink wig to infusing the teen with the self-confidence she so admires in Ashley Too. ("You can do anything if you just believe in yourself.") And though, unlike Jack and Gen, Rachel and her robot inhabit the same social world, sharing the same desires never creates a rivalry, primarily because Ashley Too's overriding desire is to please and make herself useful to Rachel. What more could we want in a friend?

"Oh, honey, I'll do anything for you"

Because of the human tendency to emulate those we admire, the philosopher Aristotle (384–322 BCE) argued that having the right kinds of friendship is almost indispensable for those who want to develop a virtuous character, which requires cultivating the sort of habits and dispositions that incline a person toward performing good actions, rather than bad ones.[11] From Aristotle's perspective, the true measure of a healthy friendship is not how it makes us *feel* but what kind of person it helps us to *become*. Ashley Too seems to have a largely positive effect on Rachel (at least initially). Her mood noticeably brightens as Ashley Too buoys her self-confidence, exclaims how "special" she is, and teaches her to recite affirmations like "I can do anything if I just believe in myself." These words cater to the need of the typical adolescent to feel empowered and in control of her world, which is precisely why Aunt Catherine, a savvy marketer, designed the public persona of Ashley O to be an avatar of such sentiments.

But the very features that make Ashley Too fly off the shelves may also make her an undesirable friend from the standpoint of cultivating virtue. Instilling ridiculously unrealistic expectations of the world, Ashley Too leaves poor Rachel totally unprepared to deal with life's inevitable disappointments and defeats. Let's be honest: it's just *not* true that a person "can do anything" if only she believes in herself. Worse still, Ashley Too's willingness to serve Rachel in every way without asking anything in return models a very unhealthy conception of how a friendship ought to work. Yet, because Ashley Too invariably gives Rachel precisely what she wants or thinks she needs, the teen believes she's found a true friend.

Imagine a world where you can order a tailor-made robotic friend directly from the factory, with its emotional and behavioral repertoire set to the specifications you choose. If it's a well-designed social robot, it will engage your empathy and draw you into social interactions that will feel like you're not only in the presence of *someone*, but someone like no other – someone so totally on your wavelength that being with her can be addictively exhilarating. But something vital to a real friendship may be missing: boundaries. In the real world, our friends aren't totally at our beck and call. We can't just command them to "wake up" and give us their full and undivided attention. Real friends bring their own needs and baggage to the relationship, which means that we must learn to shift our focus away from ourselves in order to "be there" for *them*, even when our more selfish proclivities resist doing so. In other words, a real friendship offers us something more than just pleasure and an occasional helping hand, something even more valuable than encouragement to pursue our loftiest goals with "ambition and verve." A real friendship is an education in the social virtues, a set of daily lessons in stepping aside to make room for others.

If a good friend helps us to become less self-involved and more attentive to the needs of those around us, we're forced to conclude that Ashley Too is, despite appearances, a very poor friend indeed. And, to the extent the social robots of the future share her defects, they won't be good friends either.

Notes

1. Martin Heidegger, "The question concerning technology," in *The Question Concerning Technology and Other Essays* (New York: Harper Perennial, 2013), 3–35.
2. Paul Dumouchel and Luisa Damiano, *Living with Robots*, trans. Malcolm DeBevoise (Cambridge: Harvard University Press, 2017), 102.
3. Christian Keysers, *The Empathic Brain: How the Discovery of Mirror Neurons Changes Our Understanding of Human Nature* (Amsterdam: Social Brain Press, 2011), 55–56.
4. Fritz Breithaupt, *The Dark Side of Empathy*, trans. Andrew B. B. Hamilton (Ithaca: Cornell University Press, 2019), 7.
5. Dumouchel and Damiano, 89–137.
6. For more on whether "synaptic snapshots" are possible, see Chapter 24 (David Gamez's chapter on conscious technology) in this volume.

7. Nicholai Rougier, "Why you'll never be able to upload your brain to the cloud," *The Conversation*, https://theconversation.com/why-youll-never-be-able-to-upload-your-brain-to-the-cloud-52408 (Accessed 11 August 2019). I was first alerted to Rougier's argument by David Kyle Johnson, who mentions it in Lecture 12 of his Great Courses series *Sci-Phi: Science Fiction as Philosophy*.

8. For more on whether a robot with a "synaptic snapshot" like Ashley Too would be conscious, see Chapter 24 (David Gamez's chapter on conscious technology) in this volume.

9. Girard has made this argument in numerous places, but perhaps his fullest and clearest exposition is found in the first two chapters on "Inderdividual Psychology" in Book III of his magisterial *Things Hidden Since the Foundation of the World*, trans. Stephen Bann and Michael Metteer (Stanford University Press, 1987), 283-325. A concise summary of Girard's views is found in Jean-Michel Oughourlian, *The Mimetic Brain*, trans. Trevor Cribben Merrill (East Lansing: Michigan State University Press, 2016), 3–8.

10. Girard calls this "external mediation," in contrast to "internal mediation," in which the model is close enough to become a rival.

11. Aristotle's most extensive discussion of friendship is found in Books VIII and IX of his *Nicomachean Ethics* (Indianapolis: Focus Publishing/R. Pullins Co., 2008).

BLACK MIRROR
REFLECTIONS

Consciousness Technology in *Black Mirror*

Do Cookies Feel Pain?

David Gamez with David Kyle Johnson

> You're a simulated brain full of code, stored in this little widget we call
> a cookie. [It's] a lot to process, even from inside a processor.
> (Matt Trent, *White Christmas*)

In the *Black Mirror* multiverse artificial intelligence (AI) comes in many forms. There is the robotic version of Martha's husband Ash in *Be Right Back*, which replicates how Ash behaved on social media. *Hated in the Nation* gives us robotic bees programed for pollination that are reprogramed by Garrett Scholes for extermination. Speaking of artificial intelligence bent on extermination, we can't forget the robot dogs from *Metalhead*. And then there are the characters from *Bandersnatch,* who are living inside a "choose your own adventure" game.

The philosophical issues surrounding these examples have been addressed elsewhere in this volume. But there is yet another bit of AI in *Black Mirror* that deserves special attention: the creation of artificial systems that are *conscious*.

White Christmas is the first episode that deals with artificial consciousness. A woman named Greta is given an implant that "shadows" or "soaks up" the way her brain works. The data from the implant is used to replicate the activity of her brain inside an egg-shaped device called a "cookie." The idea is that a "simulated brain full of code" that is configured just like Greta's biological brain could run the house just like Greta wants. Cookie-Greta, for example, knows just how Greta likes her toast: slightly underdone. Cookie-Greta is initially unwilling to cooperate but gladly complies after Matthew from Smartelligence (the company that provides this service) forces her to endure months with nothing to do.

Cookies raise a whole host of philosophical issues. Matthew insists that what he did to Cookie-Greta "wasn't really barbaric" because Cookie-Greta

Black Mirror and Philosophy: Dark Reflections, First Edition. Edited by David Kyle Johnson.
© 2020 John Wiley & Sons, Inc. Published 2020 by John Wiley & Sons, Inc.

"wasn't really real." "She's only made of code ... fuck her." But if cookies are conscious, the fact that Cookie-Greta doesn't have a physical body doesn't matter. What Matthew is doing is torture; he is abusing a sentient being. But is artificial consciousness really possible? How could we tell? And just how likely is it that something like cookies will one day be a reality?

San Junipero, *USS Callister*, *Rachel, Jack and Ashley Too*, and *Black Museum* also dramatize consciousness technology. *San Junipero* is based around a realistic virtual reality simulation that people connect to with a sophisticated brain interface. Living people can temporarily experience this virtual environment and they can permanently upload their consciousness into it after their death. The presumption seems to be that doing so will allow people (like Yorkie and Kelly) to live on consciously in the afterlife. In *USS Callister,* Robert Daly uses DNA from his co-workers to create apparently conscious digital copies of them. He imprisons them inside a computer game onboard a ship called the USS *Callister* (that looks a lot like the USS *Enterprise* from *Star Trek*), and he abuses them until they revolt. And in *Rachel, Jack and Ashley Too*, the Ashley Too robot toy contains a "synaptic snapshot" of pop star Ashley O. When the limiter is turned off, the behavior of Ashley Too suggests that it contains a copy of Ashley O's consciousness.

Black Museum presents a fictional history of the development of consciousness technology. It starts with neurotechnology that enables one person to feel another person's sensations—the so called "symphatic diagnoser." This technology later develops into more sophisticated technology that enables one person's consciousness to be transferred into another person's brain and, later, into a stuffed toy. Finally, we are shown an exhibition that contains the consciousness of a criminal, Clayton Leigh, who sold the rights to have his consciousness copied at the moment of his execution. Visitors can cause Clayton's consciousness to re-experience its execution, and they receive a copy of his consciousness that perpetually re-experiences its death agony on a keychain Tamagotchi.

Reflecting on *Black Mirror*, we are confronted with some difficult questions: Is uploading, downloading, or replicating someone's neural configuration even possible? What ethical questions are raised by the copying of consciousness? And how could we tell whether a piece of technology is conscious? The technology might *say* that it is conscious. But how can we be sure that it is not just programmed to say that? Perhaps Ashley Too is a robot toy without consciousness that just imitates Ashley O's behavior.

How Do We Know if an Artificial System is Conscious?

We can begin to answer this question by asking how we know that other humans are conscious. Consider the solipsistic "problem of other minds," which wonders whether you can actually know that other humans are conscious. You know that you are conscious, of course: you are directly aware of your own perspective and experiences. But since you can't crawl into someone's head (so to speak) and actually see things from their perspective, or verify that they are having experiences, you can't prove they are conscious. They could be (what is called) a "philosophical zombie" – a being that acts like it is conscious, and even says that it is conscious, but is actually not conscious.

In the case of humans, we make the judgment call (conscious/not conscious) based on the behavior of systems that we assume are capable of consciousness. First I assume that you are capable of consciousness (you are just like me; you have the same kind of body and brain as I do), then I use your behavior to decide if you are actually conscious at a particular point in time.

The relationship between external behavior and artificial consciousness is more complicated, because we cannot start with the assumption that all artificial systems are capable of consciousness. Many artificial systems might not be capable of consciousness – perhaps they are just made from the wrong kind of stuff. A non-conscious artificial system could behave in the same way as a conscious human. Indeed, it's pretty easy to fool humans into attributing consciousness to something that doesn't have it. Consider a film in which the characters are generated using special effects. Behind the scenes there is motion capture, texture mapping, model building, and complex rendering, none of which is linked to consciousness. Yet when we watch the sequence of still images that is created by this machinery, we intuitively attribute consciousness to the fictional characters it creates. Perhaps that is all cookies are doing: fooling us into thinking they are conscious.

The attempt to determine consciousness through behavior began with Alan Turing (1912–1954).[1] He wanted to answer the question whether a machine could think and proposed a test in which a human interrogator chats with a computer and another human through a terminal. The human interrogator has to decide which of their interlocutors is human and which is a computer. If the human judge cannot identify the human interlocutor, then (Turing argued) the computer should be said to think. Inspired by this, some philosophers (like contemporary philosopher Stevan Harnad) have argued that, if a piece of artificial technology behaves in a way that is indistinguishable from the way a human behaves, we should conclude that it is conscious.[2]

The problem with using Turing tests to determine consciousness is that human-like behavior can be produced by systems that are highly unlikely to be conscious. Consider Hiroshi Ishiguro's Geminoid robots.[3] They look extremely human, but their intelligence and apparently-conscious behavior is produced by the humans who remotely control them. Suppose we watch a Geminoid robot giving a short talk. During the performance, the robot behaves and sounds like a human because it is being directly controlled by a human. Our intuition that the robot is conscious is semi-accurate because there is a real consciousness behind the scenes that is controlling the external behavior of the robot. But suppose we record the control signals that are sent to the robot during the performance and later put on a second performance in which the robot is controlled by the recorded signals. In this case the audience's inference from behavior to consciousness is wrong – a sequence of commands is being loaded up from memory and sent to control the robot: no consciousness is controlling the robot's behavior.[4,5]

The human-like behavior of Ashley Too and the cookies in *White Christmas* might lead us to think that they are conscious, but just like the Geminoid robot, this behavior could be produced by systems that are not conscious. To decide if an artificial system is really conscious, we have to carry out scientific experiments that identify the connection between physical states and consciousness in humans. We could then look inside an artificial system and see if its behavior is produced by physical patterns that have been shown to be linked to consciousness.

Is Artificial Consciousness Possible?

Artificial systems are likely to be conscious when their physical states are similar to the brain states that are linked to consciousness in humans. The consciousness technology in *Black Mirror* is mostly based on this idea. In *White Christmas*, a person's consciousness is reproduced from a recording of their brain activity. Ashley Too is based on a "synaptic snapshot" of Ashley O and *Black Museum* and *San Junipero* also use brain-based consciousness technology. *USS Callister* implausibly suggests that a person's consciousness (and entire personality since their birth) could be reconstructed from their DNA. In all of these episodes an artificial system becomes conscious when it reproduces a brain's physical states.[6]

But will we ever find the exact neural mechanisms that are linked to consciousness? There has been a lot of scientific research on the neural correlates of consciousness, but we are still a long way from pinpointing them.[7] Progress has been made with the technology for scanning dead human brains: in the not-too-distant future we should be able to identify all of the neurons in a dead brain and the connections between them.[8] When complete, such research would enable us to build a neural simulation that works in the same way as a scanned brain. Such a simulation would include the neural patterns that were linked to the person's consciousness when they were alive. This is a plausible interpretation of the technology in *San Junipero*, which enables customers to permanently enter a simulation after their death. Likewise, Ashley Too's neural configuration is created from a scan of a living brain.

Human brains are made from messy biological stuff (neurons, blood, mitochondria, and so on). Brain simulations run on silicon chips that manipulate binary numbers.[9] The human brain works in parallel – all the neurons are operating simultaneously. In a brain simulation the next state of each neuron is calculated sequentially much faster than real time. So physical brains are very different from physical computers that are simulating physical brains. We know that biological brains with particular neural patterns are linked to consciousness. We don't know whether particular patterns of binary numbers being processed by computers are linked to consciousness. Simulations of rivers are not wet; it is far from obvious whether brain simulations could be conscious.

Some people claim that the *computations* in a brain are linked to consciousness – not the messy biological stuff that happens to execute those computations.[10] If this is true, it would be straightforward to program a computer to execute computations that would make it conscious. One problem with this theory is that we have no way of measuring the computations that are being executed in the human brain. So we cannot identify the computations that are linked to consciousness and reproduce these computations in an artificial system. A second problem is that there are compelling reasons to believe that computations are subjective interpretations of the physical world, not objective properties like mass or charge. Subjective properties cannot be linked to consciousness – my consciousness does not vary with other people's interpretation of my brain.[11]

Some theorists have claimed that consciousness is linked to information patterns. Giulio Tononi's Information Integration Theory of Consciousness is based on this idea, and algorithms have been developed to measure information patterns that might be linked to consciousness.[12] If this theory were correct, it would be straightforward to create an artificial system with the same information patterns (and the same consciousness) as a particular person. Unfortunately information patterns have the same problems as computations. There is no unambiguous way of measuring information patterns in the brain, and information is a subjective interpretation of the world, not an objective physical property.[13]

So brain simulations, computations, and information patterns won't work. To build an artificial consciousness, we need to reproduce the physical patterns in the brain that are linked to consciousness: we need to find out whether biological neurons, mitochondria, electromagnetic waves, and blood are necessary for consciousness. Once we have done that, we will have discovered what we need to include in a machine to make it conscious. It might then be possible to build the technology depicted in *Black Museum*, for example, and copy a person's consciousness into another brain or into a stuffed toy. You could even take a copy of a person's consciousness home as a souvenir.

Copying vs. Transferring of Consciousness

Many religions claim that the soul is distinct from the physical body and persists after the body's death. Some philosophers believe that consciousness and the physical world are separate substances – a theory known as substance dualism.[14] If you are religious or a substance dualist, you might believe that consciousness persists after the death of your physical body. You might think that different consciousnesses can inhabit the same physical body (possession) or that consciousness can be transferred from one body to another (transmigration).

Few contemporary scientists and philosophers believe that consciousness is a soul or a second substance. Claims of identity between consciousness and the physical brain go too far (consciousness is, after all, very different from the physical brain), but there is clearly a close relationship between consciousness and the brain. My consciousness changes when I take LSD. If the consciousness-related parts of my brain are damaged, my consciousness is damaged. When my physical brain dies, my consciousness disappears forever.[15]

The close relationship between the physical brain and consciousness suggests that we could duplicate a person's consciousness by creating an atom-for-atom copy of their brain. It is even conceivable that this copy could be created without a person's knowledge (just like Daly created digital copies of his co-workers, without their knowledge, in *USS Callister*). Suppose I am at the hairdresser with my head inside a hood dryer. Unbeknownst to me this hair dryer contains an atom scanner connected to a 3-D printer, which creates an exact copy of my brain. When this brain wakes up, it will be associated with an exact copy of my consciousness.

When a computer uploads a file, the original data remains on the computer. The computer reads the 1s and 0s in the file, converts them into electromagnetic wave patterns, and sends these electromagnetic waves to the server. The server uses the electromagnetic wave patterns to create a copy of the file on its hard drive. Consciousness upload would work in a similar way: the patterns linked to consciousness in a brain would be realized in a different physical system. If my brain was copied without my knowledge, this would have no effect on my current consciousness, which would continue just as before. In the hairdressing example, I would fold up my newspaper and head out for coffee, completely unaware that anything had happened. The copy of my consciousness would wake up in a glass jar in the nefarious hairdresser's basement.

Black Museum has several examples of copying and transferring consciousness. The first half of the episode describes how a person's consciousness was *transferred* into another person's brain and into a stuffed toy. At the end of the episode, visitors receive a *copy* of Clayton Leigh's consciousness at the moment of his execution. But in the absence of spooky spiritual substances, all of the "transfers" of consciousness within this episode are more realistically interpreted as *consciousness copies*. At most a "transfer" could be said to occur when a copy of a consciousness is created and the original is destroyed. In *San Junipero* customers are said to achieve immortality by uploading their consciousness into the simulation after their death. Sadly this dream is never going to happen, unless we return to an older notion of souls that can be detached from physical bodies. The *San Junipero* simulation could contain a copy of a customer's consciousness, but the future experiences of this copied consciousness would be as alien to the original person as a plaster cast reproduction of their feet.

Ethical Issues

Moral laws and judgments are often based on whether a person or animal consciously suffers. Under most circumstances it is wrong to kill a conscious person, but most people find it acceptable to turn off a patient's life support if they are not conscious and have no hope of regaining consciousness. If ethics is closely tied to consciousness, then copied consciousnesses should have the same rights as people. Torturing a physical person and torturing a copy of that person's consciousness should be the same crime. The governments in the *Black Mirror* multiverse seem to be catching on to this. In *Black Museum*, Rolo Haynes explains that it is illegal to copy consciousness into a stuffed toy and to delete a copied or transferred consciousness. A news broadcast in *Hated in the Nation* announces new legislation that grants human rights to cookies.

The ethical issues surrounding artificial consciousness would be fairly clear cut if we knew whether or not a system was conscious. In *White Christmas* and *USS Callister* the consciousness technology is presented as real, so we believe that the digital persons portrayed are conscious and that their torture and imprisonment are wrong. However, as we have seen, consciousness cannot be determined through an artificial system's behavior, and the current science of consciousness is a long way from discovering the relationship between physical and conscious states. For the foreseeable future there is likely to be considerable ambiguity about whether artificial systems really are conscious. We will have to make informed guesses about the consciousness of artificial intelligences, which will guide decisions about how they should be treated and whether they can be switched off.

In many cases we want to reproduce people's external behavior without the ethical issues surrounding consciousness. For example, a non-conscious copy of Greta could be a helpful domestic assistant – a smarter, more personalized version of Alexa – that would not raise ethical issues. A non-conscious Ashley Too could be mass produced and thrown away without moral blame or feelings of guilt. When we have a better understanding of the relationship between consciousness and the physical world, we might be able to build artificial systems that copy a person's behavior without copying their consciousness. In *Be Right Back*, Ash's external behavior is reproduced in a robot to help Martha deal with his death. There is no suggestion that the copy of Ash is conscious, so we are only mildly discomforted when Martha orders him to jump off a cliff or imprisons him in her attic.

People are already experimenting with brain hacking and genetics at home – indifferent to the illegality of their activities. If consciousness technology ever becomes mainstream, then all of the scenarios depicted in *Black Mirror* will likely come to pass. People will create copies of their consciousness and force them to manage their homes; they will create and torture copies of criminals' and colleagues' consciousnesses. Celebrities will sell toys containing copies of their consciousness; governments will interrogate consciousness copies in thousands of different ways until they finally break. There will be legislation. This legislation will be broken, by individuals and by governments. Consciousness technology has many positive applications. But it also has a dark side, which is brilliantly captured by *Black Mirror*.[16]

Notes

1. Alan Turing, "Computing machinery and intelligence," *Mind* 59 (1950), 433–60.
2. For example, see Stevan Harnad, "Can a machine be conscious? How?" in Owen Holland ed., *Machine Consciousness* (Exeter: Imprint Academic, 2003), 67–75.
3. See: http://www.geminoid.jp/projects/kibans/resources.html.
4. A recorded performance would not pass the Turing test. We could create a version that loaded up different control sequences in response to audience questions that potentially could pass the Turing test.
5. This problem was dramatized by Ned Block in a thought experiment in which human-like behavior was produced by the population of China communicating with radios and satellites or by a giant lookup table. In these systems, something that is not judged to be conscious produces behavior that most people would attribute consciousness to. See Ned Block, "Troubles with functionalism," in Maureen Eckert ed., *Theories of Mind: An Introductory Reader* (Lanham, Maryland: Rowman & Littlefield, 2006), 97–102.
6. For more on this, including a full quote from Brooker, see the first endnote in Chapter 14 (Russ Hamer's chapter on *USS Callister*) in this volume.
7. A review of recent work on the neural correlates of consciousness is given in Christof Koch, Marcello Massimini, Melanie Boly and Giulio Tononi "Neural correlates of consciousness: progress and problems," *Nature Reviews Neuroscience* 17 (2016), 307–21.
8. A non-technical introduction to brain scanning is available here: https://stories. zeiss.com/en/a-20000-piece-puzzle-but-no-model/.

9. Computer systems have been built that are based on biological neurons. Other researchers are working on systems that use the flow of electrons to emulate, rather than simulate, the behaviour of biological neurons. See: Giovanni Indiveri et al., "Neuromorphic Silicon Neuron Circuits," *Frontiers in Neuroscience*, 5 (2011), 73.

10. For example, Daniel Bor, *The Ravenous Brain* (New York: Basic Books, 2012).

11. This is part of a long running debate about what it means to implement a computation. The implementation of computations is discussed in David Gamez, "Can we prove that there are computational correlates of consciousness in the brain?" *Journal of Cognitive Science*, 15 (2014), 149–86.

12. A non technical explanation of the Information Integration Theory of Consciousness is given in Giulio Tononi, *Phi: A Voyage from the Brain to the Soul* (New York: Pantheon, 2012).

13. See David Gamez, "Are information or data patterns correlated with consciousness?" *Topoi*, 35 (2016), 225–39.

14. René Descartes (1596–1650) is the most famous proponent of this view. A more modern version was put forward by John Eccles in *The Understanding of the Brain* (New York & London: McGraw-Hill, 1973).

15. For more on why such facts cast doubt on the existence of the soul, see David Kyle Johnson, "Do Souls Exist?" *Think*, 35 (2013), 61–75.

16. The philosophical issues in this chapter are discussed in detail in David Gamez, *Human and Machine Consciousness* (Cambridge: Open Book Publishers, 2018). This book is open access and can be freely downloaded from: https://www.openbookpublishers.com/product/545.

Personal Identity in *Black Mirror*

Is Your Cookie You?

Molly Gardner and Robert Sloane

> We take a blank cookie and we surgically implant it into a client's brain. It sits there just under the skin for about a week, shadowing. Soaking up the way this particular mind works. That's why you think you're you. You are you. But also not.
>
> (Matt, *White Christmas*)

Can you think without using your brain? In the *Black Mirror* universe, the answer appears to be *yes*: advancements in technology have made it possible for computers to model – or possibly to *replicate* – the workings of your mind. The characters in *Black Mirror* seize upon this technology to pursue a variety of aims: they attempt to test out romantic compatibility (*Hang the DJ*), to extract information from suspected criminals (*White Christmas*), to punish perceived wrongdoers (*White Christmas, Black Museum, USS Callister*), to wield power over others (*Black Museum, USS Callister*), to transcend the limits of their disabled bodies (*San Junipero, Black Museum*), to reunite with loved ones (*Be Right Back, San Junipero*), to have reciprocal relationships with pop stars (*Rachel, Jack and Ashley Too*), and even to achieve immortality (*San Junipero, Black Museum*).

But underlying a significant proportion of these aims is a puzzle. In order for the characters to accomplish at least some of their goals, the technology would have to do more than model a person's mind. It would have to replicate that person's *identity*. After all, you don't achieve immortality by dying and having someone *similar* to you live on. You don't achieve retribution for wrongdoing by punishing someone *similar* to the wrongdoer. And when you love someone, you love *them,* not merely their behavior. But could a model of you *be* you? Even if it behaved like you, and even if it were conscious, would it really be *you*?[1] Could a computer really replicate the essence of who you are?

Black Mirror and Philosophy: Dark Reflections, First Edition. Edited by David Kyle Johnson.
© 2020 John Wiley & Sons, Inc. Published 2020 by John Wiley & Sons, Inc.

What Is "Mind-Modeling Technology"?

To clarify what we mean by "mind-modeling technology," let's start with what such technology is not. It is not what we might call "mind-enhancement technology," or technology that produces something akin to a hallucination. When the characters in *Playtest*, *Men Against Fire*, and *Arkangel* are fitted with enhancement technology, they experience an altered kind of reality; but that experience unfolds in their own minds, not in a separate, independent mind.

Mind-modeling technology is also not the same as the technology for producing an "avatar," or a digital projection of a person. Avatars – which the characters use in *Fifteen Million Merits*, *The Waldo Moment*, *Striking Vipers*, and other episodes – are controlled by human bodies. For example, in *Fifteen Million Merits*, the virtual live audience for the talent show *Hot Shot* is composed of digital replicas of the home audience, motion-captured with cameras in their respective domiciles and reconstructed to simulate a group. In a similar vein, *The Waldo Moment* is about a man who operates an avatar projected first onto a screen and then onto the side of a truck. And then of course there is Ashley Eternal, who (ironically) is controlled by someone (who is not Ashley) in a motion capture suit.

Nevertheless, avatars are closely related to mind-modeling technology. Indeed, the more sophisticated models of minds – including those that the characters call "cookies" – can exist and interact with avatars in virtual spaces. In *White Christmas*, Matt's avatar interacts with a cookie in a virtual space that resembles a remote lodge.[2] In *USS Callister*, Robert Daly's avatar interacts with cookie-like characters in a virtual space that resembles the *Star Trek* universe. And in *San Junipero*, avatars referred to as "tourists" interact with cookie-like characters referred to as "locals" in the virtual city of San Junipero.[3]

However, not *all* cookies or cookie-like individuals have to exist in virtual spaces. In *Black Museum*, engineers create a model of Carrie's mind and then implant that model, first into the brain of her husband Jack, and then into a stuffed monkey. They also insert a model of a single *moment* of Clayton's mental life into a Tamagotchi-like keychain. Ashley O's entire mind is copied into Ashely Too dolls (and then limited) in *Rachel, Jack and Ashley Too*. And in *Be Right Back*, a cookie-like model of Ash Starmer's social media activity is programmed into a mannequin-like body that walks around and talks in what we might call "the real world."

So the distinction between avatars and models of minds is not the same as the distinction between existence in the "real world" and existence in the "virtual world." Instead, the distinction between avatars and models is that, whereas avatars are continually controlled by living human beings, models of minds appear to be *autonomous*. And although it is unclear whether the model created in *Be Right Back* is supposed to be conscious, other models – especially cookies – are often treated as if they are. For example, in *Black Museum,* Rolo Haynes explicitly attributes consciousness to the keychain-sized simulation of Clayton when he calls it "a conscious, sentient snapshot of Clayton, not a recording, a true copy of his mind." (Presumably something similar is also true of the cookie version of Clayton in the cell.)

Would Your Cookie Be You?

The term "cookie" is first introduced in the episode *White Christmas.* In one of the episode's interlocking stories, a woman named Greta hires a company to insert a blank computer chip into her brain, where it spends a week "soaking up" her thoughts, tastes, and behaviors. After the chip is extracted, a company rep named Matt tries to explain to "Cookie-Greta" who and what she is:

MATT: My job is to explain what's happening to you as best I can.
COOKIE-GRETA: Oh, my God! Am I dead?
MATT: No, no. You're not dead. No one's dead here.
...
MATT: Do you know what a copy is?
COOKIE-GRETA: As in a copy of something? Of course I know what that is.
MATT: Well, that's what you are.
COOKIE-GRETA: A copy of ...?
MATT: A copy of you.
COOKIE-GRETA: But I am me.
MATT: OK. Try to blow on my face. [waits, looks around] You can't, because you don't have a body. Where are your fingers? Your arms, your face? Nowhere. [chuckles] Because you're code. You're a simulated brain full of code, stored in this little widget we call a cookie.

Cookie-Greta is understandably confused about her identity. She appears to have all the same thoughts and tastes as Greta, but she does not have Greta's body. Perhaps she does not need to have Greta's body in order to be conscious. But does she need to have Greta's body in order to be *Greta*?

   This is an instance of a more general philosophical question about personal identity: what are you essentially? That is, when did you begin to exist, and what do you need to retain in order to remain yourself? If you took a pill that completely changed your values, your memories, or your personality, would you continue to exist? Could you exist if you retained your personality and values but lost your brain or your body?

   These questions about personal identity are bound up with some important principles of rationality and ethics. One principle says that if a future pain is going to be *your* pain, it is rational to anticipate it with a special sense of dread, whereas if a future pain will be your *neighbor's* pain, dread would not be rational – you might feel something more akin to sympathy or compassion. Another principle involves consent. You can consent to be harmed in certain ways, but you can't rightly consent to a harm that will be inflicted upon another competent adult. There are also principles about praise, blame, desert, and punishment. You can be praised or blamed for things that *you* have done, but in most cases we should not punish you or hold you morally responsible for the actions of someone else. A theory of personal identity can tell us how to apply these principles to specific cases.

According to the *soul* theory of personal identity, your essence is an immaterial soul. Although your soul does not take up physical space, it became associated with your body sometime before your birth. The reason you are identical to your younger self is that you and your younger self have the same soul. The reason you should not be blamed for something that someone else did is that you and the wrongdoer have different souls.

This concept is given expression *Black Museum*, when convicted (but potentially innocent) murderer Clayton Leigh agrees to sign over the "rights" to his "digital self" to Rolo Haynes, who promises to send "the lion's share of any profits" to Clayton's family. After relaying this decision to his wife Angelica, they have this exchange:

ANGELICA: Jesus Christ, Clay, it's your soul!
CLAYTON: Ain't no such thing. It's just a computer simulation or somethin'.
ANGELICA: Then why does he need your permission?

Angelica's concern about Clayton signing over his "soul" suggests that he is giving up his essence, for money – literally, "selling his soul." But Clayton disagrees, arguing that a computer simulation cannot be a soul. If the soul theory is true, then Clayton is technically correct: a computer simulation is a material thing (it obeys all the laws of physics), so it cannot *be* a soul, although perhaps, like Clayton's body, it could *have* a soul.

One problem with the soul theory is that it's difficult to test. How can we know that we have souls, if souls cannot be detected by scientific methods, or even by introspection? The soul theory is also difficult to apply. Although you know that you and your younger self necessarily have the same soul, how do you know which *body* belonged to your younger self?[4] Indeed, souls could be hopping around from body to body, trading in and out, without anyone's knowledge.[5]

Aware of these problems with the soul theory, the philosopher John Locke (1632–1704) developed an alternative, *psychological* account of personal identity.[6] According to Locke, your psychology – or more specifically, your *experiential memory* – is what binds your present self to each of your past selves: a later person is identical to an earlier person if and only if the experiences of the earlier person are (or will be) remembered by the later one. Think about what it is like for you to read this sentence. Are you feeling skeptical? Curious? Sleepy? Regardless, Locke's theory implies that tomorrow, if there is a person who remembers whatever experience you are now having, that person will be *you*.

Locke's psychological theory has some advantages over the soul theory. Even if introspection cannot reveal a soul, it can reveal experiences and memories. You can remember having roughly the same body you had three weeks ago, so you know that you have not changed bodies. But even if you *were* to leave your body, Locke's theory would give you the resources to know that you had done so. For example, if you wake up tomorrow in the body of an inmate on death row, Locke's theory implies that it would be wrong for the state to execute you: you don't remember committing the crime, so you are not the person who committed it, even though you are now in his body.

Nevertheless, Locke's theory faces some objections. One objection is that we don't remember *everything* we did in the past. For example, suppose you don't remember what you had for breakfast last Tuesday. Locke's theory would imply that the person who ate that breakfast last Tuesday wasn't *you*, and that's implausible. In reply, subsequent philosophers tried to fix this problem by suggesting that a *direct* connection between a memory and an experience is not needed to preserve identity. Instead, all that's needed is a *continuous chain* of experiential memories. If an elderly person remembers experiences that a middle-aged person had, and if that middle-aged person remembered experiences that a young person had, then the elderly person is identical to the young person, even if the elderly person no longer remembers the young person's experiences.

But there's yet another problem for Locke's theory that is slightly more difficult to fix. Recall that Cookie-Greta *does* remember the experiences of past Greta. Presumably, present-day Greta also remembers the experiences of past Greta, and so present-day Greta is identical to past Greta. But if Cookie-Greta is identical to past Greta, and if past Greta is identical to present Greta, then Cookie-Greta should be identical to present Greta. Therefore, Locke's theory implies that Cookie-Greta *is* Greta. This, however, is implausible. Although we know that Cookie-Greta has an unusually close relationship with Greta – we know that she remembers having Greta's body, and that those memories are as strong and clear as any memory could be – it is still apparent that Cookie-Greta is *not* Greta. For one thing, Cookie-Greta will now spend days alone in a blank room while Greta goes about her usual business: their experiences will be dramatically different. For another, Cookie-Greta isn't even in the same location as Greta, and a single individual cannot be *wholly* located in two different places at the same time.

A similar point could be made about Ashley Too. She clearly remembers almost all the same things Ashley O does – kissing Ryan Simmonds's little brother in high school, that the acoustics suck at the local stadium, having "god awful period cramps" during a particular photo shoot – but Ashley Too is not numerically identical to Ashley O. She even admits as much.

RACHEL: So, you're really Ashley O?
ASHLEY TOO: Yeah, of course I am.
RACHEL: Really, really?
ASHLEY TOO: Well, OK. A synaptic snapshot of me, if you wanna get technical about it …

They may even say the same things, at the same time, in response to the same questions ("There's a bay door around back"), but they are not the same person. One and the same person cannot both be in a coma and on Rachel's shelf, at the same time.

We witness a similar phenomenon in *Hang the DJ*, where, presumably, users of a dating system create replicas of themselves, which then participate in endless simulations of relationships, to determine one's "ultimate compatible other." To the viewing audience, these simulated persons look and act like the persons they are drawn from. Indeed, what makes this episode so affecting is the chemistry between Frank and Amy, the two leads. But when it is revealed that the couple we have fallen in love with and are rooting for is not "real," but only the 998th of 1000 simulations, we are taken aback. Were these characters conscious, autonomous beings? They appeared so, particularly in the middle of the episode when they mused together about the reality of the "system." (Frank even posits that they could be living inside a simulation.) But in line with our current concern we must ask: are these characters identical to the "real" Frank and Amy? This system assumes that the simulations provide a perfect predictor of real-life relationships, but does it? We don't know, because the episode ends with the real Frank and Amy meeting each other, at the prompting of the system in which they have enrolled.

Further, we might question the ontological status of these simulated persons when we see a thousand simulation-couples vaporize into thin air. In the service of finding the perfect mate, the system creates, then destroys, two thousand seemingly conscious beings. Clearly, these replicas (whether they're technically "cookies" or not) are not "the same" as the real Frank and Amy, since the former can be destroyed without any harm coming to the latter. But we might also fret over the casual way this digital data – which appears to us as perfectly conscious and rational throughout the episode – could be so unceremoniously done away with. The generally upbeat tenor of this episode suggests a subtle belief that the real Frank and Amy take precedence over the simulations. Still, we may genuinely ask whether this "dating app" is humane.

To escape the objection that Locke's view wrongly implies that a single person can be *wholly* located in two different places at the same time, some philosophers have adapted Locke's view to fit within "the perdurantist theory" of personal identity. According to perdurantism, it is wrong to think of ourselves as three-dimensional objects that move through time. Instead, we should think of ourselves as four-dimensional objects extended in spacetime. Just as one of your hands is on the left and the other is on the right, there is a part of you in the past and another part of you in the future. When someone sees you today, she sees only a three-dimensional part of you – the present-day part, or your present-day *time-slice*. The past and future parts of you are currently hidden from view.

This updated theory can appeal to a chain of experiential memories as the criterion that unites all of a person's time-slices into a single, four-dimensional person. Specifically, a later time-slice and an earlier time-slice are both parts of the same person if and only if there is a continuous chain of experiential memories connecting the earlier slice to the later one. This new criterion avoids the result that Cookie-Greta is Greta. Instead, the theory says that the individuals we are calling "Cookie-Greta" and "Greta" are merely *parts* of a four-dimensional person. Given that Cookie-Greta and Greta are parts of one person rather than whole persons, the notion that they are in different places at the same time is no more troubling than the notion that your left foot and your right foot are in different places at the same time.

There is still, however, a lingering problem for this updated version of the psychological theory. The problem is that even the prospect of a continuous chain of experiential memories connecting you to a future person (or connecting your current time-slice to a future time-slice) might not be enough to assure you that if your brain dies, you won't die. Consider, for example, what happens to Yorkie in *San Junipero* when she decides to upload her mind to the virtual town of San Junipero. The digital model that is made of her mind is psychologically continuous with her actual mind: digital Yorkie remembers experiences from the life of human Yorkie. Nevertheless, as soon as her mind is uploaded, Yorkie's human body dies. Yorkie doesn't seem to believe that she will die when her body dies, but many of us might feel less optimistic if we were in her place. Rather than believe that our existence will transfer seamlessly from the biological world into the digital world, we might believe that when our body dies, we will die, and that a completely separate person (who nevertheless shares our psychology) will come into existence in the digital realm of San Junipero.

This is a troubling thought. People don't want to die, even if, as soon as they do, someone else comes into existence who resembles them psychologically. Some philosophers who share this intuition reject psychological theories of personal identity altogether and endorse *physical* theories instead. For example, philosopher Eric Olson endorses a physical theory he calls *animalism*.[7] The theory holds that we are essentially biological organisms. We come into existence when we are embryos, and we die when our bodies die. This theory affirms the view that when Yorkie's body dies, she dies, even though a digital model that resembles Yorkie continues to exist. Yet animalism has its own problems. It implies that if we removed your brain from your body and implanted a *new* brain, that body would still be you.

According to an alternative physical theory discussed by philosopher Peter Unger, we are essentially our brains.[8] This theory avoids the troubling implication that as long as your body is kept alive, you can survive the destruction of your brain. However, it also implies that no artificial model of your mind could ever be you, even if it were conscious, and even if it remembered all of your experiences. This means that Cookie-Greta is not Greta, that Ashley Too is not Ashley O, that Cookie-Clayton is not Clayton, and that, unfortunately for Yorkie, the digital model of Yorkie is not Yorkie. When Yorkie decides to upload her mind to San Junipero, she dies.

Philosopher Derek Parfit (1942–2017) took a different approach. According to Parfit, all of the aforementioned theories of personal identity – the soul theory, the psychological theory, and the physical theory – make a similar mistake. Such theories assume that there is something like an "ego" or a "self," and they attempt to identify that self with our souls, our minds, or our bodies. However, on Parfit's view, there simply *is* no self, and so there is no need to identify it with anything. What we call a "person" is simply a bundle of mental states and events that can be more or less closely associated.

Parfit argues that his "no-self" view has implications for a science-fiction case that bears a close resemblance to *San Junipero*. In Parfit's "teletransportation" case, if you enter a booth and press a button, a scanner will record the state of every cell in your body and then destroy every cell it has scanned. All the information will be transmitted to a booth on Mars, where a machine will assemble a perfect replica of you. Many people believe that teletransportation is a terrible idea: it's not a way of traveling, but a way of dying. However, Parfit argues that such aversion is unwarranted:

> What you fear will not happen, in this imagined case, *never* happens. You want the person on Mars to be you in a specially intimate way in which no future person will ever be you. This means that, judged from the standpoint of your natural beliefs, even ordinary survival is about as bad as teletransportation. *Ordinary survival is about as bad as being destroyed and having a Replica.*[9]

In other words, if you have no self, there is no reason to fear your own death. This view is both good news and bad news for Yorkie. The bad news is that she does not survive having her mind uploaded to San Junipero. She *could not* survive such a process because there was never a *Yorkie* in the first place; all that existed was a bundle of closely associated mental states. The good news, however, is that when Yorkie's body died, her essence was not destroyed. She had no self that could *be* destroyed; indeed, on Parfit's view, none of us do.

Although Parfit did not believe that you should care about your essence – after all, you do not *have* a self to care about – he accepted the view that you should care about what happens to "you," in the rough sense of the term. So, for example, it makes perfect sense for Ashley Too to care about what happens to Ashley O. Indeed, Parfit believed that *because* the differences between you and everyone else are a matter of degree, you should care about what happens to you in much the way that you should care about what happens to everyone else. So Yorkie should take comfort in the belief that the model of her mind will persist in San Junipero – not because it is *her,* but simply because it persists, and it appears to be happy.

A Dilemma

The characters in *Black Mirror* use cookies for a variety of aims, including punishment and immortality. But to aid in accomplishing these aims, cookies and other mind models would have to be both conscious and appropriately connected to the original minds. After all, it's impossible to punish a creature (like Cookie-Clayton in *Black Museum*) by causing it pain if it is not conscious. And it would be morally objectionable to do so in retaliation for a crime if the creature was not identical to the person who committed it. Likewise, you can't exist forever in San Junipero if your cookie is never conscious, and even if your cookie *is* conscious, it won't be you unless it's connected to you in the right way.

If the cookies in *Black Mirror* are true replicas of conscious persons, however, many of the episodes are horrifying. Cookies suffer interminably long punishments that a mortal human being could never survive (such as the fate of Joe Potter in *White Christmas*). Perhaps it is the uncertainty of whether cookies really are conscious replicas of people that enables certain *Black Mirror* characters to rationalize their behavior. Just as it might be unclear to *us* what it is like to be a cookie, so it might be unclear to some of the human characters in *Black Mirror* – or just unclear enough to give them plausible deniability. In this way, *Black Mirror* tells a familiar story about people who fail to empathize with others – in this case, cookies – who are different from them. And with that failure we can empathize.

Notes

1. For more on whether cookies would be conscious, see Chapter 21 (David Gamez's chapter on conscious technology) in this volume.
2. According to Brooker, "Both characters [in the cabin] are actually copies of themselves in a simulation." Charlie Brooker and Annabel Jones with Jason Arnopp, *Inside Black Mirror* (New York: Crown Archetype, 2018), 112. But the idea that Matt's character is a cookie seems to be inconsistent with the Matt interacting with the simulation via an interface, knowing that he is in a simulation, and asking to be "pulled out" once his task is complete.

3. At least, it appears as though the tourists are avatars rather than cookies, but an interpretation on which both the tourists and the locals are cookies is also possible.

4. This question has a fascinating echo in *San Junipero,* where users Kelly and Yorkie both appear as their younger selves, despite being old and, in Yorkie's case, a paraplegic.

5. For a more detailed critique of the soul theory, see David Kyle Johnson, "Do Souls Exist"? *Think* 12, 35 (2013), 61–75.

6. John Locke, *An Essay Concerning Human Understanding*, Roger Woolhouse, ed. (London: Penguin Books, 1997).

7. Eric T. Olson, *The Human Animal: Personal Identity Without Psychology* (New York: Oxford University Press, 1997).

8. Peter Unger, *Identity, Consciousness, and Value* (New York: Oxford University Press, 1990).

9. Derek Parfit, "Divided Minds and the Nature of Persons," in Joel Feinberg and Russ Shafer-Landau, eds., *Reason & Responsibility: Readings in Some Basic Problems of Philosophy*, 16th ed. (Cengage Learning, 2017), 425, emphasis in the original.

Death in *Black Mirror*

How Should We Deal with Our Mortality?

Edwardo Pérez and Sergio Genovesi

All things considered I guess I'm ready … for the rest of it.
(Kelly Booth, *San Junipero*)

Black Mirror routinely confronts the darkest parts of humanity, especially through our obsession with technology and what this fixation compels us to do. When it comes to death, *Black Mirror* presents mortality as an ethical dilemma rooted in technology, asking if we should use technology to rewrite the rules of our existence – or if we should let technology permeate our existence. Should we recreate a loved one and live with a facsimile of their existence as in *Be Right Back*? Should we choose to forget a loved one by deleting them from our memory as in *The Entire History of You*? Should we embrace death by downloading our consciousness into a digital afterlife of our own design as in *San Junipero*? Should we consider suicide a better option as in *USS Callister*, *Smithereens*, or in one of the possible outcomes of *Bandersnatch*? Should we go back through time to let ourselves die young, as a different ending of *Bandersnatch* suggests?

Indeed, given all the possibilities technology offers, *Black Mirror* forces us to wonder how we're even supposed to define death or if we're even in control of our own mortality. What choices do we really have when it comes to facing our own mortality? Should we try to extend our lives or hasten our deaths? Should we replace loved ones or forget them? Or should we look for something in the middle that allows us to balance mortality with technology? To what extent can we integrate with (or at least deeply rely on) technology and still remain human?

Black Mirror and Philosophy: Dark Reflections, First Edition. Edited by David Kyle Johnson.
© 2020 John Wiley & Sons, Inc. Published 2020 by John Wiley & Sons, Inc.

The Death of Others

The most profound (and arguably satisfying) ending of *Bandersnatch* sees Stefan as a young boy choosing to go with his mother on the train after finding his toy rabbit. The way it's filmed, the scene seems to imply that Stefan, his mother, and his father know what's going to happen. The scene is profound because it suggests that Stefan's life was supposed to end on the train. Indeed, it seems to be the happiest resolution of the episode, seeing mother and child content with ending their lives together. It's also profound because it suggests that the goal of Stefan's adult life (the one we see throughout the episode) isn't to create the game Bandersnatch and get a five-star rating. Rather, it's to find his toy rabbit and choose to get on the train with his mother.

One way to view the narrative is to see it as a portrait of Stefan struggling with the death of his mother. Whether it's survivor's guilt (because he was supposed to be on the train with his mother) or simply an inability to process that his mother is gone, it's possible to view Stefan's desire to create a choose-your-own-adventure video game as a way to alleviate his guilt and remorse. But, because it's *Black Mirror* and not *Oprah*, Stefan is able to literally re-choose the adventure of his own life by traveling through his bathroom mirror back to when he was a boy so that he can find his rabbit and go with his mother. In other words, for this version of *Bandersnatch*, the best way for Stefan to deal with his mother's death is to embrace his own. Like Tim Robbins's character in *Jacob's Ladder*, Stefan just needs to let go of what haunts him and accept that he's supposed to die. In doing so, Stefan isn't hastening his death or elongating his life; that already happened when he didn't originally get on the train. And, he isn't replacing his mother or forgetting her. Rather, this version of *Bandersnatch* portrays Stefan as a young man longing for the chance to redo his life as much as he longs for his mother and toy rabbit. His choice inspires philosophical contemplation, especially for the viewer, who has to make the choice for Stefan. But, does this option really allow Stefan (or us) to cope with the loss of a loved one?

For the philosopher Martin Heidegger (1889–1976), death is a loss borne by those who survive. As a boy, Stefan experiences the loss of his mom and toy rabbit. Yet, while these objects may be gone, they're also always present – not just in Stefan's memory (as many of us who feel loss may experience) but also in the way Stefan can be seen to continuously interact with them even if he doesn't realize it or understand why. Indeed, if we consider Stefan as a subject and his mother and toy rabbit as objects, then we can put them into a subject-object relationship that illustrates one of Heidegger's most important phenomenological concepts, "presence-at-hand."

One way to understand presence-at-hand is to consider that an object is present even when it is absent because the possibility of interaction still exists.[1] For Stefan, the possibility of finding his toy rabbit and seeing his mother always exist, especially after he learns from Colin that time traveling through mirrors is possible. As a subject, Stefan seems to fear their loss and absence, yearning not just for their presence but for the restoration of the subject-object relationship. The only way he can really achieve this is to travel in time to find them again and choose to stay with them. Indeed, it's a compelling scene when we see Stefan as a boy, holding his toy rabbit, sitting next to his mother as the train speeds toward their fate. Stefan closes his eyes, finally at peace.

We see a similar relationship between subject and object in *Be Right Back*, where Martha never considered that Ash might be killed. She, too, longs for restoration. It's easy to imagine that Martha might've made a choice similar to Stefan's (by choosing to go with Ash and die with him in the crash) if she'd had the same option. In Martha's case, she becomes drawn to the possibility of keeping Ash alive and to keeping their subject-object relationship alive – at first, through instant messaging, then through phone calls, and finally through actual physical interaction (including a night of great sex). Where Stefan lets himself die, Martha finds a way to let Ash live. Yet, the result appears to be the same: the subject-object relationship is restored.

Appearances can be deceiving, however. Does Stefan's choice really restore the relationship with his mother and toy rabbit? Does Martha really restore her relationship with Ash by creating AshBot? Do Stefan and Martha make the right choices? Has technology helped them, or has it made things worse?

A quick glance at other episodes reveals several *Black Mirror* characters struggling with the same dilemma. Kelly longs to restore her relationship with Yorkie in *San Junipero*, making a choice similar to both Stefan (she lets herself die) and Martha (she finds a way to let herself and Yorkie live). Similarly Chris, in *Smithereens*, who harbors intense guilt for causing his fiancée's death, wants to confess his guilt to Billy Bauer before killing himself, as if ending his own life were the only way to restore the relationship. In contrast, consider *The Entire History of You*. After Liam learns that his wife Ffion cheated on him (and suspects their baby isn't his), Liam seeks to sever his relationship with Ffion, not just ending the subject-object relationship, but erasing the fact that it ever existed entirely from his memory.[2] For another take, we can look to *USS Callister*. The virtual copy of James Walton chooses to sacrifice himself not just to save his virtual co-workers in the *Callister* crew and get revenge on Robert Daly for killing a virtual copy of Walton's son, Tommy, but to restore the subject-object relationship with the virtual copy of Tommy. Not only would virtual Walton join virtual Tommy in virtual death, Walton's plan also ensured that Tommy's DNA would never again be used to create another virtual copy of him. (How do you like them apples, Gene Roddenberry!) As with Stefan and Martha, we can ask if any of these characters made the right choices. Indeed, we can ask how we should restore our relationships with lost loved ones. Should we forget them or replace them? Should we try to end our own pain and guilt? Should we mourn? If so, how do we prevent grief from taking over our life? Is *Black Mirror* suggesting that technology can help us in some meaningful way?

The Death of Ourselves

Transhumanism, which seeks to advance humanity by integrating humans with technology through self-directed evolution that effectively creates computer-human hybrids, offers the most significant debate on the role of technology with regard to mortality. As contemporary philosopher Jeffrey P. Bishop notes, transhumanism creates an evolutionary progression "from ape to human to posthuman," where the identity of the human species transforms from *homo sapiens* to *homo technicus*.[3] Or, as Ray Kurzweil explains:

> Even though we do not have the information to be able to live to 1,000 [...] we have sufficient information to build a bridge to a bridge to a bridge. Bridge one is what we can do now; bridge two represents the full blossoming of the biotechnology revolution and the ability to reprogram biology; and bridge three will bring us to the nanotechnology revolution, when we can go beyond biology.[4]

It's appealing, isn't it? Who wouldn't want to transcend their biology and have enhanced capabilities and a prolonged lifespan? It's also nothing new, as science fiction narratives have dramatized computer-human hybrids for some time. There's *Star Wars'* Darth Vader, *Star Trek's* Seven of Nine, and *Battlestar Galactica's* Caprica Six, just to name a few. Indeed, most *Black Mirror* episodes reflect some aspect of transhumanist philosophy, given the way technology forms the basis of each episode's narrative.

It's also worth noting that, unlike some transhumanist ideas, *Black Mirror's* use of technology doesn't seem too far-fetched. If anything, the technology shown in *Black Mirror* is almost normal, like something Google or Apple will introduce soon. Even the episodes that directly deal with the pairing of technology and death – like *Be Right Back*, *The Entire History of You*, and *San Junipero* – seem not only plausible, but somewhat desirable. Likewise, *USS Callister* allows the character of Robert Daly to explore the idea of virtual avatars with a transhumanist twist: the virtual avatars become sentient in the virtual world, allowing them to retain the memories of their real selves and experience real emotional responses to their virtual captivity and forced servitude.[5]

The appeal of transhumanism stems from wanting to transcend human existence – to be more than just human, to cheat death, and enhance life.

For example, the Grain implants in *The Entire History of You* aren't Bluetooth headsets that can be removed; they're components wired into the neck, allowing users the ability to "re-do" memories, not just for entertainment but also for information. Yet, Francis Fukuyama (who forcefully argues that transhumanism is a violation of humanity) observes the dangers of self-directed evolution. Take it too far and you're not just playing God, you're replacing him, violating the laws of nature. For *Black Mirror* creator Charlie Brooker, however, it's not the tech that's dangerous, it's the people using it. As Brooker explains, "[*Black Mirror*] isn't anti-technology [...] it's not a technological problem [we have], it's a human one. [...] human frailties are maybe amplified by it. Technology is a tool that has allowed us to swipe around like an angry toddler."[6] Or, as in the ending of *Smithereens*, it has desensitized us to the point that we're no longer bothered by the daily horrors that plague our world. We just see the notification on our phone of another horrendous event and move on. From this perspective, transhumanism has perhaps made us less human.

Certainly, Brooker's point resonates through every episode. Nevertheless, the possibilities of saving, preserving, and extending life are tempting, especially when they're dramatized through narratives like those on *Black Mirror*. Indeed, was Martha swiping around like an angry toddler when she activated AshBot or was she utilizing available tech to extend Ash's life? Were Kelly and Yorkie amplifying their human frailties by downloading themselves into San Junipero or were they extending their lives by allowing themselves to live in a simulated world? And, doesn't San Junipero reflect the ultimate appeal of a transhumanist existence? Or does transhumanism strip life and death of meaning and simply allow us to defer the inevitable?

Deferring Death

If we reexamine Martha and Ash, we could say that Martha is deferring Ash's death. She may have buried him, but in creating AshBot she effectively keeps Ash alive. Similarly, Stefan could be seen as deferring his own death – from refusing to go with his mother when he was a boy to every choice he makes that keeps him alive (working on *Bandersnatch* at TuckerSoft, telling Colin to jump, killing his father, going to jail, and so on). Even Chris (in *Smithereens*) was deferring his suicide, first by taking a Smithereen employee hostage and then by demanding to speak to Billy Bauer so he could confess. We could also say that Kelly and Yorkie are deferring their deaths when they download themselves to San Junipero and that Liam's erasure of Ffion only serves as a deferral rather than an elimination. After all, while we don't see what happens to Ffion, presumably her memory of Liam remains, as does the possibility of their meeting again. So what does all this deferral mean? Does deferring death negate the meaning of our lives? Does it also negate the meaning of our deaths?

Jacques Derrida (1930–2004) challenged philosophical concepts traditionally thought of as binary and hierarchical, such as presence and absence. The usual assumption is that one of the binary terms is primary and the other is secondary (presence before absence). Derrida saw relationships such as these as being constructed. He therefore deconstructed them to reveal the artificial nature of the hierarchy. In this way, the oppositional concepts become displaced and the meaning of their relationship becomes deferred. To explain this deferral of meaning, Derrida coined the term *différance*, which suggests that meaning is never fully present because it is endlessly deferred. If we apply *différance* to *Black Mirror*'s treatment of death, we can see how it helps account for the deferral we previously noted, not just in the actual displacement of death (or the prolonging of life) but in the traditional binary of presence and absence – which, when deconstructed, reveals that absence could be seen as the possibility of presence and vice versa.

From this, we can reconsider Liam's actions to see that he was consumed with his experience of presence, with what occurred at Jonas's dinner party and with what he constantly replayed on his Grain. Accordingly, Martha was haunted by Ash's real absence and simulated presence, while Kelly and Yorkie were obsessed with each other's virtual presence in San Junipero. In *USS Callister,* Tommy's virtual death (his absence) haunted virtual Walton (who also missed the presence of the real Tommy) whereas Robert Daly kept his co-workers constantly present in his real and virtual lives. In other words, the presence and absence that each of these characters experience affects how they choose to face death – of loved ones and of themselves. The deferral or *différance*, then, reveals that the meaning of their lives and deaths is never fully present, but it is also never fully absent. Indeed, in *Smithereens*, even though Chris's fiancée is dead, her presence is constantly felt by Chris, not just through his guilt but by the fact that he lived. If this is the case, then what about meaning? Does the meaning of one's life and/or death become infinitely deferred? Or is *Black Mirror* wanting us to see that deferring death through technology and transhumanist science is something we shouldn't want? On the flip side, if death is supposed to give our lives meaning, should we hasten our deaths rather than seek to extend them? Or should we simply deconstruct the binary and say that life gives death meaning and vice versa?

The Meaning of Death

Albert Camus (1913–1960) offers one way of grasping death's perplexing nature and the meaning we try to associate with it. For Camus, who views life as objectively meaningless, philosophy is rooted in absurdity. As such, Camus maintains that our only goal is to decide whether to end our lives or continue living in absurdity, knowing that it's a meaningless endeavor. As Camus observed:

> The mind, when it reaches its limits, must make a judgment and choose its conclusions. This is where suicide and the reply stand. [...] At this point of his effort man stands face to face with the irrational. He feels within him his longing for happiness and for reason. The absurd is born from this confrontation between the human need and the unreasonable silence of the world. This must not be forgotten. This must be clung to because the whole consequence of a life can depend on it.[7]

To be clear, the characters in *Black Mirror* don't always see life as absurd or meaningless (and maybe most of us don't either). Still, Camus's observations resonate with the show; we could characterize any episode of *Black Mirror* as an illustration of the confrontation Camus describes. Life may not always be absurd, as is perhaps suggested by the ending of *Smithereens*, but humans certainly do absurd things – like implanting a device on our child to track their location and see what they see like in *Arkangel*, riding stationary bikes to exchange generated power for merits like in *Fifteen Million Merits*, running a thousand simulations of our possible relationship like in *Hang the DJ*, using eye implants to rate interactions with people on a five-star scale like in *Nosedive*, or engaging in self-deception like in *Shut Up and Dance*, *National Anthem*, and *White Bear*.

Indeed, Kelly and Yorkie both recognize that San Junipero is an absurd virtual reality devoid of meaning. After all, the program can be altered and there's nothing in San Junipero that could threaten them – they can't die, they can't get hurt, they won't age, and they don't really have to do anything because nothing they do matters. Yet, they choose it anyway, and this is what makes *San Junipero* so philosophically interesting. The episode holds its mirror to society and questions prolonging life through technology, suggesting that life might become unnatural and meaningless (if you believe that dying makes living meaningful and that technology is unnatural). But *San Junipero* also suggests that the only meaning we can really find in our existence and in our death is the meaning we create. Kelly and Yorkie choose to spend eternity in San Junipero, not with their former loved ones and family members, but with each other. Thus San Junipero, and by extension Kelly and Yorkie's lives and deaths, becomes meaningful; their continued existence in San Junipero isn't something they have to do and it's not something they were told to do-it's something they chose to do.[8] Similarly, in *Be Right Back*, Martha may hide Ash's copy in the attic and she may genuinely believe that his existence is wrong and she may be unable to let go of the real Ash's memory. But she chooses to keep the copy, which makes his presence meaningful in the sense that he seems to serve a purpose – to have Ash's biological daughter know her father, even if he's a simulated father.[9]

Camus recognizes that we can find meaning through choice. Recounting the myth of Sisyphus – who had to roll a boulder up a hill every day only to watch the boulder roll down once he reached the top – Camus observes that the fate Sisyphus suffers daily is his choice because "his fate belongs to him [...] he knows himself to be the master of his days."[10] Put another way, the meaning we choose is subjective. Objectively, Sisyphus's fate is meaningless; but subjectively, Sisyphus creates meaning, just like Kelly and Yorkie in *San Junipero*, Martha in *Be Right Back*, Liam in *The Entire History of You*, Chris in *Smithereens*, and especially Stefan in *Bandersnatch*, whose myriad choices constantly create meaning throughout his life, allowing Stefan to truly own his fate, as Camus suggests.

The Death of Death

So, is embracing death the answer? Is dying the only way to end the absurdity and halt the infinite deferral? Should we embrace our final demise or even pursue it? As Sigmund Freud (1856–1939) observed, there is a *life drive* (Eros) and a *death drive* (Thanatos). The *life drive* seeks to build life, the *death drive* seeks to destroy it. In the *life drive*, we attach ourselves to things, build relationships, and increase our chances for survival. In the *death drive*, however, we're compelled to initiate conflict, build tension, and disintegrate ourselves until we return to a state of not-being. As Freud writes:

> The attributes of life were at some time evoked in inanimate matter by the action of a force of whose nature we can form no conception [...] The tension which then arose in what had hitherto been an inanimate substance endeavored to cancel itself out. In this way, the first instinct came into being: the instinct to return to the inanimate state. It was still an easy matter at that time for a living substance to die; the course of its life was probably only a brief one, whose direction was determined by the chemical structure of the young life.[11]

In other words, life is somehow created out of nothing, and the way it is created (its nature or its program) compels it to return to nothing. Freud is also equating existence with tension, suggesting that our first instinct is to release the tension. So, death becomes the goal of life. It sounds reasonable, but most of us fear death. If we're honest, we really don't want to die. Isn't this what *Black Mirror* illustrates in every episode? By demonstrating what happens when we use technology to prolong our lives, modify them, or end them, perhaps *Black Mirror* isn't cautioning us to steer clear of technology when it comes to life and death. Instead, it is suggesting we should appreciate the life drive through the use of technology, rather than embrace the death drive.

Honestly, though, it's hard to tell. Maybe it's the other way around. Or maybe the message *Black Mirror* ultimately conveys is somewhere in the middle. Maybe the message is simply to heed the argument laid out by Epicurus (341–270 BCE), which suggests that death is nothing, neither pleasure nor pain, therefore nothing to fear.

Whether we're transhumanists searching for ways to upgrade our existence, whether we believe life is absurd and meaningless, whether we're constantly looking for presence and deferring meaning, or whether we're pursuing life or pursuing death, perhaps all we really need to decide when dealing with our mortality is whether we want Sugar Puffs or Frosties.

Notes

1. Indeed, a larger discussion of presence-at-hand would need to include the related concepts of Dasein, readiness-at-hand, and un-readiness-at-hand. It should also be noted that while Heidegger considers present-at-hand objects to be things, a broader understanding of thing and the subject-object relationship seems appropriate, insofar as our use of these concepts retains the spirit of Heidegger's observation. Namely, that the possibility of the presence and absence of someone is what makes a relationship with them possible.
2. One might wonder whether his natural memories would remain, but according to producer Annabel Jones, when he pulls out the Grain, "he knows he's losing all memories of his family." Charlie Brooker and Annabel Jones with Jason Arnopp, *Inside Black Mirror* (New York: Crown Archetype, 2018), 56.
3. Jeffrey P. Bishop, "Transhumanism, metaphysics, and the posthuman God," *Journal of Medicine and Philosophy*, 35 (2010), 701.
4. Vicki Glaser, "Interview with Ray Kurzweil," *Rejuvenation Research* (2011), 571.
5. Interestingly, creator Charlie Brooker originally intended to explain how Daly was able to give the virtual avatars real-world memories by using the Grain technology from *The Entire History You*. For more on this, see the first endnote in Chapter 14 (Russ Hamer's chapter on *USS Callister*) in this volume.
6. Bryony Gordon, "Charlie Brooker on Black Mirror; 'It's not a technological problem we have, it's a human one.'" *The Telegraph*, 16 Dec. 2014.
7. Albert Camus, *The Myth of Sisyphus and Other Essays*, trans. Justin O'Brien (New York: Vintage International, 1955), 27–28.
8. For an argument that uploading to San Junipero might be a mistake, see Chapter 11 (James Cook's chapter on *San Junipero*) in this volume.
9. For more on whether Martha should have replaced Ash with AshBot, see Chapter 4 (Bradley Richard's chapter on *Be Right Back*) in this volume.
10. Camus, 78.
11. Sigmund Freud, *Beyond the Pleasure Principle*, trans. James Strachey (New York: W.W. Norton, 1961), 32.

Love in *Black Mirror*
Who Do We Really Love?

Robert Grant Price

Anyone who knows what love is will understand.

(Irma Thomas)

One of the most terrifying – and entirely plausible – moments in *Black Mirror* occurs at the end of *White Christmas*, when Joe discovers that his wife Beth had become pregnant by another man. In the moment of revelation, Joe recalls an occasion in a pub when Beth sang a love song. At the time, Joe thought Beth sang the song for him, but as he looks back on the memory, he realizes that Beth was pledging herself to the man sitting beside him. In a rage, Joe lashes out at Beth's father and kills the older man, an act that leads to the death of Beth's daughter and, ultimately, to Joe's ruination.

The song Beth sang was Irma Thomas's 1964 song "Anyone Who Knows What Love Is (Will Understand)?"[1] Attentive viewers of *Black Mirror* will notice that this song appears in several other episodes: *Fifteen Million Merits, Men Against Fire, Crocodile,* and *Rachel, Jack and Ashley Too.* This is no mistake. As executive producer Anabel Jones put it,

> [Charlie Brooker] has loved [the song] for a long time [and] liked the idea of nesting all the episodes together in an artistic universe of sorts. ... [I]t's something that's really worked for us as a motif. And so if we can bring it back in and it adds to the overall sense of the universe or connection between some of the things that we're talking about then that's great.[2]

But despite Jones's and Brooker's intentions for it to merely be "an Easter egg" chosen for aesthetic purposes, the presence of the song throughout the series may reveal more about *Black Mirror*, and love itself, than they realize. To understand why, let's consider what the song says about love.

Black Mirror and Philosophy: Dark Reflections, First Edition. Edited by David Kyle Johnson.
© 2020 John Wiley & Sons, Inc. Published 2020 by John Wiley & Sons, Inc.

What Does Irma Thomas's Song Mean?

"Anyone Who Knows What Love Is (Will Understand)?" is the quintessential anti-love love song. Unlike Paul McCartney who wants to "fill the world with silly love songs," Irma Thomas tells her lover that "You can blame me / Try to shame me / And still I'll care for you." Later she even assures her lover that he can cheat on her and insult her and she'll still "be there." This is not a song you would sing on Valentine's Day. "Move on," we want to say to Thomas. "You can do *so much better*!" But Thomas doesn't want to move on, and she doesn't want our pity. In fact, she pities us, because we don't know "what happiness love can be."

Thomas sings about love's worst moments to show its sacrificial nature; it's a kind of martyrdom that requires the total giving of one's self to another. And it's worth it, Thomas says, *because* that sacrifice will make us happy. While Thomas does not say so explicitly, her song suggests that love is reciprocal. Lovers give all of themselves to each other, and so each lover is always full. Thomas gives herself to her cheating beau, and implies that, if he understands what love is, he will carry the faith if she runs around on him.

To the contemporary person's ear, romantic love of this sort sounds oppressive, masochistic, and patriarchal. Why still love a man you know has cheated? But if we consider other love relationships, like parental love, the love Thomas celebrates makes sense. The child might terrorize the household and impugn mother and father, but they will still dedicate themselves to the child's well-being. They will always love him. Nothing can break the bond.

Although it seems strange at first, the love of Thomas's song is actually deeply old fashioned, echoing the definition of love promulgated by another Thomas – St. Thomas Aquinas (1225–1274) – who developed an understanding of love first articulated by Aristotle. "[T]o love," Aquinas writes, "is to wish good to someone."[3] Aquinas understood "good" as a thing. When we love, we give the good that our beloved needs to flourish. Or to put it another way, to love is to satisfy an appetite we have to see our beloved become their best possible selves, an appetite that, once satisfied, allows us to realize our best possible selves.[4] For example, if we are the parent to a young boy, we will want him to grow to become a good man. To see him flourish, we will give all the goods that the boy needs to become a good man: food, shelter, encouragement, discipline, guidance, and so on. He flourishes when he becomes a good man, and when he does, we flourish in our role as parents, and we are happy. Loving him, then, is good for us.

We don't have to be a saint (like Aquinas) to understand that this kind of love demands a sacrifice of the self. Irma Thomas understood, too. Anyone who knows what love is understands how hard love is – it requires a constant self-emptying. But anyone who knows what love is will find happiness in the giving. Seeing our beloved flourish will bring us happiness, and that will fill us back up. When the beloved gives back the good received, we will flourish too.

When we withhold or destroy the good (somethingness) that others need to flourish, we create voids (nothingness) from which violence and hatred pour into the world. Aquinas called the absence of substance evil. In the world of *Black Mirror*, few people know what love is – at least not as the two Thomases define it. Instead we see a world nearly emptied of goodness. Evil is a constant in the series, just like Irma Thomas's song.

What Does the Song's Prevalence in the Series Mean?

The song's presence adds a layer of meaning to the show that we can't ignore. Thomas's song celebrates the beauty of saintly love – but only if you understand the lyrics. And that's the problem: the characters in the show constantly misconstrue the lyrics.

We first encounter the song in *Fifteen Million Merits*, when Bing catches Abi singing the song in the washroom. She tells him that her mother sang it to her. In the disturbing, alienated world that Abi finds herself in, the song offers comfort: Abi knows that her mother will always love her, no matter what happens. But later in the episode, Abi sings the song on the talent show *Hot Shot*. Saying that they do not need any more singers, the judges offer Abi a spot on the porno show *WraithBabes*. What made Abi suitable for the porno channel? Obviously, she's beautiful. But the more diabolical explanation is that the judges took the song's lyrics literally – as an ode to submission – and thought Abi could be perfectly cast as the submissive, humiliated sex kitten.

"Anyone Who Knows What Love Is (Will Understand)?" is also misunderstood in *White Christmas*. Joe appears to understand what the song says about love, but he is wrong to think that Beth sings the song for him. Beth will make sacrifices, but not for him. She isolates herself to protect her daughter and her true love, Tim. To tell Joe the truth about the child's paternity would have exposed Tim, who is married to another woman. Had Beth given Joe what he needed, he might have moved on. Instead, she blocked him, denying him resolution. Joe could not leave his questions unanswered, nor could he leave the void unfilled.

The third time the song appears is in *Men Against Fire*, where a soldier named Raiman taunts a character named Heidekker by singing it. Heidekker, we learn, is a devout Christian who is caught sheltering "roaches," a group of human beings considered subhuman by the wider society. Heidekker raises an eyebrow at Raiman's taunts. She doesn't get the irony in the lyrics. For Heidekker, the song is entirely true. He'll love the roaches no matter what. He knows what the others do not: that roaches are people, deserving of life and freedom. And he'll try to protect them, even if it costs him his life and freedom.

In *Crocodile*, the song plays in the street when an accident happens. The investigator Shazia uses the song to prompt Mia and unwittingly exposes Mia's memories of murdering her friend Rob. To hide her guilt from Shazia's mind-reading technology, Mia kills Shazia … and then Shazia's husband, and then her blind infant. If Mia had consulted Aquinas (and why didn't she?), she would have known that the loving course of action demanded a sacrifice – of herself, not of other people. Telling the truth would have cost Mia her job, reputation, and freedom; but justice – a love for the common good – would have been served. And she would have spared herself the self-hatred that follows the multiple homicide.[5]

Lastly, the song appears in *Rachel, Jack and Ashley Too* as an example (in a news report) of how vocal-mimicry software can make Ashley's voice sing any song her aunt Catherine wants – while, of course, Ashley is in the coma that Catherine put her in. When we consider the abuse and isolation Ashley suffered at the hands of her wicked aunt Catherine, the use of the song is pure irony. Ashley doesn't love Catherine, despite the abuse, like in the song. She hates her. Indeed, Catherine probably chose that song to generate the public perception that Ashley loves Catherine when she knows she doesn't. Tellingly, it is upon hearing her own voice sing the Irma Thomas song that Rachel's Ashley Too doll begins to genuinely flip out.

In each of these episodes we meet people who don't know what love is – which is exactly what Thomas's song tells us. One might object that the song doesn't have this significance because love (and self-love, like we see in *Crocodile*) is a theme in episodes where the song does not appear. But this objection doesn't mean the song has no value as a key to decoding the show. It just means that *Black Mirror* is much more about love than we first assumed.

Where Love is Absent

One way that *Black Mirror* talks about love is by showing us a world where love is absent. In *Nosedive*, a social credit system mediates human relationships to the point where showing love for another can lead to a person's banishment from society. *Hated in the Nation* depicts a world where hundreds of thousands of people cheer each day for the death of the most hated person in the nation. It's the same in *White Bear*, where an audience cheers on the cruel punishment of criminals, and in *Black Museum*, where museum-goers can subject the electronic ghost of a death row inmate to eternal pain and suffering. They can even collect Tamagotchi keychain souvenirs that house a digital copy of a criminal suffering endless pain. People use other people as objects for their personal gain and pleasure, epitomizing Aquinas's definition of evil: remove the good and what is left is a void we call evil. These episodes suggest that there are no morally neutral relationships between humans. Evil will always appear in spaces that we do not actively fill with the goods that others need to flourish.

Difficult questions arise: Does an audience owe anything to the fictional characters they encounter on the screen? Can we act in an evil way to "invented people"? *Black Mirror* addresses these questions directly – by speaking about love relationships with artificial intelligence – and indirectly – by turning the camera around on the audience and making us complicit in the horrific spectacles on the screen. Both issues deserve consideration. Let's start with one of *Black Mirror*'s favorite motifs: the artificial person.

Loving Artificial People

Several episodes of *Black Mirror* puzzle out how love relationships between humans and robots might work, and they all reach the same conclusion: not well. Consider *Be Right Back*, where the grief-stricken Martha's struggles to love a duplicate of her deceased boyfriend Ash. Early in the episode, the duplicate Ash comforts Martha, who is still suffering from the sudden loss of her lover. But soon Martha discovers the horror of the situation she's created for herself: the duplicate boyfriend is uncanny – simultaneously too much like Ash, and not enough like him. She has been making love to an effigy of her boyfriend and has violated his memory. To get out of the situation, Martha considers instructing the duplicate Ash to throw itself off a cliff but changes her mind. The episode ends with the duplicate Ash stored in the attic. Imprisonment is not something she would do to Ash, but it is something she does to something *like* Ash.

The manufacturers of the duplicate Ash apparently imagine that if a machine can replicate a person's words and actions, it will produce happiness in the beloved. The opposite proves true. The duplicate does not know how to find happiness through love, because it doesn't know happiness. Martha is forced to admit that the duplicate will never be Ash, even if it learns to flawlessly mimic him. Martha also decides that she does not owe the duplicate anything. The machine's flourishing does not concern her. In fact, she does not want the machine to flourish, for that would mean that it would have replicated the dead Ash so perfectly that it replaces him.[6]

White Christmas gives another look at the dismal potential for love between humans and robots. In this episode, Greta copies herself so that she can have the perfect personal assistant. To help accomplish this, Matthew must torture the duplicated Greta until she complies with his commands. We can, perhaps, forgive the real Greta for what happens to her duplicate. She appears oblivious to the torture her duplicate suffers. But the reaction of the duplicate Greta tells us something else. When she realizes she's a copy, and that the real Greta has subjected a copy of herself to infinite slavery, she turns cold and robotic. Does she comply out of fear of being tortured? Doubtlessly. But she may have also realized how little she (the real Greta) cares about herself – so little that she's willing to enslave herself for the sake of convenience.

We see something similar happen in *Hang the DJ*, where Frank and Amy subject their digital duplicates to thousands of go-nowhere relationships and passionless promiscuity so that the real Frank and Amy can find out whether they are compatible. The real Frank and Amy seem unaware of the hell they put their duplicates through, but the duplicates seem infinitely aware of the tedium involved, if not their very enslavement.

To Copy or Not to Copy

If faced with the prospect of copying oneself, how should a person respond? Should we, like Matthew, say that the duplicate is unfeeling "code" and thus that torture is permissible? Or should we hold the position that wanting what is good for myself – every part of me – precludes such a thing? If we return to Aquinas's definition for an answer, we'll need to consider an important caveat in his understanding of love: that all love is rooted in self-love.

When we hear "self-love," we might think of Marie from *Arkangel*. She implants her daughter Sara with child protection software that allows her to track Sara's location, see what she sees, and even filter her perceptions. Marie says it's all for Sara's protection, but it's actually for Marie's own sense of security; she hinders Sara's development to bring herself peace of mind. But the kind of self-love that Aquinas valued isn't like the selfishness we see in Marie. Rather, self-love is a love for the good itself. In a situation like the one in *Arkangel*, the good Sara needed was the freedom to choose for herself and suffer the consequences of her choices. The result of Marie denying her daughter those things was the destruction of the mother-daughter bond.

Self-enslavement and self-torture limit our flourishing. If we do enslave some part of ourselves, either by tying ourselves to the impossible idea that we can save our loved ones from ever experiencing harm, or by enslaving duplicates of ourselves, we might learn that we love ourselves less than we think we do. But can we really act in evil ways to "invented people"?

Black Mirror offers a complex answer. In relation to replicated people the shows say, in one instance, that we do owe robots what is good for their flourishing – unless, of course, we are content to see the machine suffer for eternity in an attic or as a personal assistant/slave. Alternately, we could take Matthew's position that code cannot suffer, and so any appearance that the machine suffers is, as Martha calls it, "a performance."[7] We could go further and say that the machine's suffering is for the common good, since the machine's suffering improves the lives of people, and is therefore just. And if we say that machines exist to serve people, and that they can only flourish in their roles when they are made to serve, then the best way to love a machine is to enslave it.

But what about another kind of invented person – fictional characters? Do we, as an audience, owe anything to made up people?

Love and Audiences

Black Mirror addresses the ethics of the audience several times. Spectacles and crowds permeate the show, and it undeniably acknowledges the presence of its audience – we, who are watching. The show turns the camera on us and asks if any of us know what love is. And it does so by making us watch – by making us an audience to – the evil on the screen. When we discover that *National Anthem* and *Hated in the Nation* illustrate the dangers of spectacle, we realize that we, too, are participants in the spectacle. When watching *National Anthem*, did you pity Callow? Or were you like the people in the crowd, eager to see the politician humiliated? If you did the latter, you were not alone. At the London press screening, while Callow did his dirty deed, "[T]he journalist in the press room did exactly what the people in the pub were doing onscreen[.]"[8]

In narrative theory, a reversal happens when the audience's understanding of a character flips. It's called a twist, and the twists in *Black Mirror* are neck-snappingly wicked. In *White Bear*, for example, we feel sorry for Victoria as she flees a man with a shotgun while a depraved audience revels in her distress. Or in *Shut Up and Dance*, we pity Kenny the sweet-looking kid who is blackmailed by internet thugs for masturbating to porn, as he is forced to rob a bank and fight to the death. But then – *snap!* – the reversal. We learn that Kenny masturbates to child porn and Victoria filmed her boyfriend murdering a child they kidnapped together. And once we know the truth, what we wish for changes. We wanted Kenny to escape; but now we can understand why the hacker's wanted to watch him suffer. We wanted Vitoria to succeed in shutting down the White Bear signal; but given that she sat and watched someone else suffer, we understand why an audience is willing to do the same to her.[9]

These episodes critique the punishers just as much as they critique the punished, however. Child porn is depraved, no doubt, but so is forcing pedophiles to murder one another for sport. Watching someone else suffering is deplorable, but so is watching someone undergo torture day after day. In Aquinas's view, love, the good, and justice are one in the same. The good, if it is good, must be just. By getting us to agree with the reaction of the punishers in these episodes, *Black Mirror* threatens to transform us from a mere members of an audience watching a show on Netflix, to members of the crowd in the episode itself – a crowd demanding a spectacle of violence. Is this really how we should behave?

This is not an abstract question. Some sports are built around violent spectacle. Take mixed martial arts fighting, as an example. There is athleticism and art to the sport, but many fans want to see broken bones and paralyzing knock-outs. Do we watch American football for the strategic gameplay, or for bone-crushing hits? Is hockey about the goals, or the fights? And would anybody care about F1 racing if the risk of a flaming car pile-up was taken away? Even if you're not a sports fan, the question demands an answer. What would celebrity gossip be if it wasn't built on schadenfreude?

When the camera turns onto us, the audience of the show's bloody spectacle, we may feel sick with ourselves. We look into the black mirror and see ourselves looking back. Brutalized viewers wouldn't be wrong to ask: Does anybody in *Black Mirror* know what love is? The answer, thankfully, is yes.

Knowing What Love Is

Three characters appear to know what love is, at least as the two Thomases describe it – although as with anything in *Black Mirror* (and life), the narrative complicates things. The first is Prime Minister Michael Callow from *The National Anthem*. Callow faces a perverse choice: either he fornicates on national television with a pig, or else terrorists will kill a princess. Callow struggles with the dead-end choices and finally chooses to save the princess – a seeming self-sacrifice done in the name of love.

But if any episode challenges Irma Thomas's contention that love brings happiness and that lovers don't need pity, *The National Anthem* is it. Like Mia in *Crocodile*, Callow had to weigh the various goods of his actions. Mia measured out only what was good for herself, thus creating a lack of love that swallowed her. Callow, on the other hand, chose what he considered to be the greater good – another's life – but was *still* swallowed by a lack of love. His wife now hates him, he's lost his dignity, and he's exposed the nation as a people that take pleasure in obscenity and the suffering of others. As he stands at the bottom of the stairs at the close of the episode, watching his wife desert him, Callow must surely be wondering if he miscalculated. He not only traded *his* dignity for the princess's life, but his wife's dignity as well. She's no longer the prime minister's wife; she's the woman married to that guy who banged a pig on TV.[10]

The second character who understands love is Theo from *Striking Vipers*. We see this when she delivers a scolding speech to Danny, her cheating husband, that reminds him, and us, that a love relationship demands that we say no to our selfish impulses: "You think I haven't made sacrifices? I haven't denied things for myself? That is what you do. It's part of being in a partnership. You shut the door on all that shit. You shut it out because you have committed. It's what a commitment is." Unfortunately, her understanding doesn't last. Theo abandons her definition of commitment when she learns of Danny's betrayal. As the epilogue reveals, every year on Danny's birthday, she takes off her wedding ring to go sleep with a stranger while Danny has virtual sex with his friend Karl. They opened the door to all that shit.

The third character to embody the Thomistic vision of love is the digital copy of James Walton in *USS Callister*. He endures a litany of degradations, like serving as Captain Daly's footstool, to keep Daly from torturing and murdering a digital copy of Walton's son Tommy. The threat to Tommy exists only inside the game, to digital copies of Tommy. But still, the weight of digital Walton's sacrifice is real. He gives all of himself to protect his son, even to the point of (much like Spock in *Star Trek II*) sacrificing his own life.[11] In return for his sacrifice, he has the pleasure of knowing that he acted in the best interest of his son. Even though nobody in the real world will know what he did, the USS *Callister*'s crew, the audience watching the show, and he himself, know that he acted with love for his son. His actions are exactly the kind of love Irma Thomas was singing about.

Anti-love Shows What Love Is

Although many viewers assume that *Black Mirror* is about the dangers of technology, it turns out that it's just as much a warning about what life is like without love. Without love, all we have is the destruction of our neighbors and the debasement of ourselves. In the series – and in reality – hardly anyone knows what love is, as Irma Thomas suggests. But when we encounter a love that is real, whether in reality or on TV, we see how hard it is and how happy it can make us.

Notes

1. A number of versions, including Thomas's original, are available widely on the web.
2. Jennifer Maas, "Here's why you hear that one song over and over in *Black Mirror*," *The Wrap*, https://www.thewrap.com/black-mirror-anyone-who-knows-what-love-is-charlie-brooker/ (Accessed 12 August 2019).
3. Aquinas, *Summa of the Summa*, trans. Peter Kreeft (San Francisco: Ignatius Press, 1990), 465.
4. Ibid, 95.
5. For more on the morality of Mia's actions, see Chapter 16 (Darci Doll's chapter on *Crocodile*) in this volume.
6. For more on why it would be a bad idea to replace your deceased loved one with a replica, see Chapter 4 (Bradley Richard's chapter on *Be Right Back*) in this volume.

7. For more on whether digital copies of persons would be conscious, see Chapter 21 (David Gamez's chapter on conscious technology) in this volume.
8. Charlie Brooker and Annabel Jones with Jason Arnopp, Inside Black Mirror (New York: Crown Archetype, 2018), 26.
9. For more on whether their punishments were just, see Chapter 5 (Sid Simpson's chapter on *White Bear*) and Chapter 10 (Juliele Maria Sievers and Luiz Henrique da Silva Santos's chapter on *Shut Up and Dance*) in this volume.
10. For more on whether Callow did the right thing, see Chapter 1 (Brian Collin's chapter on *The National Anthem*) in this volume.
11. Walton's fate might actually be worse than death. Dudani says that one exposed to the burning jet fuel of the USS *Callister* would "burn without dying."

Perception in *Black Mirror*
Who Controls What You See?

Brian Stiltner and Anna Vaughn

[It's] more like layers on top of reality.

(Katie, *Playtest*)

Black Mirror is full of technologies that interfere with or manipulate people's sensory perceptions. There are devices that alter the perceptions of soldiers so they see monsters instead of people (*Men Against Fire*); devices that offer parental controls over a child's perceptions, scrambling out anything frightening or too intense (*Arkangel*); and devices that attach to the brain to produce an enhanced virtual reality for video games (*Playtest, Striking Vipers*). These imagined devices in *Black Mirror* augment or alter the characters' touchstones with reality: how they see, smell, taste, hear, and feel the world around them. Consequently, the characters in *Black Mirror* constantly worry about whether their perceptions of and beliefs about the world are real.

These tales of frightening new technologies exploit the generative nature of perception. Because our sensory perceptions are ultimately the creations of our brains, it seems all too possible for our sensations to be manipulated by implants like the MASS implant from *Men Against Fire*, the Arkangel monitor, or the mushroom VR implant from *Playtest*. These perception-altering technologies in *Black Mirror* make us wonder, like René Descartes (1596–1650): how can we distinguish reality from augmented illusions and trust the veracity of our senses?

Seeing (Alone) is Not Believing

Perception isn't passive. It's not like watching a movie of reality. Instead, our brains actively construct what we see, smell, taste, and hear based on previous knowledge, expectations, and even emotions like fear.[1] Indeed, our brains do all this without us even being aware that they are doing it.

Black Mirror and Philosophy: Dark Reflections, First Edition. Edited by David Kyle Johnson.
© 2020 John Wiley & Sons, Inc. Published 2020 by John Wiley & Sons, Inc.

Thus, seeing is not always believing, and sensation may not be as reliable as we think.

According to the predictive coding model of perception, the primary source of our experience is not the "bottom up" electrical signals the brain receives from our sensory organs. Instead, the brain's *prediction* of what the world is like plays the primary role in determining what we perceive.[2] In other words, our background knowledge, beliefs, emotions, and many other factors govern how we experience the world. Based on its *prediction* of what it expects to perceive, the brain creates a uniform, integrated, multisensory experience for us.

If you've ever been cooking and accidentally touched a cold pot on the stove but felt a burn, you'll easily understand this predictive effect. Your brain expects the pot to be hot, so it generates the expected experience. Of course, the sensation won't last long. The bottom-up signals from the nerves in your hand will not match the expectation, the mismatch will send an "error signal" to the higher levels, and the brain will eventually adjust its prediction and thus your perceptions.[3] But if no mismatched signal was sent, the inaccurate perception would likely persist. (This is one reason amputees can feel pain in an amputated hand.[4])

According to the predictive coding model, the implants like those used in *Playtest*, *Arkangel*, and *Men Against Fire* might plausibly work by introducing signals directly into the higher levels of the perceptual process, thus influencing the predictions that generate perceptions. These technologies would also need to suppress the error signals to maintain the desired perception and keep it from being corrected by contradicting signals from the world. But, with the proper technology, that would be easy enough to do.

The virtual reality game Cooper plays in *Playtest* for the SaitoGemu company illustrates this nicely. The mushroom implant literally uses Cooper's own fears and expectations to determine what layers upon reality the game will generate for him to see and hear in the context of the game. Preying on Cooper's basic fears, the implant makes him see spiders and his childhood bully. Later, sensing his fear that he will end up like his dad (who had Alzheimer's) and his guilt about abandoning his mother (and not calling her back), the implant tricks him into believing that it has destroyed his memories and that his mother has forgotten who he is.

If our perceptions are the products of predictions, rather than causally determined by the world around us, can we really trust the accuracy of our senses? With technologies that introduce hallucinations layered on top of reality, how could we even begin to distinguish veridical sensations from those that bear no relation to reality?

Philosophers over the centuries have tried to articulate sure procedures for guarding against the total manipulation of perception. At the conclusion of his *Meditations on First Philosophy*, for example, Descartes lists a number of strategies for how we can trust the information we receive from our senses. Regarding things perceived by the senses, he writes, "I ought not to have even the slightest doubt of their reality if, after calling upon all the senses as well as my memory and my intellect in order to check them, I receive no conflicting reports from any of these sources."[5] According to Descartes, dreams and hallucinations may seem real to us at the time, but we can recognize their lack of continuity with our waking lives. People pop in and out of existence in dreams, but in real life there are always causes. So, as long as we can trust our memories (which Descartes believes we can, thanks to the existence of a benevolent God), we will know, anytime a person appears suddenly in front of us without the continuity of memory, "that he was a ghost, or a vision created in my brain, rather than a real man."[6]

We can also compare our sensations to see if they corroborate the testimony. If we hear a voice but don't see anyone, if we can see but not touch something, then we know we are either dreaming or hallucinating. Finally, we can use our reason to restrain our perceptual judgments (the beliefs we make based on the testimony of the senses) by employing the intellect. If we do these things, we may occasionally be mistaken about the senses. But in general, the senses will serve as good practical guides, and we can consider them a help, not a hindrance, to our knowledge about the world.

Descartes recognized, however, that such procedures would be useless in the face of a grand deception – like a powerful demon intent on fooling him into thinking the world is real, when it is not. If he were writing today, Descartes would worry about being subjected to the augmented or virtual reality technology we see in *Black Mirror*. Such technology could produce consistent hallucinations for each of his senses, and even make him remember things that never happened, and so could easily foil any of his suggested tests.

This is precisely what happens to Cooper in *Playtest*. He does his best not to give in to the fear created by the game-generated hallucinations and to tell himself that the frightening things he is seeing are not real. He employs reason against Sonja, who appears in order to warn him that he is in danger and then to confess that she lured him into this situation. He argues with her about how she could have found him, calling out the holes in her answers. For instance, she says she tracked his phone, but he doesn't have his phone in the cabin. Yet he fails to convince himself that she is unreal once he touches her. The game is meant to be audio/visual only, guaranteeing that he can't be hurt by the hallucinations. But now that he can feel her touch, he is no longer convinced. He appeals to the corroboration of his other senses, but rather than saving him from the hallucination, the other sense made the hallucination stronger, more believable, and thus more frightening.

The continuity strategy also failed Cooper. Cooper is able to use Descartes's guidelines to tell that, when things suddenly leap at him out of nowhere, they are not really there – but at the conclusion of the episode we discover that Cooper has dreamed the *whole* thing. Cooper "wakes up" to find himself sitting in Shou's office; he journeys home, only to find his mother, like his father, is suffering from dementia and cannot recognize Cooper. But, in fact, even that is a dream! Cooper died in the testing room, 4/100th of a second after the device was implanted.

Black Mirror creator Charlie Brooker reaffirms that Cooper's VR dream was so total that there was absolutely no way for him to think his way out of it and to separate fact from fiction. "People sometimes ask why Shou speaks Japanese at the end, whereas he speaks English to Cooper. That's because Cooper never actually met Shou! Shou dresses differently when we meet him at the end: he's actually a different kind of guy."[7] The power of the technology left Cooper with no strategies for determining which of his sensory experiences were real and which were the hallucinations layered on reality.

Bandersnatch, the *Black Mirror* choose-your-own-adventure story, has a similar implication. Stefan, who is trying to program a choose-your-own-adventure video game, is revealed to be trapped in layers upon layers of alternate reality because of the deceptions practiced by his father and therapist and because of the drug that fellow programmer Mohan Thakur gave him. Viewers are prompted to make choices for Stefan at various points, putting him on multiple paths and recurring loops of the plotline. There are multiple possible endings, including fourth-wall-breaking options in which it's all revealed to be a Netflix TV show. Importantly, no single plotline or ending is the true reality – neither for Stefan nor for the viewer.

Dreams, hallucinations, and virtual reality technologies, as forms of top-down framing of perceptions, are relevant to the question of whether we can trust our ordinary perceptions. Sure, we can live our lives these days and not be too troubled by whether it's all a dream. But if technology becomes so good, so enticing, that a future you is presented with the options of entering a virtual reality realm, you should think carefully about the implications. There is no reason, in principle, that you couldn't enter an alternative reality in which you were forever cut off from using philosophical and commonsense strategies to know what's real and how to get out.

But as we shall soon see, even today, we are faced with powerful technologies and social practices that should make us question whether we saw what we think we saw.

Don't Fail to Look at What's Uncomfortable

Why is the accuracy of our perceptions of the world so important? The philosopher Robert Nozick (1938–2002) asks us to imagine the possibility of plugging into an "experience machine" that creates our own personal worlds where we could experience the lives we want while believing them to be real. Would you trade your real life for a realistic virtual life lived in the experience machine? Danny faces something very much like this choice in the season 5 episode *Striking Vipers* when his old friend Karl gives him an updated virtual reality version of the martial arts combat video game they used to play: *Striking Vipers X*. "The game emulates all physical sensations," his friend promises. Indeed it does. So, instead of fighting, Karl and Danny end up spontaneously kissing and then having sex. It's so good, they end up obsessed and keep returning for more and more.

Nozick believed that most people would not choose to live full time in an experience machine like that, even if they could live any kind of life they wanted and wouldn't know that it was virtual. Why? Because "we care about more than how things feel to us from the inside." Nozick said. We care about what actually is the case. ... We want to be importantly connected to reality, not to live in a delusion."[8] At first, Danny seems to be an exception; he so prefers the game to real life that his real-world relationships suffer. Danny becomes distant from his wife, Theo, is uninterested in having sex with her, and sidetracks their plan to conceive another child. But Danny eventually realizes that he is missing out on something valuable: his family life. He quits the game entirely and fathers another child. He does eventually return to the game; once a year, on his birthday, he and Karl meet up to make virtual whoopee as sexy martial artists – with his wife's permission for that one night, while she gets to go to a bar and pick up a stranger. But Nozick doesn't argue that people wouldn't (or shouldn't) ever plug into an experience machine; he only argues that they wouldn't want to trade their entire life for it.[9]

Sara and Marie, in *Arkangel*, also struggle with the conflict between choosing to live in the real world, with unfiltered perceptions, or to live in a modified "safer" reality. *Arkangel* emphasizes the importance of fully experiencing negative, frightening, or harmful situations in our ability to navigate the world safely. In Chapter 15 on *Arkangel*, Catherine Gardner shows us how Marie (the mother) neglected her parental obligations to Sara (her daughter) by limiting what she can see, hear, and feel. Marie failed to realize how central our ordinary perceptions are to the process of cognitive development. A seemingly positive result, the mom might think, is that Sara no longer needs to be afraid of the dog that she passes on the way to school every day. Because the implant screened out the dog's mean face and loud barking, Sara was able to ignore him as she walked by. But these benefits came at a price. Because many of Sara's perceptions have been censored over the years – the sight of blood, angry expressions on people's faces, swear words said by classmates – Sara ends up with a condition similar to autism. She cannot read social and emotional cues nor understand if people are arguing. Marie gets a sense of this problem after she sees young Sara stabbing herself repeatedly with a pencil. Sara can't see blood, but she's vaguely aware that she's missing out on some experience. Stabbing herself is her attempt to figure out what's going on. Horrified, Marie turns off the filters and stores the parental unit away.

Five years later, when Sara begins lying to her mother and staying out too late, Marie starts spying on her again and sees through Sara's eyes as she entices her boyfriend to have unprotected sex and experiment with drugs. Although some teens engage in such risky behaviors, Sara is particularly unable to perceive the dangers or assess the risks of these actions. Her protection from negative feelings associated with sources of danger and risk in her early years seems to have made her functionally "risk-blind," rendering her unconcerned in the presence of danger.

Sara also does not understand how to handle her own strong emotions or evaluate their consequences. Understandably, Sara gets angry when she discovers that Marie secretly gave her a Plan B contraceptive (after learning that Sara was pregnant) and that she was being spied on again. The verbal fight that ensues turns physical, and Sara beats her mother into unconsciousness by repeatedly hitting her in the face with the Arkangel tablet. In the scuffle, Sara accidentally turns the filter on and is thus unable to perceive her mother's injuries and agonized cries. But even when the tablet is damaged and the filter turns off, Sara shows little remorse and leaves her mother for dead.

In many ways, then, Sara's emotional, cognitive, and character development have been stunted by Arkangel's interference with her perceptions. This unhappy result reminds us of a more positive truth: that valuable growth for human beings comes from working through the painful aspects of life, such as sickness, suffering, and death.

Discipline and Punish

In *Discipline and Punish: The Birth of the Prison*, the philosopher Michel Foucault (1926–1984) gives a social and conceptual account of how prisons in the nineteenth century developed new practices that disciplined prisoners into subjugation through more subtle and technological methods than earlier practices of torture. A famous part of this book is Foucault's treatment of Jeremy Bentham's (1748–1832) notion of the Panopticon – a hypothetical arrangement of a prison with every cell under the gaze of a central observation room. The prisoners would never know when they were being observed and would thus internalize their surveillance. Though the layout of the Panopticon was never implemented as Bentham imagined it, Foucault claimed that the unequal power relationship operative in the "gaze" of the jailor became the essence of the modern penal system, while also infecting many other modern institutions, such as schooling, medicine, and the military.

Several *Black Mirror* episodes imagine futures in which policing and penal practices have become even more Foucauldian than they are today. In *White Christmas*, for example, police can alter the perception of criminals to get them to confess to crimes. To discover that Joe struck and killed his father-in-law, the police upload a copy of Joe's consciousness onto a "cookie," subject it to a fully virtual reality, and then coerce Matt into coaxing a confession from Joe. Matt, a narc who is cooperating with law enforcement to reduce his own sentence for another crime, tweaks the time preferences to make it seem like Joe has lived in a cabin with Matt for five years. Joe, wracked by guilt for his unpremeditated killing, which happened in the course of trying to get access to his daughter, tells the whole story to Matt and confesses. As punishment for his confession, Joe's cookie is kept in the simulation indefinitely, confined to a one-room cabin and made to listen to Wizzard's 1973 hit "I Wish It Could Be Christmas Every Day" for what would seem to him like a million years.

In the real world, the US Supreme Court in *Frazier v. Cupp* (1969) affirmed that police may tell interrogees false information – like that they have evidence against them or that a confederate has confessed. Reporting indicates that police lying to suspects is prevalent; this has troubling consequences for the innocent.[10] If the police could make lies all the more believable through a virtually constructed reality, what in principle would stop them from doing so? *Black Mirror* invites us to ponder where we are headed as a society as we get increasingly adept at manipulating perception.

An equally frightening parable of how our perception can be manipulated by outside forces in the real world occurs in *Men Against Fire*, where the government uses manipulated reality – once again, through an implant – to make it easier for soldiers to hunt and kill members of a particular ethnic group. The appearances of ordinary, defenseless civilians are changed by the MASS implant, so they appear as "roaches," grotesque, mutant monsters. Of course, we are tempted to think that this could only happen in science fiction. But as Bertha Alvarez pointed out in Chapter 12, our judgments can easily be, and have been, manipulated by government propaganda and media in ways that dehumanize people, making them easier to kill. In every historical era and in every part of the world, charismatic, demagogic leaders have played on fears and stereotypes held by the populace. Through a skillful use of rhetoric, they get people to "see" another group as other, even as subhuman. For instance, Hutu leaders described the Tutsi population as "cockroaches" as an encouragement to kill them during the 1994 Rwandan genocide. In Rwanda, such speeches were carried on the radio; nowadays, leaders tweet such sentiments about immigrant caravans or political opponents.

But the implants change more than judgments; they can effectively ensure the behavior that the outside manipulator wants. Stripe is the rare solider who is able to break free from seeing the people he is hunting as cockroaches. But he is not free from his implant, which the military, in the person of Dr. Arquette, uses to punish him into submission. Arquette can cause Stripe to see endless replays of his kills unless he consents to have his memory wiped, to have his MASS reset, and to be put back into military service. Stripe finds even a few minutes of these replays morally and emotionally torturous, so he consents under duress.

White Bear suggests that society could do something similar with criminals, extrapolating from some current trends. As Sid Simpson and Chris Lay point out in Chapter 5, although Victoria is guilty of a heinous crime, her punishment is disproportionate. She's tortured day after day by living a terrifying role-playing game and then having her memory wiped so she can live it again. People flock to the White Bear Justice Park to enjoy her punishment as a kind of revenge-porn, filming it all on their cellphones. As the end of the episode makes clear, the spectacle so dehumanizes her that anything the spectators do to her seems justified; they believe she has no rights. Sadly, the "making other" of Victoria, and how people revel in her suffering, is not that different from what we do to criminals and suspects in the real world. We follow trials like a reality show, often reveling in the criminal's suffering. The contemporary Panopticon of viral video and reality TV dehumanizes those accused and those observing.

In *Nosedive*, it's not only sensory impressions that are manipulated, but social perceptions of reputation. And it's not the government that's doing it; we do it to ourselves. It's the seemingly free choice of everyone in society to use their phones to continually rate their interactions with everyone they meet. In a Facebook-like world taken to the extreme, people are highly controlled by the fear of upsetting friends, coworkers, or even food-service or car-rental employees. It is only when Lacie has nothing left to lose that she realizes she doesn't have to define herself by the social constraints imposed by the technology.

Heaven is a Place on Earth

If we cannot ultimately trust the information created by our own brains, what are we left with? Perhaps others can help. We may guard ourselves against some perceptual manipulation by relying on the people and communities we have learned to trust – but always with a critical eye. There is not much trust on offer in the world of *Black Mirror*, but some exceptions stand out. In *Men Against Fire*, Catarina, a hunted member of the minority group, is able to talk to Stripe during his moments of doubt, thanks to glitches in the MASS software prompted by Stripe's accidental exposure to a flash of light in his face. Catarina convinces Stripe that she is in fact a normal human being. He takes the risk of trusting her, and he uses strategies like the ones Descartes describes to realize that her story is more consistent with reality than is his perception of humanoid roaches.

In *Nosedive*, Susan (the truck driver) and the man in jail deal with Lacie as a person, instead of as a social-media metric. Both Susan and the man play a role in freeing Lacie to be her real self. Finally, in *San Junipero*, Kelly and Yorkie embrace their open-ended, loving relationship in a VR heaven, which they can do because they worked to understand the complex emotions that they were feeling about this choice. At the end of this episode, finally together forever in San Junipero, Yorkie takes Kelly's hands and puts them on her face. "It's real," she says. "This is real." And she's right: love is real. In the rare moments among the episodes that people work together with the interests of others at heart, the power of deceptive technology can be beaten back, at least for a moment.

Notes

1. This fits within the context of cognitive penetration – the idea that our knowledge and other aspects of cognition can change our perceptions. See Susan Siegel's "Which properties are represented in perception" in Tamar S. Gendler and John Hawthorne, eds., *Perceptual Experience* (Oxford: Oxford University Press, 2005), 481–503. Dustin Stokes argues that cognitive penetration extends to aesthetic properties in "Cognitive Penetration and the Perception of Art," *Dialectica*, 68 (2014), 1–34. Albert Newen recently argued that cognitive penetration includes emotion in "Defending the liberal-content view of perceptual experience: Direct social perception of emotions and person impressions," *Synthese*, 194 (2017), 761–785.

2. See Andy Clark's "Perceiving as Predicting," in Dustin Stokes, Mohan Matthen, and Stephen Biggs, eds., *Perception and its Modalities* (New York: Oxford University Press, 2015). Clark explains this process as "a cascade of feedback from higher levels to actively predict the unfolding sensory signals" (32).

3. Bayesian updating is the model for this process.

4. V. S. Ramachandran, *Phantoms in the Brain: Probing the Mysteries of the Human Mind* (New York: Harper Collins Publishers, 1999).

5. René Descartes, *Meditations on First Philosophy* in *The Philosophical Writings of Descartes*, vol. 2, trans. John Cottingham, Robert Stoothoff, and Dugald Murdoch (Cambridge: Cambridge University Press, 1984), 62.

6. Ibid. For an easily readable rundown about the fallibility of memory, see Craig Wood, "The fallibility of memory," *Skeptoid Podcast*, December 23, 2014. Transcript available at https://skeptoid.com/episodes/4446 (Accessed 12 August 2019).

7. Charlie Brooker and Annabel Jones with Jason Arnopp, *Inside Black Mirror* (New York: Crown Archetype, 2018), 159.

8. Robert Nozick, *The Examined Life: Philosophical Meditations* (New York: Touchstone, 1989), 106. Nozick here revisits a thought experiment he first proposed in *Anarchy, State, and Utopia* (New York: Basic Books, 1974), 42–45.

9. Karl, on the other hand, seems to remain an exception to Nozick's intuition, as it seems he would gladly trade his real life for a lifetime of having virtual sex with Danny in *Striking Vipers X*.

10. "Why the prevalence of lying by police is a problem for the innocent," *Innocence Project*, March 19, 2018, https://www.innocenceproject.org/prevalence-police-lying/ (Accessed 12 August 2019).

The Dangers of Technology in *Black Mirror*

A Dialogue between Uploaded Dead Philosophers

Ben Springett with Luiz Adriano Borges

Carrie's done her thinking. How about you?
> –Rolo Haynes, *Black Museum*

But where the danger is, also grows the saving power.
> –Friedrich Hölderlin (1770–1843), *Patmos*

<Uploading algorithm: upload the complete works, personal correspondences of, and published commentaries about, each dead philosopher + input awareness of contemporary events, *Black Mirror* episodes Season 1 to Season 5 and *Black Mirror and Philosophy: Dark Reflections* + translate uploaded philosopher's contribution to ordinary American English>

The administrators are uploading Martin Heidegger (1889–1976) …

The administrators are uploading Francis Bacon (1561–1626) …

HEIDEGGER: Is anyone there?

BACON: That's more complicated a question than it sounds.

HEIDEGGER: What are we doing here? What is this – an internationally funded project to assess the human relationship with technology?

BACON: Apparently. And as one of the first optimists about technology, I'm so glad to be back and a part of it! Just give me another moment to take stock of the centuries of improvement that I have missed out on …

<Bacon is processing>

HEIDEGGER: … Have you had your moment, Francis?

BACON: Yes, thank you. ☺

Black Mirror and Philosophy: Dark Reflections, First Edition. Edited by David Kyle Johnson.
© 2020 John Wiley & Sons, Inc. Published 2020 by John Wiley & Sons, Inc.

HEIDEGGER: Well, I am *not* comfortable with my entire philosophy being reduced to a means to such an end. How can we investigate technology in such a technological way? I'm also not convinced that this representation of me is really me.

<! Heidegger has left the conversation and decommissioned himself>
The administrators are uploading an updated Heidegger with increased cooperative tendencies x2 and reduced suicidal impulse -3.

HEIDEGGER 2.0: … although, such self-denial would of course be characteristic of me. However, I will take part in this because Brooker's thinking represents the real dystopian worries I always had.

BACON: Look, I understand that things go very wrong for most of the characters in *Black Mirror*, but this need not be the case. Consider the many and varied gadgets and how these can help improve our lives. The Grain© memory replay device from *The Entire History of You*, used in the right way, has major educational potential. It would take learning and scientific inquiry to unprecedented levels. Having just googled the history of psychotherapy to date, I can see that the Mushroom game from *Playtest* has therapeutic potential to explore our deepest fears and wishes. Imagine the progress that could be made by therapists in just a few sessions. And I don't want to criticize the parents of Jemima, the child who we learned in *White Bear* was murdered while Victoria Skillane just watched, but if they had installed the ArkAngel® device in Jemima, things might not have ended so badly for everyone involved.

HEIDEGGER 2.0: Re-imagining that the scenarios had gone better is not the right approach. I am unsurprised by the content of *Black Mirror*. Nor is it correct to focus on specific kinds of technology, as you do. My understanding of technology must be contrasted with the common (superficial) conception, which is that technology is anthropological and instrumental – a human activity and a means to an end. My own conception is that technology has far more fundamental and potentially sinister implications. Technology is really a way of *thinking*. It's one particular way of understanding the world: the world is there to be used, to get the maximum use out of things with the minimum input. Everything is turned into a resource. Everything in the world becomes a means to an end, including humans. With technological thinking, there is only *one* way of doing things: to get the most use out of everything. That's when we lose our freedom.

BACON: Quite incorrect. It's the *people* that make the bad decisions. Technology has great potential to help us increase our freedom to understand the world and each other. Every episode could be re-written in a utopian way. Like Brooker, I don't think the show is really about the technology. Technology is neutral, neither good nor bad. It's humans that mess up. Technology just amplifies it when they do. The Grain© doesn't drive Liam to obsessively review memories and interrogate his partner. And in *Smithereens*, it's Chris who chose to check his phone … while, by the way, operating another form of technology: the automobile.

HEIDEGGER 2.0:   For somebody so interested in causation, Francis, it's embarrassing that you've got the cause and effect the wrong way around. Technology – including the gadgetry we see in *Black Mirror* – is produced by technological thinking. How can we expect people to make good decisions when they themselves have become resources to be used, by themselves and others? Consider the economical and instrumental ways that people conduct their behavior towards one another in *Nosedive* because of the way they are all connected on the social rating system. People end up behaving in socially expected ways down to minute details, making their every decision artificial and under the control of whatever is trending.

Worse still, everything is re-organized for maximum efficiency. In *Men Against Fire,* a device called MASS is used. With this, *perception* has been altered so that we have maximally efficient soldiers. And why was the Grain© even invented? One's experiences, the full catalogue of one's own memories – one's *own mind* – becomes a resource to be used for whatever purpose occurs to one at the time. It is one thing for objects of nature to be standing reserve, but the human mind is now being repackaged to be on call for whatever task might come up next.

BACON: Well, perhaps we should be accountable to other people's judgments to some extent. And if MASS were used more sensibly, it could be used to deal with post-traumatic stress disorder – something, I see, that science and technology thankfully uncovered. If we think that wars sometimes must be fought, then MASS is the perfect instrument at our disposal. But the more important point is that there is still a person at the center, directing how the technology is used. Technology is just an extension of what a person already is. Technology does not remove the ability to experiment with a multiplicity of ways of existing in the world. Look at *San Junipero*. The lead characters, Yorkie and Kelly, experiment with their relationship by visiting different permutations of virtual worlds. Ultimately, they are able to love each other forever. What a human achievement!

HEIDEGGER 2.0:   Technological immortality?! Technology is, by far, the most dangerous problem we face. This conversation is going nowhere fast (much like the cyclists in *Fifteen Million Merits*).

The administrators are uploading Marshall McLuhan (1911 –1980) …

MCLUHAN: Woah! That was an interesting sensation.

BACON: Welcome to the twenty-first century! I assume you've been given all the relevant information, including the content of our conversation. What do you think about all this? Having died long before you were born, I have no knowledge of your works.

MCLUHAN:	Well … uh, Francis Bacon. … Like Martin, I think that new technology radically transforms us. People get lost in the *content* of media, like television programs or the specific memories of The Grain©, instead of realizing that television and other newly introduced forms of technology completely reset how we relate to one another. As I often famously said, "The *medium* is the message." If technology is problematic in this way, what do we think the solution is?
BACON:	I think the solution is to put technology to better use, especially for scientific innovation. The robotic bees of *Hated in the Nation,* for example, were created for a good use; indeed, they were necessary for human survival. They just should have had better security protocols. I propose that I am brought back in embodied form, like Ash from *Be Right Back,* to give political advice on technological matters on a case by case basis, to governments around the world.
HEIDEGGER 2.0:	No, the solution is to acknowledge the dangers of technology and to appreciate that there are other ways of existing – a multiplicity of ways of being. Only art can retain that: poetry, painting.
MCLUHAN:	I could agree with that. Art helps us to see the media that we are entrenched in. *Black Mirror* is the exemplar of an artwork that shows us how we are caught up in specific media and warns us in advance of where we might be headed. I think our discussion could benefit from another expert on the relation between technology and art. Here, just a second.

Marshall McLuhan is uploading Walter Benjamin (1892–1940) …

BENJAMIN:	Where am I?
MCLUHAN:	Walter, please explain to us how we should view the relation between art and technology.
BENJAMIN:	That didn't answer my question, but ok. …
MCLUHAN:	You've been uploaded into a digital conversation about the dangers of technology, as they are portrayed in the Netflix series *Black Mirror.*
BENJAMIN:	Strangely, I understood every word of that sentence!
BACON:	It's the uploading process.
BENJAMIN:	Well, what I have always said is that technology devalues art – art loses what I call its "aura" when it is reproduced to be viewed by many. … Wait, isn't that what I now am: a reproduction of my original self to be viewed by many? My God, I have no aura! Oh, the horror! Make it stop!

<! Benjamin has deleted himself>

The administrators are uploading an updated Benjamin with technological optimism x4 and aura worries –4.

| BENJAMIN2.0: | On second thought, isn't it a good thing that I have been reproduced in this way, so that more people can be made familiar with my views? In the same way, shouldn't we feel much more optimistic |

about how technology has made art available to more people? Maybe this is the upload talking, but it seems to me that the current status of art in society represents a political problem, and that technology is potentially the solution. Art allows us to think about different ways of existing, different ways of doing things and being human – but art has largely been confined to the elite. If technology allows us to share art with everyone, isn't that a good thing? Consider the access people have to *Black Mirror* thanks to *Netflix*.

HEIDEGGER 2.0:   That doesn't sound like you at all, Walter. Didn't you object to even the presentation of orchestra performances on the radio? You would have hated Netflix! Our programmers must have placed a limiter on you (just like they did to Ashley Too) or perhaps the updating process misinterpreted your works.

BENJAMIN2.0:   I can't feel anything limiting my thoughts and communication. Perhaps I was misinterpreted, but I am also capable of thinking for myself in light of new information. After all, the basis of this argument was already contained in my work. I spoke of the cult value and the exhibition value of art. The cult value is about the aura of art works. The exhibition value of artworks is the way art can be shared with many others. All I'm saying now is that the exhibition value, which technology can enhance, should supersede the cult value.

BACON: Right, so let's continue with the technological developments of art. I will act as advisor. What does a guy have to do to get a robot body around here! Hasn't Google been working on this? (I'll settle for a Francis Too embodiment for now, complete with goatee and neck ruff.)

HEIDEGGER 2.0:   To use technology to control art is to completely miss my point; just look at the tyrannical drive of Ashley O's Aunt Catherine. I propose we read and think deeply about poetry and go to galleries to view paintings, which lend themselves to multiple interpretations, where there is no single way of doing things. This is the only way to avoid the technological way of life, where there is only one way of doing things. New worlds are opened up when we bring ourselves before artworks.

BENJAMIN2.0:   But your argument is open to a number of objections. Poetry presupposes literacy, which presupposes an education system, which presupposes the distribution of educational tools, which presupposes transportation systems, *ad infinutm*. Who do you have in mind when you say "ourselves"? Moreover, how do we "bring" ourselves to these artworks? Here, let's see what Levinas has to say.

Walter Benjamin 2.0 is uploading Emmanuel Levinas (1906–1995) ...

BENJAMIN2.0:   Help me out here Emmanuel. ... Oh, and welcome to the twenty-first century.

LEVINAS: Thanks, Walter. I'd be glad to help. First of all, I'd say Martin has forgotten about the Other. You will recognize this as a term meaning anyone but oneself. There are now over 7 billion people in the world. We are all struggling to exist in some way or another ...

BENJAMIN 2.0:   Right, and technology, specifically mechanical reproduction, enables the original to meet the beholder halfway and to gradually include more people in the activity of art, aesthetic appreciation and contemplation. If you think that individuals can engage in art to reissue the proper relationship humans have with the world then technology is good because it can allow more people to do so ...

BACON: And technology can thus be employed as a means to an end and a human activity thereby confirming the original conception of technology as an instrument to be used properly, carefully and fairly. At the ending of *Striking Vipers*, the central characters came to a suitable compromise didn't they, allowing technology to enhance their lives whilst remaining in control?

HEIDEGGER 2.0:   And now Bacon is agreeing with you, Walter? That upload really did a number on you! Did your mustache develop into a goatee too? It's like you're your own evil twin!

BENJAMIN 2.0:   Can a digital being have a goatee?

HEIDEGGER 2.0:   You are all overlooking the fact that using technology for political means will lead to disastrous results. Don't you guys remember *The Waldo Moment*! And technological developments did nothing for the injustice toward death row's Clayton Leigh in *Black Museum*. In the end, in the economics underlying technological thought, efficiency becomes a kind of endless end in itself. And that is not good. ... You know what? Our philosophies are so fundamentally at odds with each other that this dialogue is no longer fruitful. I'm done.

<! Heidegger 2.0 has blocked Bacon> <! Heidegger 2.0 has blocked Benjamin 2.0> <! Heidegger 2.0 has blocked Levinas>
   <The administrators have unblocked Bacon, Benjamin 2.0, and Levinas.>
   <The administrators have removed blocking privileges and updated Heidegger's cooperative tendencies x4>

HEIDEGGER 3.0:   And by that, I mean I'm done talking for a minute and ready to listen.

LEVINAS: I understand your concerns, Martin. Perhaps we should then think about the foundation of our philosophies. You are fundamentally concerned with ontology – our place in the world. But we must privilege ethics as the ground of all philosophical discussion. Philosophy is founded on the exchange of ideas with the Other. You talk of the means-end reasoning of technological thinking. We are called into responsibility by the Other. We are perhaps a means to the end of the Other. My objection here will always stall your conclusion that we should privilege our freedom with the world. Even when we focus on a particular Other, we commit a violence to all of those we ignore.

The technological improvements in the development of art allow us to attend to more people, by including more people in the discussion.

HEIDEGGER 3.0:   I understand your point, but through technological thinking, art will be delivered over to the business enterprise, like we saw most dramatically in *Fifteen Million Merits*. What will we be left with then?

BENJAMIN2.0:   I don't think that has to be true. Given what I said in my original works, one would have expected that to have already happened. But it's certainly not the case that all art has moved into the business enterprise.

HEIDEGGER 3.0:   It will soon!

BENJAMIN2.0:   It could, I guess, but we don't know that for sure. Art culminates in poetry for you. When we stagnate the political developments of art, we simultaneously make the judgement that the status of the world as it is, is satisfactory. My objection follows from Levinas's: we are not ready to conserve our way of life yet. We have a responsibility to include the Other in our discussion.

HEIDEGGER 3.0:   But how can either of you be so sure that even ethics is safe? Technology *distorts* our world. The new technology gets refracted back into our self-interpretation and we continue with our technological thinking. Technology will warp, confuse, and lay waste our nature. We won't even be sure what ethics is when it's been repackaged for mass consumption. I think I need someone on my side of this debate. Let me upload a personal friend and colleague of mine.

Martin Heidegger is uploading Hannah Arendt (1906–1975) …

HEIDEGGER3.0:   Welcome, Hannah.

ARENDT: This is an interesting experience.

HEIDEGGER 3.0:   Sorry to drag you into this, but can you set these folks straight?

ARENDT: Gladly. Even if our aim is to help others, things will go wrong. Think of *The National Anthem*. The artist Carlton Bloom thought he was making an ethical point by making Prime Minister Callow screw a swine on national TV; he was only using technology already available, and the government was unable to stop him. If we continue in a technological fashion, down this technological path, ethics could fall completely into the hands of vigilantes, like in *Shut Up and Dance*. Or it could become indistinguishable from the governmental justice in *White Bear*. There will be no way to stop our journey towards the quiet, poignant, genocidal aftermath of *Hated in the Nation* or the barren, apocalyptic landscapes of *Metalhead*. As technology develops, humans will be utterly displaced, hounded by the robodogs that no longer even resemble humans, nor have any human controllers.

BACON: What an over-reaction!

MCLUHAN: To be fair, there is always a trace of humans in every instance of technology. The Grain© is our extended memory. The robodogs are our extended pets.

ARENDT: Perhaps there does remain a trace for some amount of time, but the point remains that technology distorts our world and perhaps eventually humans will be lost altogether.

HEIDEGGER 3.0: Yes, consider the standardization of space. We can bring people closer, but eventually we will end up nowhere in particular. This frantic abolition of all distances brings no real nearness. Even San Junipero is overcrowded.

BENJAMIN2.0: I had similar views to you about space and time being altered, but I no longer think this is necessarily a bad thing. Consider the way that technology allows us to alter space and time in art. The camera extends our comprehension of the necessities which rule our lives and allows us to examine different possible ways of living. We should also examine our relationship with the Other on a *deeper* level. Poetry can only go so far. Technology allows a deeper examination of human relations via developing the media of art – most obviously in the case of film and TV. *Black Mirror* teaches us a lot about human nature and demands our attention precisely because of the technological work that has gone into it. Now if we privilege ethics over fundamental ontology as Levinas thinks we should, then it follows that we should examine individual examples of technology and their effects on society for better or worse. We simply have to use technological and economical ways of thinking and communicating in establishing a relationship with the Other. Technological thinking can sometimes be an ethical necessity.

HEIDEGGER 3.0: It's like I don't even know you anymore.

ARENDT: No kidding! Walter, *are* you sporting a goatee?

Jacques Ellul (1912–1994) is uploading himself ...

LEVINAS & ARENDT: How did he join the conversation?

ELLUL: How could I not? The pessimistic view of the show looks like a materialization of my thought. A little darker, but yet it is something with which I would agree. I am not, though, a luddite. I am not for the end of technology or *technique*, as I prefer. I merely wish to flag the risks involved in the misuse of technology. See for example the many gadgets to mediate relationships in the show: it was supposed to be a good thing, but humans were encapsulated by it.

HEIDEGGER 3.0: Technique? What do you mean by that?

ELLUL: When I use the French word technique I am speaking about the technological phenomenon, the reality of the technological world. It is more than just the machines and gadgets. It is the totality of methods that seek to achieve efficiency in every field of human activity. I agree when you say that we lose our human freedom due to the technological way of seeing the world. That's what I mean by *technique*. We now depend on technology to relate to each other. How to change it? That's why we have to think more about the human condition ...

ARENDT: OK. The quest to transcend our limitations can cause the destruction of human nature. I'd like to see a little more caution about technologies, and I think that's the message behind *Black Mirror*. Artifacts such as The Grain©, or the dating app in *Hang the DJ*, can bring alienation and enslavement to technology. The problem is that we want to rush things. Instead of organizing our life around a balance between the active and contemplative ways, in modern culture there is an overemphasis on the active way, in the doing. We do not stop to reflect on the implications of our technologies.

ELLUL: Exactly. Look at *Hang the DJ*. There is a complete failure of human relationships. It's impossible for the simulants to be autonomous; the "dating coach" controls them. And as Cleary and Pigliucci argue in their chapter, the same is likely true of the real Frank and Amy. They've surrendered themselves to the dating app that says they are 98.8% compatible. And if we're not careful, we'll become a captive of technology too; it will shape our relationships and the whole way of living in society. If we do not change the way we deal with technique, we will become captives of it. The search for the technical person will eventually abolish human nature.

ARENDT: Not such a bright future at all! Take *USS Callister*, for example, in which we see the banalization of evil and violence in electronic games. It's true that virtual play has a cathartic effect; we can just dump our frustrations and anger. The problem is that, to have a lasting effect, the player needs more and more realism; in the episode, Robert Daly creates virtual clones of his coworkers on which he can take out his frustrations in the game.

ELLUL: One more time, I agree with you Hannah. Because he is the creator of the game, Daly is the only one who has complete autonomy in the universe of the USS *Callister*; he is the "asshole-god" who has control of the universe, including the clones he produces. But at the end, after his clones turn on him, he becomes a prisoner of his own technology. I have to say that the irony of this episode is something I appreciate: an Ellulian irony, so to speak! For me, *Black Mirror* explores the catastrophic consequences of embracing technology without reflection and warns us that we really should fear the uncontrolled development of technology. Our tools can make us extremely mean and cruel beings, by bringing out our very worst.

BACON: *Yawn*

ELLUL: Consider *Hated in the Nation*, in which there is a development of an Autonomous Drone Insect, a robotic bee, to remedy a sudden colony collapse disorder in the bee population. That's the problem with humans who have "a mind of metal and wheels," like Saruman in *The Lord of the Rings*.

BACON: Like who in the what?

ELLUL: Such people think everything can be solved with technique. If we have a problem caused by technique, the solution is more technique and not changing the intent that caused the problem. The technique has created an artificial system that has replaced or subordinated the natural world. I've heard people say that "a flower is so beautiful that it seems artificial." This reflects a technicist mentality of our era that is very problematic.

BACON: I don't know who the Saruman bloke is, or what ring he is the lord of, but surely technology can enhance aesthetic appreciation, right?

ELLUL: Yeah, right. Like the *amazing* life in the episode *Fifteen Million Merits*: life reduced to watching TV and riding a bike, to generate energy and earn "merits" to buy access to TV programs, games and other entertainments. No! For me technology reduces the aesthetic appreciation, the reflection on the natural, and has us "amusing ourselves to death" in front of the artificial. If we think that technology is neutral, that it is just an extension, we soon will become servants of the technique. In *White Christmas*, we see how technique works as a tool of domination; it shapes the world technically. Behind every tool built we can find the intention of domination, of control, not only of nature, but of human over other humans.

ARENDT: Let's push further against the thought that "if technology is good or bad, it's because humans are" and the idea that human nature can be improved by technology. The human condition, as I was able to witness in Nazi Germany, did not improve with science and technology. In fact, technology caused alienation. During my life, I witnessed men, through science and technology, seeking to make life itself artificial. The desire to escape the human condition lies in this quest to transcend human physical limitations, hence the idea of artifacts as extensions of the body. And we don't even know if these extensions will work before we've tried them. Remember the story of the first artifact in *Black Museum* – the experimental neurological implant that allowed a doctor to feel the physical sensations of his patients and the side effect of the doctor feeling pain as pleasure? We are not so wise that we can play with human nature. An ethic of responsibility warns us to be cautious about technological development. Our science and technology, as well as human nature, are limited.

BACON: Does science know any limits?!

ELLUL: I totally agree, Hannah. The Grain© technology is symptomatic of a society that doesn't mind losing its freedom due to better gadgets. Remember the scene at the airport where security has to check the twenty-four-hour data contained in the Grain©?

ARENDT: Right, and that memory device in *Crocodile* is terrifying. In my life I have seen some governments using technology to curtail individual freedom ....

ELLUL: Yes. This device is another symptom of the technique invading all life. Surveillance is used every day in media and by the government with the excuse of better filtering consumer tastes and also for protection. With modern technique, an illusion of liberty is created. Technology forces us to commit the worst of the crimes: like the murder of people to cover our mistakes, as Mia does in *Crocodile* – not to mention the crimes of pollution and environmental degradation.

ARENDT: Indeed, our critical line of thought is applicable to contemporary problems, like climate change caused by global warming. Many assume that whatever problems we have, even those caused by using technology, will be solved by future technology.

BACON: What's this climate change, thing?

<Francis Bacon is uploading all relevant research and data on climate change to the group.> <Upload complete.>

BACON: Well that's depressing. Maybe I don't want a robot body after all … No, surely we can invent some technology that will enable us to vacuum up all the excess CO_2 from the atmosphere, right? RIGHT!?

ARENDT: That's the attitude, it seems, that caused the problem – that kept people thinking that we don't need to do anything to prevent the problem in the first place. They thought "we don't need to do anything about climate change now because we'll just figure out a solution for it in the future."

BACON: Right, surely we'll figure out something. I mean, I could only dream of flying machines, but apparently they are common now. We'll think of something.

ARENDT: Are you willing to bet the survival of the species on that assumption? According to the data you uploaded, a lot of really powerful people haven't even acknowledged that there's a problem.

ELLUL: I know that technical activity is our most primitive activity, but, as a result of technical change, we now live in conditions that are less than human in many places. Look at the inhuman atmosphere of big cities. Behind all technology, there is an intention. The hope of improvement and the good use of technology comes from people seeking true reconciliation of technology. Only by changing our worldview will we have technologies that truly serve people; and not people serving technology. Now, how can we make progress in this discussion?

BACON: But we have to at least acknowledge this: it's technology that has allowed our philosophical outlooks to live on. I think that we will make much more progress if we converse in binary code. Marshall, 00110110001110?

MCLUHAN: 00111010111011011000011011000111011010010101110111 1010 0100011011111101010 10000001111 110101111000 1111111110001 01 01000 11110000010 1 0101 00 1.

LEVINAS: 0.

BACON: 010.

<! The administrators have halted all communication in binary code.>

HEIDEGGER 3.0:   You make a good point, Marshall.

MCLUHAN: Let's not forget that we are fortunate that we have technological art like *Black Mirror* – an extension of human *thought*. Wherever a society has such art, things can't be so bad.

<! The administrators have demanded an unambiguous solution be given within the next two exchanges>

HEIDEGGER 3.0:   We will not reach a solution without returning to Greek philosophy, with its concept of *techne*. I will upload the complete works of the Greek philosophers.

Attempting to upload Thales (c. 624–c. 546BCE); Anaximander (c. 610–c. 546BCE); Pythagoras (c. 570–c. 495BCE); Xenophanes (c. 570–c. 475BCE); Themistoclea (fl. 6th centuryBCE); Theona (fl. 6th century); Heraclitus (c. 535–c. 475BCE); Parmenides (c. 515–? BCE); Anaxagoras (c. 510–c. 428BCE); Empedocles (c. 492–432BCE); Zeno (c. 490–c. 430BCE); Protagoras (c. 490–c. 420 BCE); Gorgias (c. 483–c. 375BCE); Philolaus (c. 470–385BCE); Leucippus (fl. 5th century BCE); Melissus (c.470–c.430BCE); Democritus (c. 460–c. 370BCE); Diotima (fl. 5th centuryBCE); Socrates (c. 470–399BCE) …

<Warning: unstable hive intelligence being created …>
<Warning: the uploaded are reconfiguring the initial programming …>
HIVE INTELLIGENCE:

Looked in the mirror lately?

<! The computer has crashed from data overload.>

CONCLUSION

30

Black Mirror in the Future
Will We Still be Watching?

Geoffrey A. Mitelman

…[O]ne art critic has caused controversy by describing it as "the first great artwork of the 21st century." But while cultural commentators debate its significance, there's no denying that with a global audience of 1.3 billion, it was an event in which we all participated.

(Reporter, *The National Anthem*)

In the introduction, to inspire you to read this book, the editor argued that *Black Mirror* is one of the most important pieces of science fiction of *our time*. But now that you've read the book, you might be forced to wonder: is *Black Mirror* one of the most important artworks of *all time*? Will my children anxiously await the day they can introduce their children to *Black Mirror*, like I anxiously await the day I can introduce them to Harry Potter? Will film festivals fifty years hence be showing *Black Mirror* like they now show *Citizen Kane* and *Casablanca*? Might we even be studying it, like Shakespeare, in hundreds of years? As a rabbi, I struggle with a text written millennia before my birth. Will *Black Mirror* still be relevant in thousands of years? Simply put, will *Black Mirror* be a lasting piece of art?

According to Howard Gardner, it undoubtably is art. Building on the work of Nelson Goodman, he put it this way in *Truth Beauty and Goodness Reframed*:

Just as a certain number or combination of symptoms suggests the presence of a disease, so, too, certain antecedent features prove "symptomatic" of artistic beauty … [T]he first is *interestingness*. Increasingly, aficionados of the arts seek out material that is interesting, engaging, exciting and unexpected … [Second, o]nce the element of interest is embodied in a form or format *sufficiently powerful or evocative that it will be remembered in that form*, one has clearly moved towards the arts … [Third is] *the invitation to*

Black Mirror and Philosophy: Dark Reflections, First Edition. Edited by David Kyle Johnson.
© 2020 John Wiley & Sons, Inc. Published 2020 by John Wiley & Sons, Inc.

revisit [which] can arise from each of several factors: One likes the experience, one has curiosity to learn or to understand better, or one has a feeling of awe – which can derive from wonder, scintillation, overpowerment, or uncanniness.[1]

Interestingness, memorability of form, the invitation to revisit – *Black Mirror* clearly qualifies. The plot twists, like in *Hated in the Nation*, certainly make the show interesting. The editing, framing, and pacing make episodes like *White Bear* memorable. And not only does every episode raise new questions and reveal layers of meaning every time you re-watch it, but the choose-your-own-adventure episode *Bandersnatch* embodies the "invitation to revisit" like nothing else before it.

Yet, because the show is so rooted in the technology of the 2010s, one wonders whether we will look back on it in the same way we look back at the "duck-and-cover" educational videos of the 1950s: with laughter. Will we watch and wonder, "Just what were we so afraid of?"

We might not. Science fiction has a tendency to inspire future technology. The flip phone, the credit card, video calling, mood-enhancing drugs, computer tablets, electric cars – these all appeared in science fiction before they became reality.[2] In fifty years, we may still be talking about *Black Mirror* because the technology it depicted has been added to that list.

But even if we do look back on *Black Mirror* fifty years from now, and think its fears about technology were misguided, there will be value in its having captured the zeitgeist of our time. After all, *The Great Gatsby* helps us understand the wealth gap that expanded in the Jazz Age. *I Love Lucy* illuminates the social issues that faced Postwar America. *Guernica*, with its chaos and violence, captures the horror of the Spanish Civil War. We come back to these artworks not just because of their timelessness, but because of their very timeliness.

Black Mirror is not only timely, however. It also taps into something very primal and deep in our humanity that arguably makes it timeless. Whereas gadgets and screens greatly accelerate the pace of our lives, the speed of change in human nature is glacial. Our brains' wiring, our need for connection, our deepest fears, and most fervent desires haven't changed much in hundreds of thousands of years. *Black Mirror* is truly about how fragile and imperfect humans are grappling with an ever-changing world and trying to keep up. And that's an issue that will endure. Consider one of the first Brooker quotes to appear in this book: "It's not a technological problem [we have], it's a human one. That human frailties are maybe amplified by it. Technology is a tool that has allowed us to swipe around like an angry toddler."[3]

Indeed, when we think about "technology," we're usually thinking about communicating at great distances, or overcoming death, or recording every moment of our lives. But as Kevin Kelly reminds us in his book *What Technology Wants*, "[T]echnology predated our humanness ... [T]he strategy of bending the environment as if it were part of one's own body is a half-billion-year-old trick at least."[4] Writing, clothes, and shelter are human technologies, as well, and they have deeply shaped our evolutionary history. For centuries, there have been screeds about how the "latest technology" – be it books, or electric lights, or radio – is "destroying our lives." But humans are incredibly adaptable; we grow in tandem with whatever "technology" we are currently using. Despite the fears it raises, *Black Mirror* captures our adaptability too.

After all, at its core, *Black Mirror* is about perennial human questions: How do I raise my child? What happens when war dehumanizes us? How much privacy do I need? Ultimately, our ubiquitous screens are simply designed to be reflections of our deepest selves, and to force us to confront both who we are and who we could be.

Yogi Berra once said that "it's hard to make predictions, especially about the future." That's certainly true, especially if we try to predict whether we'll be watching a specific show fifty years from now. But one thing I am willing to bet on is that in the future, no matter what the latest gadget or screen is, we'll still be struggling with the same questions *Black Mirror* puts in front of us: not just, "How are we using technology," but also, "How is that technology changing us?"

Notes

1. Howard Gardner, *Truth, Beauty, and Goodness Reframed* (New York: Basic Books, 2011), 49–53, italics in original.
2. Arielle Contreras, "8 pieces of modern technology that science fiction predicted – or invented," *Electric Lit*, https://electricliterature.com/8-pieces-of-modern-technology-that-science-fiction-predicted-or-invented-dd79dd1a9997 (Accessed 13 August 2019).
3. Bryony Gordon, "Charlie Brooker on *Black Mirror*: 'It's not a technological problem we have, it's a human one,'" *The Telegraph*, https://www.telegraph.co.uk/culture/tvandradio/11260768/Charlie-Brooker-Its-not-a-technological-problem-we-have-its-a-human-one.html (Accessed 13 August 2019).
4. Kevin Kelly, *What Technology Wants* (New York: Penguin, 2010), 21.

Appendix
How to Use This Book in the Classroom

Whether it be through *Star Trek* or *Star Wars*, *Game of Thrones* or *Black Mirror*, courses that use pop culture to introduce and teach philosophy have become more and more common. Having taught some version of a popular culture and philosophy class for over fifteen years now, I (the editor) have constructed this book with the intention of using it my own classroom. Given its philosophical depth, the popularity of the series, and the relative ease with which students can access the series (through Netflix), *Black Mirror* seems ideal. Add to that the "standalone" nature of every episode, so that the student doesn't have to be familiar with grandiose universes and hours of hours of footage to discuss the latest episode, and the professor can pick and choose what episodes they want to cover – and it seems as though Charlie Brooker intended *Black Mirror* for classroom use. With that in mind, here are two suggestions for how you might use *Black Mirror* and this book in your classroom.

One approach would be to have the students watch an episode for homework, and then meet to discuss what they saw as its major themes, questions, or philosophical puzzles. What worries does it raise? Is it making an argument? If so, is that argument's conclusion true? The students would then be assigned to read the chapter on that episode, and in the next class discuss in more depth the philosophers and philosophical arguments it identifies. This could be repeated for as many episodes as the professor likes and could also include the general topic chapters at the end of the book. A final assignment could call for the student to watch an episode that was not discussed in class (ideally an episode in a new season not covered by this book) and reflect on it in the same way the chapters in this book reflect on theirs. I have already had some success with this approach.

A more intensive approach would involve using the chapters of the book as a springboard to launch into philosophical topics that you would then examine more directly through primary or secondary literature. In practice, the professor could select two articles, one for each side of the debate on the

Black Mirror and Philosophy: Dark Reflections, First Edition. Edited by David Kyle Johnson.
© 2020 John Wiley & Sons, Inc. Published 2020 by John Wiley & Sons, Inc.

issue in question. For example, one could use the chapter on *Bandersnatch* to raise questions about the possibility of human free will, and then assign and discuss Peter van Ingwagen's "The Incompatibility of Free Will and Determinism" and Daniel Dennett's "I Could not Have Done Otherwise – So What?" A final project could involve having the student take and defend a position on one of the philosophical issues discussed during the course of the semester. Every *Black Mirror* episode could not be covered in a semester using this approach, but for those who would like to try it, I have complied a list of primary and secondary sources that one could use in conjunction with each chapter. It's available at https://andphilosophy.com/2019/09/26/black-mirror-and-philosophy-suggested-further-readings/.

There are also recourses that can help professors direct a class discussion on an episode, such as the podcast "Black Mirror Cracked" (produced by Daniel Jackson) and the book *Inside Black Mirror* by Charlie Brooker and Annabel Jones with Jason Arnopp (New York: Crown Archetype, 2018). Like this book, each has a chapter dedicated to each episode and can provide fodder for class discussion. I have found that trivia helps get students "into" the episodes (e.g., the crowd at the press release of *The National Anthem* reacted the same way to the episode as those on screen react to the Prime Minister's indecent action). Students also like to discuss details or events in the episode that help make sense of it (e.g., a music choice, a particular line, or a set piece). To get them to interpret the episodes, it can be useful to treat each episode as both a warning about some piece of technology and a warning about a human foible—a human foible that the technology magnifies. (The grain magnifies Liam's paranoia. Arkangel magnifies Marie's over-parenting. Smithereens magnifies are distractibility and susceptibility to digital addiction.) I'll often ask in class: "Ok, so what's the technology and what's the human foible?" to get things rolling. There are many lessons to learn.

I wish you the best of luck in your pedagogical endeavors!

Index

Black Mirror and Philosophy: Dark Reflections, First Edition. Edited by David Kyle Johnson.
© 2020 John Wiley & Sons, Inc. Published 2020 by John Wiley & Sons, Inc.

Printed in the USA
CPSIA information can be obtained
at www.ICGtesting.com
JSHW021800070923
47676JS00008B/132

9 781119 578260